Latin America in the 1940s

Sponsored by the Joint Committee on Latin American Studies of the Social Science Research Council and the American Council of Learned Societies, with funds from the Andrew W. Mellon Foundation.

Latin America in the 1940s

War and Postwar Transitions

EDITED BY DAVID ROCK

University of California Press
BERKELEY LOS ANGELES LONDON

University of California Press
Berkeley and Los Angeles, California

University of California Press, Ltd.
London, England

Latin America in the 1940s : war and postwar transitions / edited by
David Rock.
p. cm.
Includes bibliographical references and index
ISBN 0-520-08416-0 (alk. paper). — ISBN 0-520-08417-9 (pbk.:
alk. paper)
1. Latin America—Politics and government—20th century. 2. Latin
America—Economic conditions. 3. Latin America—Social conditions.
I. Rock, David, 1945-
F1414.L279 1994
980.03'3—dc20 93-29798
CIP

Printed in the United States of America
9 8 7 6 5 4 3 2 1

The paper used in this publication meets the minimum requirements of American National Standard for Information Sciences—Permanence of Paper for Printed Library Materials, ANSI Z39.48–1984. ♾

Contents

Figures

Tables

Contributors

CORINNE ANTEZANA-PERNET is a member of the Department of History, University of California, Irvine. She is working on a doctoral dissertation on the growth of the women's movement in Chile.

RUTH BERINS COLLIER is associate professor of political science at the University of California, Berkeley, and coauthor (with David Collier) of *Shaping the Political Arena: Critical Junctures, the Labor Movement, and Regime Dynamics in Latin America.*

JOSEPH COTTER is a lecturer in the Department of History at the University of California, Santa Barbara. His Ph.D. dissertation was entitled "Before the Green Revolution: Mexican Agricultural Policy, 1920–1949."

PAUL W. DRAKE is chair of the Department of Political Science at the University of California, San Diego. His books include *Socialism and Populism in Chile, 1932–52.*

E. V. K. FITZGERALD is professor of economics at the Institute of Social Studies, the Hague, Netherlands. Among his books is *The Political Economy of Peru, 1956–1978: Economic Development and the Restructuring of Capital.*

JOHN D. FRENCH is assistant professor of history at Duke University, and author of *The Brazilian Workers' ABC: Class Conflict and Alliances in Modern São Paulo.*

DANIEL LEWIS is a former lecturer in the Department of History, University of California, Santa Barbara. His Ph.D. dissertation was entitled "A Political and Economic History of Grain Farming in Buenos Aires Province, Argentina, 1914–1943."

FERNANDO LOPEZ-ALVES is assistant professor of political science at the University of California, Santa Barbara. His published articles include "Explaining Confederation: Colombian Unions in the 1980s."

DAVID ROCK, the editor of this volume, is professor of history at the University of California, Santa Barbara. His books include *Argentina, 1516–1987: From Spanish Colonization to Alfonsín.*

IAN ROXBOROUGH is professor of sociology at the State University of New York, Stony Brook. Among his books is *Unions and Politics in Mexico.*

ROSEMARY THORP is a fellow of St. Antony's College and lecturer in economics at the Institute of Economics and Statistics, University of Oxford. She is coauthor (with Geoffrey Bertram) of *Peru, 1890–1977: Growth and Policy in an Open Economy.*

Acknowledgments

This book was conceived during a conference at the University of California, San Diego, in early 1986 in which a group of specialists reviewed and discussed recent scholarship on modern Latin America. Among the conclusions of these discussions was that the 1940s, the period coinciding with World War II and the beginning of the Cold War, represented a crucial historical bridge in modern Latin America, but that many of the features of this period remained unknown, ignored, or forgotten.

Thanks to the support of the Social Science Research Council (SSRC) of New York, in December 1987 a second interdisciplinary group of Latin Americanists met at the University of California, Santa Barbara, to arrange a collaborative research project on Latin America in the 1940s. This meeting became the prelude to a third conference in Santa Barbara in December 1989, at which the decision was made to prepare papers with a view to eventual publication. The participants in the project have changed over time although, as I hope the introduction acknowledges, several past participants who were unable to submit papers for this volume had an important part in shaping and defining the issues it addresses. I am particularly grateful to Charles Bergquist, Leslie Bethell, and Joseph Love.

I owe a heavy debt to Paul Drake, who as a member of the Joint Committee on Latin American Studies of the Social Science Research Council gave me enormous assistance in raising the funds for the two conferences in Santa Barbara and in advising on the selection of participants. In 1989, Valpy

Fitzgerald, who replaced Drake on the Joint Committee, had a similarly helpful role. I must thank the three staff members of the SSRC with whom I had contact during the planning, execution, and follow-up phases of the project: Joan Dassin, Silvia Raw, and Eric Hershberg. At the University of California, Santa Barbara, my home campus, I received additional support and funding from the Interdisciplinary Humanities Center. A willing group of graduate students provided indispensable assistance during the two conferences in Santa Barbara. I should mention in particular Daniel Lewis (now a contributor to this volume), Karen Mead, and Jan Sallinger-McBride. Anthony O'Regan assisted me in the final stages of editing the papers.

David Rock
Santa Barbara, California

Introduction

David Rock

The central theme of this book is the relationship between the "global shocks" of the 1940s, induced by World War II and the onset of the Cold War, and the political development of Latin America. First, the 1940s brought the Latin American republics into a new international order in which old ties with Western Europe crumbled and sometimes disappeared while relations with the United States assumed greater importance than ever before. Second, many parts of Latin America in the 1940s, especially in 1944–1946, witnessed an unprecedented, though not entirely uniform, shift from conservative or authoritarian rule toward democracy and the rapid growth of labor unions. By the end of the decade, however, the infant democratic movements had all collapsed, labor was in disarray, and conservatives were once more in power.

The chief aim of our inquiry was to establish and to illustrate the extent to which international and domestic political changes were linked. A second aim—since the 1940s were so crucial to the formation of the contemporary world, at least until the recent demise of the Cold War—was to measure the long-term impact of these changes in Latin America. Some of our early discussions, for example, suggested that this period represented a vital historical watershed in that it produced the intense opposition between popular and authoritarian forces which later became one of the chief distinguishing features of Latin American politics. Finally, we intended to compare the democratic experience of the 1940s with that of the 1980s and to explore the extent to which the failures of the earlier period offered lessons for the later.

During the initial planning of the project in 1986, Joseph L. Love addressed one of the main aspects of the political transition of the 1940s, as he linked the collapse of the democratic movements in Latin America toward the end of the decade with the beginnings of the Cold War. "The Rio Treaty of 1947," Love wrote,

> the OAS [Organization of American States] Treaty of 1948, and the pressure by the U.S. to outlaw domestic Communist parties—all these steps seem to have been part of an American Cold War strategy with major influence, for example, on the internal politics of Brazil and Chile. The United States' 'disinterest' in the region in the latter 1940s . . .has to do not only with the requirements of European policy but with the judgment that the region was now 'under control,' in terms of dealing with Communism. Furthermore, the onset of the Cold War was surely related to the end of the 'democratic opening.' (letter of July 19, 1986)

During subsequent stages of the project, both during the preconference of 1987 and the full conference of 1989, several contrasting and divergent viewpoints emerged: some participants expressed their skepticism over the importance of this period, but others called it "a crucial decade." A second striking difference of opinion lay between those who minimized the external global shocks as a factor in political change in Latin America and therefore emphasized "internal trajectories," and those, like Love, who regarded the changing international environment of this period as critical.

In a preliminary statement during the meeting in 1987, Paul W. Drake characterized the 1940s as "regressive and conservative." Comparing regime changes over the period he found little to support the view that there were regionwide trends toward enhanced political participation and social reform or that the United States actively encouraged such trends. Drake noted a few "political openings" around 1945 but emphasized their brevity and their eventual failure. Except in Argentina under Juan Perón and in Guatemala under Jacobo Arbenz, Drake saw this decade as a period of relative political inertia in which the populists and democrats generally fared badly.

Drake illustrated these observations by the examples of Chile and Peru. In both countries, populism emerged in the 1930s; the 1940s, by contrast, saw the consolidation of antipopulist, "ideologically cooling" regimes emphasizing growth at the expense of redistribution and reform. Labor unions remained weak, and reformist forces ended the decade less powerful and effective than at the beginning. At most a mere "nudge to the left" occurred in 1944–1947 in the "artificial climate" at the end of World War II.

In another preliminary statement in 1987, Ruth Berins Collier, citing the examples of four Latin American nations, presented a second, broadly similar view. She argued that except in Peru, Argentina, and in lesser degree Venezuela, reformist efforts, and the political incorporation of "popular groups," predated the 1940s. During the period 1943–1946, which marked the high point of the popular front movements in Latin America, the Communist parties of Mexico, Brazil, Venezuela, and Chile abandoned their confrontations with conservative regimes and attempted to arrest and contain popular pressures.

Broadly speaking, Collier shared Drake's view that in Chile in the 1940s reform efforts were suspended and greater repression prevailed than in the preceding decade. In Brazil, social reform affecting the urban working class occurred before 1946, and Mexico in the 1940s underwent a transition to more authoritarian forms under the reconstructed ruling party, the Partido Revolucionario Institucional (PRI). In all four countries, the later 1940s witnessed a further tightening of political controls in response to renewed labor pressure. In Chile, greater labor militancy provoked a ban on Communists and rural strikes; Brazil too under the Dutra regime banned the Communists; Mexico intensified earlier trends toward the co-optation and repression of labor; in Venezuela, where the government initially sought to exploit rising labor militancy, the late 1940s saw the collapse of earlier reform initiatives under the Acción Democrática (Democratic Action).

Leslie Bethell, by contrast, argued that the "postwar conjuncture" (1944–1946) marked a "critical moment" in the development of modern Latin America. He observed that wartime inflation spurred an "unprecedented (political) mobilization," a profusion of new parties, and a widespread sense of "something different" about to take shape in many parts of the region. At the end of the war, already existing democratic institutions were strengthened; elsewhere came a succession of "political openings" and "windows of opportunity." Bethell provided examples from Brazil. The war, he claimed, at first strengthened authoritarianism under Getúlio Vargas. But in 1945, a "dramatic opening" revived many of the reformist impulses that had lain dormant over the past decade. Bethell noted a rapid expansion in rates of unionization and intense competition for the labor vote during this period.

In 1945, the Brazilian Communist party gained unprecedented prominence.

Even so, Bethell acknowledged that these trends proved short-lived. By 1948–1950, the effort to consolidate democratic institutions had disintegrated, as military and traditional elites successfully neutralized the new forces. In Brazil, the 1945 election was followed by a deliberate policy of containing earlier democratic advances, eliminating Communist influences, and enforcing new controls over organized labor.

Charles W. Bergquist argued that the distinctive feature of the 1940s was the resolution of "the crisis of world capitalism" that had begun upon the outbreak of World War I and then intensified at the onset of the Great Depression in 1929. The "crisis" period marked an era of opportunity for Latin America because it reduced the influence of the industrial capitalist powers in the region and enabled several nations to pursue structural change and social reform. However, "the 1930s," Bergquist declared, "came to an end in 1948," when a new, relatively stable order that crystallized in the North Atlantic nations "resolved the crisis." This resolution was achieved principally by the postwar agreement between capitalists and the labor unions in the United States and in several leading European nations that traded social reform and welfare concessions by capital for labor's commitment to increase productivity and to oppose communism.

The new "structure of accumulation" among the Western industrial nations, Bergquist continued, underlay the extinction of the "windows of opportunity" of the mid-1940s in Latin America and the shift into conservatism during the late 1940s. Thereafter, the interests and needs of the industrial nations led by the United States forced the Latin American nations to continue as exporters of primary goods and at the same time to open the door to the multinational corporations that eventually dominated their economies. In a system and a structure that perpetuated monopoly and privilege in Latin America, there was no longer any scope for democracy and reform. The 1940s were therefore "crucial" to Latin America in that they established the region's place within the new global system of capitalist accumulation. In Bergquist's view, the 1940s was a "pivotal watershed," since in that period the basic frameworks were erected in which Latin America developed during future decades.

In later discussions, another marked difference of opinion emerged between those who saw the political trends of the 1940s as merely one stage in an unfolding set of separate national histories in which internal forces strongly predominated and those who emphasized the novelties of the period that were shaped primarily by the external global shocks, that is, World War II and the Cold War. Ruth Berins Collier, Paul W. Drake, and Fernando Lopez-Alves argued strongly in favor of the "internal-historical" dynamic, as opposed to Leslie Bethell and John D. French, who took the "external-conjunctural" approach.

The chapters assembled in this volume reflect the debates of 1987 and 1989 and introduce several new subjects, participants, themes, and broader perspectives. Chapter 1 by David Rock, a historian, reviews the dynamics of change in Latin America during this period and its chief manifestations: population growth and urbanization, the spread of popular nationalism, the acceleration of industrial development, the expansion of the interventionist state, and the emergence of populist movements stressing industrial development and social reform. Some of these conditions were present during earlier periods, particularly in the 1930s. In the 1940s, however, they rapidly intensified and started to emerge in conjunction with one another as part of a multilayered, reciprocal process of change.

A second section of this chapter evaluates the policies and attitudes of the United States toward Latin America between the late 1930s and the early 1950s. Immediately before the war, the United States sought to extend its links with Latin America for both economic and security reasons. The attempted economic linkages sprang from fears in the United States at the formation of trading blocs in other parts of the world, and the security issue reflected apprehensions that Latin America would be penetrated and taken over by Germany and Japan.

The position of the United States began to change, however, as early as 1940–1941, following the Nazi conquest of Western Europe. Henceforward, American policymakers increasingly recognized that the key to mastery over Latin America, particularly South America, lay in control over Western Europe, because many of Latin America's principal markets were there. Subsequently, the policymakers focused increasingly on Europe and away from Latin America. The support of the United States for democratic change in Latin America in 1945 was mainly due to a desire to establish client states that could be used to support the United States in the newly formed United Nations. The United States abandoned its support for democracy in Latin America as its Western European commitments grew and as the Latin American democracies became increasingly tied to economic nationalists and populists who resisted American influences. By the end of the decade, and throughout the early 1950s, conservative and antidemocratic regimes in Latin America were perceived as the best vehicles to protect U.S. interests. Thus, according to this view, the decline in the involvement of the United States in Latin America began much earlier than the onset of the Cold War, and the Cold War served mainly to consolidate a swing away from Latin America that was already well under way.

Chapter 2 by the economist Rosemary Thorp is a survey of the economic development of the region during this period. The chapter once more highlights the acceleration of industrial and population growth and provides additional insight into the wartime activities of the United States in Latin America. Thorp points to the apparent paradox between the wartime growth of the state in Latin America and the expanding linkages with the United States. The chapter provides data on and an interpretation of the growth of foreign trade, the impact of inflation, and trends in foreign investment. During the early postwar period, the Latin American coffee exporters prospered, but grain exporters such as Argentina became increasingly stagnant. The issue of Argentine grains is taken up in more detail in chapter 10.

Chapter 3 by Ruth Berins Collier, a political scientist, focuses on regime change and the political position of labor. The chapter skillfully measures the relative impact of international factors against internal historical trends or "trajectories" in four Latin American nations: Brazil, Chile, Mexico, and Venezuela. Changing international conditions strongly influenced the two phases Collier discerns in the postures and activities of leftist organizations led by the communist parties and the labor unions and another two phases in the "opening" and "closing" of regimes and of reformist initiatives, which together resulted in four overlapping phases. From this perspective of "opening" up to 1945 and "closing" after 1945, international pressures strongly influenced the formation and disintegration of internal political alliances.

A second part of this chapter examines political change from the contrasting perspective of "internal trajectories." The 1940s is seen not as a period of international influences that produced similar outcomes across Latin America but as a decade that catches countries at different phases in the unfolding of their own histories. From an analysis that combines the two perspectives, Collier argues that international forces could complement and reinforce internal trends, or influence their timing, but could neither derail nor eliminate the internal trends.

Chapter 4 by the economist E. V. K. FitzGerald reflects recent interest in the formation of the United Nations Economic Commission for Latin America (ECLA), founded in 1948, and in the origins of the doctrine of "unequal exchange" disseminated by Raúl Prebisch. FitzGerald notes that after the war Latin America began to seek a new and more salient position in the world economic order to reflect its wartime economic growth; its expanding share of world trade; its need for new sources of employment, particularly in manufacturing; and its determination to conquer the destabilizing effects of wartime inflation. After 1945, however, the interests of the great powers led by the United States frustrated this quest. Following the creation of ECLA, Prebisch enunciated the doctrine of unequal exchange, which has been commonly understood as an indigenous expression of the growing sense of frustration in Latin America by the late 1940s. In this guise, unequal exchange strongly influenced the succeeding generation of Latin American economists, particularly those on the left.

Yet as FitzGerald shows, unequal exchange was not original, indigenous to Latin America, or leftist in pedigree. The idea had a long history that in Latin America alone stretched as far back as the late eighteenth century. The version of unequal exchange publicized by Prebisch closely resembled one popular among extreme right-wing economists in Germany and Romania between the wars. Unequal exchange filtered into Latin America from Central and Eastern Europe during the 1930s and early 1940s and reappeared in Prebisch's formulations, although Prebisch himself continually claimed the idea as his own invention. Seen in this light, unequal exchange became another illustration of the importance of international influences in Latin America and another chapter in the long story of the region's ideological colonization by Europe.

Chapter 5 by Paul W. Drake, another political scientist, employs Chile and Peru as case studies, presenting a modified and more extensive version of his preliminary ideas. Drake stresses the divergent political outcomes of the 1940s in different parts of the region, among them Chile and Peru. The divergences, he argues, reflected differences in social and class structures that sprang from the specific character of each national economy. In Chile, these structures engendered a relatively powerful left with the result that Chilean politics became dominated by transactions and coalitions in which the left became one of the main participants. In Peru, in contrast, oligarchic forces commanded more power and found it easier to weaken and to restrain popular forces. Thus in Chile, the left gained some power through the popular front of the late 1930s, and the defeat of the Chilean left in the late 1940s was neither total nor final. In Peru, however, the left, represented mainly by the APRA (Alianza Popular Revolucionaria Americana), invariably proved more easily subdued and contained; indeed APRA remained excluded from government until the mid-1980s.

In this chapter, Drake upholds his earlier view that the depression of the 1930s, as opposed to World War II or the Allied victory of 1945, became the principal activator of new forms of mass politics. Even so, Drake acknowledges some general similarities in political trends in Chile and Peru during the 1940s that are observable elsewhere. During the war, for example, the left in both Chile and Peru abandoned anti-imperialism, supported the Allies, and participated in an alliance of democratic forces that was more broadly based than any of its predecessors. Similarly, both countries participated in some degree in the continental shift to the left in 1945–1947 followed by the general strong counterswing to the right at the end of the decade. Despite the marked differences between Chile and Peru, similar coalitions of industrialists, middle-class groups, and labor dominated both governments in 1945–1948. (In Chile, this coalition ruled from 1938 to 1948.)

Chapter 6 by the political historian John D. French is a detailed account of Brazilian politics in 1945, which marked the downfall of Getúlio Vargas in the military coup of late October and the rise of new popular political forces. French traces Vargas's ideological shift from authoritarianism to populism in 1943–1945. The chief ingredients of populism were economic nationalism and the search for a new political constituency among the urban working class, but with a continuing retrospective emphasis on "class collaboration" and "social peace." French contrasts this outlook with that of Brazil's conservative-minded liberals, who in 1945 were led by Brigadier Eduardo Gomes. He also examines the extraordinary alliance between Vargas, the erstwhile authoritarian whom many considered a fascist, and Luis Carlos Prestes, who emerged from lengthy imprisonment under Vargas to lead the newly legalized Brazilian Communist party.

Thus fundamental realignments occurred in Brazilian politics in 1945. French illustrates the links between Vargas's shift to populism and the vast expansion of the electorate in 1945: "the forceful and irreversible entrance of the urban working class into national political life." Despite the victory of the right-wing Gen. Eurico Dutra in the elections of late 1945, the conservative right led by Gomes suffered a definitive defeat; these elections thus began the political eclipse of the Brazilian rural oligarchy. Although he proved to be a conservative, Dutra's allegiances lay not with the landed classes but with the nascent Brazilian industrial sector, and following Vargas's removal by the military coup, Dutra inherited the deposed president's popular support.

Chapter 7 on Chilean women during the 1940s by the historian Corinne Antezana-Pernet demonstrates with particular clarity the political cycle of the 1940s: the sudden eruption of new democratic forces toward mid-decade and the gradual fading of those forces at the end of the decade. To some extent, this chapter follows Drake's view in locating the beginnings of the politicization of women in the 1930s, but it differs from Drake in presenting the mid-1940s as a second, more intense stage in this process. Antezana-Pernet, however, confirms the picture presented in several other chapters that the late 1940s was a period of marked regression. At this point in Chile, almost all the numerous women's associations founded earlier disintegrated and disappeared despite the legislation of 1949 that gave women the right to vote. Women's political organizations did not reappear in Chile until the late 1960s; the chapter also suggests the linkages between the radical movements of the 1940s and those of almost thirty years later.

Antezana-Pernet's study is an important new addition to the burgeoning historical literature on Latin American women. The author captures the diversity and heterogeneity of the women's movement in Chile and its relationship with the process of social change sparked by the depression and the war. Antezana-Pernet shows further that the rise and fall of the women's movement in Chile was closely linked to changes in international relations during this period. Thus the final stages of World War II gave rise to the spread and intensification of democratic forces, while the coming of the Cold War closed the avenues toward democracy and ruptured the alliances of 1944–1946.

Chapter 8 by Fernando Lopez-Alves, another political scientist, represents one of the first detailed surveys of politics in Uruguay during the 1940s. In certain respects, Uruguay resembled its neighbor Argentina under Juan Perón: the political influence of the rural sectors was in rapid decline; successive governments grew increasingly committed to industrial development through protectionism and by taxing the rural sector; the state was growing rapidly as an employer and extending its activities in the economy.

In other respects, however, Uruguayan politics pursued an entirely different course from that of Argentina: rather than implementing Perón-style corporatist institutions, Uruguay restored a pluralist democracy.

Lopez-Alves endorses Collier's view that national history, rather than external conditions, proved the dominant force shaping the direction of Uruguayan politics. At the heart of the Uruguayan political system stood the two great political parties, the Colorados and the Blancos, and the legacies of *batllismo*, the political movement established during the first two decades of the twentieth century by President José Batlle y Ordoñez. The 1940s marked the resurgence of a *batllista* democracy. In this period, new laws prevented the formation of new political parties and therefore consolidated the duopoly of the Colorados and the Blancos. Other measures revived the *batllista* practice of confining the labor unions to wage bargaining and channeling workers' political demands away from the unions and into the Colorado party. In the 1940s, the labor unions became more consolidated and centralized, but a labor or a social democratic party in Uruguay never formed nor were unions controlled by the state or the parties as in the corporatist model adopted by Perón. In this period, Uruguay thus underwent a "democratic reconstruction," based on continually rising state spending, that it managed to sustain into the 1950s without the sharp turn to the right at the end of the 1940s that occurred elsewhere.

Lopez-Alves concludes by pointing to some of the most striking contrasts between the Latin American democracies of the 1940s and those established during the 1980s. In the 1940s, state power was growing rather receding as in the 1980s; economic development in the 1940s focused on the expansion of the internal market as opposed to the effort during the 1980s to develop internationally competitive exports.

Chapter 9 by an economic historian, Daniel Lewis, returns to the themes of the internal trajectories and the global shocks in an analysis of the Argentine agricultural sector. In the 1940s and early 1950s, acreages and production of wheat, corn, and other crops in Argentina fell spectacularly. Commentators have commonly attributed the decline to the policies of Perón that raised farmers' costs while heavily taxing their earnings. Another long-established interpretation links the decline of agriculture to the dependent and vulnerable position of the mostly tenant farmers with respect to the landowning ranchers. Whenever world prices favored cattle over grains, as they did during most of the 1940s, the landowners displaced the farmers and shifted to cattle production.

Lewis, however, offers a much broader historical picture of the decline of Argentine agriculture. He points to the wide-ranging conditions that were already seriously undermining Argentine farming during the 1930s: the trend in Europe after 1918 toward agricultural protectionism; technological advance and rising productivity in the farm sector of the United States during the late 1930s; the reliance in Argentina itself on stopgaps such as government price supports for farmers and the unwillingness to take steps to increase agricultural investment; the need to import increasingly expensive agricultural machinery; the growing proportion of grain consumed domestically by a population becoming increasingly urbanized. During the mid-1930s, Argentine farmers gained a temporary boost as drought and land fatigue afflicted their competitors abroad. But the boost was only temporary and by 1938–1939, immediately before the outbreak of the war, the markets of Western Europe were becoming glutted. In that period, Argentina managed to remain competitive in wheat, but the corn sector was already in steep decline.

Already struggling to survive, the Argentine farmers were then hit by the effects of World War II: the European markets were eliminated, prices collapsed, and production surpluses rapidly mounted. Between 1940 and 1944, thousands of tenants were evicted from the land, as acreages devoted to farming plummeted. In the early 1940s, the farm sector plunged into a decline from which there was probably no escape, since by this point farmers abroad, particularly in the United States, were using new technology to achieve massive increases in productivity. Lewis acknowledges that after the war Perón's policies toward farming were ill-conceived and misdirected, but the chief reasons for the downfall of farming, as he sees it, stemmed from the years preceding Perón's presidencies.

A second analysis of agricultural issues is presented by Joseph Cotter, a historian of science, in chapter 10, focusing this time on Mexico. Cotter's chief concern is with the diffusion and adoption of U.S. technology in Mexican farming and in particular with the origins of the "Green Revolution," which from the 1940s onward effected profound and enduring changes in farming techniques and the structure of rural society.

In this chapter, Cotter presents a revisionist view of the coming of the Green Revolution in Mexico. In contrast with the established view that the technological linkages between Mexican farming and the United States began during the early 1940s, he argues from extensive documentation that these connections were present much earlier. The links took numerous forms, among them the widespread use of foreign seeds and crop varieties, the importation of machinery and fertilizers from the United States, the translation of scientific texts, the adoption of pest control practices, and the creation of agricultural secondary schools modeled on those of the United States.

In Cotter's view, Mexico's commitment to "scientific nationalism" was largely rhetorical. The country lacked a scientifically trained corps of agronomists, and the aspiration for autarkic agrarian development was doomed from its beginnings. A willingness to accept foreign assistance prevailed throughout even among many leftist and ostensibly anti-imperialist groups. Indeed, extensive contact with the United States in the sphere of agricultural technology survived even at the height of the nationalist policies of President Lázaro Cárdenas that led to the expropriation of British and American oil companies in 1938. At this point, Mexico continued to send students of agronomy to the United States for training and to bring in American technical experts. Soon afterward, the ties between Mexico and the United States through agriculture became even stronger, although they were not, as the generally received view holds, the result of the shift to the right in Mexico after the outbreak of war. Instead, Cotter argues, the increased willingness to draw upon foreign expertise reflected the gathering crisis in Mexican agriculture: the falling production of food crops, led by corn, and the country's growing reliance on imports.

Chapter 11 by the sociologist Ian Roxborough returns to the themes of labor control and capital accumulation originally raised by Charles Bergquist at the preconference of 1987. In 1944–1948, Roxborough shows, two rival approaches to future economic development appeared in Latin America. The first, supported by the communist parties, the labor unions, and reformist groups in general, stressed land reform, income redistribution, and "class collaboration" between labor and capital to achieve both industrial development and a form of Latin American social democracy. The second approach, upheld by conservatives, stressed development through close linkages with the United States and a Latin American version of the "politics of productivity" in which labor would accept discipline, and subject itself to state corporatism, in return for a share in the fruits of future economic growth. By the late 1940s, the latter approach had gained supremacy, although uneven economic growth during subsequent periods provoked periodic political breakdowns and military coups in most parts of the region.

Although conservatives finally emerged dominant during the 1940s, Roxborough argues that this period marked an advance on the past in that the power of the oligarchic landed classes dwindled and that of the urban sectors and the state increased. Even so, the decline of the landed classes in Latin America was not nearly as great as in other parts of the underdeveloped world, particularly parts of Asia. In Latin America, the ability of the landed classes to defeat most of the projects for land reform proved in the long term one of the major constraints on successful industrial development. After the 1940s, Latin America also proved to be unlike Western Europe, where the relative success of the left during the immediate postwar period led to successful social democracies, a progressive form of corporatism, and the growth of the welfare state. Finally, the enduring importance of the 1940s stemmed from the conscious adoption during that period of import-substituting industrialization, the growth model that prevailed until its breakdown during the debt crisis of the 1980s.

The subject matter, the interpretations, and the disciplinary approaches of this book are thus multiple and varied. Five chapters in the volume address more than one Latin American nation or the region in its entirety, and six examine specific nations. We approach the development of Latin America during this period from economic, social, political, and ideological perspectives. In several cases, the analysis focuses on the "long" 1940s and therefore includes data and issues from earlier and later periods; elsewhere the emphasis is on a specific moment during this period, such as the year 1945. Aside from the issue of Argentine agriculture, the authors agree that the 1940s had a greater impact in urban rather than rural Latin America; we therefore focus more strongly on the labor movements in the cities rather than on the peasantry. Some authors, particularly those dealing with the Atlantic states of South America led by Brazil and Argentina, stress the importance of the 1940s as the great turning point in the region's development. Others, in contrast, especially those focusing on nations such as Chile that were hit hardest by the depression, see the 1930s as a more significant transition. From a third perspective, the 1940s began the consolidation of existing trends whose origins lay in the past history of each separate country.

The concluding chapter in this volume suggests looking at the 1940s as a new beginning, not so much because of the appearance of entirely new conditions but because of the resynthesis of already existing conditions in a radically different way. The stirrings of popular nationalism and the intensified quest for industrial development during the 1940s possessed strong roots in the region's past. But it was the "global shocks" of the 1940s that strengthened these forces and brought them to the fore to a much greater extent than ever before. The 1940s created a new political dialectic in Latin America. On the one hand, the "window of opportunity" of 1944–1946 led the region toward what the historian E. H. Carr once called "the socialization of nationalism, and the nationalization of socialism."[1] On the other hand, the resurgent authoritarian rulers of the late 1940s became the immediate precursors of the "bureaucratic authoritarians" and the "state terrorists" of the 1960s and 1970s. Finally, the 1940s marked the emergence of a conjunction of forces that carried Latin America back into an international system profoundly and irreversibly different from its predecessors.

Notes

1. E. H. Carr, *Nationalism and After*. London: Macmillan, 1945, 18.

1 War and Postwar Intersections

Latin America and the United States

David Rock

The 1940s brought some striking changes in many parts of Latin America. Population and the cities were growing as never before. Nationalism suddenly became "rampant" in the region, and the "leaven of economic nationalism [was] working overtime."[1] A "dynamic of rising expectations" erupted in the cities, as the "masses [became] increasingly class conscious and politically potent."[2] Advancing techniques of mass communication led by film and radio "enabled [Latin Americans] to glimpse the way others live[d] [and] they [were] asking why they should not live as well."[3] "People were demanding a voice in government, and. . .they were getting it. With this new voice they demanded economic independence and progress, social justice and political sovereignty."[4] "It seemed only a matter of time," commented another observer, "before popular pressures would break through the dikes, and bring in a flood of political and social changes."[5]

This period marked the consolidation of a new type of Latin American state, one committed to greater public ownership, economic change, and rising standards of living. At the helm of the state stood a new brand of populist political leader who "claimed to represent the people and. . .treated social and economic problems as fundamental."[6] Instigated by the populists, Latin Americans demanded "a higher standard of living, and [became] convinced that industrialism was the way to get it."[7] From the emergent new political order came the "the impulse to build strong, independent nations, to mold broader and more efficient economies, and to create new social forms and institutions."[8] Instead of seeking to modernize by attracting European immigrants—the nineteenth-century liberal-positivist program—the Latin American nations would now "increase their manufacturing efforts as a base for a larger population."[9] A growing middle class of entrepreneurs and managers employed by manufacturing would "provide a broader base for political responsibility."[10] Higher tariffs were "part of the whole fabric of the New Nationalism," while numerous reform movements emerged "designed to bring about a broader distribution of wealth."[11]

Around the mid-1940s—in some parts a little earlier and in others a little later—the demand for industrial development began to fuse with the aspiration for social reform, whereas before, if these conditions existed, they had tended to remain separate. Under the Estado Nôvo (new state), established by Getúlio Vargas in 1937, Brazil, for example, enacted one of the highest tariffs in the world and constructed a heavily regulated and increasingly centralized economy.[12] But it was only around 1945 that the attempt to promote economic change became linked with the emergence of new popular movements and with attempts to promote greater social equality.[13] In Mexico during the late 1930s, in contrast, President Lázaro Cárdenas greatly intensified land reform, nationalized oil, and supplanted clerical power in the schools by "socialistic education." But in Mexico reform and mass mobilization were as yet unaccompanied by the other component of industrial development and structural change: industrialism became the priority in the 1940s.

Before the mid-1940s only Chile effected the synthesis of social reform and industrial development, although somewhat exceptional conditions prevailed there. The Great Depression had a deeper impact in Chile than in any other country. Imports in the early 1930s were around 80 percent lower than in the late 1920s, and gross national product fell by around 40 percent.[14] In Chile the depression fanned a premature populism that in 1938 led to the formation of the Popular Front administration. Under the slogan of "bread, roof, and coat" (*pan, techo, y abrigo*), Chile pursued state-led industrial development that for a time at least was combined with an attempt at social reform.[15]

But in most of Latin America until toward the end of World War II, the old-style oligarchic or autocratic state remained intact. Under leaders such as Oscar Benavides in Peru or Agustín P. Justo in Argentina, politics in the 1930s stuck firmly in the molds of the past. Most governments reacted to the depression not by fostering structural change but by attempting to revive primary exports. As yet industrial and urban growth remained too incipient, the deflationary effects of the depression too deadening, labor markets too slack, markets too fragmented, and popular leaders too defensive to create a climate for political change. The "rebellion of the masses," or as he also labeled it, the "sovereignty of the unqualified," predicted by the Spanish philosopher José Ortega y Gasset had as yet failed to materialize.

The late war years came much closer to fulfilling Ortega y Gasset's prophecies. Change sprang from the reversal of conditions prevalent during the depression. These new conditions included war-induced inflation, accelerating industrial growth, and the rapid growth of urban employment; meanwhile, new democratic and reform currents redefined concepts of participation and economic progress.

Inflation occurred chiefly from the impact of the war on Latin America's foreign trade. In the Allied nations millions of farmers, miners, and factory workers became soldiers; women workers operated the factories that now produced munitions instead of civilian goods. During the war Latin America's imports of manufactured consumer and capital goods fell sharply, but its exports grew, with trade tilting away from Europe and toward the United States.[16] Import shortages, rising shipping freights, and large balance of payments surpluses all contributed to rising prices in Latin America; inflation then spurred the rapid expansion of the Latin American labor movements. In 1945 workers "heightened the tempo of their struggle for economic and social status," as the Latin American labor unions emerged larger and more powerful than ever before. At this point "labor. . .received more recognition as an actual or potential political force than in any previous year."[17]

Wartime inflation fostered new forms of political instability. In many parts of Latin America the export boom shifted labor from subsistence or local farming into export production but in doing so provoked a contraction in domestic food supplies. Parts of Mexico, Haiti, Cuba, Venezuela, Peru, the Dominican Republic, and the rubber region of the Amazon, into which the Brazilian government deployed thousands of peasant workers, all suffered outbreaks of political unrest stemming from the rapid expansion of export production, the disruption of peasant communities, and urban food shortages. In 1944 corn riots set the scene for the overthrow of the Hernández Martínez dictatorship in El Salvador. In Bolivia falling real wages among tin miners, alongside pressures from employers to raise export production, provoked the unrest that led to the "Catavi massacre" of 1942 and then the nationalist revolution of December 1943 led by Víctor Paz Estenssoro.

A second feature of the war period was accelerating industrial growth that built on the expansion of manufacturing during the late 1930s. Although they could no longer import capital goods and raw materials, the industrial producers of Argentina, Brazil, Chile, Mexico, and other countries managed to increase production and, despite the parallel growth of agricultural and mineral exports, to draw growing quantities of labor from the export sectors. Peasants and other rural workers thus swarmed into the cities, contributing to the expansion of the labor unions. In Colombia, for example, President Alfonso López Permejo attributed his fall in July 1945 to "that active industrial development which is causing and creating interests of such magnitude that they openly defy the force of the laws." The expansion of industry, he added, had produced the "awakening of a sleeping social consciousness."[18]

The growth of manufacturing encouraged the growth of state planning and the spread of the interventionist state. The disruption of foreign trade during the 1930s suggested the end of the liberal international economy; the early 1940s displayed the power of the mighty industrialized war economies in Europe and North America. These conditions combined convinced Latin American political leaders, particularly in the military, that planned state-led industrialization offered the key to national progress and national power. A senior Argentine military officer writing in 1944, for example, argued that greater self-sufficiency was essential to his country's future. The war showed that the small, weak nations had no protection against the strong, and therefore "the current war demand[ed] healthy and powerful industries." After the war, he predicted, the reemergence of the trade blocs or "spheres of influence" of the 1930s controlled by the great powers would make it impossible to return to the free trade economy; the key to the future therefore lay in "economic independence." Economic development, moreover, should be led by the state, which was "no worse or more bureaucratic an administrator than a company that possesses a monopoly."[19]

In Mexico industrial development became state policy following the assumption of the Manuel Ávila Camacho government in December 1940. In April 1941 the Law of Manufacturing Industries granted tax incentives and tariff protection to designated sectors of manufacturing; in 1942 the National Chamber of Industry was established to foster public support for industrial development; in 1944 the state-owned Nacional Financiera was revamped into an industrial bank to support manufacturers; in 1944 too Mexico extended import controls.[20] In 1940 Brazil launched a five-year plan to establish a chemical industry and negotiated a large loan in the United States to build the Volta Redonda steel plant. In Argentina a greater commitment to industrial development also began in 1940 led by Federico Pinedo, the finance minister, and then intensified after the military coup of June 1943. In 1944 the Argentine military junta established a state-controlled industrial bank, and in 1945 another government agency, the Instituto Argentino para la Promoción del Intercambio, began diverting profits from agricultural exports into urban industries.[21] By the end of the war even the smallest and poorest countries of the region such as Haiti and the Dominican Republic were laying ambitious plans for industrial diversification.[22]

In the large Latin American nations, governments embarked on projects to increase power supplies from oil and hydroelectricity and to develop roads and air transport. Supporting these ventures were associations like the "New Group" of manufacturers in Mexico, which campaigned for government-subsidized industries in Mexico City, Guadalajara, and Monterrey. The New Group demanded government investment in chemical and machine tool industries, export duties on industrial raw materials to safeguard supplies for local producers, the lowering of railroad freights, and the establishment of new regional industrial banks.[23]

State planning initially went furthest in Chile, where government institutions controlled industrial, mining, and farming credit and financed large-scale power and transportation projects. Chile became a leader in utilizing the profits from wartime exports to finance government corporations led by the state development company, the Corporación de Fomento.[24] The Chilean Economic Powers Law of December 1943 embodied the type of government intervention now starting to appear in many parts of the region. This legislation fixed urban rents; controlled prices, profits, and internal commerce; and supervised tax subsidies for local industries.[25]

Lastly, the mid-1940s marked the rise of new forms of popular politics. Their origins lay partly in the growth of the cities and the labor unions and in the activities of the Communist parties that between 1942 and 1947 functioned in greater freedom than ever before. But change also sprang from the great blasts of wartime propaganda by the Allies, which fostered, as one commentator defined it, a new "democratic faith."[26] As early as 1941 Arthur P. Whitaker correctly recognized the likely impact in Latin America of the principles and ideals the Allies were brandishing in the war against fascism. Latin American conservatives, he noted, were cooperating with the Allies in an effort to safeguard "the defense of the status quo, [but] Washington's emphasis on inter-American cooperation for the defense of democracy had revolutionary implications."[27]

Three years later Whitaker identified "the wartime contagion of liberal ideas" as the main reason for the downfall of Fulgencio Batista in the Cuban elections of 1944.[28] Similarly, in the struggle against dictatorship in El Salvador in 1944, "it was possible for the *Diario Latino* to conduct an anti-[Hernández] Martínez campaign."[29] This campaign constantly echoed the phrases and speeches of Roosevelt and Churchill.

In Guatemala the overthrow of Jorge Ubico in July 1944 followed a student-led uprising that invoked the "Four Freedoms" (freedom of speech, freedom of worship, freedom from want, and freedom from fear) proclaimed by Franklin D. Roosevelt in 1941.[30] Among the manifestos that appeared in Guatemala in the weeks preceding the fall of Ubico was that of the "311" (leading citizens). "Guatemala cannot remove itself from the democratic imperatives of the era," the manifesto proclaimed. "It is impossible to frustrate by coercion the uncontainable impulses of that great ideology now being reaffirmed in the conscience of the world by means of the bloodiest of struggles between oppression and liberty."[31] Even in reactionary Nicaragua "the international context at the end of World War II with its rhetoric of democracy and anti-fascist united fronts provided a supportive milieu for Somoza's (brief) turn to the left."[32]

The sweep toward free elections and popular democracy began in 1943–1944, and in 1945 nine states including Brazil fell to movements pledged to democratization. "The years 1944 and 1945," commented Whitaker, "brought more democratic changes in Latin America than perhaps in a single year since the wars of independence. The victory of the United Nations over fascist totalitarianism in Europe and Asia galvanized the democratic forces. . . .There were renewed discussions of fundamental problems of democracy all over Latin America."[33]

In Latin America, however, these nascent democratic forces often possessed a somewhat different content from the democratic movements typical of the United States. In a 1945 piece entitled "Rise of the Common Man," Whitaker noted that "the underlying discontent had been stirred into action by the war, with its economic dislocations and the impulse. . .for social justice [generated] by the. . .Four Freedoms and the higher standard of living in the United States. But in several Latin American countries the resultant popular movements diverged widely from the pattern of liberal democracy in the United States."[34] Going far beyond the demand for the vote, in Latin America "democracy" implied popular mobilization and social reform. Thus in one typical Latin American definition during this period, democracy signified an "awakening of conscience and a concern with the problems of social welfare."[35] In Mexico democracy was understood as "satisfying the hunger of the people," and in Colombia as "an equalization [of] liberty and social justice."[36] In many cases European influences made a stronger impression in Latin America than those from the United States. "Among Latin American progressives," remarked an observer in late 1945, "there is a growing eagerness to look at the British experiment in democratic socialism (under Clement Atlee) for possible guidance and inspiration."[37]

In Latin America the most typical expression of political change was "populism," the unique blend of popular participation, charismatic leadership, corporatism, nationalism, and social reform. The populists were often conservatives at heart, and among their main political objectives was the creation of mass movements under their own control as a barrier to the expansion of the Communist parties. Meanwhile, their economic objectives were to expand the domestic market as a basis for "inward-led" industrial development. Miron Burgin, an American academic historian then working for the State Department, recognized this trend in 1943 and judged it both desirable and inevitable. "Manufacturing industries in Latin America," he wrote,

> must for some time to come depend on domestic markets. The broader the internal market the more secure is the foundation for the continuing growth of domestic industries. This in turn presupposes a higher standard of living of the population at large. . .[and] a reorientation in the economic thinking and policies concerning the national dividend. Standards of living rather than exports [are now] the index and criterion of economic well-being. Consequently the primary objective of economic policy centers around the problems of placing higher real incomes in the hands of consumers, as this provides the best means of insuring economic diversification and stability.[38]

The Hemispheric Alliance

Toward the mid-1940s these trends in Latin America toward social reform, industrial development, and nationalism began to collide with the interests and policies of the United States. Immediately before World War II Latin America as a whole, as opposed to the traditional bulwarks of U.S. influence in the Caribbean basin, was central in U.S. foreign policy and strategic planning.[39] At that point Americans embraced the Pan-American movement "with all the fervor of a religious crusade. Latin America [was] the fashion; it [was] more, it [was] a mission."[40]

The chief foundation of these attitudes was "isolationism": with closer access to the markets, raw materials, and agricultural resources of Latin America, the American isolationists of this period argued, the United States could establish a self-contained commercial bloc insulated from all economic and military threats from abroad. In 1933 Franklin D. Roosevelt proclaimed the "Good Neighbor" policy, which pledged that the United States would abandon the use of military force in Latin America and no longer seek to undermine nondemocratic governments by tactics like the withdrawal of diplomatic recognition. "The maintenance of constitutional government in other nations is not, after all, a sacred obligation devolving upon the United States alone," Roosevelt declared.[41] During the prewar years Roosevelt greeted Gen. Rafael Trujillo of the Dominican Republic as his "great and good friend" and Vargas of Brazil as "co-author of the New Deal."[42] As observers recognized, the main purpose of these gestures was to enable the United States to dominate Latin American trade. The Good Neighbor policy, declared one commentator, was a "supercolossal trade promotion scheme in dignified attire."[43] "Pan-Americanism is a trade term made in the United States. It means buy from us. . . .It proclaims that those who live in the hemisphere should love one another and must buy one another's pots and pans."[44]

The pursuit of Latin America intensified after 1935, as hemispheric control came to be seen as still more imperative to balance the growth of German and Japanese influence in Europe and Asia and to prevent Germany and Japan from expanding into Latin America. Americans feared that growing trade between Germany and parts of Latin America, particularly Brazil, would serve as the springboard for the expansion of German political influences in the region. Similarly, if war occurred, "there could be no great war industry in North America without free access to the mines and fields of the southern continent. . . .[A] struggle for the hegemony of Latin America [was] therefore [to] be one of the most important phases of the Second World War."[45] The nationalization of Mexican oil in 1938 alarmed the United States not only because U.S. properties were confiscated but also because of fears that Germans would be brought to Mexico to run the industry and the Nazis would gain control over supplies and prices.[46]

Between 1936 and 1940 the United States sponsored a sequence of inter-American conferences that established elaborate procedures for consultation among the American republics on defense and security issues.[47] At Lima in 1938, for example, the republics resolved to block the spread of "totalitarian ideologies," and in the Declaration of Lima they proclaimed that "American solidarity" was founded in republican institutions, national sovereignty, and individual liberty.[48]

After the outbreak of war in Europe in September 1939, all the American nations again supported the United States by subscribing to the "Declaration of Neutrality of the American Republics." At the Havana conference of 1940 the United States sponsored resolutions in which the republics undertook to share information on Axis attempts at "subversion." An increasingly dense web of U.S. federal government agencies led by the Inter-American Development Commission and the Reconstruction Finance Corporation sought to strengthen American political and economic interests in the region.[49] In July 1940 the Export-Import Bank, founded in 1934, received a large quantity of additional funds to be used to stabilize Latin American trade and currencies and to assist the United States in winning control over the region's raw materials.

Behind all these measures lurked the fear that an unguarded Latin America would fall prey to an Axis takeover.[50] Germany would fight "a civil war in every nation of the hemisphere" in its own quest for Latin America's foodstuffs, minerals, and markets, claimed one observer.[51] The Nazis, suggested another commentator, were plotting to flood Latin America with manufactured goods produced by slave labor, and a string of pro-Nazi coups d'état would immediately follow German commercial expansion in the region.[52]

The tactics employed to strengthen the position of the United States in Latin America rapidly grew more forceful. For example, Nicholas John Spykman from Yale University, urged "total war" along the lines of recent Nazi practice in Europe, recommending "propaganda attacks on the ideology of the opponent, fifth columnists, trade embargoes," blacklists, and close associations with the Latin American military, or in other words "ideology blended with coercion," in which "military assault [became] only the last weapon in the struggle. . .used only if other forms of coercion fail[ed] to bring surrender."[53] In 1940 the United States used strong-arm diplomacy to nullify the influence of the German settler community in Guatemala, and in October it supported the overthrow of Panamanian president Arnulfo Arías, an early nationalist reformer whom the State Department regarded as a supporter of the Axis.[54]

Links between the United States and Latin America continued to strengthen throughout the early 1940s, with trade acting as the main bond. After mid-1940 all the markets of continental Europe except Spain and Portugal lay under German control, blockaded by the British, and beyond the reach of Latin American exporters. Consequently, by early 1941 the U.S. share of trade with Latin America, at 54 percent, had already climbed beyond the peak of 52 percent attained during World War I in 1917; in the first half of 1941 more than 60 percent of Latin America's imports came from the United States compared with only 55 percent in 1917.[55] The flow of minerals from Latin America to the United States intensified, as exports of Chilean copper, Brazilian rubber and manganese, Mexican zinc and other commodities swiftly doubled.[56] Growing numbers of Latin American officers attended military schools in the United States. In October 1941 the United States extended the Lend-Lease Act to include Latin America, and soon after Pearl Harbor in December 1941 nearly all the Latin American republics broke diplomatic relations with the Axis powers as the prelude to a declaration of war.[57]

This swift realignment behind the United States became particularly striking in Mexico and Brazil. In 1938 the nationalization of oil by Cárdenas led to serious tensions between Mexico and the United States, but the conflicts swiftly subsided in 1940 when the war closed Mexico's access to Western Europe, leaving the United States as its only large foreign market and source of imports.[58] By early 1942 the oil dispute was indefinitely shelved, and during subsequent years economic ties between the United States and Mexico became closer than ever before.[59] As the United States poured resources into Mexican railroads and mines, thousands of Mexican *braceros* (farm workers) crossed the border to labor in the United States.

In Brazil, in language reminiscent of the Fascists, Vargas greeted the fall of France in June 1940 as the "new age" that marked the end of "improvident liberalism."[60] But as his contacts with the Axis powers dwindled and the United States flooded Brazil with military and economic aid, Vargas too crossed over into the inter-American alliance. Soon there were American military bases in the strategic Brazilian northeastern "bulge," the closest part of the American continents to Europe and Africa, which the military strategists feared would be the most probable target of a German invasion.[61] At the inter-American conference at Rio de Janeiro in February 1942 the United States promised military supplies to the Latin American nations and preferential access to its shrinking pool of manufactured goods; in return the Latin Americans agreed to the "economic mobilization of the Americas" to support the war effort.[62]

Throughout this period the only country to resist the Pan-American alliance was Argentina, a country with close commercial and cultural links with Europe but very few ties with the United States. In 1940–1941 the Argentine government attempted to increase exports of grains and meat to the United States, but when these efforts failed it became increasingly obstructive. At the Rio de Janeiro conference in early 1942 Argentina attempted to create a neutral bloc of Latin American states opposed to the United States. Although this move failed, the Argentine delegation succeeded in modifying a resolution to break relations with the Axis from an obligation into a mere recommendation. During the next two years, despite growing U.S. opposition, Argentina stood alone among the Latin American nations in upholding relations with the Axis.[63]

The chief objective of the United States during the war was to increase the flow of exports from Latin America, in particular the minerals needed to feed defense production. As a result wartime investments by the United States in Latin America focused on extending railroad links between the mining regions and the ports. In 1940 the United States financed the Volta Redonda steel project in Brazil but only because Vargas threatened to approach Nazi Germany for assistance. Overall, U.S. agencies like the Export-Import Bank favored much smaller projects that once peace returned were likely to extend or protect markets for U.S. exports. The United States invariably opposed the industrial development of Latin America by protectionist tariffs.[64] Similarly, trade concessions by the United States to Latin American nations during the war applied mostly to minerals and raw materials rather than industrial goods. As critics such as the hostile Argentines suggested, the "partnership" proclaimed by the United States was all too obviously both one-sided and short term.

Growing contact with the United States during the war thus fostered an export boom in much of Latin America but did little to meet growing aspirations in the region for industrial development and higher living standards. In the United States liberals often recognized these limitations and led campaigns for a broader commitment to Latin America's future. "The best way to improve trade with Latin America," argued Samuel Inman, for example, "is to raise its standard of living. A modest industrialization, with working conditions guarded by enforcement of labor laws, is one way for countries to modernize their colonial economies."[65]

However, most conservatives in the United States condemned increased aid to Latin America as "boondoggling."[66] The conservative position was to "deny that the other American republics, even those most favored. . .[could] ever attain a high degree of industrialization. [The conservatives] consign[ed] these countries to the status of large-scale producers of foodstuffs, minerals and other raw materials, and small-scale manufacturers of easily worked goods for local consumption."[67]

As the war progressed, there were signs of growing disenchantment among Latin Americans with the limited scope of U.S. policy. Latin Americans demanded broader trade concessions from the United States in favor of their expanding manufacturing sectors; they criticized the preferences of the United States to offer loans rather than trade in manufactures as a recipe for eventual stagnation and chronic indebtedness; growing numbers of Latin Americans found the United States insensitive to the mounting social problems of the region that resulted from inflation and the rapid growth of the cities. "To achieve a (genuine) common front," declared the leftist Peruvian writer Luis Alberto Sánchez, "the United States must demonstrate that it is concerned with the welfare of the common man in Latin America."[68] Throughout Latin America fears of U.S. domination were reviving. "We see the United States advancing as a giant," declared a Mexican diplomat in 1943, "but in the degree the giant grows, its shadow falls upon us."[69]

Growing Rifts, 1940–1948

By this point, around 1943, other issues were pulling the United States and Latin America still further apart. The Pan-American movement was based on the isolationist assumptions of the 1930s that were now glaringly outdated. From the fall of France in mid-1940 onward, growing numbers of Americans recognized that "if the battle for Latin America was going to be won at all, it would have to be won on the other side of the Atlantic, for a Hitler who triumphed in Europe would be a Hitler capable of triumphing in much of Latin America."[70]

As the commitments of the United States spread to a world arena far beyond the confines of the hemisphere, Latin America's privileged standing under the Good Neighbor and the Pan-American movements was threatened. After the war, declared Secretary of State Cordell Hull in 1943, "there [would] be no longer any need for spheres of influence, for balance of power, or any other of the special arrangements" that guided policies before the war.[71] By 1944, as the United States steadily focused its attention away from Latin America and toward Europe and the Pacific, "all was far from well in the inter-American family." The Pan-American movement, complained Whitaker, was "a living organism; it need[ed] sunshine and exercise, and by 1944 it was growing pale and wan through lack of both."[72]

The change in attitude toward Latin America in the United States during the war found a striking illustration in Nicholas John Spykman's *America's Strategy in World Politics*. Written in 1940–1941 and published soon after Pearl Harbor, this often meandering but revealing tract began on the isolationist assumption of Latin America's critical importance to the United States; it ended, however, by suggesting entirely the opposite.

On the isolationist premise that the "struggle for the hegemony of Latin America [would] be one of the most important phases of the war," Spykman first conducted a long review of inter-American relations. This review, however, led him to conclude that the United States could not survive an Axis takeover of Europe and the Far East, as the isolationists argued, by retreating into a closed hemispheric system. Much of South America, above all Argentina, Spykman observed, depended heavily on trade with Europe. These areas had to "find a market or perish, [and] our good neighbors [had to], therefore, continue their efforts to balance our power by means of European or Asiatic affiliations."[73] Because of trade, countries like Argentina remained constantly vulnerable to Axis penetration and were likely to enlist immediately with Germany in the event of a German conquest of Europe.

The "closed New World" of the isolationists, Spykman continued, was unsuited to American interests for other reasons. If Germany defeated Britain, as seemed quite possible in late 1940 and 1941, it could then impose an embargo on European imports of U.S. and Canadian grain. Such an embargo, Spykman believed, would be "fatal for the temperate zone of North America." Alternatively, as some American policymakers were urging, the United States could acknowledge South America's links with Europe and abandon this part of the continent to the Axis while keeping control over the "quartersphere" north of Panama. Withdrawal to Panama, however, Spykman retorted, could not be justified from a military standpoint, since it would leave the United States without access to the mineral wealth of South America and would place the Axis in a position to attack the Panama Canal.[74] The obvious solution to the whole problem, Spykman concluded, was winning control over Europe:

> [Victory in Europe is] an absolute prerequisite for the independence of the New World. . . .There is no safe defensive position on this side of the oceans. Hemispheric defense is no defense at all. . . .The Second World War will be won or lost in Europe and Asia. The strategic position demands that we conduct our military operations in the form of a great offensive across the oceans. If our Allies in the Old World are defeated, we cannot hold South America; if we defeat [the Axis] our good neighbors will need no protection.[75]

In the postwar period, Spykman continued, it would be "cheaper in the long run to remain a working member of the European power-zone than to withdraw," since withdrawal risked allowing the rise of a new dominant force in Europe that would again threaten the western hemisphere.[76] Thus having begun by focusing on the inter-American issues stressed by the isolationists, Spykman ended his study by concentrating exclusively on the interests of the United States in what he called, in the language of geopolitics, the "rimlands" of Western Europe and Asia.

Spykman died within a year of the appearance of this book, but in a second work published immediately after his death in 1943 he did not once mention Latin America. His new position found expression in a single maxim: "Who controls the rimland rules Eurasia; who rules Eurasia controls the destinies of the world."[77] Spykman now urged that after the war Germany "should be broken up to prevent European unification on the basis of German domination."[78] He foresaw a successful balance of power in postwar Europe based on an Anglo-American alliance in control of the Western nations, which he thought would remain stable so long as the Soviet Union stayed out of the "rimlands."[79]

By late 1944 an element of friction had appeared in inter-American relations. Latin Americans objected strongly to the plan produced by the Allied conference at Dumbarton Oaks for a future United Nations dominated by a Security Council that would include the great powers alone. This concept, the Latin Americans held, contradicted the idea of the equality of sovereign states embodied in the Pan-American movement.[80] In 1944 Latin Americans objected too to the Bretton Woods conference on monetary and trade issues, in which the Allies pledged themselves to free trade and opposed protectionism.[81]

In this period Argentina remained a third major source of friction. In June 1943 a military coup in Argentina brought a faction of anti-American nationalists to power. In March 1944 the United States finally forced Argentina to break diplomatic links with Germany after discovering that the nationalist regime was attempting to purchase weapons from the Nazis. But in 1944 the diplomatic break brought no immediate improvement in U.S.–Argentine relations, and this issue became a pretext for Latin American critics to accuse the United States of returning to the bullying interventionism that had preceded the Good Neighbor policy.

In this atmosphere the rifts between north and south continued to widen. In February 1945 the United States sponsored a Pan-American conference at Chapultepec, Mexico, to gather Latin American support for the launching of the United Nations at a second conference in San Francisco in March. Although the Latin American nations did pledge their support in San Francisco, Chapultepec again exposed the deep divisions in the Pan-American movement. U.S. delegates led by Undersecretary Will Clayton urged free trade and private enterprise throughout the hemisphere and opposed Latin American pressure for continuing economic aid after the war; the Latin Americans, in contrast, demanded more economic aid and vigorously defended protectionism and state corporations.[82] Overall Chapultepec produced nothing but "a clarification of [divergent] attitudes."[83] "The long range consequences of this rift," predicted Whitaker, were "very serious, if the economic policy question. . .should prove a decisive factor."[84] The United States, he pleaded, should "revise its policies" to prevent the "dismantling of Pan-American morale."[85]

But the next twelve months brought more conflicts as the United States launched an attack on economic nationalism in Latin America. According to Spruille Braden, the undersecretary of state for Latin America, "the exaggerated nationalism, now so prevalent everywhere" had to be "completely extirpated."[86] The disputes over economic nationalism appeared in the wake of Braden's acrimonious conflict with Juan Perón, now the leading figure in the Argentine junta, while Braden served as American ambassador in Buenos Aires in mid-1945. As ambassador, Braden campaigned against the Argentine junta's nationalist policies and its "fascist" affiliations while supporting the "democratic" opponents of Perón. But in this battle Perón emerged the victor. In September–October 1945 Perón survived the attempts of his opponents to overthrow him, and in February 1946 he routed his opponents in elections.[87]

In 1944–1945, particularly during the preparations for the San Francisco conference to establish the United Nations, the United States supported the democratization of Latin America. But it then grew noticeably less interested in democracy once the United Nations had been formed and as the realization grew that democracy was likely to cast up popular nationalists like Perón.

Immediately after the war the United States canceled its contracts for minerals and other strategic supplies from Latin America. Trade boomed in the region in 1945–1947 as the Latin American nations used their dollar reserves accumulated during the war to finance a flood of imports from the United States. But as exports to the United States started to fall, and the wartime dollar reserves in Latin America disappeared, the trade boom abruptly stalled. In Mexico a balance of payments deficit forced a devaluation in July 1947.[88] Brazil devalued its currency in 1948. In Argentina imports from the United States increased fourfold in 1945 and 1946 and by an additional two and a half times in 1947. Yet there too the postwar boom collapsed in 1948, and Argentina's imports failed to regain the level of 1947 until 1960.[89]

By 1945–1946 only a shrinking group of liberals in the United States continued to demand policies to accelerate the economic development of Latin America. Sumner Welles, for example, one of the architects of the Good Neighbor policy but now retired from the State Department, acknowledged that isolationism was defunct and that the United States was bound to assume a world role. Yet he urged his country to seek "the continuous perfection of the existing inter-American system. The United States [had to] continue wholeheartedly its policy of economic cooperation with its American neighbors. Such bread cast upon the waters [would] come back to this country a hundredfold. One of the most profitable opportunities for American investment and for American foreign trade [lay] with the neighboring republics of the hemisphere."[90]

In 1945 Laurence Duggan, another State Department liberal, perceived "a militant determination" in the United States "to protect fundamental human rights, . . .encourage democratic institutions, and promote the transfer of political and economic power to more progressive classes" in Latin America. But he criticized the abrupt termination of wartime trade contracts by the United States and its failure to assist Latin America to adjust to the new peace economy. The United States, Duggan argued, should adopt "an understanding and tolerant attitude toward tariff protection in Latin America."[91]

In a second book published in 1946 Welles claimed that "good relations" with Latin America were "of vital significance [to] security [and] prosperity. . . .The survival of democracy and the peace of the world depend[ed] on the restoration of the inter-American system."[92] Unless economic aid were resumed, Welles predicted social and economic dislocation in Latin America and the further spread of communism. Already "Communists were taking advantage [of] recent United States policy. . .to arouse suspicions and hostility toward the American people," he declared.[93] To end this threat the United States should support the rapid industrialization of Latin America "as the best means of raising living standards."[94]

But warnings and appeals like these passed unheeded. As the Cold War supervened and the Soviet Union intensified its pressure on the European "rimlands," the position that Spykman had advocated in 1941–1943 continued to gain strength. The wartime flow of funds from the United States to Latin America rapidly dwindled and in 1946–1950 amounted to only 2 percent of total U.S. foreign assistance.[95] After the war Latin America received virtually no foreign aid from the United States, and for around a decade, except in Mexico and oil-rich Venezuela, the inflow of private foreign investment was negligible. In contrast, between July 1945 and December 1951 the United States provided $8.6 billion to its former enemies, led by Germany and Japan, and $5.6 billion to its former Western European allies, led by Britain and France. The sum allotted to Latin America during the same period was a mere $2.6 million, mostly for defense.[96] In 1947 the U.S. Congress at first rejected new military aid to Latin America ostensibly on the grounds that such aid upheld the power of "dictators," but the fact was, at least for the time being, that no military aid was needed.[97] According to Welles the "good relations" between Latin America and the United States during the depression and early war years now lay in "advanced disintegration. . . .Suspicions and animosity toward the United States" prevailed throughout Latin America.[98]

As Arnold Toynbee described the year 1947, "the governing event in world history. . .was the failure of the victors in the Second World War to maintain their war-time co-operation, and the consequent re-partition of the world into two hostile camps."[99] The decisive stage in the development of U.S. policy occurred that same year as the Truman administration committed itself to the defense of Western and Southern Europe and Japan against the threatened encroachment of the Soviet Union. In March 1947 the Truman administration was compelled by the imminent withdrawal of Britain from the Balkans to pledge financial aid to Greece and Turkey in the struggle against Communist insurgents. The breach between the two superpowers became final following the conference of foreign ministers in Moscow in March and April. In May 1947 Communists were expelled from the cabinets in France and Italy. In June Secretary of State George C. Marshall proclaimed the plan bearing his name for the reconstruction of Western Europe.

The same year, the U.S. Congress appropriated $1.6 billion in foreign aid for the support of "free" Europe, 25 percent of which was destined for Greece and Turkey alone. The year 1947 also marked the failure of the campaign led by former vice president Henry Wallace, another of the leading champions of Latin America during the era of the Good Neighbor, to secure a rapprochement with the Soviet Union based on joint support for the United Nations. Meanwhile, Communist-orchestrated coups d'état, starting in Poland and ending in Czechoslovakia, consolidated the rule of Stalin throughout Eastern Europe.[100] In 1947 too a succession of Latin American governments, led by Brazil, Chile, and Cuba, banned the Communist parties, purged Communists from the labor unions, or severed diplomatic relations with the Soviet Union.

The same year, Marshall himself attended the inter-American conference at Rio de Janeiro. In this meeting he reiterated the views of the United States expressed at Chapultepec two years before. Unlike Europe, he argued, the development of Latin America required private enterprise, "a type of collaboration in which a much greater role [fell] to private citizens than in a program [like the Marshall Plan] designed to aid European countries to recover from the destruction of war."[101] A year later at another inter-American conference in Bogotá, Marshall took the same line. "The basic economic trouble," he declared, in an argument that once again evoked Spykman,

> has been the collapse of the European economy. . . .The recovery of Europe is therefore a prerequisite to the resumption of trade relationships. . . .We propose to provide the free nations of Europe with that marginal material strength they require to defend the free way of life and to preserve the institutions of self-government. If human rights are blotted out in Europe, they will become increasingly insecure in the new world as well. This is a matter of as much concern to your countries as it is to mine."[102]

Concerning U.S. assistance to Latin America, Marshall stated:

> We have already agreed to certain principles. . .in the Economic Charter of the Americas [at Chapultepec]. . . .The American republics proclaimed their common purpose to promote the sound development of their national economies. The Charter pointed the way toward the realization of their aim through the encouragement of private enterprise and the fair treatment of foreign capital. . . .My government is prepared to increase the scale of assistance it has been giving to the economic development of the American republics. But it is beyond the capacity of the United States government itself to finance more than a small proportion of the vast debt needed. The capital required during the coming years must come from private sources, both domestic and foreign.[103]

As the United States focused on Europe and the Far East and away from Latin America, the Good Neighbor lapsed into the "Good Spectator." "Today," wrote Duggan in 1949, "we are paying a minimum of attention to New World problems, and this neglect is all the more marked because only yesterday we were making an all-out effort to persuade our neighbors of our friendship."[104] Surveying political conditions in Latin America, Duggan concluded pessimistically: "In general the situation is not at all encouraging."[105]

Contemporary observers like Duggan and Welles thus regarded the early postwar period in the same way as many Latin Americans: the United States had been ready to support Latin America with funds, technical assistance, and market incentives while its interests in the region were threatened, but as it emerged victorious from the war and then faced the new threat from the Soviet Union, it began focusing exclusively on Europe. Latin Americans were now constantly complaining about the reorientation in policy and the growing fixation of the United States on Western Europe. The United States, they declared, was interested only in "defense treaties" to consolidate its grip over Latin America. During the war the United States had purchased Latin American commodity exports at fixed and relatively low prices, but these prices had now fallen even lower as the world market was reconstructed and alternative sources of supply emerged. In the discussions on continental security—now virtually the only issue the United States would allow to enter the agenda—the Latin Americans vainly attempted to redefine the concept of aggression to include "economic aggression" of the type they accused the United States of inflicting on them.

During the late 1940s and 1950s Latin America paid a price for its physical location "outside the main international arena."[106] By the time of the inter-American conference held in Bogotá in 1948, Latin America's democratic opening of mid-decade was collapsing. In Venezuela and Peru new democratic regimes were overthrown in 1947 and 1948; in Colombia in 1948 the popular reformist leader Eliécer Gaitán fell to an assassin's bullet. In Argentina, Chile, Brazil, Paraguay, Bolivia, and many of the Caribbean and Central American countries incumbent regimes moved sharply to the right, launching repressive campaigns against the Communist parties in each country, repressing the labor unions, and silencing the reformers.[107] Typical of the trend were the breakdown of democratic practices and the brief civil war in Costa Rica in 1948. If José Figueres, the leader of this rebellion, later won a reputation as a leading Latin American democrat, in 1948 he stood at the head of a conservative movement opposed to the so-called *caldero-comunistas* who had hitherto dominated the country.[108]

Thus popular government was becoming extinct. Writing in 1952, Germán Arciniegas perceived a "vast conspiracy against democracy, liberty, and respect for human rights" in Latin America: "Congresses have been closed by force. Universities have been brought under government domination. . . .The judiciary has been packed. Political leaders have been reduced to silence."[109] In this era the United States protected its interests in most of

Latin America through conservative oligarchs or military dictators. In supporting the dictators, the United States invoked the provisions of the Military Security Act of 1951 that allowed military assistance "to any nation whose ability to defend itself is important to the United States."[110] In the early 1950s Secretary of State John Foster Dulles advanced Marcos Pérez Jiménez, the dictator of Venezuela, as an "ideal leader" for Latin America, because he made his country "attractive to foreign capital." If all Latin America were like Venezuela, Dulles held, "the danger of Communism and social disorder would disappear."[111] After a fact-finding tour of Latin America in 1953 Milton Eisenhower acknowledged the region's need for capital investment but insisted that capital had to be "attracted" not "induced." Eisenhower condemned economic nationalism in Latin America as the work of "Communist agitators."[112] The bilateral defense pacts, Eisenhower declared, that Washington was now pursuing were the key to the hemispheric system: they would protect the access of the United States to the raw materials of Latin America, safeguard U.S. property and investments, and protect the region against Communist infiltration.[113] In a message to the U.S. Congress in 1954 President Dwight D. Eisenhower echoed these ideas as he urged: "Military assistance [to Latin America] must be continued. Technical assistance must be maintained. Economic assistance can be reduced."[114]

Conclusion

World War II and its aftermath thus promised radical change in Latin America but eventually failed to deliver it. In Latin America there were attempts to link social and economic change to a transition to popular government. By 1945 the transition was taking shape, but it then collapsed on the advent of the Cold War and the slump in foreign trade in 1947–1948. The 1940s began in an atmosphere that suggested the United States might eventually align itself with progressive forces in Latin America and have a leading part in the region's economic and political development. This atmosphere was gradually stifled, however, as the United States turned its attention first to the destruction of Nazism and then to the containment of communism. Policy followed the directions Spykman had suggested: if the United States defeated its enemies abroad, its "good neighbors [would] need no protection." The lesson of the 1940s was that when powerful foreign nations dominated the strategic regions of Europe and Asia the United States turned toward Latin America; if the United States itself controlled these regions, it turned away from Latin America almost to the point of forgetting its existence.

For more than a decade after 1945 the United States was closely involved in Latin American affairs in one issue alone: that of the ill-fated Arbenz regime in Guatemala, the single survivor of the progressive movements of the 1940s. But by the late 1950s, as Richard Nixon discovered during his uncomfortable tour of the region in mid-1958, new radical forces were emerging in Latin America as the region faced endemic inflation, burgeoning population growth, stagnant industry, and escalating popular discontent.

Notes

1. *Inter-American Affairs, 1943*, edited by Arthur P. Whitaker. New York: Columbia University Press, 1944, 203; Russell H. Fitzgibbon, "Latin America," in *Problems of the Post-War World*, edited by T. C. McCormick. New York: McGraw Hill, 1945, 476.

2. Donald Marquand Dozer, *Are We Good Neighbors? Three Decades of Inter-American Relations, 1930–1960*. Gainesville: University of Florida Press, 1959, 226–27; *Inter-American Affairs, 1945*, edited by Arthur P. Whitaker. New York: Columbia University Press, 1946, 232.

3. Laurence Duggan, in George Wythe, *Industry in Latin America*. New York: Columbia University Press, 1945, vi.

4. Edwin Lieuwen, *Arms and Politics in Latin America*. New York: Praeger, 1960, 32.

5. Arthur P. Whitaker, quoted in Lieuwen, *Arms*, 51.

6. Ibid., 50.

7. Duggan, in Wythe, *Industry*, v.

8. Wythe, *Industry*, 1.

9. Ibid., 3.

10. Ibid., 4.

11. Ibid., 61, 65.

12. See ibid., 182.

13. See John D. French, "The Populist Gamble of Getúlio Vargas in 1945: Social, Political, and Ideological Transitions in Brazil," this volume.

14. See Charles P. Kindleberger, *The Great Depression*. Berkeley and Los Angeles: University of California Press, 1973, 190.

15. See Paul W. Drake, "International Crises and Popular Movements in Latin America: Chile and Peru from the Great Depression to the Cold War," this volume; Brian Loveman, *Chile: The Legacy of Hispanic Capitalism*. 2d ed. New York: Oxford University Press, 1988, 231–52.

16. These trends are discussed in more detail in Rosemary Thorp, "The Latin American Economies in the 1940s," this volume.

17. Whitaker, *Inter-American Affairs, 1945*, 145, 147.

18. R. A. Humphreys, *Latin America and the Second World War*. Vol. 2. London: Athlone Press, 1982, 34.

19. Lt. Col. Mariano Abarca, *La industrialización de la Argentina*. Buenos Aires: Ministerio de Agricultura de la Nación, 1944, 17–32.

20. Sanford A. Mosk, *Industrial Revolution in Mexico*. Berkeley and Los Angeles: University of California Press, 1950, 63, 80.

21. See David Rock, *Argentina, 1516–1987: From Spanish Colonization to Alfonsín*. Berkeley and Los Angeles: University of California Press, 1987, 262–89.

22. *Inter-American Affairs, 1944*, edited by Arthur P. Whitaker. New York: Columbia University Press, 1945, 107.

23. Mosk, *Industrial Revolution*, 36–53.

24. See Whitaker, *Inter-American Affairs, 1943*, 130.

25. George Wythe, "Industry, Commerce, and Finance," in Whitaker, *Inter-American Affairs, 1943*, 105.

26. Dozer, *Neighbors*, 226–27.

27. Whitaker, *Inter-American Affairs, 1941*, 47.

28. Whitaker, *Inter-American Affairs, 1944*, 42.

29. See William Krehm, *Democracies and Tyrannies in the Caribbean*. Westport, Conn.: Lawrence Hill, 1984, 19.

30. R. A. Humphreys, *Latin America and the Second World War*. Vol. 1 (1939–1942). London: Athlone Press, 1981, 13.

31. Quoted in Ronald M. Schneider, *Communism in Guatemala, 1944–1954*. New York: Praeger, 1958, 11. (I have slightly modified Schneider's translation of this document to make the English more idiomatic.) In Schneider's own view of Guatemala in 1944: "In a world which was talking of the Four Freedoms and the triumph of democracy, the personalistic dictatorship of Ubico. . .seemed outdated. The students and young professional men were most affected by the democratic propaganda of the allies which served to awaken their sense of civic consciousness" (ibid., 9).

32. Ian Roxborough, personal communication.

33. Whitaker, *Inter-American Affairs, 1945*, 137.

34. Ibid., 239.

35. Otis E. Milliken and Sarah E. Roberts, "Labor and Social Welfare," in *Inter-American Affairs, 1943*, edited by Arthur P. Whitaker. New York: Columbia University Press, 1944, 66.

36. Whitaker, *Inter-American Affairs, 1945*, 137.

37. Ibid., 136.

38. Quoted in Whitaker, *Inter-American Affairs, 1943*, 127.

39. See David G. Haglund, *Latin America and the Transformation of United States Strategic Thought*. Albuquerque: University of New Mexico Press, 1984.

40. Nicholas John Spykman, *America's Strategy in World Politics: The United States and the Balance of Power*. New York: Harcourt, Brace, 1942, 247.

41. Quoted in J. Lloyd Mecham, *The United States and Inter-American Security, 1889–1960*. Austin: University of Texas Press, 1961, 116.

42. Hubert Herring, *Good Neighbors: Argentina, Brazil, Chile, and Seventeen Other Countries*. New Haven: Yale University Press, 1941, 4.

43. Spykman, *Strategy*, 235.

44. Quoted in Carleton Beals, *America South*. Philadelphia: J. Lippincott, 1938, 492.

45. Spykman, *Strategy*, 315.

46. See David Green, *The Containment of Latin America: A History of the Myths and Realities of the Good Neighbor Policy*. Chicago: Quadrangle Books, 1971, 43.

47. See Mecham, *Security*, 125–40.

48. Mecham, *Security*, 142.

49. Ibid., 203–7.

50. See Green, *Containment*, 33.

51. Spykman, *Strategy*, 209.

52. Robert Angell, *America's Dilemma, Alone or Allied?* New York: Harper and Brothers, 1940, 105.

53. Spykman, *Strategy*, 198, 261.

54. See Humphreys, *Latin America*, 1, 99–102.

55. See George Wythe, "Economics and Finance in 1941," in Whitaker, *Inter-American Affairs, 1941*, 77.

56. Mecham, *Security*, 243.

57. See Michael J. Francis, *The Limits of Hegemony: United States Relations with Argentina and Chile during World II*. Notre Dame, Ind.: University of Notre Dame Press, 1977.

58. See Whitaker, *Inter-American Affairs, 1941*, 67.

59. See Mosk, *Industrial Revolution*, 84.

60. Humphreys, *Latin America*, 1, 63.

61. Whitaker, *Inter-American Affairs, 1941*, 64; Humphreys, *Latin America*, 1, 144.

62. Humphreys, *Latin America*, 1, 180.

63. On these issues see Joseph S. Tulchin, *Argentina and the United States: A Conflicted Relationship*. Boston: Twayne Publishers, 1990, 63–96; Francis, *Limits of Hegemony*; Carlos Escudé, *Gran Bretaña, Estados Unidos, y la declinación argentina, 1942–1949*. Buenos Aires: Belgrano, 1983; U.S. Department of State, *Memorandum of the United States among the American Republics with Respect to the Argentine Situation*. Washington, D.C.: Department of State, 1946.

64. See Lloyd C. Gardner, *Economic Aspects of New Deal Diplomacy*. Madison: University of Wisconsin Press, 1963, 130; Green, *Containment*, 76.

65. Samuel Guy Inman, *Latin America: Its Place in World Life*. 2d ed. New York: Harcourt, Brace, 1942, 413.

66. See the "Butler Report" of 1943, named after its sponsor, Senator Hugh A. Butler from Nebraska. See Whitaker, *Inter-American Affairs, 1943*, 41.

67. Laurence Duggan, in Wythe, *Industry*, v.

68. See Green, *Containment*, 62–64; Mecham, *Security*, 259.

69. José Rubén Romero, quoted in Mecham, *Security*, 258.

70. Haglund, *Transformation*, 220.

71. Quoted in Whitaker, *Inter-American Affairs, 1943*, 47.

72. Arthur P. Whitaker, "Summary and Prospect," in *Inter-American Affairs, 1944*, edited by Arthur P. Whitaker. New York: Columbia University Press, 1945, 209.

73. Spykman, *Strategy*, 320, 470.

74. Ibid., 456.

75. Ibid., 457, 470.

76. Ibid., 467.

77. Nicholas John Spykman, *The Geography of the Peace*, edited by Helen R. Nicholl with an introduction by Frederick Sherwood Dunn. New York: Harcourt, Brace, 1944, 43.

78. Ibid., xi.

79. Ibid., 57.

80. Robert Burr, "United States Latin American Policy," in *The Dynamics of World Power: A Documentary History of United States Foreign Policy*, edited by Arthur M. Schlesinger, Jr., Vol. 3. New York: Chelsea House Publishers, 1973, xxvii.

81. Whitaker, *Inter-American Affairs, 1944*, 148.

82. Arthur P. Whitaker, "Politics and Diplomacy," in Whitaker, *Inter-American Affairs, 1945*, 12–13.

83. Whitaker, *Inter-American Affairs, 1945*, 120.

84. Ibid., 238.

85. Ibid., 244.

86. Dozer, *Neighbors*, 219.

87. For a detailed account of the events of 1945 in Argentina see Felix Luna, *El '45*. Buenos Aires: Sudamericana, 1971.

88. Mosk, *Industrial Revolution*, 75.

89. Louis Rodriguez, "A Comparison: U.S. Economic Relations with Argentina and Brazil, 1947–1960." Ph.D. diss., Louisiana State University, 1963, 86.

90. Sumner Welles, *The Time for Decision*. New York: Harper and Brothers, 1944, 403–4.

91. Laurence Duggan, *The Americas: The Search for Hemisphere Security*. New York: Henry Holt, 1949, 130, 156, 203.

92. Sumner Welles, *Where Are We Heading?* New York: Harper and Brothers, 1946, 182, 185.

93. Ibid., 240.

94. Ibid., 241.

95. Mecham, *Security*, 352.

96. These figures appear in Peter Calvocoressi, *Survey of International Affairs, 1953*. London: Oxford University Press, 1956, 353; for other figures showing a similar general trend see Tulchin, *Argentina and the United States*, 102–4. According to

Tulchin, Belgium and Luxembourg received more aid from the United States than the whole of Latin America. In these calculations, however, military aid to Latin America after the war was negligible. As late as 1958 Latin America's share of foreign aid from the United States was barely 3 percent of the total.

97. Juan Archibaldo Lanús, *De Chapultepec al Beagle: Política exterior argentina, 1945–1980*. Buenos Aires: Emecé, 1984, 142–43; Lieuwen, *Arms*, 197; Gardner, *New Deal Diplomacy*, 259.

98. Welles, *Where Are We Heading?*, 185.

99. Arnold Toynbee, "Introduction," in *Survey of International Affairs, 1947–1948*, edited by Peter Calvocoressi. London: Oxford University Press, 1952, 1.

100. These events are discussed in Calvocoressi, *Survey of 1947–1948*.

101. Lanús, *Chapultepec*, 142.

102. Marshall's address at Bogotá, 1 April 1948. Quoted in Burr, "Latin American Policy," 44.

103. Burr, "Latin American Policy," 44–45.

104. Duggan, *Americas*, viii.

105. Ibid., 127.

106. Toynbee in Calvocoressi, *Survey of 1947–1948*, 9.

107. The impact of the Cold War is discussed in more detail in Drake, "International Crises and Popular Movements."

108. For a recent analysis of the 1948 revolution see Fabrice Edouard Lehoucq, "Class Conflict, Political Crisis, and the Breakdown of Democratic Practices in Costa Rica: Reassessing the Origins of the 1948 Civil War," *Journal of Latin American Studies* 23 (February 1991), 37–60.

109. Germán Arciniegas, *The State of Latin America*, translated by Harriet de Onís. New York: Knopf, 1952, xi, xiv.

110. Lieuwen, *Arms*, 198.

111. Gordon Connell-Smith, *The United States and Latin America: An Historical Analysis of Inter-American Relations*. London: Heinemann, 1966, 208.

112. Mecham, *Security*, 371.

113. On the Eisenhower mission see Calvocoressi, *Survey of 1953*, 352.

114. Connell-Smith, *Relations*, 209.

2 The Latin American Economies in the 1940s

Rosemary Thorp

In the 1940s Latin America achieved satisfactory growth, even in per capita terms, and the share of industry in gross domestic product rose from 15 percent in the last five years of the 1930s to 18 percent by the early 1950s. Population growth accelerated, rising from an average of 2.1 percent in the early 1940s to 2.5 percent in the second half of the decade. Rising population was reflected in the growth of major Latin American cities. The global experience of growth and industrial expansion is presented in table 1.

In this chapter I explore the conditions that underlay these broad trends, dividing the 1940s into two halves: first, the war years and the economic effects of the war, and second, developments during the late 1940s in conjunction with the reshaping of the international political economy. The discussion focuses chiefly on foreign trade, industrial growth, and the role of the United States, and given the limitations of space, treats these themes only in a global Latin American perspective. I show that in many ways the war years had rather positive economic effects, but for various reasons events in the rest of the decade did not lead to a consolidation of the different positive elements.

World War II and the Latin American Economies, 1939–1945

Arthur Lewis has described the period 1913–1939 as "the longest depression" of the world economy.[1] World War I opened the cracks in the existing

Table 1 Latin America: Growth Rates of Real Income and Population; Share of Industry in GDP; Percentage of Urban Population

	Real Income	*Population*	*Real Income Per Capita*	*% Industry in GDP*	*% Urban Population*
1935–40	4.5	1.9	2.5	15.2	17
1940–45	4.8	2.1	2.7	16.7	20
1945–50	6.8	2.5	4.2	18.0	25
1950–55	4.5	2.7	1.7	18.7	33

Source: United Nations, *The Economic Development of Latin America in the Post-War Period.* New York: United Nations, 1964, 5, 27.

system and exposed shifting structures. By 1918 the old Victorian system centered on London and the gold standard was in disarray, and the new dominance of the United States in trade and capital flows was apparent. With hindsight, we understand that the stability of the old system was based not on gold but an on underlying equilibrium in trade and capital flows, now being disrupted by the entry of new members and shifting relative positions. But at the time, the relevant actors were unready for change. Contemporary thinking could only seek to reinstate a return not only to the gold standard but also, quite unrealistically, to the prewar currency parities. The extent to which the old system had depended for its success not only on an underlying equilibrium but also on a single center, London, was ignored. Since there was now more than one financial center, and a much larger supply of volatile short-term funds, the system became dangerously unstable. By the end of the war the United States showed a long-term credit balance of $3.3 billion, but its leaders failed to understand that they needed to encourage imports and to export capital to keep the system alive. Instead they adopted protectionist policies, and in the 1920s capital exports from the United States comprised only some inexperienced private lending, much of which flowed into unproductive projects.

The crash of 1929 highlighted the fundamental weaknesses of the whole system. Subsequently, during the 1930s most governments pursued purely defensive policies dominated by increasing protectionism and exchange controls that permitted only the slow growth of world trade. There was little foreign investment during this period; indeed the main capital flow was toward the United States, which once more became a net debtor.

By the late 1930s, however, the United States was once more becoming the leading actor in the world economy. Even before Congress declared war on Japan and Germany in December 1941, war production and the protection of strategic raw materials had become an issue of central importance. In 1940 the United States government established the Metals Reserve Company, whose task was to stockpile raw materials used to produce weapons and munitions, and began pressuring American business interests to cooperate in obtaining supplies of oil, tin, copper, and other minerals. U.S. public and private investment in Latin America now began to rise, particularly in the crucial fields of transport and communications, which in 1943 accounted for 31 percent of total direct investment to Latin America compared with 15 percent in 1924.[2]

Simultaneously, the United States sought to assist Britain in the desperate struggle against Nazi Germany, although for some time legislation left over from the isolationist period between the wars made it difficult to offer credits. In 1942 these obstacles were overcome by the Lend-Lease Act under whose provisions the United States retained nominal title to the weapons and munitions exported to Britain and its allies, while the issue of paying for goods imported by Britain was deferred until the end the war. Between 1942 and 1945 supplies worth $44 billion in current dollars were exported under lend-lease, the great bulk of them to the British Empire.

Throughout this period the United States economy grew rapidly. While Europe was suffering enormous war damage, productive capacity in the United States rose by 50 percent. By 1945 the United States produced more than half the worldwide total of manufacturing goods and owned half the world volume of shipping, compared with only 14 percent in 1939. The United States now supplied one-third of world exports, but it took only one-tenth of world imports.[3]

Even though profoundly affected by the weakness and disruption of the international system, Latin America, unlike the United States and the leading European nations, did not experience this period as "the longest depression." On the contrary, particularly in the 1930s, the region achieved substantial growth (see table 2). Import-substituting industry emerged as the leading sector in most of the larger countries, and agriculture for domestic use in most of the smaller countries. In several notable cases, like Brazil and Colombia, overall economic recovery occurred before exports returned to the levels of the 1920s and owed much to unorthodox policy management:

trade, exchange and capital controls, and countercyclical government spending. With growing urbanization and industrialization, the expansion of state intervention, and a declining reliance on primary exports, a new structure began to take shape in Latin America.

World War II had a major part in shaping the new model by delivering another severe shock—this time from the supply side, unlike during the depression—to the old export-led structure. The shock of the early 1940s came on top of those of earlier periods and intensified the growing conviction, particularly in the larger countries, that it was unsafe to depend on traditional export-led growth and that new sources of dynamism within Latin America itself had to act as a substitute. The unusual feature of the shock represented by World War II, however, which helped to account for the ambiguities in the subsequent evolution of Latin America, was that it failed to increase the region's autonomy. Instead, as the struggle began to safeguard supplies and to develop new sources of vital raw materials, the war marked a major advance in the influence of the United States in Latin America.

The transition was particularly striking in Mexico. There the transformation of relations with the United States became so far-reaching that by 1942

Table 2 Selected Countries: Comparison of Real GDP, 1929–1940 (Index 1929 = 100)

	Argentina	*Brazil*	*Colombia*	*Mexico*	*U.S.*	*U.K.*	*France*
1929	100	100	100	100	100	100	100
1930	96	98	99	96	90	99	97
1931	89	95	98	99	83	94	93
1932	86	99	104	84	72	95	89
1933	90	108	110	98	71	98	93
1934	97	118	117	103	76	104	93
1935	102	121	120	112	83	108	90
1936	103	136	126	121	94	113	91
1937	111	142	128	128	99	117	96
1938	113	148	136	130	94	118	96
1939	117	152	145	140	102	120	100
1940	114	150	148	142	109	132	83

Sources: Latin American countries: Rosemary Thorp, ed., *Latin America in the 1930s*. London: Macmillan, 1984, Statistical Appendix, Table 4. United States, United Kingdom, and France: A. Maddison, *Phases of Capitalist Development*. Oxford and New York: Oxford University Press, 1982, 174–75.

the Mexican foreign minister described the frontier as "a line that unites rather than divides us." Remarks like these were almost astonishing in light of the bitter clash over oil between the two countries only four years earlier. In 1942 an agreement was reached between the Mexican government and the Export-Import Bank to develop a steel- and tin-plate-rolling mill in Mexico. A Railroad Mission established by the U.S. government worked on expanding Mexico's communications infrastructure, and agreements were reached for the purchase of numerous raw materials.[4] Similarly, when Brazil joined the Allies, the United States supported attempts to strengthen the Brazilian industrial base. The Cooke Mission of 1942, for example, was described as "lay[ing] the foundations of the long range strength of Brazil's whole industrial economy." During this period the United States also helped to bolster the growing links between Brazilian industry and the military. In Peru, U.S. funds and exports assisted in establishing the Corporación Peruana del Santa to produce iron and steel. There were numerous examples elsewhere of similar trends. Among the larger Latin American nations, Argentina alone avoided this process of penetration.[5]

Among the striking paradoxes of the war years, and one of the major consequences of the war itself, was the growing involvement of the United States in Latin America alongside the expanding role of the Latin American states and the use of direct controls. Over many parts of Latin America the private sectors were becoming more closely tied to government in much the same way that in the United States business leaders were co-opted by the government to plan and to execute a whole range of new projects.

THE ECONOMIC EFFECTS OF THE WAR ON LATIN AMERICA

The war quickly intensified demand for Latin American primary products, spurring export revenues, although growth varied over different parts of the region. Some nations, led by Ecuador, Venezuela, Brazil, Colombia, and some of the Central American states, experienced annual growth rates of more than 6 percent; elsewhere, as in Bolivia and Chile, growth was negligible. Even so, on average Latin America's export revenues rose by more than 4 percent a year at constant prices (table 3).

The capacity of each country to benefit from the growth of exports varied widely, because in many cases, particularly as with minerals, price controls or delayed payments meant that little additional revenue was actually re-

Table 3 Latin America: Average Annual Growth Rates of Exports, 1940–1945

Argentina	4.0	Honduras	4.6
Bolivia	2.4	Mexico	4.6
Brazil	12.1	Nicaragua	4.3
Chile	1.5	Panama	2.5
Colombia	6.6	Paraguay	20.9
Costa Rica	−1.3	Peru	4.5
Ecuador	18.9	Uruguay	5.4
El Salvador	8.1	Venezuela	9.7
Guatemala	12.0		

Sources: South America: James W. Wilkie, *Statistics and National Policy*, Supplement 3. University of California, Los Angeles, 1974. Central America: Victor Bulmer-Thomas, *The Political Economy of Central America since 1920*. Cambridge: Cambridge University Press, 1987.

Note: Figures are based on constant 1970 dollars.

ceived. Thus countries such as Chile, Bolivia, and Peru gained relatively few benefits from huge increases in export volumes. But even where additional revenues were available, as in Brazil, Colombia, and Mexico, there was little to spend them on, and in these countries the reserves grew rapidly (table 4).

Import scarcities undoubtedly prompted new efforts at substitution, but these efforts were limited by shortages of crucial imports and machines. The net result was a continuation of the industrial growth of the type already experienced during the 1930s but with a much stronger bias toward capital goods and basic inputs. During this period, for example, some of the firms that later achieved prominence in the Brazilian capital goods industry evolved from workshops to factories.[6] For the first time ever manufactured

Table 4 Latin America: Percentage Change in Reserves, 1940–1945

Argentina	+156	Mexico	+480
Brazil	+635	Peru	+ 55
Chile	+214	U.S.(export prices)	+174
Colombia	+540		

Source: R. A. Ferrero, *La política fiscal y la economía nacional*. Lima: Editorial Lumen, 1946.

Note: Figures are based on current dollars. The U.S figure represents export prices in 1945 indexed for inflation (1939 = 100).

goods were being traded within Latin America: Brazilian, Argentine, and Mexican textile exports to other Latin American countries, for example, rose from almost nothing in 1939 to 20 percent of total exports by 1945. The emphasis of the missions and advisers from the United States on iron and steel and other basic inputs helped to push industrial development in new and healthy directions, although these trends were later reversed by the renewed emphasis on consumer goods.

The results of industrial growth on per capita income also varied (table 5). In contrast with earlier periods there was now little correlation between the growth of per capita incomes and that of exports.

In addition, in many cases rising exports combined with import scarcities inevitably meant inflation that climbed beyond the rates of rising world prices (see table 6).

During the war only Colombia appeared to learn how to apply a sophisticated system of containing inflation. Robert Triffin, the well-known U.S. economist and expert in monetary matters, visited Colombia in 1944 and wrote a brief history of Colombian banking published in Bogotá as a supplement to the *Revista del Banco de la República*. Triffin detailed the measures between 1941 and 1943 to increase savings and to counter the effect of the

Table 5 Selected Latin American Countries: Growth Rates of Real Per Capita GDP and Exports, 1940–1945

	Real Per Capita GDP	*Exports*
Argentina	1.2	5.0
Brazil	0.3	8.1
Chile	2.4	2.2
Colombia	0.4	17.5
Ecuador	1.5	17.0
Honduras	0.8	22.4
Mexico	4.6	11.7
Paraguay	−0.1	3.1
Uruguay	1.3	10.7
Venezuela	2.6	23.1

Source: United Nations, Comisión Económica para América Latina, *Series históricas del crecimiento de América Latina*. Santiago de Chile: CEPAL, 1978.

Note: Figures are based on constant 1970 dollars.

Table 6 Latin America: Cost of Living Indicators

	Wartime (1939 = 100)		*Postwar (1945 = 100)*	
	1945	*1948*	*1950*	*1955*
Argentina	133	156	256	587
Bolivia	320	144	187	2,525
Brazil	247	159	173	383
Chile	233	186	253	1,440
Colombia	161	151	193	242
Costa Rica	189	119	133	125
El Salvador	191	106	130	166
Guatemala	191	146	156	165
Honduras	146	106	116	145
Mexico	200	126	148	248
Nicaragua	433	83	95	166
Paraguay	233	172	229	2,060
Peru	183	182	236	333
Uruguay	133	129	129	220
Venezuela	134	129	122	131
U.S. (export prices)	174	120	107	122

Source: James W. Wilkie, *Statistics and National Policy*, Supplement 3. University of California, Los Angeles, 1974.

inflow of foreign exchange. He concluded that "the anti-inflation measures taken in Colombia comprise[d] perhaps the most complete and balanced system introduced to date to deal with inflation in Latin America."[7] He estimated that the measures effectively sterilized at least half the inflow of foreign exchange.

The more common pattern was one of inflation and accompanying exchange rate overvaluation. During the war many countries allowed significant overvaluation to develop, since nothing appeared to be gained from devaluation when many exports were being sold at fixed prices in direct purchase agreements with the United States. A beneficial effect of accumulating reserves and rising inflation was that the defaulted foreign debt of the 1930s could now be paid. Brazil and Mexico, for example, both settled with their creditors in 1943, thus clearing the way for their renewed integration with international capital markets: debt resolution became one of the main ingredients of the growth model adopted during the postwar period.

Despite these elements of disequilibrium, on balance the wartime period introduced some interesting and potentially healthy economic trends in the form of the broader base of industrialization, new areas of state activity, greater collaboration between the state and the private sector, and even experience with exports of manufactures in the context of a new interest in regional integration. How did these aspects fare as the war ended?

The Aftermath of War

THE POSTWAR ECONOMY

World War II thus brought conditions similar to those that followed earlier external shocks, although the new relationship between the private sector and the state marked one striking contrast with the past. An even greater contrast with the past, however, lay in the new international system that appeared after 1945. In earlier decades the signals pointing to the need for change were present but had remained weak and conflicting. Now it was clearly recognized that the old international system was bankrupt and in need of fundamental restructuring. Furthermore, the United States was now fully prepared for deliberate and positive action to lead institutional change and to support economic recovery. At the end of World War II American policymakers had a relatively clear idea of the changes that were necessary to reconstruct the international economy. First, there had to be a complete dismantling of the controls established during the 1930s and expanded during the war. Second, inflation, an unavoidable wartime evil, now had to be conquered.

The Bretton Woods agreement of 1944 marked the start of the new system. The chief purposes of the agreement were to return to stable exchange rates and to ensure that the supply of long-term capital was put to productive use. The creation of the International Monetary Fund (IMF) and the World Bank at Bretton Woods aimed to achieve those two goals. Bretton Woods established a "gold-exchange" standard in which convertible currencies led by the dollar became accepted as part of exchange reserves. For the next two decades this measure established the dollar as the leading reserve currency. Both the IMF and the World Bank were committed to supporting the liberalization of trade and capital accounts.

In 1944 there were hopes that after the inevitable emergency aid of the immediate postwar period these new institutions would facilitate a sufficient flow of funds to "grease" the system. In fact, the problems caused by the U.S. trade surplus and the resulting dollar shortage, and the urgent needs of the Europeans for funds, were not so easily resolved. As a result, in 1947 the Marshall Plan was launched, providing for a four-year recovery program for Europe, with Europe pledging in return for Marshall Aid to raise productivity and lower trade barriers and inflation. Between 1945 and 1953 foreign loans from the United States totaled $33 billion, of which $23 billion went to Europe. By the latter year the recovery of Europe was in full swing, and world trade in manufactures began to rise sharply.

How did all of this affect Latin America? Not quite in the expected manner. The trade boom that followed the early postwar period derived mainly from an exchange of manufactured goods between the developed countries. Earlier, expansion of world trade had tended to result in declining terms of trade for manufactures. This time, as a result of postwar shortages and accelerating technical progress and substitution, terms of trade moved slightly in their favor. This trend intensified as the European Common Market took shape during the late 1950s.

Under these conditions the performance of primary products became extremely varied. Following the price boom of 1943–1948 temperate agricultural products performed poorly throughout the 1950s, as they were adversely affected by the expansion of agriculture in the developed countries. Coffee, by contrast, did spectacularly well until the mid-1950s, while on the whole tropical products fared better than temperate goods. Minerals behaved erratically, receiving a boost during the Korean War but falling afterward. In Latin America oil became the great winner, and Venezuela was thus the striking exception to the general trend throughout this period.

During the postwar period capital flows followed the trends in trade. The Korean War brought a repetition of 1939–1945 as the United States sought to extend its grip over mineral supplies in Latin America: American private capital sought to control oil in Venezuela, copper and lead in Mexico and Peru, and bauxite in the Caribbean. Unlike in the aftermath of World War I, when such steps had been regarded as threatening the interests of home industries, the United States was no longer opposed to American firms investing abroad in manufacturing: after World War II economic growth in Latin America came to be seen as the best protection for democracy. U.S. private investment in Latin America increased during the late 1940s, but the rise was very small compared with that of later periods, partly because of the discouraging climate that prevailed in Latin America at this point. Meanwhile, U.S. public funds went elsewhere. Thus in 1945–1950 the capital inflow to Latin America was positive, but negative if Venezuela and Cuba were excluded; in 1951–1955, in contrast, the capital inflow increased by almost five times.[8] Aside from the Communist world, in 1951 Latin America stood out as the single regional bloc that was not covered by a U.S. aid program; in 1945–1951 Belgium and Luxembourg together received more aid than the whole of Latin America.[9]

Behind these trends lay the fact that Latin America had ceased to be an area of much interest to the United States, since it was regarded, at least for the time being, as relatively safe from the threat of communism. After World War II Latin America, in contrast, was now acutely aware of U.S. dominance in the region, which found reflection in the new patterns of trade and investment. Trade patterns for Argentina, Brazil, Chile, and Mexico shifted dramatically, primarily toward the United States (see table 7).

In all four cases, between 1938 and 1950 the European share of exports fell at least 20 percentage points, while that of the United States and Canada rose steeply, particularly with Mexico. Trade within Latin America declined

Table 7 Comparison of Export Share to Principal Markets, 1938 and 1950

	% Exports		
	To U.S. and Canada	*To Europe*	*To Latin America*
Argentina			
1938	9.0	72.0	8.7
1950	20.4	51.4	11.1
Brazil			
1938	34.6	49.1	4.8
1950	55.9	29.7	8.0
Chile			
1938	15.9	52.4	2.5
1950	54.1	24.7	17.5
Mexico			
1938	67.4	27.4	6.7
1950	93.5	4.9	93.5

Source: United Nations, *Yearbook of International Trade Statistics*. New York: United Nations, 1951.

after the war but, except in Mexico, not to its prewar levels. Even so, trade within the region remained relatively marginal.

Although Latin America received very little U.S. investment after 1945 compared with Europe, the 1940s marked the consolidation of a pattern first visible in the 1920s in which the dominant capital flow came from the United States. In the 1920s a larger quantity of investment income flowed back to Europe than to the United States, but by 1949 the United States was receiving ten times more income from Latin America than the income flowing from Latin America to the rest of the world (see table 8). Of the increment in the book value of investment from the United States in Latin America between 1936 and 1950, 42 percent was in Venezuela, followed by 23 percent in Brazil and 17 percent in Panama.[10]

But the United States of course remained interested in Latin America. In particular, after strongly supporting the expansion of the Latin American

Table 8 Latin America: Commodity and Capital Flows, 1925–1929, 1949, and 1950 (Millions of U.S. Dollars)

	Exports (FOB)[a]	*Imports (FOB)*	*Investment Income (Net)*[b]	*Long-term Capital (Net)*[bc]
1925–29 (annual average):				
United States	990	840	−300	200
Europe	1,460	910	−360	30
Total	2,450	1,750	−660	230
1949:				
United States	2,503	2,624	−550	588
Rest of world	2,592	1,845	−47	−104
Total	5,095	4,469	−597	484
1950:				
United States	3,090	2,658	−748	194
Rest of world	3,020	1,837	−7	161
Total	6,110	4,495	−755	355

Source: United Nations, Economic Commission for Latin America, *Foreign Capital in Latin America.* New York: United Nations, 1955.

[a]Including nonmonetary gold.

[b]Including reinvested earnings of subsidiaries.

[c]Including amortization and repurchase of foreign long-term debt and transactions with the International Bank for Reconstruction and Development; excluding government grants.

states during the war, from 1945 the United States sought to restrict power in the region. At the inter-American conference held at Chapultepec, Mexico, in early 1945 the United States demanded a blanket commitment from Latin America to reduce tariffs and open the gates to foreign capital. The Latin Americans countered with requests for similar concessions for their exports to the United States. The Chapultepec meeting failed to reach any final agreement on tariffs, although the Latin Americans pledged to accept foreign investment but on condition it did not run "contrary to the fundamental principles of public interest."[11] In Latin America protectionist sentiments were becoming stronger. As a Mexican entrepreneur later remarked: "What we need is protection on the model of the United States."[12]

In 1945–1947 the Latin American nations continued to urge the United States to increase aid as the United States continued to drag its feet. Finally, during the inter-American conference in Bogotá of 1948, it became clear that the United States had no intention of offering a Marshall Plan for Latin America. In other international meetings Latin American protectionist proposals failed, although the Latin Americans managed to defeat counter-proposals from the United States requiring them to lower tariffs.[13] Subsequently the Latin Americans secured another victory with the creation of the United Nations Economic Commission for Latin America (ECLA) in 1948, whose role was to defend and publicize the region's commitment to industrial development to escape dependence on unstable and undynamic primary exports.[14]

ECONOMIC TRENDS, 1945–1950

As we have seen, the first half of the 1940s favored a major shift in the development of Latin America: industry and trade within Latin America grew, the role of the state advanced, and the weaknesses of dependence on primary exports were once more exposed. In comparison the second half of the 1940s marked a step backward, as the effort to discredit state intervention also weakened the commitment to developing basic industries. During this period too little was done in Latin America to correct economic distortions caused by overvalued currencies. Exaggerated fears of the inflationary consequences of devaluation tended to breed an undue reliance on import controls, particularly as imports grew rapidly during the early postwar years. Despite overvaluation, however, exports grew strongly and indeed helped to sustain the prevailing exchange rates (see table 9). Bolivia alone remained outside the process, as international demand for tin fell sharply after the war.

Export growth in Latin America after 1945 was based almost entirely on primary goods, and once international trade resumed the new manufactures of Brazil, Mexico, and Argentina were immediately displaced by U.S. and European suppliers. The flood of imports into Latin America, along with often poorly managed import controls and protectionism, now slowed down the process of import-substituting industrialization. Brazil and Chile, the two countries most firmly established on the path toward import substitution, succeeded in increasing the share of industry in gross domestic product.

Table 9 Latin America: Annual Growth Rate of Exports and Per Capita GDP, 1940–1950

	Exports	*Per Capita GDP 1940–45*	*Per Capita GDP 1945–50*
Argentina	5.0	1.2	1.6
Bolivia	−1.2	–	0.0
Brazil	8.1	0.3	3.3
Chile	2.2	2.4	1.0
Colombia	17.5	0.4	1.8
Costa Rica	30.1	–	4.2
Dom. Rep.	–	–	5.3
Ecuador	17.0	1.5	6.9
El Salvador	21.7	–	6.7
Guatemala	16.1	–	−0.9
Haiti	–	–	−0.5
Honduras	22.4	0.8	1.7
Mexico	11.7	4.6	3.0
Nicaragua	16.8	–	4.1
Panama	29.8	–	−2.5
Paraguay	3.1	−0.1	0.0
Peru	8.8	–	2.4
Uruguay	10.7	1.3	4.1
Venezuela	23.1	2.6	6.9

Sources: Exports: James W. Wilkie, *Statistics and National Policy*, Supplement 3. University of California, Los Angeles, 1974. GDP: United Nations, Comisión Económica para América Latina, *Series históricas del crecimiento de América Latina*. Santiago de Chile: CEPAL, 1978; and Victor Bulmer-Thomas, *The Political Economy of Central America since 1920*. Cambridge: Cambridge University Press, 1987.

Note: Figures are compound growth rates, based on constant 1970 dollars.

Colombia also increased industry's share, but there industry was beginning from an exceptionally low base. Among the small countries El Salvador alone achieved an increase in industry's share of gross domestic product. Overall, the figures for share of industry in gross domestic product over 1940–1950 show either stagnation, declining rates of industrial expansion, or even actual reductions (see table 10). The general trend was downward from the perhaps artificial levels of industrial development achieved during the war.

Meanwhile despite overvalued currencies and the abundance of imports, inflation was typically increasing, even though by this point inflation abroad was declining. Albert Hirschman, in his classic study of inflation in Chile during 1939–1952, argued that inflation became the preferred escape valve for social tensions. In his view several of the following conditions prevailed: "fiscal deficits, monetization of balance of payments surpluses, massive wage

Table 10 Latin America: Industry as a Percentage of GDP, 1940–1955

	1940	*1945*	*1950*	*1955*
Argentina	23	27	24	25
Bolivia	—	—	12	15
Brazil	15	20	21	23
Chile	18	22	23	23
Colombia	8	12	14	15
Costa Rica	13	12	11	12
Dom. Rep.	—	—	12	13
Ecuador	16	—	16	15
El Salvador	10	12	13	14
Guatemala	7	13	11	11
Haiti	—	—	8	8
Honduras	7	12	9	12
Mexico	17	21	19	19
Nicaragua	11	12	11	12
Panama	—	7	8	10
Paraguay	14	18	16	16
Peru	—	14	14	15
Uruguay	17	21	20	23
Venezuela	14	16	11	13

Source: United Nations, Comisión Económica para América Latina, *Series históricas del crecimiento de América Latina*. Santiago de Chile: CEPAL, 1978.

and salary increases, . . .bank credit expansion, war-induced international price booms, [and] Central Bank credit to state sponsored development agencies."[15] One of the common elements of this period was the near absence of significant anti-inflation measures.

In addition to Chile, the countries that suffered the highest rates of inflation were Argentina, Bolivia after the revolution of 1952, and Paraguay. Other countries experienced more moderate inflation that was nevertheless higher than in previous decades. In Argentina inflation was fed by Perón's failed attempts to reverse his damaging relative prices policies that had initially discriminated against farmers and ranchers. In Paraguay stagnation and an isolated, closed economy allowed fiscal deficits to precipitate inflation. In Bolivia the revolutionary government encountered a depleted tin sector, international recession, and imperative political demands. The countries that managed to avoid inflation, such as Venezuela, Ecuador, Peru, and most of the Central American states, were those in which exports were rising rapidly and currencies were overvalued. Only Colombia achieved a coherent anti-inflation policy, while in Mexico the rapid expansion of agricultural production played a major part in keeping food prices stable.

At least during the 1940s the falling rate of industrial expansion, along with the growth of inflation, did not prevent overall growth. A large majority of nations, both large and small, experienced high per capita growth. The two countries that displayed the weakest export growth, Bolivia and Paraguay, were the most conspicuous cases of stagnation. Gross domestic product in Panama also stagnated because of the fall in exports of services as the United States scaled back its activities in the canal zone immediately after the war.

For most of the smaller countries the return to the old model of primary export-led growth during the latter 1940s was definitive, and they remained excluded from the subsequent boom in import-substituting industrialization. Venezuela and Peru, as exporters of oil and minerals, followed a similar path. In the larger countries, where industrial interests were becoming more important and the new urban masses were demanding new sources of employment, it was clear that industry had to be supported. But the inefficient continuation of controls, the unclear signals given to foreign capital, the unfulfilled hopes for Marshall aid, and the new strength of labor movements were all reasons for investors to hesitate. It was only in the 1950s that the conditions for industrial development, the so-called ISI (import-substituting industrialization) model, were fully worked out.

Conclusion

The 1940s was thus a decade of considerable promise, in that it gave an impetus to industrialization, intraregional trade, and the expansion of the state. Expectations rose partly as a result of those trends and partly because of hopes for a "Marshall Plan for Latin America." However, instead of a Marshall Plan came a wave of tariff-hopping direct investment geared to the production of consumer goods for the local market. The elements of promise were by the end of the decade unfulfilled, with the result that the ISI model that emerged after the 1940s lacked a strong emphasis on state-promoted basic industries or intraregional trade, became consumer oriented and import dependent, and largely ignored issues of economic efficiency.

Notes

The author acknowledges the assistance of Marta Delgado in preparing this article.

1. W. Arthur Lewis, *Economic Survey, 1919–1939*. London: George Allen and Unwin, 1949.

2. United Nations, *Foreign Capital in Latin America*. New York: United Nations, 1955, 155, 160.

3. J. Ashworth, *A Short History of the World Economy since 1850*. London: Longman, 1975, 258.

4. See Stephen R. Niblo, "The Impact of War: Mexico and World War II." Occasional Paper no. 10, La Trobe University, Institute of Latin American Studies, Melbourne, 1988, 7ff.

5. The linkages are detailed in R. A. Humphreys, *Latin America and the Second World War*. 2 vols. London: Athlone Press, 1981–1982.

6. Bishnupriya Gupta, "Import Substitution in Capital Goods: The Case of Brazil, 1929–1979." D. Phil. diss., University of Oxford, 1989.

7. Robert Triffin, "La moneda y las instituciones bancarias en Colombia," supplement to *Revista Banco de la República*. Bogotá, August 1944.

8. United Nations, *The Economic Development of Latin America in the Post-War Period*. New York: United Nations, 1964, 3.

9. Stephen G. Rabe, "The Elusive Conference: United States Economic Relations with Latin America, 1945–1952," *Diplomatic History* 2, no. 3, 288.

10. United Nations, Economic Commission for Latin America, *Foreign Capital in Latin America*. New York, 1955.

11. Sanford A. Mosk, *Industrial Revolution in Mexico*. Berkeley and Los Angeles: University of California Press, 1950.

12. R. J. Shafer, *Mexican Business Organizations: History and Analysis*. Syracuse: Syracuse University Press, 1973.

13. Karin Kock, *International Trade Policy and the GATT, 1947–1967*. Stockholm: Almquist and Wiksell, 1969.

14. See E. V. K. FitzGerald, "ECLA and the Formation of Latin American Economic Doctrine," this volume.

15. Albert O. Hirschman, *Journeys towards Progress*. New York: Twentieth Century Fund, 1963, 183.

3 Labor Politics and Regime Change

Internal Trajectories versus External Influences

Ruth Berins Collier

Social analysts have long been fascinated with the idea of critical junctures or historic watersheds—particular "moments" or transitions of fundamental political reorientation. It is this fascination that has inspired the present volume, the guiding hypothesis of which is that the 1940s represents precisely such a moment of reorientation. In this chapter I examine the politics of labor and regime change in Latin America during the 1940s from two analytical perspectives, each related to a different critical juncture. The first perspective emphasizes the influence of international events: World War II and the international realignments that accompanied the advent of the Cold War.[1] The second perspective views the development of Latin America in the 1940s as part of a longer evolution within each country: the unfolding of an internal trajectory of change, the parameters of which derive from the initial incorporation of labor.[2] This incorporation was part of a major and multifaceted socioeconomic transformation, which brought with it a set of political changes: the shift from a laissez-faire to an activist state; the appearance of a formal industrial sector regulated by the state; the change in forms of social control from clientelism to corporatism; the advent of mass society and mass politics; and the emergence of capital-labor relations as a major social cleavage accompanied by new forms of social protest. The analysis of these changes focuses on three phases: the incorporation period itself, the initial reaction in the "aftermath" period, and the longer-term legacy that is labeled the "heritage" of incorporation. These two perspectives represent quite different approaches to the politics of labor and regime change in Latin

America in the 1940s. Instead of arguing the merits of one perspective at the expense of the other, I shall attempt to combine them through a comparative analysis of four Latin American countries: Brazil, Chile, Mexico, and Venezuela.

Figure 1 schematically represents the intersection of the two perspectives in the four countries. The skeleton of the internal trajectories argument is laid out horizontally. The period of the initial incorporation of labor occurred differently in the different countries, setting in motion distinct trajectories of change that unfolded during the subsequent aftermath and the heritage periods.[3] The alternative perspective that emphasizes the role of international forces is shown by the long box in the middle of the figure.

As figure 1 shows, the two perspectives differ in their treatment of time. First, the international forces perspective is synchronic and cross-sectional; the internal paths approach is diachronic and longitudinal: while the former examines a slice of time, the latter employs a historical, over-time approach. Second, while the international perspective uses real time (i.e., the 1940s), the internal paths perspective is based on analytical time, so that the analytically defined periods of incorporation, aftermath, and heritage vary in historical timing as well as duration.

A word might be added about the types of causes that are the focus of each of the perspectives. Although generated within each country, the various elements of the internal forces are more generic and structural than unique or idiographic, since they constitute a common social transformation based on the institutionalization of labor-capital relations and the integration of the working class in the political system. The transformations are therefore parallel or similar in the various countries.

An international perspective may focus on a variety of external causes. One is the diffusion or contagion of models or ideas from abroad: for example, the international appeal of fascism, communism, or democracy. A second is common or repeated pressures from abroad: for example, American or Soviet foreign policy toward Latin American countries. A third issue refers to the impact in Latin America of fundamental shifts in the international order that had an impact on the world at large: a bipolar international system, world hegemonic leadership of a hemispheric power, the salience of the Cold War with its competing ideologies, and the dominance of a world capitalist order characterized by a Keynesian compromise between labor and capital.

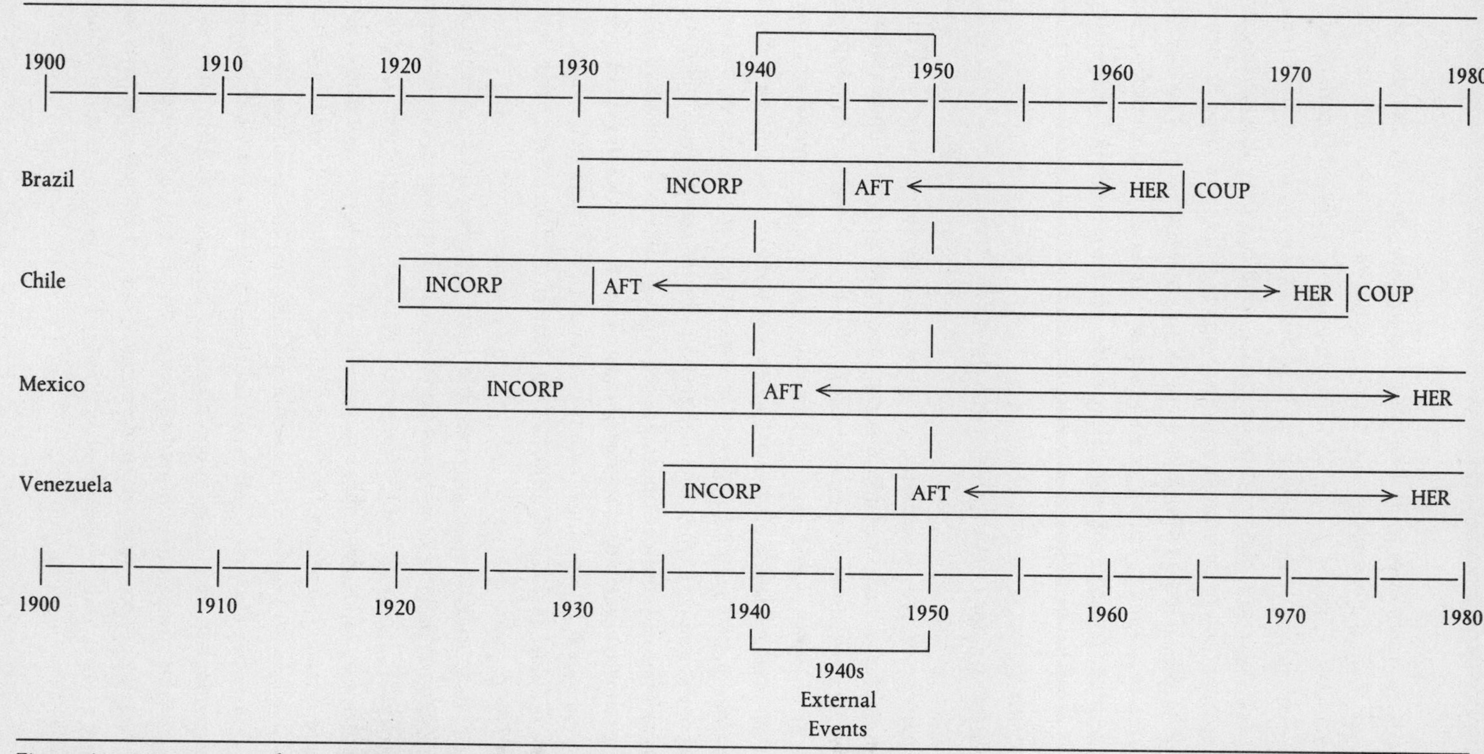

Figure 1. Intersection of Two Analytic Perspectives: Internal Trajectories (incorporation, aftermath, and heritage periods) and External Events

We have, then, two quite different perspectives. They are not mutually exclusive; each may be rounded out by reference to the other. For example, it is important whether or not labor incorporation occurred before or after the rise of fascism or the adoption of a popular front policy by the Comintern, since these were the types of external conditions that affected internal development. But equally important, the impact of these external influences was affected by a nation's position along its internal trajectory. Thus the two perspectives are not rival but complementary approaches that can be usefully combined. Before assessing the nature of this complementarity, however, I begin by treating each view separately.

The International Conjuncture of the 1940s

Though the external forces unleashed during the 1940s may have had wide-ranging political and economic impacts, I focus here on their impact on two related dimensions of domestic change. The first concerns coalitions and patterns of political and class collaboration or conflict. Specifically, were labor unions and leftist parties collaborating with other political and economic actors, or were they engaging in strikes and other forms of working-class protest and confrontation? The second dimension concerns patterns of democratization, political opening and closing, and reformist initiatives. That is, to what extent does regime change in Latin America during the 1940s reflect or match international events or trends? Those external events most likely to influence these features of Latin American politics are presented in table 11.

A first consideration is the possible links between these international events and the patterns of political and class collaboration in Latin America. The popular front policy of the Comintern was clearly important. Originally adopted in the mid-1930s, this strategy was abandoned temporarily following the German-Soviet pact of August 1939 and then renewed in a more radical form after the German invasion of the Soviet Union in June 1941. The subsequent popular front policy advocated the formation of broad anti-Fascist alliances, including cooperation with bourgeois parties, anti-Fascist governments, and non-Communist groups within the labor movement. It meant class collaboration, the moderation of labor demands, and in its most extreme forms, the dissolution of Communist parties and the abandonment of strikes for the duration of the war. In 1943, consistent with the priority

Table 11 Key Events in the 1940s

1939	German-Soviet pact
1941	German invasion of Soviet Union
	Popular Front policy of Comintern restored
	Pearl Harbor
1943	Comintern disbanded
1944	D Day
1945	V-E Day
	V-J Day
	U.N. Charter
1946	Iron Curtain speech
	Communist governments installed in Bulgaria and Romania
1947	Cominform founded
	Communist governments installed in Hungary and Poland
	Truman Doctrine
	Rio Treaty
	Taft-Hartley Act
1948	Organización Regional Interamericana del Trabajo

given to a broader anti-Fascist alliance, the Comintern was disbanded, signifying the dissolution of the international revolutionary alliance. Because Communist parties were influential in labor movements throughout Latin America, we would expect to see reverberations of Comintern policy throughout the region.

The spirit of multiclass solidarity and the support for a new coalition against fascism were not limited to the Communists. The same sentiments flourished in the United States and through this route too reverberated in Latin America. The same year that the German invasion brought the Soviet Union into the war, the Japanese attack on Pearl Harbor provoked the United States to join the Allies. U.S. sentiment toward collaboration with the Communists changed accordingly. This flip-flop was reflected in *Time* magazine's two descriptions of Vicente Lombardo Toledano, the Marxist leader of Mexican labor. The first, published in 1940 before the United States entered the war, referred to the "large-eared, hot-eyed, Communistic little Vicente Lombardo Toledano" and ridiculed *his* "screaming" and "unblushing" shift of policy following the change in Comintern line after the German-Soviet nonaggression treaty.[4] In 1942, just a year and a half later, however, *Time* described Lombardo as "the brilliant, aggressive and fluid leader of Mexican labor, . . .a slight, gentle little man with big ears and dreamy eyes, . . .a

Puritan in his personal life, abstemious, logical in argument, part-Indian, part-Italian, philosopher, archaeologist, scientist, scholar."[5]

We might expect this change in the attitude of the United States to be reflected in pressure on non-Communist factions within the labor movement to pursue a more moderate course, as well as on various other groups to recognize that the struggle against fascism was of paramount importance. International influences created a context in which many Latin American governments and bourgeois parties might be receptive to the line of collaboration proposed by Communist parties. These changes in international influence might thus lead us to expect a brief period of multiclass collaboration starting in 1942.

By 1945 the conclusion of the war brought an end to the rationale for political and class collaboration. External alliances were quickly reordered, and those changes had implications for internal alliances as well. At this point we would expect the reemergence of a postponed reformist or radical political agenda, ideological polarization, and a renewal of class conflict and labor protest.

The second issue concerning the impact of international forces relates to regime change. Here the expectation would be that the victory of the Allies and the triumph of democracy over fascism led to the diffusion of democratic and reformist values throughout the world, a process reinforced by the United Nations Charter. Moreover, from 1943 the United States began to press for political liberalization and democratization in Latin America. By 1945 and the beginning of Cold War hostilities over the issue of democracy in Eastern Europe, "it became even more imperative that the allies of the United States in Latin America were seen to be democratic."[6] If international influences were important, we would expect at this point a pattern of democratization and political opening in Latin America. We might also expect a period of new reformist initiatives, both because popular demands could be expressed more openly and because the models of social democracy, the welfare state, and a Keynesian class compromise were taking shape in the United States and Europe.

International pressures for reformist democracy in Latin America were short-lived. New international forces unleashed by the Cold War tended to support a political closing, as democracy-versus-fascism became superseded by the new cleavage of capitalism-versus-communism. If during the war the Soviet Communists subordinated class struggle abroad for the anti-Fascist fight, after the war the Western democracies, particularly the United States, subordinated the prodemocracy struggle to the struggle against communism. Though it is hard to date the onset of this period, any ambiguities were resolved by 1947. In that year the Soviet Union established the Cominform to replace the dissolved Comintern and reinstate Moscow discipline, and the United States proclaimed the Truman Doctrine to contain communism and aid other governments in the anti-Communist struggle. Nineteen forty-seven was also the year of the Rio Treaty, a pact of hemispheric solidarity and mutual assistance that brought the Cold War to the Western hemisphere. Finally, it was in 1947 that the battle against communism penetrated the labor arena. In the United States the Taft-Hartley Act barred Communists from union leadership; in Latin America the anti-Communist labor confederation, Organización Regional Interamericana del Trabajo, was formed under the auspices of the American Federation of Labor.

The impact of international influences on the two dimensions of multiclass collaboration and democratization might thus be expected to produce four partially overlapping periods. These periods, which are presented in the upper half of figure 2, are summarized as follows:

1941–1945: After the greater level of class conflict and strikes during the period of the German-Soviet pact, renewal of popular front strategies, class cooperation, decline in strikes, and labor peace.

1944–1946: Democratization, political opening, and reformist initiatives.

1945–1946 (or later): Ideological polarization, greater class conflict, labor protest, and political opposition.

From 1946–1947 on: Political closing, restored labor discipline, and a retreat from reformist politics.

To what extent did these hypothesized phases actually occur in the four Latin American countries under examination?

1. *Multiclass Collaboration and Political Cooperation by Left and Labor (1941–1945)*. The popular front policy of the Comintern had an important effect throughout Latin America, and all four countries underwent this phase. In each of these countries the Communist party was influential among organized labor, pursued a policy of cooperation with governments, and encouraged the moderation of industrial conflict. For their part centrist groups were willing partners to collaboration.

The influence of the popular front policy was strongest in Chile. In the mid-1930s the Communist, Socialist, and Radical parties established a Popu-

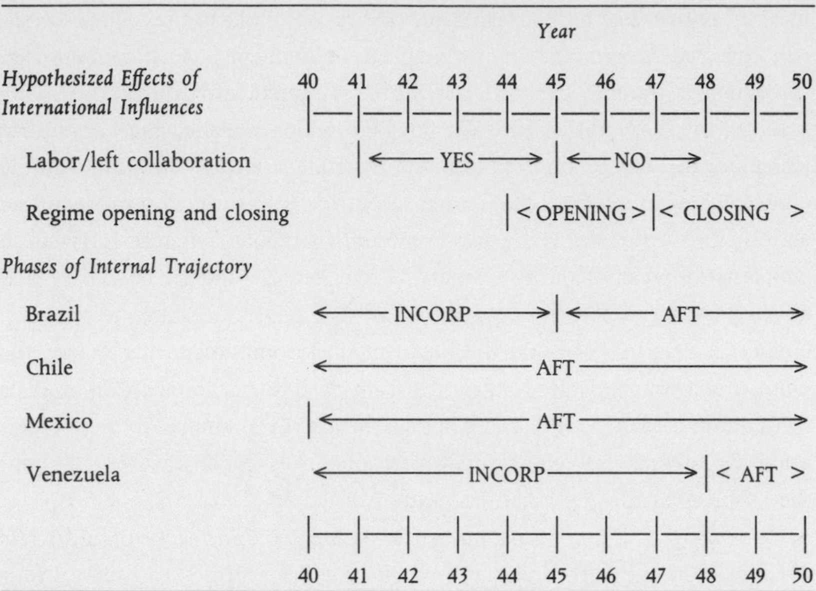

Figure 2. Timing of Expected Outcomes of International Events and the Incorporation and Aftermath Periods

lar Front that unified large segments of the working and middle classes. A Popular Front government under Radical leadership was elected in 1938, and it held together despite the German-Soviet pact. Elections were held again in 1942, after the adoption of the Comintern's more extreme version of popular frontism. Although the Popular Front as a formal coalition was not renewed, the Communists and Socialists continued to collaborate with the Radical party and supported its more conservative presidential candidate, Juan Antonio Ríos Morales, and subsequently his government.

In Brazil popular front collaboration occurred in the mid-1940s. At first, in 1941–1942 under the still heavily authoritarian government of Getúlio Vargas, the popular front policy had little impact. At this point there were no elections, labor was controlled through a corporatist system, and the Communist party was banned. Conditions began to change, however, in 1943 as the expectation grew that after the war the authoritarian regime would yield to a democratic regime. By 1945 a coalition of the Vargas forces, the working class, and the Communist party began to form. The pro-Vargas forces now took the initiative by founding the Partido Trabalhista Brasileira (PTB), aiming to mobilize labor support. Vargas and the Communists then struck a deal, which led to a political amnesty for imprisoned Communists and the legalization of the Brazilian Communist party. Both the PTB and the Communist party participated in the *queremista* movement that urged Vargas to become a presidential candidate, and in 1945 they organized the Movimento Unificador dos Trabalhadores as a political vehicle to enlist working-class support.

Mexico was another example of popular front collaboration. In the second half of the 1930s the Mexican Communist party (PCM) shifted from an anticollaborationist stance to support for the Cárdenas government. This posture continued for the duration of the war despite the election of the more conservative government of Manuel Ávila Camacho in 1940. Under Cárdenas the Communists promoted the reorganization of the governing party to resemble a popular front coalition. In the 1940 election the PCM withheld its support from a reformist successor to Cárdenas in favor of Ávila Camacho, for whom it pledged to act as a "shock brigade."[7] Following the German invasion of the Soviet Union, the Confederación de Trabajadores de México, the major national labor confederation, entered into pacts with business to promote collaboration and in 1942 renounced the use of the strike for the duration of the war.

Venezuela deviated only partially from the general pattern. During the popular front period of the 1930s the Communists collaborated with the reformist opposition in an antigovernment front, which collapsed at the time of the German-Soviet pact. With the renewal of the popular front policy in 1941 the Venezuelan Communist party began to collaborate with the government in a "marriage of convenience"[8] that emphasized class harmony and political stability. The following year the party supported congressional candidates loyal to President Isaias Medina Angarita. Until 1944 the Communist party remained the dominant influence within the working class and brought the bulk of the urban labor movement into the coalition. For his part Medina established a more open atmosphere, allowing political freedom, party activities, and the formation of new unions. During this period, however, the reformist opposition under Acción Democrática rejected collaboration and remained in opposition. Acción Democrática had considerable popular support: it was the dominant influence among the peasantry, and after 1944 it became the dominant force in the working class as well. Because of the continued opposition to the government by Acción Democrática and its affiliated popular groups, Venezuela constitutes a partial exception to the hypothesized pattern of broad anti-Fascist collaboration.

2. *Political Opening and Reformist Initiatives (1944–1946)*. Evidence of this trend is more mixed. During this brief period new democratic regimes were created in both Brazil and Venezuela, but Mexico and Chile did not experience reform or opening. In Brazil a combination of international diffusion and direct pressure from the United States contributed to the downfall of the Vargas government in 1945 and the inauguration of a new, electoral regime. Besides adopting a more open political system, Brazil enacted a number of labor reforms beginning in 1943 when Vargas himself began attempting to construct a new constituency among the urban working class. These reforms, which continued until around 1946, included a greater toleration of strikes, wage increases, the cancellation of a loyalty test for labor union leaders, the introduction of union elections, the legalization of the Brazilian Communist party, and the political amnesty of 1945. Similarly, despite a seemingly improbable beginning in which Acción Democrática achieved power through a coup, in 1945 Venezuela witnessed the advent of a more democratic government. Although a reformist opening had already begun under Medina, the year marked a deepening of the commitment to reform. A constitutional convention wrote a new democratic charter, which was quickly implemented in subsequent elections. Reformist changes were also made in labor policy, including a more favorable labor law, some labor participation in government, rising wages, and the spread of collective bargaining.

These trends were absent in Chile and Mexico. Even though democratic rule had already prevailed in Chile for more than a decade, the mid-1940s were an antilabor period. The interim Duhalde government of 1945–1946 was hostile to labor and repressed strikes and demonstrations led by the Communists. In Mexico the antireformist trend was even more marked, as this period brought greater control of labor and the tightening of authoritarian one-party dominance. Real wages fell steeply, especially in the unionized industrial sector, even as the economy grew. Unionization stagnated, and a change in labor law restricted the right to strike and made it easier to dismiss workers. The government used a newly enacted "crime of social dissolution" to persecute dissident union leaders, while changes in the structure of the ruling party reduced the relative weight and influence of labor within it. These steps culminated in January 1946 with the reorganization of the ruling party into the Partido Revolucionario Institucional (PRI), a measure that further subordinated labor and the other organized "sectors" of the party and concentrated power in central party organs. Finally, again in early 1946, changes in the electoral law made it more difficult for dissident groups to register as political parties and therefore helped to insulate the PRI from challenges by the opposition.

3. *The New Combative Posture of Labor and the Left (immediate postwar years).* All four countries underwent heightened class conflict and growing political opposition during the immediate postwar period coinciding with the end of the popular front policy and the onset of the Cold War. This pattern was particularly striking in Brazil and Mexico. In Brazil the opening years of the Dutra government saw an intensified process of the repoliticization and reactivation of the working class begun during the last years of the Vargas government. The trend became visible in the party system and in the sphere of industrial relations. In the newly opened political arena, parties with a base in the working classes achieved unprecedented electoral success. In the presidential and congressional elections of December 1945 the Communists won 10 percent of the national vote and achieved pluralities in major industrial cities and a number of state capitals. The Partido Trabalhista Brasileira won another 10 percent, giving the two parties based in the union movement approximately one-fifth of the vote. This electoral mobilization was accompanied by a more militant political posture on the part of both the Communists and the PTB.

As John French has argued, during this period the working class attained a new level of consciousness that marked a radical break with the past. Even in this early period, shortly after its founding, the PTB could not be seen merely as an instrument created from above by Vargas. Instead, as competition from the Communist party put the PTB under pressure to be responsive to the rank and file, the PTB came to represent an independent working-class voice.[9] In addition to the electoral sphere the new militancy of the Brazilian working class was also evident in the labor unions, which became more democratic and activist. Major changes in the leadership of the unions occurred as Communist party and PTB militants began to take control. In 1945 an attempt by the government to curb these trends by instituting plural unionism failed in the face of working-class opposition. In 1946 Communist leaders organized a major wave of strikes affecting many rural as well as urban areas.

Mexico experienced similar heightened political and class conflict during this period. When the war ended, the Confederación de Trabajadores (CTM) split on the issue of continued collaboration with the government. Dissidents under Communist influence now portrayed collaboration as a wartime expedient and declared their determination to return to a more militant and aggressive posture. Accordingly, a number of important national unions left the CTM and formed the rival Central Única de Trabajadores. Somewhat later Lombardo was expelled from the CTM and formed his own movement, the Alianza de Obreros y Campesinos de México—later the Unión General de Obreros y Campesinos de México (UGOCM). The two dissident confederations supported a more combative and independent stance, and at their height they represented around 40 percent of the organized labor movement. This split became reflected in politics, as Lombardo founded the Partido Popular Socialista (PPS) as an opposition party based on working-class support. In the long run the PPS did not fare particularly well, but these developments illustrate the greater intensity of labor militancy during the immediate postwar period.

Chile and Venezuela present a somewhat different picture in that political collaboration continued even with the expected rise in class conflict. In Chile the Communist party became more aggressive, and under its leadership labor conflict, including rural strikes, rose substantially. The growth of the Communist left was also reflected in the party's increased share of the vote in the 1947 municipal elections. Yet at the very time they were becoming more active and combative the Communists supported the Radical party candidate, Gabriel González Videla, in the presidential elections of 1946 and even joined González Videla's new government despite its rejection of their formal participation in Radical-led governments throughout the period of popular front policy. In Venezuela the particular twist was that the growing radicalization and militancy of the labor unions took place in the context of expanded collaboration between the labor movement and the government. During the *trienio* of 1945–1948 Acción Democrática was in power, and affiliated unions strongly supported and collaborated with the government. The Communist party also commanded influence in the labor movement, and it too decided to support what it considered the progressive policies of the government, although a dissident Communist group, the Machamiques, rejected this position.

4. *Collapse of Reformist Initiatives and Political Closing (from 1946–1947 on).* The onset of the Cold War undoubtedly had a major impact in Latin America. In all four countries the Communist party was banned, strong antilabor measures were adopted, the earlier reformist tide was reversed, and in some

cases democratic regimes were overthrown. Although the democratic regime in Chile remained intact, the opportunities for reformist initiatives rapidly dwindled. These trends appeared in response to rising labor militancy and in conjunction with the anti-Communist atmosphere sparked by the Cold War. In 1947 legislation drastically restricted rural unionization and outlawed strikes in the rural sector. The González Videla government embarked on a vigorous anti-Communist campaign, denouncing all strikes as the products of Communist subversion. The Communists were ousted from the cabinet, and in 1948 the Communist party was banned.

In Brazil the transition to a new electoral regime continued on track, but beginning in mid-1946 the government reasserted control over the unions and oversaw a period of retrenchment with respect to labor reforms. The government intervened in union elections, placed many unions under the direct control of the Labor Ministry, and hardened its position on strikes, either restricting them by legislation or repressing them by force. In addition the government reinstated the loyalty test used under Vargas to prevent Communists from becoming union leaders and then banned the Movimiento Unificador dos Trabalhadores (the Communist labor front), the Confederação dos Trabalhadores do Brasil (a new labor central), and finally in 1947 the Communist party itself.

Mexico experienced a similar antireformist period in the late 1940s. In 1946, as we have seen, the government moved to limit political opposition and strengthen one-party dominance. The party sphere was further restricted in 1949, when the Communist party lost its registration. From 1947 to 1949 the government reacted to the growth of a dissident labor movement by intervening in union elections and denying recognition to the new labor central, the UGOCM, created by Lombardo. The result by 1950 was a heavily controlled labor movement from which leftists were excluded.

Venezuela became the most dramatic case of political closing during the second half of the 1940s. In 1948 the coup led by Marcos Pérez Jiménez and his co-conspirators overthrew the electoral regime and brought an abrupt end to the period of reform under Acción Democrática. The military regime, which remained in power until 1958, became synonymous with extreme political and labor repression. Although the first two years of the regime under Carlos Delgado Chalbaud were milder than the dictatorship established by Pérez Jiménez in 1950, the first junta nevertheless quickly moved against Acción Democrática and thereby also the labor movement.

Table 12 Assessing International Influences

Hypothesized Outcomes	*Brazil*	*Chile*	*Mexico*	*Venezuela*
Labor/left collaboration (1941–45)	Yes	Yes	Yes	Yes*
Democratic opening and reformist initiatives (1944–46)	Yes	No	No	Yes
Increased labor protest and class conflict (1945–)	Yes	Partial	Yes	Yes**
Collapse of reformist initiatives and political closing (from 1946–47)	Yes	Yes	Yes	Yes

*Did not involve Acción Democrática.

**With major government support.

Table 12 summarizes the impact of international forces on domestic trends and indicates that the relationship between them was very close. At this broad correlational level the general hypothesis about the causal importance of the international conjuncture seems to hold up quite well, and events in Latin America demonstrate a substantial fit with the cross-sectional explanation that focuses on external causes. We can now turn to the second perspective.

The Initial Incorporation of Labor as a Critical Juncture

Like the perspective that focuses on international forces, the perspective based on the incorporation of labor offers a set of predictions about labor protest, state-labor relations, political coalitions, governmental reformist initiatives, and political openings and closings. Yet unlike the first perspective it examines the unfolding of internal trajectories of change over time.

According to this argument, the type of initial incorporation of labor marks the critical transition that sets each country along a particular trajectory. The argument centers on change in the historical development of the relations between the state and the working class. It focuses on the politics of the emergence of an organized labor movement, specifically on the domestic political conjuncture that prevailed at the time the labor movement first achieved legal recognition and became incorporated as a legitimate social actor. According to this view, labor incorporation contains some important common features, but different patterns can be distinguished. These differences had lasting impacts on trade union politics and, more broadly, on the general trajectory of political change and the shaping of the political arena in each country. The argument presents three sequential analytical phases: incorporation, aftermath, and heritage. In the first phase different types of incorporation experiences are identified with their own specific dynamics and contradictions. The contradictions are worked out or resolved during the subsequent aftermath period. These two phases together establish a particular political heritage.

INCORPORATION PERIOD

Throughout Latin America the state undertook the incorporation of labor to address the "social question": the rising level of working-class protest triggered by dismal labor and social conditions. The response to this question was the creation of institutionalized channels for the resolution of labor-capital conflict. The period of incorporation is identified by the shift in the relationship between the state and labor from one based on repression to one in which state control was exercised through a legalized state-sanctioned labor movement. In this period the state moved to legitimate, support, and shape an institutionalized labor movement.

This change—from repression to legitimation, from exclusion to incorporation—occurred in most of Latin America during the first half of the twentieth century. In Brazil the period of incorporation came during the first Vargas presidency, beginning in 1930, and reached its climax with the creation of the Estado Nôvo in 1937. In Chile the same process occurred in the Alessandri-Ibáñez period, starting with the election of Alessandri in 1920 and reaching its height after Ibáñez formally assumed power in 1927. Mexico had the most extended period of incorporation, beginning in 1917 and culminating during the Cárdenas presidency in the 1930s. Finally, in Venezuela incorporation occurred in the period following the death of Juan Vicente Gómez: it began in 1935 and culminated during the *trienio* of 1945–1948, when Acción Democrática came to power. (The time lines in figure 2 show the incorporation periods.)

These incorporation periods were the political outcome of economic growth and social change. The rapid expansion of Latin American economies that began during the late nineteenth century led to urbanization and the development of a broad range of new economic activities in commerce and manufacturing. The new economic sectors spawned two new social groups:

the working class and a broad range of middle-sector groups, which included owners, managers, professionals, and other intermediate sectors. These emerging social actors put new items on the political agenda, including the resolution of industrial conflict that arose with growing worker protest and organization, and the transformation or reform of the oligarchic state demanded by the middle sectors.

Incorporation did not occur until the oligarchy had lost control of the state and representatives of middle-sector reformers came to power. This change represented a transition from a laissez-faire state controlled by the traditional oligarchy to a more activist and interventionist state, one more responsive to the urban middle sectors. Even though the oligarchy itself had in some countries put forth an incorporation proposal of its own, no such project was carried out while the oligarchy retained power. Rather it was introduced only as part of a larger transformation of the state—from a laissez-faire state to a more activist state. The new state upheld traditional liberal property rights but took on new social, welfare, and economic responsibilities. Along with these new responsibilities the state adopted a paternalistic stance toward labor, manifested in legislation on such issues as working conditions, the minimum wage, and social security. At the same time, the state attempted to create an institutionalized system of labor relations, casting itself in the role of mediator of class conflicts and arbiter of labor-management relations. These measures as a whole signified the advent of state corporatism, new structures that vertically integrated the emerging urban, industrial society.

Such, then, is the sociological commonality of labor incorporation in Latin America. In the course of economic growth two new emerging classes, the middle sectors and the working class, were integrated into the polity in dominant and subordinate positions, respectively. However, important differences existed among the countries. Though nowhere did the oligarchic state remain intact, oligarchic interests remained powerful to varying degrees in the new, "postoligarchic" state. Hence, a major issue was the relationship—or cleavage—between the traditional oligarchy and the middle sectors seeking to reform the state. The nature of this relationship is reflected in the different types of incorporation projects that were adopted.

Although the middle sectors generally succeeded in challenging oligarchic hegemony, they often found it difficult to establish their own political dominance and to consolidate a more interventionist state. In all four cases under consideration here, political stalemate between the older and newer dominant classes prevented or stymied reform. Two solutions to the deadlock emerged. In Brazil and Chile the military played a key role in breaking the political impasse and intervened to oversee the introduction of the new state. In Brazil this stage occurred in 1937 when Vargas exploited his military support to abandon the electoral regime and install the authoritarian Estado Nôvo. In Chile the same process began in 1924 when army officers, including Carlos Ibáñez del Campo, intervened in the political process, and it took a more definitive form in 1927 when Ibáñez formally assumed power. In these two cases the authoritarian state enforced a modus vivendi between the traditional oligarchy and the reformist middle sectors. The middle sectors were able to effect the transformation to an activist state while the traditional oligarchy, despite its loss of political control, was able to protect its interests.

In Mexico and Venezuela the oligarchies were relatively weak, and traditional clientelist relations were eroding in the rural societies of these two countries. An alternative strategy to overcome the deadlock became available through the mobilization of labor and the peasantry. In Mexico the protracted stalemate after the revolution of 1910–1917 ended by virtue of the continuous mobilization of popular-sector support by successive governments during the 1920s and 1930s. The height of the incorporation period in Mexico occurred during the government of Cárdenas between 1934 and 1940. In Venezuela, following the death of Gómez in 1935, successive governments embarked on indecisive reforms, failing to satisfy the reformist middle-sector groups, which remained in opposition. During the decade 1935–1945 the reformers mobilized popular support, and finally Acción Democrática, the leading opposition party, gained power in 1945.

The political mobilization of the popular sectors, particularly the working class, represents the critical difference between these two types of incorporation, which may be called state and party incorporation, respectively. In both types of incorporation political leaders sought to respond to the growth of labor unions and class tensions through control over the working class. However, in the two cases of party incorporation, Mexico and Venezuela, political leaders sought not only to control labor and the peasantry but also to win their popular support. State and party incorporation are thus distinguished by this difference in the balance between the control and mobilization of the popular sectors. The main features of the two types of incorporation are outlined in figure 3.

	Party Incorporation (Mexico and Venezuela)		State Incorporation (Brazil and Chile)
Incorporation Period	[—— Pattern of Incorporation ——]		
	Electoral regime	v.	Authoritarian regime
	Populist alliance	v.	Accommodationist alliance
	Political mobilization	v.	Depoliticization
	Major concessions to labor	v.	Paternalistic benefits
	Populist party	v.	No party or minimal party role
	[—— Dynamics at End of Incorporation ——]		
	Polarization and alienation of right Conservative reaction	v.	Absence of working-class participation and partisan identities Regime terminated in democratic opening
Aftermath	Transformation of majority coalition Reintegration of right	v.	Failure to establish centrist majority bloc
	Components: 1. Programmatic conservatization of populist party 2. Exclusion of left from coalition 3. Retention of working class in coalition 4. Mechanisms to limit political conflict		Stages: 1. Reactivation and repoliticization of labor 2. Creation of populist party and center-left coalition politics 3. Failure and discrediting of populism and coalition politics: radicalization and polarization
Heritage	Integrative party system Hegemonic, stable regime	v.	Polarizing multi-party system Opposition and conflict Coup and long-term military rule

Figure 3. Party versus State Incorporation: Contrasting Patterns of Change

In cases of party incorporation sufficient benefits were offered to induce the dominant part of the labor movement to cooperate with the state, and labor became part of a multiclass alliance. In cases of state incorporation, in which such mobilization was not pursued, labor retained greater political autonomy. This difference in the political position of labor had important and enduring consequences.

Thus, although the two types of incorporation have certain common features, they produced quite different political alliances. State incorporation, as in Brazil and Chile, was based on an accommodationist alliance consisting of an uneasy truce between the reformers and the oligarchy. The emphasis lay on the depoliticization of the working class and the control of the union movement. A highly elaborated labor law defined the system of union representation and exercised control over unions in such spheres as union tactics (particularly the use of the strike), internal governance, and the selection of labor leaders. Independent and leftist unions were repressed and replaced by a state-sponsored and state-penetrated labor movement. With this strong emphasis on control little or no political mobilization of either the urban or rural popular sectors occurred, and little effort was made to incorporate the popular sectors into a populist political party.

Mexico and Venezuela, in contrast, became examples of the alternative model of party incorporation. There, incorporation was based on a populist alliance between elements of the new urban middle sectors, the working class, and, in these two cases, the peasantry.[10] Unlike the attempt to depoliticize the labor movement under state incorporation, the mobilization strategy central to party incorporation entailed the politicization of the working class. In this way incorporation involved as a first priority not only the integration of labor as a functional group but also its integration as a political movement. The result was the creation of a broad multiclass coalition that found expression in a political party—Acción Democrática in Venezuela and what became the PRI (Partido Revolucionario Institucional) in Mexico. These parties institutionalized the populist alliance and channeled working-class political activity into support for the government. In addition to attracting the working-class vote these parties established organizational links with the labor unions.

The dynamics or logic of support mobilization meant that, compared with state incorporation, party incorporation implied more concessions and a stronger political position for the labor movement. Instead of leftist and independent unions being repressed, they were tolerated or even became part of the governing coalition. Corporatist labor codes were promulgated, but they imposed fewer constraints on unions and union activity. The same kind of state-penetrated union movement was not established, although mobilization induced the labor movement to support the government and, by virtue of the benefits it received from it, to become dependent on the state. In general the adoption of a mobilization strategy entailed an increase in the political power of labor since its very utility to the political leadership as a political resource depended on its strength.

Party incorporation and the political mobilization of labor did not threaten the basic capitalist orientation of the state but rather did much to co-opt the working class. Nevertheless, working-class mobilization threatened important sectors of society. Thus the dynamic of party incorporation was political polarization: a progressive coalition in power was opposed by the dominant economic sectors, which formed a counterrevolutionary or counterreform alliance.

AFTERMATH

Each type of incorporation established a distinctive political agenda for the following period—the aftermath—ultimately producing different types of regimes as a political heritage. Here we are concerned with the aftermath period alone, since the heritage period in all four countries occurred after the 1940s (see figure 1). Hence, issues relating to regime outcomes in the heritage period will be mentioned only briefly.

The aftermath of state incorporation unfolded in three steps: (1) conservative governments protected established interests while labor was becoming a participant in the reopened, democratic regime; (2) attempts were made to form populist coalitions both through the formation of a populist party and through multiclass alliances of working-class and middle-sector parties; and (3) these populist experiments collapsed.

The aftermath began when authoritarian regimes that had established state incorporation became discredited and were superseded by democratic openings. At this point labor, which had hitherto been denied a role in the earlier period of demobilization, became an important political actor. Under state incorporation institutional channels for the political participation of workers had not been established, partisan identities among workers had not been consolidated, and coalitions had not been formed between labor and other classes or political actors. As a result the working class was politically autonomous from governing parties at the same time that it was tightly constrained under the prevailing system of industrial relations.

Labor's role in competitive party politics became a central issue in the aftermath period. With a new opportunity to enter the political arena the labor movement was swiftly revitalized and politicized. In both Brazil and Chile the Communist party quickly reestablished its influence among unionized workers. Meanwhile, middle-sector reformers sought to fill the void left by state incorporation and to shape labor's participation. In this effort the reformers made what might be called, from a comparative perspective, a "belated" attempt to establish a populist party in order to mobilize and channel working-class political participation and to enlist the support of labor for the electoral coalitions they were seeking to construct. These efforts were made by the original leaders of the middle-sector reform movements. In Brazil Vargas himself in 1945 took the initiative in creating the Partido Trabalhista Brasileira as the vehicle for labor representation and participation. In Chile Marmaduque Grove, Ibáñez's original coconspirator in 1924, along with other reformers sought to mobilize the support of the working class through a new populist Socialist party.

This attempt to establish populist parties, however, proved unsuccessful. The middle sectors failed to unite around these parties and instead for the most part supported center or center-right parties that lacked a large working-class base of support. As a result the new movements failed to achieve power and were therefore never in a position to offer sufficient concessions to satisfy their labor constituency. Instead, the aftermath of state incorporation brought a period of coalitional politics in which center or center-right parties, the Partido Social Democrático in Brazil and the Radical party in Chile, won power on the basis of electoral coalitions with the populist parties (and, in Chile, with the Communist party too). However, because oligarchic groups retained substantial influence in Congress, the centrist parties were as strongly drawn toward an accommodationist coalition with the conservatives as they were toward a populist alliance with the working class. As a result the populist parties remained only junior partners in the coalitions and from this position were not able to extract enough from their collaboration to satisfy the working class. In reaction an increasingly radical, anticollaborationist wing emerged within both the populist parties and the labor movements. In both Chile and Brazil these tendencies were reinforced by relatively powerful Communist parties competing for working-class support. Disillusioned by coalition politics and pressured by the Communists, the populist parties developed strong left-wing factions. A process of polarization began, and the period ended with the abandonment of the now discredited pattern of coalition politics. By 1952 in Chile and by 1960 in Brazil the labor movement and the parties or party factions that had attracted working-class support abandoned collaboration with the political center. The aftermath period ended with the collapse and discrediting of populism and coalition politics.

The outcome of state incorporation and its aftermath was a failure to create a strong, stable political center. The weakness of the political center subsequently became one of the most striking features of the party systems of both Brazil and Chile. The long-term legacy of state incorporation during the heritage period may be labeled *multiparty polarizing politics*. Although Brazil and Chile were far from identical cases, the two countries had in common highly fragmented party systems with a built-in tendency toward polarization. In both countries, in the context of the political and economic pressures of the 1960s, polarization intensified until a broad coalition favoring a military coup emerged. In Brazil in 1964 and in Chile in 1973 the military intervened to establish the two most durable bureaucratic-authoritarian regimes in South America.

In Mexico and Venezuela the main feature at the end of the period of party incorporation was a conservative reaction as the dominant economic sectors resisted the mobilization of labor, the progressive reforms, and their own exclusion from the governing coalition. In Venezuela the conservative reaction culminated in a military coup in 1948 and a decade of repressive, counterreformist rule. In Mexico the same polarization and rightist opposition occurred, but the party managed to stay in power by electing a conservative successor to Cárdenas in 1940. In the effort to regain power in Venezuela or to retain power in Mexico, the populist parties attempted to construct a new centrist bloc to end the political polarization provoked by the populist coalition.

The aftermath period in Mexico and Venezuela thus formed a striking contrast with that of state incorporation in Brazil and Chile. In Mexico and Venezuela the conservative reaction signaled the political limits of reform in late capitalist development. It provided a big incentive to avoid the polarization of the immediate past, to include the bourgeoisie and middle sectors in the dominant political coalition, and to reconstitute the multiclass coalition based this time in the center right. This effort to reintegrate the right and to create a new governing coalition had four chief features: a programmatic turn to the right; the exclusion of the left from the alliance; the retention of the labor movement (urban and rural) in the alliance by maintaining union-party linkages and labor support; and finally the establishment of conflict-limiting mechanisms to avoid the kind of polarization that had led to the toppling of the Acción Democrática–dominated regime in 1948 and had threatened the dominance of the ruling party in Mexico in 1940. In Mexico the mechanism was the strengthening of one-party dominance and in Venezuela the use of party pacts.

The heritage of party incorporation in Mexico and Venezuela was very different from that of state incorporation in Brazil and Chile. It consisted of a party/political system that was integrative, rather than polarizing, and that institutionalized something approaching a coalition of the whole in contrast to the unstable coalitions in Brazil and Chile. These regimes developed sophisticated conflict-limiting mechanisms that facilitated the formulation of consistent, sustainable policies and avoided the zero-sum conflicts and policy vacillation and immobilization that became the chief features of policies in Brazil and Chile. Mexico and Venezuela also developed strong centrist parties supported by a substantial proportion of the working-class as opposed to a party system that relegated parties with substantial working-class support to a position of nearly permanent opposition. The heritage phase in Mexico and Venezuela was thus characterized by the emergence of a stable, hegemonic regime able to weather the economic crises and the political challenges that confronted the countries of Latin America throughout the 1960s and 1970s and that in Brazil and Chile led to prolonged and repressive military rule.

Combining Perspectives

The above discussion summarizes two quite different approaches to understanding labor politics and regime change. The first examines the course of Latin American politics during the 1940s in light of powerful international factors reflecting the changing relationships among the major world powers.

The second, which focuses on a formative internal transition that in most instances occurred earlier in the century, does not focus on the 1940s per se. Instead, it develops an account of different paths or trajectories of change followed by Latin American countries during periods that do not necessarily coincide and at rates of change that vary considerably among them. From this point of view the 1940s is a rather arbitrary decade that catches countries in different phases in the unfolding of their trajectories. How do the two explanatory schemes intersect? How may they be combined or juxtaposed?

We begin by noting which of the internal phases occur in the 1940s. This decade corresponds to the incorporation or aftermath periods, or both, in all four countries (see figure 1). Two countries, one an example of state incorporation and the other of party incorporation, underwent the transition from incorporation to aftermath. In the other two cases the entire decade corresponded to the aftermath phase. (Figure 2 presents a more detailed chart of the intersection of the two perspectives.)

In an attempt to link the two perspectives we might ask three questions. These questions, as well as an outline of the answers, are presented in figure 4.

The first question considers the two strands of analysis as rival hypotheses. It asks to what extent the outcomes are caused by international events as opposed to internal dynamics. In other words, is the internal explanation spurious? The answer seems to be negative because for each pair of cases (of party and state incorporation) similar or parallel internal dynamics and steps unfolded in different decades, quite independently of the international context.

The second question considers international factors as a complement to internal trajectories. Did the international events of the 1940s affect the *timing*, *intensity*, and *variations* of outcomes that formed part of the internal dynamic? In Brazil there appears little doubt that this was the case. The authoritarian regime of the incorporation period was certainly not going to last forever, and in Latin America the typical pattern is for authoritarian regimes to be replaced by electoral regimes. Nevertheless, according to standard accounts of the period, the international climate as well as direct pressure from the United States favored democratic opening at this time. International factors also appear to account for the particular intensity with which Brazil experienced certain phases of the aftermath period. The end of the popular front policy of the Communists abroad and their readoption of strategies of class confrontation help explain why Brazilian labor experi-

1. *EXTERNAL EVENTS AS RIVAL EXPLANATIONS FOR THE SAME OUTCOMES.*
   Are the phases that appear to derive from internal trajectories of change really the product of international factors?

   Conclusion: No.

Cases of Party Incorporation

	Mexico	*Venezuela*
Height of Incorporation (Resolution of Stalemate)	1934–40	1945–48
Transition to Aftermath	1940	1948
Conservatization of Populist Party	1940–	1957/58–
Conflict-Limitation Measures	1946	1957–58
Exclusion of Left	1947–48	1958–62
Retention of Labor Support	1940–	1958–

Cases of State Incorporation

	Brazil	*Chile*
Transition to Aftermath	1943–45	1931
Labor Reactivation Under Conservative Government	1946–50	1932–38
"Populism"	1950–55	1938–41
Coalition Government	1955–60	1942–48
Ultimate Failure of Populist Attempt	1960	1948

2. *EXTERNAL EVENTS AS COMPLEMENTARY EXPLANATIONS FOR THE SAME OUTCOMES.*
   Where external and internal factors appear to push political dynamics in the same direction, do the international events affect the timing, intensity, or variation of phases associated with internal trajectories of change?

   Conclusion: Often.

3. *RELATIVE EXPLANATORY POWER OF EXTERNAL AND INTERNAL FACTORS.*
   Where external and internal factors appear to push political outcomes in different directions, do the internal dynamics deflect the international influence?

   Conclusion: Yes.

Figure 4. Role of External versus Internal Factors in Explaining Political Phases in the 1940s

enced an unprecedented, almost explosive reactivation and repoliticization during the immediate aftermath period of 1945–1947. Equally, the international conjuncture often affected the intensity of the conservative orientation of the government in the early aftermath period. Conservative from the start, in 1947 the Dutra government cracked down on labor, reintroduced a number of Estado Nôvo controls, and restored the ban on the newly legalized Communist party. The conservative reaction in Brazil during the late 1940s was stronger than that in the analytically comparable period in Chile in the 1930s. While specific conditions in the two countries help to explain this difference, there is no doubt that the contrasting international context was important.

International factors also affected the distinct features of Chile's aftermath period, in particular, the timing, duration, and specific character of the coalition governments. In Chile the coalitions of the aftermath period included the participation of the Communists and took the form of the Chilean Popular Front, a direct reflection of Comintern policy and the general international context of anti-Fascist collaboration. In Brazil, in contrast, the entire coalitional period corresponded to the Cold War so that Communist party participation was precluded from the beginning. The timing of the Cold War was also significant in Chilean politics. According to the internal trajectories thesis, the aftermath of state incorporation consisted of an abortive attempt to establish a viable, multiclass political center. Looking at this issue from the vantage point of the international conjuncture creates new perspectives on the degree of this populist failure. In Chile the onset of the Cold War and the regionwide move to proscribe the Communist party came at the end of the aftermath period, when the populist experiment and coalition politics were breaking down of their own weight, rather than at the beginning of the period as in Brazil. This contrast in timing helps explain why in Chile collaboration and coalition politics were discredited in the eyes of the labor movement and the left much more decisively than in Brazil. The discrediting of coalition politics in turn might have contributed to the more intense radicalization and polarization that subsequently occurred in Chile in comparison with Brazil.

In Mexico international factors might also explain some of the distinctive aspects of the aftermath period, in particular why the conservative reaction to party incorporation remained relatively mild, that is, why in Mexico, unlike in most countries, the incorporating party avoided a military coup. Perhaps these distinctive features reflected the timing of the initial aftermath period during the Comintern's second, more extreme, popular front line favoring multiclass collaboration. During this period, as we have seen, most sectors were willing to support broad anti-Fascist fronts while labor remained pledged to restraint in support of the war effort. Under these circumstances labor proved more willing to acquiesce in the conservatization typical of the aftermath period of party incorporation. Thus international factors facilitated the transition to conservatism and the avoidance of an institutional breakdown. In other countries, such as Venezuela, in contrast, the aftermath period coincided with the Cold War and the internationally influenced period of political closing during the late 1940s, when international trends may have encouraged a harsher, more repressive conservative reaction. In these countries a military coup overthrew the incorporating regime and banned the incorporating party.[11]

The timing of the internally unfolding steps in relation to the international events illuminates another aspect of Mexican politics in the 1940s. Because of Mexico's success in maintaining institutional continuity, a populist party rather than a counterreformist, anti-populist military government was in power during the internationally defined phase of political closing during the Cold War. The existence of a governing populist party may have contributed to the development of an alternative to conventional labor repression in the form of the distinctive Mexican institution known as *charrismo*: the informal coercive control exercised by the party over unions to eliminate leftist or independent leadership. In this way the transition to Cold War politics in the late 1940s might help to explain the distinctive character of state-labor relations in Mexico.

In Venezuela, despite the coincidence of timing, regime change did not seem to be strongly influenced by the international conjuncture. There the high point of party incorporation began in 1945. Though Venezuela's democratic, reformist period coincided with pressures pushing in the same direction as international factors, the latter did not appear very significant in determining either the timing or the type of labor incorporation. The timing itself seems more closely related to the internal situation, particularly the breakdown of negotiations over the selection of candidates for the forthcoming elections. This episode provoked the military coup that carried Acción Democrática to power and initiated the *trienio*. Nor did international factors influence the type of incorporation period. The mobilization of the popular sectors began in the mid-1930s at a time when the mobilizing parties remained in opposition. Similarly, it was in the 1930s that Acción Democrática adopted a democratic and reformist position. Thus when it gained power in 1945 its populist coalition and its commitment to democracy and reform were already in place.

The end of the incorporation period in Venezuela occurred in 1948 when a military coup ended the *trienio*. The timing of this event too appeared predictable in light of prevailing international conditions. However, accounts of Venezuelan politics rarely refer to the international context, and other considerations cast doubt on its importance. The impact of the international conjuncture in the late 1940s is usually understood in light of the turn against the Communists, but in Venezuela it was the populists and Acción Democrática, rather than the two competing Communist factions, that became the target of the conservative military. Indeed for several years afterward one of the Communist factions collaborated with the government.

Thus, international factors obviously had important consequences in

Latin America. Yet the international conjuncture was never more powerful in shaping political outcomes than the internal trajectory. In a number of instances international factors affected the timing and intensity of the stages following labor incorporation; they help to round out the picture and explain some of the variations within patterns of change for which the internal argument alone could not account.

Finally, the third question raises the issue of how the internal dynamics explain the differential impact of international events. As table 12 showed, sometimes the expected outcomes of the 1940s did not occur. The deviation can often be explained by internal trends. Thus, when the two logics contradicted one another and pointed toward different outcomes, the internal dynamic took precedence.

Among the four countries considered, Brazil appeared to follow most closely the periodization suggested by international forces; yet even in Brazil the deviations can be explained by the internally driven logic. An example is the political opening that occurred at a time when the Cold War might have suggested a political closing. In 1950 a reformist opening began that could be understood only as an integral part of the aftermath of state incorporation—as part of the attempt to establish acceptable channels for the political participation of labor. Mexico too generally conformed to the phases suggested by the 1940s conjuncture but again with an exception: the period of political opening and reform in 1944–1946 failed to occur. Instead Mexico was moving in the opposite direction toward political closing, the strengthening of one-party dominance, and the marginalization of labor—a pattern explained by the internal dynamics perspective. In Mexico this period marked the aftermath of party incorporation and hence constituted a period of conservative reaction to the prior reformist period. In this case, then, the logics of the two perspectives led in opposite directions, and the internal trajectory proved stronger than the international conjuncture.

In Chile international influences became most visible in the relationship between the policy of the Comintern and the formation of the Chilean Popular Front in the mid-1930s and in the subsequent coalitions among the Communist, Socialist, and Radical parties in the 1940s. Although the formation of the Popular Front cannot be understood without reference to international factors, these factors alone are insufficient to explain the persistence of the coalitions during the 1940s. Contrary to the internationalist hypothesis, the Chilean Popular Front survived the German-Soviet pact, and the coalitions that followed the Popular Front continued for some time beyond the end of World War II, when international factors pointed to increased class conflict and protest. Although there was a wave of strikes in Chile after 1945, in other respects the shift to the politics of confrontation was limited despite strong ties between a relatively strong, class-conscious labor movement and Marxist political parties—conditions that might have suggested particular receptivity to the influence of international communism. In 1946, when Communist parties elsewhere in Latin America were returning to confrontation, the Chilean party not only joined the governing coalition but also for the first time formally joined and participated in the government—a step it had declined to take during the years of Comintern's popular front policy. The various deviations from the expected patterns of the 1940s reflected the playing out of the attempts at coalition politics typical of the aftermath phase. At the end of World War II the possibilities and drawbacks of collaboration were still being explored, the issues remained unresolved, and all parties were vacillating. Thus although ultimately discredited, at this point coalitional politics temporarily continued despite pressures from the international conjuncture toward renewed political confrontation.

Venezuela too conformed to the expected patterns of the 1940s except in one instance. Although labor protest increased dramatically in the immediate postwar years, this activity was less a result of the end of popular front collaboration on the part of the Communist-influenced labor movement than a reflection of the new activism of Acción Democrática unions undertaken with the support of the *trienio* government. This outcome reflected the general pattern of party incorporation and the mobilization of labor support that characterized it.

Conclusion

This analysis has juxtaposed and combined two different analytic perspectives on labor politics and regime change in Latin America. Both the international and the internal perspectives contribute to our understanding of Latin America during the 1940s and hence should be viewed not as rival but as complementary explanations. There is no doubt that the international events of the 1940s left a strong imprint on the political landscape of Latin America. Yet these events failed to deflect the unfolding of internal trajectories set in motion by the initial incorporation of labor. Overall, the internal dynamics prove stronger causal factors. However, the international factors do help explain the distinctive features and variations of the internal patterns, filling in some of the details and helping to account for the timing and intensity of the steps as they unfolded in each country.

Notes

1. This argument has been explored in Leslie Bethell and Ian Roxborough, "Latin America between the Second World War and the Cold War: Some Reflections on the 1945–1948 Conjuncture," *Journal of Latin American Studies* 20, no. 1 (May 1988), 169.

2. See Ruth Berins Collier and David Collier, *Shaping the Political Arena: Critical Junctures, the Labor Movement and Regime Dynamics in Latin America*. Princeton: Princeton University Press, 1991. A similar argument for European countries appears in Gregory Luebbert, *Liberalism, Fascism, or Social Democracy: Local Classes and the Political Origins of Regimes in Interwar Europe*. New York: Oxford University Press, 1991.

3. The concepts of "aftermath" and "heritage" are explained on page 73.

4. *Time* (7 October 1940).

5. *Time* (13 April 1942).

6. Bethell and Roxborough, "Latin America," 171–72.

7. Liisa North and David Raby, "The Dynamic of Revolution and Counterrevolution: Mexico under Cárdenas, 1934–1940," *Latin American Research Unit Studies* 2, no. 1 (October 1977), 51.

8. Romulo Betancourt, *Venezuela: Oil and Politics*. Boston: Houghton Mifflin, 1979, 72.

9. John D. French, "Industrial Workers and the Birth of the Populist Republic in Brazil, 1945–1946," *Latin American Perspectives* 16, no. 4 (Fall 1989), 5–27.

10. Collier and Collier, *Shaping the Political Arena*, also examined party incorporation in Colombia, Uruguay, Peru, and Argentina, where mobilization was limited to organized labor.

11. In Collier and Collier, *Shaping the Political Arena*, Uruguay presented the only other case of party incorporation in which the incorporation period was not terminated by a military coup that ousted the incorporating party. It was also the only other country in which the transition from party incorporation to the aftermath period was made before the onset of the Cold War.

4 ECLA and the Formation of Latin American Economic Doctrine

E. V. K. FitzGerald

Introduction

The foundation of the United Nations Economic Commission for Latin America (ECLA) in 1948 was recognized at the time as a crucial step in the postwar construction of a regional doctrine of trade and industrialization. More recently, significant scholarly reassessments have related the body of economic ideas associated with ECLA to the wider tradition of late-industrialization ideology and subsequent Latin American debates on structuralism and dependency theory.[1] However, these ideas are still generally regarded as an autochthonous critique of orthodox trade theory arising from the Latin American experience of the Great Depression. In this chapter I "relocate" early ECLA theory in the specific context of the international debate on the organization of the world economy in the aftermath of World War II.

Technical accounts of *cepalino* (from CEPAL, Comisión Económica para América Latina, the Spanish name for the commission) economic propositions, and the institutional history of ECLA itself can be found elsewhere.[2] Drawing on those accounts, in this chapter I offer three propositions on the history of Latin American thought. First, the institutional context within which ECLA and its doctrine were established is best understood in terms of the frustrated Latin American aspiration to move from the periphery to the industrialized center of the world economy. Second, the issues of unequal exchange and late industrialization developed by ECLA had a long intellectual history that was well known in Latin America by the 1940s, to which the Prebisch model was an addition rather than a departure. Third, a rereading of the early *cepalino* publications in the light of these two propositions provides new evidence of the Latin American perception of the world economy in the immediate postwar period. This historical and theoretical contextualization is not intended to question the originality of the "center-periphery model" of trade and industrialization. Locating early ECLA thought in the appropriate intellectual and practical context can only emphasize the significance of economic doctrine at this crucial moment in modern Latin American history.[3]

The Postwar Reinsertion of Latin America in the World Economy

The concern in Latin America over the region's role in postwar economic arrangements formed part of wider international debate throughout the decade about the organization of the world economy.[4] In 1942 the United States and Britain reached a preliminary agreement on the need to reshape global trade and payments systems that stemmed from a shared interpretation of the dangers of a return to the protectionism of the interwar years: between 1929 and 1933 world trade had declined by 65 percent in value and 25 percent in volume.[5] To complement free trade in manufactures, Keynes and others pointed out the need to avoid disastrous fluctuations in raw materials prices and to coordinate national macroeconomic policies.

Before World War II European views on the economic development of Africa and Asia were, quite naturally, derived from colonial policy. Until the 1920s the United States held similar views about its southern neighbors, which, along with the Monroe Doctrine, had traditionally generated considerable resentment in Latin America. Indeed, between the wars Latin America could not be considered "poor" since average incomes were well above subsistence levels and comparable with those obtained in Southern and Eastern Europe.[6] Industry in the region was viewed by outside observers as relatively dynamic, even if much of the impetus was considered to come from foreign corporations and immigrants rather than from the local elites, who were characterized as traditional landlords and bureaucrats.[7]

After the Great Depression views on world economic development began to change and found reflection within the United States in the influential books by Eugene Staley published in 1939 and 1944. Staley called for support for the industrialization of the so-called noncolonial South to ensure its integration with the international division of labor.[8] For this purpose he classified Argentina and Chile with France and Australia, and Mexico, Peru, and Colombia with Spain, Portugal, and the USSR.[9] He also argued that state intervention as well as international help were needed in the South, citing Japan, Turkey, Mexico, and Egypt as leading examples. The concern of the League of Nations during the 1920s for the economic development of poorer European nations (and, by implication, for Latin America) was manifested in a report drawn up by Stanley Bruce, the Australian delegate to the League in 1939. His plan for world socioeconomic development strongly influenced the creation of the United Nations Economic and Social Committee in 1944.[10]

In fact, more than a decade earlier, in 1928, the Conference of American States held in Havana had already ostensibly reoriented U.S. policy toward Latin America and the Caribbean. At the Seventh Pan-American Conference in Montevideo in 1933, Cordell Hull announced the demise of "dollar diplomacy"; what the new "Good Neighbor" policy could achieve was symbolized by the material reconstruction of Puerto Rico. Latin American governments now began to perceive a permanent change in their hemispheric status, and this outlook seemed to be confirmed at the Panama Conference in 1939 when the United States announced its commitment to industrial investment in Latin America and the establishment of the Export-Import Bank to provide federal funding for capital equipment exports to the region in 1940.[11] At Bretton Woods in 1944 agreement was reached to establish the International Trade Organization, the International Monetary Fund, and the International Bank for Reconstruction and Development in order to stabilize primary commodity prices, promote world trade in manufactures, and plan investment. The Latin American delegations at Bretton Woods seemed justified in assuming that although the Allies were committed to the U.S. position that the postwar world economy would be based on free trade, such a system would both provide for Latin American access to U.S. markets and for assistance in their own industrialization.[12]

In Latin America little new investment had been undertaken during the war years because of restricted supplies of capital goods from the United States except in those sectors producing strategic exports for the Allies. Nonetheless, industrial employment had expanded rapidly, and the incorporation of urban groups within the political system created new pressures for industrial expansion and the provision of social infrastructure. Moreover, Latin American governments could no longer rely on the supply of cheap local wage goods, particularly peasant-produced food, to protect the incomes of urban industrial workers during adjustment to export decline, as had been the case in the 1930s.[13] Latin American governments logically anticipated that the strategy of increased industrial investment and manufactured exports necessary to ensure both economic development and social stability would receive strong support from the United States.

Although the Latin American share of world trade had risen from 8 percent in 1938 to 13 percent in 1946, much of this was due to the growth in commerce between the republics during the war and the collapse of European trade. To the general arguments for a new international economic order was added the alarming fact that Latin America's terms of trade in 1940 stood at 33 percent below their 1928 level and by 1946 had fallen by a further 23 percent (see table 13).[14]

The per capita purchasing power of exports, taking into account volume changes, from Latin America in 1940–1944 was little more than half what it had been in 1925–1929. The considerable accumulation of dollar reserves during the war reflected the contraction of import volumes far below those experienced during the Great Depression.[15] In consequence, the fact that gross domestic product had grown by 3.4 percent annually between 1939 and 1945 was seen at the time as a rearguard action against trading odds and not, as later interpretations would suggest, as a positive result of import substitution.[16] Moreover, as Carlos Díaz-Alejandro has pointed out, the expansionary macroeconomic monetary policy that supported demand for the output of domestic industry during the 1940s was essentially the unintended conse-

Table 13 Latin America: External Trade, 1925–1949

Indices (1937 = 100)	*1925–29*	*1930–34*	*1935–39*	*1940–44*	*1945–49*
Export volume	97	88	94	89	113
Price index:					
Exports	124	69	86	110	194
Imports	124	91	97	138	185
Terms of trade	100	75	89	79	104
Import capacity:					
Total	96	66	84	71	118
Per capita	114	72	84	64	96

Source: United Nations, Economic Commission for Latin America, *Economic Survey of Latin America, 1949*. New York: United Nations, 1951, 17.

quence of the abandonment of the gold standard and the collapse of fiscal revenues from trade.[17]

At the inter-American conference at Chapultepec in early 1945 the Latin American governments expressed strong views on the organization of markets for raw materials, particularly the issues of price stability and access to the United States for manufactured exports, especially from those industries set up to support the Allied war effort.[18] Washington, however, refused to commit itself to aid or tariff preferences and condemned Latin American proposals for development planning. The United States now appeared to regard the economic problems of the region as essentially internal rather than as bound up with the international trade system and seemed mainly interested in the allegiance of Latin America in the emerging struggle against communism.[19] Even though this major shift in the U.S. position evidently reflected new strategic priorities, it was still widely assumed in Latin America that industrial investment would be supported by the resumption of the concessionary credits required to purchase technology from the United States. A regional version of the Marshall Plan for Europe was even proposed at the 1948 Inter-American Conference in Bogota, albeit without success.[20]

Nonetheless, there was still some expectation that new international arrangements would be more favorable to the region. The establishment of the International Trade Organization (ITO) was confirmed in Havana in 1948, although U.S. support turned out to be one of the last manifestations of the "Freedom from Want" policies of the Roosevelt-Truman era. The Latin Americans regarded the "Havana Charter" as legitimizing their aspirations to the status of membership in the "North" that was accorded to Central Europe between the wars and was now being granted to the dominions of the British Commonwealth. The Havana meeting also seemed to the Latin Americans to imply the continuation of the wartime export stabilization schemes and technology transfers that had been denied at Chapultepec. However, the U.S. Congress subsequently refused to ratify the ITO and the initiation of the Cold War transformed the international agenda for the 1950s.

The failure of the Havana Charter was perceived by Latin American governments as representing rejection by the United States and the region's unwilling inclusion in a "Third World" emerging from decolonization.[21] The nature and objectives of inter-American economic cooperation as set out by Staley were among the first victims of the Cold War. The failure of the Havana Charter was thus seen as a profound political rebuff, a "shift that was regarded as a betrayal by Latin America" and that was to have a radical effect on regional economic doctrine.[22]

Contemporary Theories of Trade and Development

The growth of the Latin American economies was in the 1940s, and still is, driven by the income from raw materials exports and dependent upon imported capital goods for investment. The terms of trade were seen as exogenously determined and inevitably became the central focus of economic debate in the region. The idea that the prices of primary commodities, both minerals and agriculture, were in some sense unfairly depressed relative to imported manufactures went back as far as the era of the viceroyalties during the eighteenth century. Equally, the concept of "unequal exchange," in the broad sense of the "North" setting prices so that the return on its own resources is higher than that of the "South," had a long history in economic thought extending back to Ricardo and Mill.[23] Ricardo had based the classical concept of comparative advantage on the technical conditions governing the labor inputs to traded commodities, which permit the product of a days' work in one country to be exchanged for that of several days' work in another. Neoclassical trade theory broke away from the labor theory of value through the introduction of the concept of "reciprocal demand" in which the market for the products determines their price. Both variants were to reappear in the postwar debates initiated by ECLA.[24]

The concept of unequal exchange had been widely employed in Central Europe during the 1920s to justify planned industrialization, although the need for tariff protection in order to "catch up" with technologically more advanced industrial nations had been advanced in the mid-nineteenth century by Friedrich List.[25] The Central European theorists regarded unequal exchange as the key feature of trade between *groups of nations* at the "center" and the "periphery" of the world economy. This specific terminology was apparently first used by the German economic historian Werner Sombart, whose analysis of European history published in 1928 described a dominant center—Great Britain supported by the United States—surrounded by an exploited and dominated periphery consisting of Central, Eastern, and Southern Europe.[26] The economists of the Frankfurt School hotly contested this view on the orthodox Marxist grounds that exploitation by one proletariat (and thus one "country") by another was theoretically impossible.[27] Nonetheless, Sombart's theory enjoyed considerable support among Central European nationalists promoting state-led industrialization and economic autarky to overcome technological disadvantage. Another strand of Ricardo's model was taken up in 1929 by the Romanian economist Mihail Manoïlescu who argued that surplus labor and low productivity in the agricultural sector resulted in depressed export prices and that the substantial urban-rural wage differential was a handicap to the expansion of industrial demand.[28]

By the early 1930s the debate in Europe on center-periphery relations was well known and widely discussed in Latin America, including Argentina, although there was no formal theory for Latin America as such.[29] Sombart was initially read in German but was translated and published in Mexico in 1946. He defined the "center" and "periphery" as follows: "To find our way through the chaos of events [in the world economy], we should distinguish between the central capitalist countries and a mass of peripheral countries. . . .The former are active directive nations, the latter are passive and directed."[30]

Ernest Friedrich Wagemann, a Chilean who had studied in Germany in the 1920s, published his *Evolución y ritmo de la economía mundial* in 1933, which was based on the ideas of Sombart and widely read in Latin America at the time; a Portuguese translation of Manoïlescu's *Theory* was published in São Paulo in 1931.[31] It therefore appears most unlikely that Prebisch himself, who was not only of German origin and a professor of economics but also actively involved in debates on international trade, was unaware of the origins of the contemporary center-periphery concept.

Nationalist views on unequal exchange were an integral part of Argentine political discourse at the time. It was also common to make comparisons between Argentina and the British dominions, and Prebisch visited Australia during the 1930s.[32] The influence of List is explicit in the writing of Alejandro E. Bunge and his Revista de Economía Argentina group that then went on to influence the early stages of Peronism. Indeed throughout this period there was constant discussion in Argentina about state-led industrialization that involved both military figures and "*ingenieros*" like Bunge and Adolfo Dorfman.[33] Prebisch himself seems to have remained more interested in international monetary issues during this period, although after 1940 he did come under the more liberal political influence of Federico Pinedo, who as finance minister pressed for proindustrial policies based on market mechanisms.[34]

During the 1940s major European and North American debates took place on issues of world trade, monetary policy, and economic development, with particular attention being paid to the consequences of the mismanagement of international economic relations between the wars.[35] Much of the most important contemporary work in economic theory was rapidly translated by *El Trimestre Económico* and the Fondo de Cultura Económica from the early thirties onward as were significant local contributions on postwar economic prospects.[36] The ideas of Keynes on both macroeconomic management and international economic organization were also well known in the region by the mid-1940s, and in fact Prebisch himself published a short summary of the *General Theory* in 1947.[37] In this way, despite the comparative isolation of Latin America from Europe during the Second World War, young economists were well aware of contemporary European economics and social theory.[38]

The combination of these prewar debates on industrialization in the "South" and the emergence of new theories of trade and macroeconomic management in the "North" provided the intellectual context within which Latin American economists reacted to the failure of the Havana Charter in 1948. The establishment of the United Nations Economic Commission for Latin America (ECLA) in the same year provided an ideal vehicle for their views. The United Nations Economic and Social Council founded ECLA, with strong support from Secretary-General Trygve Lie, two years after it had been proposed at the first session of the United Nations General Assembly in 1946.[39] At that time Latin America accounted for twenty out of the total U.N. membership of fifty-one nations and having been allies of the victors during the war logically expected considerable external support for their regional organization. However, the industrialized countries led by the United States resisted the idea from the start on the grounds that ECLA might become a platform for international trade claims, which were better contained within the more docile Organization of American States. As a result, after some hard bargaining ECLA was originally founded for a three-year probationary period and only became a permanent body within the U.N. system in 1951.[40]

The View from Santiago

The first product of the newly founded ECLA was the *Economic Survey of Latin America, 1948*, which appeared before Prebisch became a member of the commission.[41] The report presented a structuralist interpretation of the development of the main Latin American economies since 1937. The main difference from subsequent *Surveys* was the relatively uncritical evaluation of foreign trade. Prebisch was in charge of the 1949 *Survey*, but before this was released he published his celebrated essay *The Economic Development of Latin America and its Principal Problems.*[42] The propositions put forward in this essay, and their subsequent incorporation into the 1949 *Survey*, generated considerable discussion and much hostile criticism, rapidly becoming identified with the ECLA position as a whole.[43]

The 1948 *Survey* was overshadowed by the political impact of the 1949 *Survey* but presented valuable insights on the origins of ECLA doctrine. Part 1 ("Growth, Disequilibrium, and Disparities: An Interpretation of the Process of Economic Development") of the 1948 *Survey* brought together valuable data on the main economies of the region for the first time. In the analysis of foreign trade and industry considerable use was made of the earlier League of Nations methodology, particularly the effect of the lower income elasticity of demand for primary commodities as compared with industrial goods, in order to explain the deterioration of the terms of trade (for which data since 1870 is presented).[44] The text also shows that many of the premises of the industrialization strategy that ECLA was to develop in the 1950s were already widely accepted, such as the need for planning and the attribution of low manufacturing productivity to the lack of private investment and the availability of cheap labor.[45]

Part 2 of the 1948 *Survey*, entitled "Economic Development of Selected Latin American Countries," contained much excellent data derived from detailed appendixes on industrialization in the larger countries of the region.[46] The data substantiated empirically the negative effect on growth of changing world trade conditions. These studies, which were partly based on research carried out by the authors before the foundation of ECLA itself, helped to define *cepalino* ideas on industrialization. The aggregate data (see table 14) illustrate the rapid expansion of "import capacity" (a statistical concept apparently invented by ECLA) immediately after the outbreak of peace, followed by stagnation: actual imports rose rapidly between 1945 and 1947 as accumulated reserves were spent and then dropped back as the terms of trade effect and profit outflows squeezed liquidity.[47]

The effect of this import constraint was reflected more in the stagnation of consumption than in investment (see table 15), therefore implying that unequal exchange was leading to severe social tensions. The country studies were also the prelude not only to a number of important ECLA ideas about

Table 14 Latin America: The External Constraint, 1945–1949 (in billions of constant 1950 U.S. dollars)

	1945	*1946*	*1947*	*1948*	*1949*
Exports	4.2	5.3	6.3	6.6	5.7
Capital inflow	0.3	0.4	0.7	0.5	0.6
Gross receipts	4.5	5.7	7.0	7.1	6.3
Terms of trade effect[a]	–	1.9	2.6	2.8	2.4
Factor outflow[b]	0.5	1.0	1.0	1.5	0.6
Imports:					
Capacity	4.0	4.7	6.0	5.6	5.7
Actual	2.8	4.0	6.3	5.8	5.3

Source: United Nations, Economic Commission for Latin America, *Economic Survey of Latin America, 1951–1952*. New York: United Nations, 1954, 16.

[a]"Loss" due to deterioration of terms of trade since 1945.

[b]Profits, interest, and repatriation of capital.

technology itself but also to an appreciation of the domestic constraint placed on the expansion of modern industry by "traditional" ownership forms in sectors such as agriculture.[48]

Immediately after the Havana meeting ECLA economists embarked on the final version of the 1949 *Survey*, which was intended to give substance to the original, somewhat rhetorical presentation of a year earlier.[49] The personal standing of Prebisch as a central banker had probably been crucial in causing the stir at the Inter-American Conference at Havana about the analysis of international trade. By the same token, however, his conservative views on fiscal and monetary matters were also evident in the final version that was presented at the meeting of ECLA at Montevideo in 1950.[50] The 1949 *Survey*

Table 15 Latin America: Production and Accumulation, 1945–1949 (in billions of constant 1950 U.S. dollars)

	1945	*1946*	*1947*	*1948*	*1949*
GDP	27.4	30.9	33.6	34.6	35.7
Investment	3.3	4.3	5.1	6.1	6.3
Consumption	22.7	25.2	28.5	27.7	29.1
Investment (as a percentage of GDP)	11.9	13.9	15.3	17.7	17.6
Per capita consumption ($)	164	179	198	188	192

Source: United Nations, Economic Commission for Latin America, *Economic Survey of Latin America, 1951–1952*. New York: United Nations, 1954, 5 and 9.

was mostly made up of the expanded version of the Prebisch model of trade relations and a critique of the then orthodox monetary approach to balance of payments theory. His view implied not only a radical analysis of the economic problems of the periphery but also an outspoken criticism of the behavior of the center in setting high prices, wages, and profits for itself on the one hand and retarding the spread of technology and industry on the other. The 1949 *Survey* suggested an industrial policy based on domestic markets not as an optional solution, however, but rather as the only alternative to the expansion of manufactured exports and thus more import openness on the part of the center.[51] The "center-periphery" model set out in the 1949 *Survey* contained four key points:

1. The terms of trade reflect a combination of collusive behavior by labor and business at the center, which can "make" prices because of its market control, and of surplus labor at the periphery, which must "take" prices because of competition between suppliers. The result is a built-in balance of payments disequilibrium.[52]
2. The diffusion of technology from the center to the periphery is retarded by institutional constraints, lack of investment, and poor labor mobility. The control of world market prices by the central economies means that any increase in productivity at the periphery leads only to increased profits at the center as export prices fall.
3. Import substitution is a "second best" alternative to fair prices for primary commodities and access to center markets for manufactured exports, but it may be necessary in order to create employment.[53]
4. National planning is legitimated by the experience of state intervention at the center during the war and the need to ensure that domestic profits are used for industrial investment rather than luxury consumption.

The crucial step in the argument, upon which the force of the ECLA critique depended, was thus the *lack of competition* at the center: "the theory also refutes the classical assumption of competition. . . .both the factor and product markets of the Center [are] operating under monopolistic markets, while competitive markets prevail at the periphery."[54] As Fernando Henrique Cardoso has pointed out, Prebisch's position was therefore not a repudiation of Ricardo—as neoclassical critics incorrectly stated—but rather a protest that the mutual Ricardian benefits from trade were being inequitably distributed because of northern protectionism.[55] Indeed Furtado states that Prebisch himself was initially not interested in an ECLA post but rather was engaged as a consultant and produced the "polemical text" for Havana at the last moment. The text did *not* criticize neoclassical theory as such but rather the lack of diffusion of technological progress due to international arrangements. Furtado defines Prebisch's position as follows: "to escape the constraints of the existing international order, the peripheral countries had to adopt the road of industrialization, the high road for access to the fruits of technical progress. . .[although in proposing this, Prebisch] . . .exposed his flank to an easy counter-attack from the academic world, which demanded a conceptual rigor he did not possess."[56]

In the wake of the international furor that followed the 1949 *Survey*, the official ECLA view of international trade was considerably modified for the 1950–1951 *Survey*.[57] This document marked a major statistical advance on its predecessor by using a series of national accounts, which permitted international comparisons. However, the center-periphery model was drastically changed. The radical Ricardian critique of terms of trade deterioration as a reflection of world power was replaced by an interpretation based on the difference between the income elasticity of demand for imports of raw materials and that for manufactures. In other words, the problem was contingent on the nature of the commodities and consumer demand rather than on the process of capital accumulation and state power. The 1950–1951 *Survey* was essentially a more elaborate version of the trade model given in the 1948 *Survey*, even though the structuralist analysis of supply determination and income distribution at the periphery was retained.

Even this modified ECLA view on the historical trend in the terms of trade was mercilessly attacked by neoclassical economists as being both empirically and theoretically untenable.[58] The surveys of the early 1950s continued with the essentially Keynesian approach, and although the management of international finance and the lack of development aid were still criticized, the center was no longer held to be exploiting the periphery through unequal exchange.[59] This domesticated version of *cepalino* doctrine rapidly became an integral part of governmental discourse in the region—and ECLA survived its probation to became a permanent part of the U.N. system.

ECLA Doctrine in Retrospect

Although the systematic exposition of the center-periphery model and the statistical support provided by the surveys were very welcome, ECLA theory did not come as a great surprise to Latin American economists. The reaction against the theory came from neoclassical economists at the center, particularly because the critique came from a U.N. institution led by a respected central banker. It is probably inaccurate to regard the origins of the center-periphery model as essentially autochthonous and based on the experience of the interwar years.[60] Nor can ECLA thought be reduced to an expression of regional nationalism in the tradition of earlier thinkers such as José Carlos Mariátegui and Víctor Raúl Haya de la Torre because ECLA economists, with the exception of Juan Noyola, seem to have been largely innocent of Marxism.[61] Prebisch himself, abetted by his biographers, claimed to have thought up the idea of the center-periphery model by himself.[62] In his account the pathogenesis was due to his experience of the forced delinking of America from the world economy during the interwar period, an interpretation that has been extended to the origins of Latin American dependency theory as a whole.[63] Cardoso and Aníbal Pinto are rather more circumspect: they attribute the center-periphery model to Prebisch but view it as a technical critique of neoclassical trade theory.[64] The most comprehensive study of ECLA economics, by Octavio Rodríguez, discreetly avoids the whole question of theoretical antecedents, referring only to the influence on Prebisch of the experience of central banking in Argentina between the wars.[65] Furtado, probably the outstanding Latin American economist of his generation, implies that the essence of the model was based on neither theory nor experience but rather was a nationalist statement.[66]

It is perhaps understandable that in the immediate postwar period Prebisch preferred to overlook the Central European antecedents of his model. Sombart had become a convert to National Socialism, to which Prebisch was particularly antipathetic, and Manoïlescu had been a member of the Iron Guard. To the untutored eye, like that of businesspeople in the United States, the center-periphery model appeared if anything to reflect Leninist theories of imperialism, an error subsequently compounded by dependency theorists.[67] This confusion was exacerbated by the statements of Prebisch himself concerning his intellectual formation. For example, he dismissed the "first stage" of his thought, before ECLA, in a few words: "important theoretical problems emerged in my mind," he remarked vaguely.[68] He acknowledged no intellectual mentors, even for the subject of his doctoral dissertation on Pareto, and omitted his 1947 book on Keynes from his bibliographical curriculum vitae.[69] Above all, Prebisch continually claimed the sole authorship of the ECLA model, scarcely mentioning the work of his colleagues in Santiago or elsewhere in Latin America.

Such criticism of Prebisch does not necessarily imply a denial of either his or ECLA's originality. As Alexander Gerschenkron has pointed out, theorists faced with similar circumstances, in this case late- industrializing countries facing an adverse organization of world trade, will tend to reach similar conclusions.[70] Faced by similar statistical evidence for the South as a whole, and exposed to the same contemporary debates among academics and policymakers, Hans Singer at the headquarters of the United Nations in New York put forward independently a theory so similar to the "elasticities" version of the ECLA model that the two became known as the single "Prebisch-Singer theory of terms of trade deterioration."[71] The Ricardian implications of surplus labor present in ECLA analysis had also been developed earlier and the implications for trade theory more rigorously defined.[72]

In the late 1950s ECLA surveys incorporated the pioneering work by Osvaldo Sunkel and Pinto on the structuralist theory of inflation.[73] These authors explicitly based their interpretation on earlier work by Juan Noyola, which in turn was influenced by the work of Michael Kalecki, but their framework was the same Ricardian value theory used in the first center-periphery model. Nonetheless, Prebisch's own ideas on inflation and monetary policy remained unrepentantly orthodox.[74] The theory of unequal exchange as an explanation of underdevelopment was taken up some decades later by Samir Amin and Arghiri Emmanuel as part of a wider Marxist critique of capitalist accumulation on a world level.[75] Nicholas Kaldor also constructed post-Keynesian models, possibly under some ECLA influence, to demonstrate how a long-term downward trend of the terms of trade could arise from diminishing returns to agriculture and rising wages in the North.[76] However, the ordinal "ECLA model" of international trade in the 1949 *Survey* was only set out much later with proper neo-Ricardian rigor by Oscar Braun, another Argentine economist, who returned to the consequences for world prices of the oligopolistic position of the center as a producer of not only manufactures but also raw materials.[77]

Conclusion

The International Trade Organization was never established. The General Agreement on Tariffs and Trade (GATT) set up in 1947 protected the interests of the industrialized countries. The United Nations Conference on Trade, Aid, and Development (UNCTAD) was created in 1964 with Prebisch as its secretary-general but without the power to counterbalance unequal exchange. In recent years the United States has attempted to extend to world trade in services the same protectionist measures it refused to lift on goods at the Havana conference nearly half a century ago.[78]

We can draw only tentative conclusions as to the formation of modern Latin American economic doctrine from the argument presented in this chapter, particularly because so much research on national economic debates in the postwar period remains to be done. Yet it does seem clear that early *cepalino* theory is best understood as part of a wider postwar debate on the world order and not as a delayed reaction to the Great Depression or a precursor of Third World developmentalism. In the event, by promoting import substitution, ECLA may even have contributed to the failure to establish a permanent system of international economic management more conducive to sustained industrialization in Latin America.[79] Nevertheless, the lasting influence of ECLA doctrine is still to be found in the shared premises of regional political debate.

Notes

My thanks are due to Edgardo Floto for our original conversations on the topic at Cambridge over a decade ago; Joseph Love and Cristóbal Kay for helpful comments on an earlier draft; and Sylvia Raw for her generous gift of Celso Furtado's postmodernist autobiography *A fantasia organizada*. Rio de Janeiro: Editorial Paz y Tierra, 1985.

1. H. W. Arndt, "The Origins of Structuralism," *World Development* 13, no. 2 (1985), 151–59; José Hodara, *Prebisch y la CEPAL: Sustancia, trayectoria, y contexto institucional*. México, D.F.: Colegio de México, 1987; Cristóbal Kay, *Latin American Theories of Development and Underdevelopment*. London: Routledge, 1989; Joseph L. Love, "The Origins of Dependency Analysis," *Journal of Latin American Studies* 22, no. 1 (1990), 143–68; Felipe Pazos, "Cincuenta años de pensamiento económico en la América Latina," *El trimestre económico*, no. 50 (1983), 1015–48, and Octavio Rodríguez, *La teoría del subdesarrollo de la CEPAL*. México, D.F.: Siglo XXI, 1980; Osvaldo Sunkel, "The Development of Development Theory," in *Transnational Capitalism and National Development*, edited by José Villamil. Atlantic Highlands, N.J.: Hassocks, Harvester, 1979, 19–31; for a self-appraisal see Raúl Prebisch, "Five Stages in My Thinking on Development," in *Pioneers in Development*, edited by Gerald M. Meier and Dudley Seers. New York: Oxford University Press, 1984, 175–91.

2. The propositions are well set out in Octavio Rodríguez, *Teoría del subdesarrollo*, and Edgardo Floto, "The Center-Periphery System and Unequal Exchange," *CEPAL Review* 39 (1989), 135–54; institutional history can be found in Gabriel Guzmán, *El desarrollo latinoamericano y la CEPAL*. Barcelona: Editorial Planeta, 1976, and Hodara, *Prebisch y la CEPAL*.

3. Karl Mannheim, *Estado y planificación demócratica*, México, D.F.: Fondo de Cultura Economica, 1945, stresses the role of the intelligentsia in moments of crisis. The contemporary influence of this book in Latin America is noted by Furtado, *A fantasia organizada*.

4. Karin Kock, *International Trade Policy and the GATT, 1947–1967*. Stockholm: Almquist and Wiksell, 1969.

5. League of Nations, *Economic Stability in the Postwar Period*. Geneva: League of Nations, 1945.

6. Colin Clark, *The Conditions of Economic Progress*. London: Macmillan, 1940.

7. J. Fred Rippy, *Latin America and the Industrial Age*. New York: Putnam, 1947.

8. Eugene Staley, *World Economy in Transition*. New York: Council on Foreign Relations, 1939; idem, *World Economic Development*. Montreal: International Labour Office, 1944.

9. Staley, *World Economy*, 70.

10. Francis Paul Walters, *A History of the League of Nations*. Oxford: Oxford University Press, 1952.

11. Xavier Alcalde, *The Idea of Third World Development*. Lanham, Md.: University Press of America, 1987, 120.

12. See Abba Lerner, "Economic Liberalization in the Postwar World," in *Postwar Economic Problems*, edited by Seymour Edwin Harris. New York: McGraw Hill, 1943, 71–103.

13. E. V. K. FitzGerald, "A Note on Income Distribution, Accumulation, and Recovery in the Depression," in *Latin America in the 1930s: The Role of the Periphery in World Crisis*, edited by Rosemary Thorp. London: Macmillan, 1984, 242–78. On the impact of inflation see Rosemary Thorp, "The Latin American Economies in the 1940s," this volume.

14. United Nations, Economic Commission for Latin America and the Caribbean, "Series históricas del crecimiento de América Latina." *Cuadernos estadísticos de la CEPAL*, no. 3. Santiago: CEPAL, 1978.

15. Richard Lynn Ground, "The Genesis of Import Substitution in Latin America," *CEPAL Review* 36 (1988), 179–203.

16. United Nations, Economic Commission for Latin America, *Economic Survey of Latin America, 1948*. New York: United Nations, 1949; idem, *Economic Survey of Latin America, 1949*. New York: United Nations, 1951.

17. Carlos F. Díaz-Alejandro, "The 1940s in Latin America," in *Economic Structure and Performance*, edited by M. Syrquin, L. Taylor, and L. E. Westphal. New York: Harcourt, Brace, 1984, 341–62.

18. Daniel Cosío-Villegas, *American Extremes*. Austin: University of Texas Press, 1964.

19. Simon Gabriel Hanson, *Economic Development of Latin America*. Washington, D.C.: Interamerican Affairs Press, 1951; William Adams Brown and Redvers Opie, *American Foreign Assistance*. Washington, D.C.: Brookings Institution, 1954.

20. Cosío-Villegas, *American Extremes*.

21. United Nations, Economic Commission for Latin America, *Report on the First Session of the ECLA, 7–25 June 1948*. New York: United Nations, 1953.

22. Alcalde, *Third World Development*, 179.

23. Phyllis Deane, *The State and the Economic System: An Introduction to the History of Political Economy*. Oxford: Oxford University Press, 1989.

24. Octavio Rodríguez, "On the Conception of the Center-Periphery System," *CEPAL Review* 3, (1977), 195–239.

25. Kurt Mandelbaum, *The Industrialization of Backward Areas*. Oxford: Blackwell, 1945; Friedrich List, *The National System of Political Economy*. London: Longman, 1909 (first published in Geneva, 1844).

26. Werner Sombart, *Der Moderne Capitalismus*. Munich and Leipzig: Dünscker und Humblut, 1928.

27. Martin Jay, *The Dialectical Imagination: A History of the Frankfurt School and the Institute of Social Research, 1923–1950*. London: Heinemann, 1973.

28. Mihail Manoïlescu, *The Theory of Protection and International Trade*. London: King, 1931.

29. Love, *Dependency Analysis*.

30. My translation from the Spanish edition of Werner Sombart, *El apogeo del capitalismo*. México, D.F.: Fondo de Cultura Económica, 1946, 3: 10.

31. Ernest Friedrich Wagemann, *Evolución y ritmo de la economía mundial*. Barcelona: Editorial Labor, 1933. On the influence of Wagemann in Latin America see Hodara, *Prebisch y la CEPAL*, and on that of Manoïlescu see Joseph L. Love, "Manoïlescu, Prebisch, and the Thesis of Unequal Exchange," *Rumanian Studies* 5 (1980–1986), 125–33.

32. Aldo Antonio Dadone and Luis Eugenio di Marco, "The Impact of Prebisch's Ideas on Modern Economic Analysis," in *International Economics and Development: Essays in Honor of Raúl Prebisch*, edited by Luis Eugenio di Marco. New York: Academic Press, 1972, 15–34.

33. Adolfo Dorfman, *Desarrollo industrial en la Argentina*. Buenos Aires: Escuela de Estudios Argentinos, 1942 (republished in 1970 as *Historia de la industria argentina*. Buenos Aires: Solar Hachette); Alejandro E. Bunge, *Una nueva Argentina*. Buenos Aires: Kraft, 1940. For discussion of this particular debate see Juan Carlos Korol and Hilda Sabato, "Incomplete Industrialization: An Argentine Obsession," *Latin American Research Review* 25, no. 1 (1990), 7–30; and for the context of Argentine economic nationalism see David Rock, *Authoritarian Argentina: The Nationalist Movement, Its History, and Its Impact*. Berkeley and Los Angeles: University of California Press, 1993.

34. Carlos H. Waisman, *The Reversal of Development in Argentina*. Princeton: Princeton University Press, 1987.

35. Roger Blackhouse, *A History of Modern Economic Analysis*. Oxford: Blackwell, 1985. The contemporary liberal critique of international economic management is well represented by Albert O. Hirschman, *Power and International Trade*. Berkeley and Los Angeles: University of California Press, 1945, and W. Arthur Lewis, *Economic Survey, 1919–1939*. London: George Allen and Unwin, 1949. For contemporary views on late industrialization see Paul N. Rosenstein-Rodan, "Industrialization of Eastern and Southeastern Europe," *Economic Journal* 53, no. 3 (1943), 202–11.

36. Pazos, *Pensamiento económico*; Victor L. Urquidi, "La postguerra y las relaciones economicas internacionales de Mexico," *El Trimestre Económico* 11, no. 2, (1944), 20–345; Victor L. Urquidi and Ernesto Fernández-Hurtado, "Diversos tipos de disequilibrio económico internacional," *El Trimestre Económico* 13, no. 1 (1946), 1–33.

37. Roy F. Harrod, *The Life of John Maynard Keynes*. London: Macmillan, 1951; Raúl Prebisch, *Introducción a Keynes*. México, D.F.: Fondo de Cultura Económica, 1947. See also Aldo Ferrer, "The Early Teaching of Raúl Prebisch," *CEPAL Review* 42 (1990), 27–34, who states that Prebisch was one of the first economists to recognize the Keynesian revolution and make it known in Latin America.

38. Furtado, *A fantasia organizada*.

39. Alcalde, *Third World Development*; David H. Pollock, "Some Changes in United States Attitudes toward CEPAL over the Past Thirty Years," *CEPAL Review* 6 (1978), 57–80.

40. Hodara, *Prebisch y la CEPAL*.

41. United Nations, Economic Commission for Latin America, *Economic Survey of Latin America, 1948*. New York: United Nations, 1949.

42. United Nations, Economic Commission for Latin America. *Economic Survey of Latin America, 1949*. New York: United Nations, 1951; Raúl Prebisch, *The Economic Development of Latin America and Its Principal Problems*. New York: United Nations, 1949.

43. Pollock, "United States Attitudes"; Hodara, *Prebisch y la CEPAL*.

44. Economic Commission for Latin America, *Survey 1949*, xix. For a remarkably similar model derived from the statistical analysis in League of Nations, *Economic Stability*, see Hans Singer, "The Distribution of Gains between Investing and Borrowing Countries," *American Economic Review* 40, no. 2 (1950), 473–85.

45. Economic Commission for Latin America, *Survey 1948*, 15.

46. Furtado, *A fantasia organizada*, lists the authors of these appendixes, including himself on Brazil and Víctor Urquidi on Mexico.

47. The data have since been revised in United Nations, Economic Commission for Latin America, *The Economic Development of Latin America in the Postwar Period*, New York: United Nations, 1964, but the figures presented here reflect contemporary perceptions and thus are more relevant to the argument of this chapter.

48. Rodríguez, *Teoría del subdesarrollo*; Raúl Prebisch, *Algunos problemas teóricos y*

prácticos del crecimiento económico. Santiago: Comisión Económica para América Latina, 1951.

49. Furtado, *A fantasia organizada*, 76–80.

50. Economic Commission for Latin America, *First Session of the ECLA*.

51. Rodríguez, *Teoría del subdesarrollo*.

52. For an algebraic formulation see Floto, "The Center-Periphery System." The essence of this approach had been earlier stated by Urquidi; see note 36.

53. "The peripheral countries have no means of absorbing the surplus of their gainfully employed population except by developing their own industrial activity." Economic Commission for Latin America, *Survey 1949*, 49.

54. Werner Baer, "The Economics of Prebisch and the ECLA." *Economic Development and Cultural Change* 10, no. 2 (1962), 169–82. See also M. June Flanders, "Prebisch on Protectionism: An Evaluation," *Economic Journal* 74, no. 294 (1964), 305–26.

55. Fernando Henrique Cardoso, "The Originality of the Copy: CEPAL and the Idea of Development," *CEPAL Review* 4 (1977), 7–40; Jacob Viner, *International Trade and Economic Development*. Glencoe, Ill.: Free Press, 1952; Gottfried Harberler, "Los términos de intercambio y el desarrollo económico," in *El desarrollo económico y América Latina*, edited by Howard Ellis. México, D.F.: Fondo de Cultura Económica, 1960, 325–62.

56. Furtado, *A fantasia organizada*, 61–62.

57. Rodríguez, *Teoría del subdesarrollo*.

58. Cf. Viner, *International Trade*, and Harberler, *Términos de intercambio*, respectively; according to Furtado (*A fantasia organizada*, 140), Viner had debated this theme with Manoïlescu too.

59. Cf. United Nations, Economic Commission for Latin America, *Economic Survey, 1951–1952*. New York: United Nations, 1953.

60. As for instance Kay does in his otherwise excellent survey of modern social theories in Latin America. Cf. Kay, *Latin American Theories*.

61. Albert O. Hirschman, "Ideologies of Economic Development in Latin America," in *Latin American Issues: Essays and Comments*, edited by Albert O. Hirschman, 3–42. New York: Twentieth Century Fund, 1961, 3–42.

62. Prebisch, "Five Stages"; Dadone and di Marco, "The Impact of Prebisch's Ideas"; Guzmán, *El desarrollo*.

63. Sunkel, "The Development of Development Theory."

64. Cardoso, "The Originality of the Copy"; Aníbal Pinto and J. Kñákal, "The Center-Periphery System Twenty Years Later," in di Marco *International Economics*, 97–128.

65. Rodríguez, *La teoría del subdesarrollo*.

66. Furtado, *A fantasia organizada*, 62.

67. Pollock, "United States Attitudes"; Kay, *Latin American Theories*.

68. Prebisch "Five Stages," 176.

69. Prebisch, "Five Stages."

70. Alexander Gerschenkron, "History of Economic Doctrines and Economic History," *American Economic Review* 59, no. 2 (1969), 1–17.

71. Singer, "Distribution of Gains"; Baer, "The Economics of Prebisch."

72. Furtado (*A fantasia organizada*, ch. 4) claims to have "conceived" this idea himself in 1949. This may be so, but the concept is not a new one: for example, see the elaboration of Marx's formulation in Mandelbaum, *Industrialization*, written five years earlier. "The Law of Comparative Costs is just as valid in countries with surplus labor as it is in others. But whereas in the latter it is a valid foundation of arguments for free trade, in the former it is an equally valid foundation for arguments for protection." W. Arthur Lewis, "Economic Development with Unlimited Supplies of Labour," *Manchester School of Economic and Social Studies* 22, no. 1 (1956), 139–91.

73. Osvaldo Sunkel, "La inflación chilena: Un enfoque heterodoxo," *El trimestre económico* 25 (1958), 570–99; Aníbal Pinto, *Chile: Un caso de desarrollo frustrado*. Santiago: Editorial Universitaria, 1958.

74. Carlos Bazdresch, *El pensamiento de Juan Noyola*. México, D.F.: Fondo de Cultura Económica, 1984; E. V. K. FitzGerald, "Kalecki on the Financing of Development," *Cambridge Journal of Economics* 14, no. 2 (1990), 183–203; Arndt, "The Origins of Structuralism"; Guzmán, *El desarrollo*.

75. Samir Amin, *Accumulation on a World Scale*. New York: Monthly Review Press, 1974; Arghiri Emmanuel, *Unequal Exchange*. London: New Left Books, 1972.

76. Anthony P. Thirlwall, "A General Model of Growth and Development on Kaldorian Lines," *Oxford Economic Papers* 38, no. 2 (1986), 199–219.

77. Oscar Braun, *Comercio internacional e imperialismo*. Buenos Aires: Siglo XXI, 1973.

78. Ground, "The Genesis of Import Substitution."

79. José Antonio Ocampo, "New Economic Thinking in Latin America," *Journal of Latin American Studies* 22, no. 1 (1990), 169–81.

5 International Crises and Popular Movements in Latin America

Chile and Peru from the Great Depression to the Cold War

Paul W. Drake

In export economies highly susceptible to foreign influences, international crises have presented unusual opportunities for and obstacles to political change. The myriad ways in which Latin America's reform movements have interpreted, responded to, and been molded by external shocks have, along with domestic factors, determined the fate of those movements. Common outside forces have engendered similar political phenomena in many of the republics. At the same time, distinctive local reactions and conditions have produced divergent political outcomes.

In this chapter I sacrifice the intricacies of national histories and variables in the interest of highlighting the impact of international changes on the evolution of popular movements in Chile and Peru. The term "popular movements" mainly refers to the major reform parties representing organized labor: in Chile the Socialist and Communist parties, and in Peru the Communist party and the American Popular Revolutionary Alliance. My analysis emphasizes how similar external influences were refracted through different internal political prisms.

Global events exerted exceptional influence during three great, interconnected transformations in the twentieth century: the Great Depression, World War II, and the Cold War. Throughout the period 1930–1945 Latin America had to adjust to the massive disruption of the global economic and geopolitical order; after 1945 it had to respond to and accommodate the consolidation of U.S. hegemony in the name of capitalism and anticommunism. In the late 1940s reinvigorated capitalist growth within the orbit of the United States called for containment of demands from labor and the left.

In many parts of Latin America the Great Depression ignited a crisis of the oligarchic order, which had been under stress since World War I. The collapse of the international economy called into question the nineteenth-century model of elite rule based on laissez-faire and free trade. The depression capsized international flows of trade and finance and in some countries activated the masses as a political contender while energizing the reform parties. These reform parties demanded simultaneous state action on industrialization and social reform, especially in the mushrooming cities.

The way countries dealt with the crisis, and with the resulting populist challenge, shaped political developments for decades to come. By the time World War II was over and the Cold War had set in, a new international order had been established under the auspices of the United States. Latin America accommodated itself to the international regime by resolving the political conflicts spawned by the Great Depression. The key issue for Latin American politicians was how to adapt to the changing world system and simultaneously cope with labor and the left. [1]

Analytical Framework

This prolonged process of adaptation can be illuminated by comparing Chile and Peru, which offer both striking commonalities and striking contrasts. In some political aspects both cases approximated the norm in Latin America as a whole. Although certain regional political patterns were discernible in Latin America in the 1940s, the decade overall did not display a lasting secular pattern toward either democracy or dictatorship. After authoritarianism swept the hemisphere in the 1930s, a mixed picture emerged in the early 1940s. Then, from 1944 to 1950, ten governments switched from being nonelected to being elected, but seven others reverted from democracy to dictatorship. [2] From this perspective the 1940s brought no clear trend toward democracy.

Yet from another angle this period marked some important changes and political reorientations. In the 1930s populist reform movements convulsed both Chile and Peru, though rightist governments prevailed. In the mid-1940s, as World War II drew to a close, both Chile and Peru—like most of the hemisphere—experienced an opening to democracy and the left. With the onset of the Cold War in the latter years of the decade, however, the mid-decade opening to mass politics swiftly closed; both nations joined most of Latin America in turning to the right and aligning with the United States. By the early 1950s both governments were ruled by strongman presidents aloof from party politics. Throughout these years the two countries were caught between the United States and domestic popular movements; the external and internal forces that appeared reconcilable at the end of World War II soon after proved to be incompatible.

Despite the common tendencies noted above, Chile and Peru followed opposite paths of political economy from the Great Depression through World War II. The two countries present contrasting developmental responses to the crises of growth, distribution, participation, and legitimation during the 1930s and World War II (see table 16).

Why were their responses to similar international crises and popular movements so different? If we follow the analytical approach employed by Cardoso and Faletto, the answer lies mainly in the different ways the two countries were connected to the international economy and in their contrasting domestic social structures and political systems. These differences—as mediated through intervening political variables and national peculiarities—helped produce divergent governing coalitions and policies.[3]

Partly because Chile relied overwhelmingly on sales abroad of nitrates and copper controlled by U.S. corporations, its upper class was weaker than its counterpart in Peru, less dedicated to export-led development, and more amenable to populist promotion of industrialization and mild welfare measures for urban groups. The Chilean elites were more willing to allow the

Table 16 Chile and Peru: Crises and Responses, 1930–1945

Crises	*Responses*	
	Chile	*Peru*
1. Growth	Import-substituting industrialization and diversification	Export promotion
2. Distribution	Inclusion of middle and working classes	Upper-class accumulation
3. Participation	Inclusion of urban groups	Exclusion of populists, urban groups
4. Legitimation	Elections/populist state	Coercion/oligarchic state

state to interfere in the foreign sector to protect domestic capitalists. Moreover, Chile was already more industrialized and urbanized than Peru, and therefore possessed a stronger basis and constituency for the promotion of manufacturing and welfare in the cities through forms of state capitalism. The larger middle class and labor sectors had a much greater role in Chile than in Peru, where the agro-exporting elites and the military remained more powerful.

The Peruvian oligarchy kept popular movements at bay from the depths of the depression until the close of World War II. The Peruvian export sector suffered less from the depression than its counterpart in Chile and recovered more quickly. In contrast with Chile the leading export products in Peru from 1930 to 1950 were mainly in local hands; whereas foreign companies accounted for over 60 percent of Peru's exports at the end of the 1920s, they produced less than 30 percent by the close of the 1940s.[4] Control over most export production helped the Peruvian oligarchy to continue to rule directly through its own representatives or the armed forces. In sum, the relative success of the more diversified export economy in Peru protected the political standing of the domestic owners of many of those means of production.

While the ruling class in Peru relied on the military to protect its interests, upper-class groups in Chile discovered that the armed forces were unreliable. The Chilean military was closer to the middle than the upper class, divided ideologically, and discredited politically. Having ruled the country from 1927 to 1931, the armed forces took the blame for the depression and the chaotic conditions it provoked. From 1931 the Chilean military returned to its traditional role outside the civilian political arena. In contrast to the violent confrontations between the military and the American Popular Revolutionary Alliance in Peru, a leader of the Chilean armed forces gave birth to the Socialist party, and despite the military's ingrained anticommunism, it did not oppose the Popular Front. By the same token, fueled by higher levels of urbanization and industrialization, the left and organized labor were stronger in Chile than in Peru. A stronger tradition of democratic party politics also facilitated the expansion and inclusion of new popular forces. As a result the reform movement was able to climb to power in Chile but remained blocked in its northern neighbor.

After success in the 1930s reformers in much of the hemisphere encountered frustration and failure in the 1940s under the constraints of World War II and the ensuing Cold War. The political shifts from left to right in the latter half of the 1940s occurred within the international and national frameworks erected from 1930 to 1945. By the start of the 1950s the popular challenge had been contained almost throughout Latin America through co-optation and repression.

Even when both Chile and Peru curved left in the mid-forties and then right at the end of the decade, the cumulative differences between them established earlier remained. Within Chile's more open, progressive system the leftward turn after World War II gave a greater role to the Communists than in Peru. Similarly, although the rightward turn in Chile during the Cold War excluded the Communists, it did not include a crackdown on the populist Socialists. Chile's veer to the right, unlike Peru's, did not entail a restoration of oligarchic authority and laissez-faire economics. Instead, Chile retained a significant role for the middle class, the state, and import-substituting industrialization. The defeat of the left in Chile in the late 1940s was only partial, and by the 1950s and 1960s the leftists were reasserting themselves.

In Peru during the late 1940s, in contrast, the agro-exporting, free trade elites reestablished their hegemony. They had emerged victorious during the depression and, after a brief opening to popular forces in 1945–1948, continued to prevail thereafter. In comparison with Chile, Peruvian industrialists, middle sectors, organized laborers, mass parties, and democratic institutions were still too frail to dislodge the traditional ruling class. From the late 1940s onward the more effectively repressed popular movement in Peru capitulated to the established order.

The dominant sociopolitical coalitions in the two countries is summarized in table 17.[5]

Chronological Framework

In the wake of the depression both countries witnessed an upsurge of mass movements, headed by the Socialists and Communists in Chile and the Apristas, followers of the American Popular Revolutionary Alliance (APRA), in Peru. The Chilean Socialists and the Peruvian Apristas, despite important differences, saw each other as kindred spirits and aligned themselves with similar populist brethren throughout the hemisphere. Although more Marxist in orientation, the Chilean Socialist party resembled APRA in its populist emphasis on nationalism, statism, industrialization, and the unification of the middle and working classes against the oligarchy and the imperialists.

Table 17 Chile and Peru: Dominant Social-Political Coalitions

Chile	*Peru*
1932–1938	*1933–1945*
Agriculturalists	Agro-exporters
Industrialists	Military
Middle class	
1938–1948	*1945–1948*
Industrialists	Industrialists
Middle class	Middle class
Labor	Labor
1948–1950s	*1948–1950s*
Foreign capitalists	Foreign capitalists
Industrialists	Agro-exporters
Middle class	Military

Both parties blamed the depression on the United States and the local ruling class, vowed to eliminate international as well as local inequalities, and rejected ties with political organizations outside Latin America. Equally, both parties were committed to a "third path" to national development that was neither capitalist nor communist. Indeed, much of their political history was bound up with their tensions with the United States externally and the Communists internally.[6]

From 1932 to 1945, however, the trajectories of these popular movements sharply diverged, as they encountered inclusion in Chile and exclusion in Peru. At the start of the 1930s the Socialists as well as the Apristas missed chances to seize power and subsequently concentrated on the electoral route to political supremacy. Both countries possessed rightist governments in the mid-thirties that were succeeded by more centrist (and in Chile slightly left-of-center) administrations at the end of the decade. Both these centrist governments at the end of the 1930s ruled under the slogan To Govern Is to Educate. Presidents Pedro Aguirre Cerda and Juan Antonio Ríos Morales (1938–1945) in Chile and Manuel Prado y Ugarteche (1939–1945) in Peru presided over a cooling of ideological and class conflicts from the 1930s. Both the right and the left moderated their antagonisms toward each other and toward the United States and the Soviet Union during World War II.

In the early 1940s these civilian governments tried to consolidate liberal democracies, although to a much more restricted extent in Peru. The military seldom threatened to overthrow these moderate presidents. Under the constraints of wartime the administrations of both countries increasingly preferred to place growth before redistribution. Both nations suffered from inflation, agricultural stagnation, and shortages, especially of imports and capital goods. Their exports, however, did relatively well, and foreign exchange accumulated. Even though to a much lesser extent than in Chile, the Peruvian government expanded, as it sought to reward urban industrialists and the middle class. In both countries demands from workers and peasants were stifled, and most gains accrued to the middle or upper classes.

Despite their broad similarities the Aguirre Cerda–Ríos and Prado administrations were built on very different political coalitions. While the Chilean rulers welcomed support and participation from Socialists and Communists, the Peruvians outlawed the Apristas. Chile handled rising demands from middle- and working-class sectors in the cities through popular front politics: incorporating labor and the left into the electoral system and the populist state. It was easier to integrate the left while the United States was crusading against fascism. Without destroying the oligarchy, the Chilean governments before 1948 promoted state expansion, industrialization, and welfare benefits for the most highly organized employees and workers.[7]

In Peru the traditional elites continued to rule directly in collusion with the armed forces and kept the growth of the state, import-substituting industrialization, and social reforms at lower levels than in Chile. Despite international shocks they retained more elements of laissez-faire. In Peru during this period populism was postponed.[8]

At the end of World War II, as politicians temporarily revived the reformist rhetoric and expectations of the 1930s, both countries provided a release for pent-up demands by swerving to the left. For two years Presidents Gabriel González Videla (1946–1952) in Chile and José Luís Bustamante y Rivero (1945–1948) in Peru led prolabor coalition governments that included the parties most despised by the armed forces: the Communists in Chile and the Apristas in Peru. Both countries, however, quickly switched to the right and banned those parties.

The right-wing reactions of the late 1940s responded mainly to mounting economic difficulties and labor unrest, but at the same time to pressures from the United States at the inception of the Cold War. The involvement of the United States in Chile was much more intense than in Peru because of larger investment and the greater strength of the Chilean Communists. Nevertheless, the basic pattern in both countries was similar to that continentwide: as the reserves accumulated during the war ran out and inflation intensified, governments cracked down on workers and their political allies. The broader objectives of these actions were to favor capital accumulation, encourage foreign investment, and promote stable growth in alignment with the United States. In this way the Chilean and Peruvian governments moved more closely to the United States and in return received investments, loans, and military assistance. Even some Chilean Socialists and Peruvian Apristas aligned with the United States in the Cold War and with the Inter-American Confederation of Workers (Confederación Interamericana de Trabajadores [CIT]), a body of the American Federation of Labor and the Congress of Industrial Organizations (AFL-CIO). The pattern was particularly marked in Peru. Having been less willing to adopt state expansion and industrialization during the depression, Peru now adopted an unusually strong commitment to economic liberalism.

By the end of the decade and the beginning of the 1950s labor and the left were demobilized in both countries. Independent unions were crippled and in disarray, their federations divided by repression and by the competition between Moscow and Washington for their allegiance. Peasants remained on the margins of political life. Finally, at the close of the period under study both countries turned to militaristic, personalistic leaders: Presidents Carlos Ibáñez del Campo (1952–1958) in Chile and Manuel A. Odría (1948–1956) in Peru. These conservative caudillos were influenced in some degree by the populist style of Peronist Argentina but avoided its laborite policy orientation.

At the termination of this era both Chilean and Peruvian reformers expressed severe disappointment with their meager achievements. Although Chilean popular movements had participated in government and accomplished far more than their Peruvian counterparts, at the end of the 1940s both were seeking new ways to fulfill unkept promises to their followers. Center-left coalitions had failed to produce nationalistic development or significant benefits for the masses, even in the burgeoning cities. Many of APRA's former comrades in the Chilean left decided that more radical, ideological, independent politics were necessary to advance their agenda. In contrast, APRA concluded that it would have to moderate further, intensify its anticommunism, and collaborate with more rightist groups to win acceptance from the oligarchy and the military. In subsequent years the Chilean left attempted to move beyond Popular Front politics, while APRA aimed for electoral and office-holding successes similar to those the Chileans had gained earlier.

In this essay I compare these two experiences by stressing the impact of international influences on the thought, behavior, and trajectory of these popular movements. I shall attempt to underscore the elements of cross-fertilization among Chilean, Peruvian, and other Latin American reformers. The emphasis on interaction between external and internal forces, however, is not meant to deny the often primary importance of domestic factors in national political development. Instead I use the international framework to spotlight and to reexamine certain neglected commonalities and contrasts among these labor parties during this period.

The Depression

CHILE, 1930s

As in Peru the government that restored order in Chile soon after the onset of the depression represented the right: the economic magnates and the Conservative and Liberal parties.[9] In contrast with Peru, however, the Chilean right managed to resist the most reactionary and intransigent right-wing elements and gradually responded to the new threat from popular forces by means of inclusive, flexible strategies. By acquiescing in democratization and state activism, the elites opened the door to the eventual victory and incorporation of the left and urban labor. Since the upper class saw the military as unreliable, it opted for piecemeal concessions to preserve its privileged position. The bargain that evolved in the 1930s and 1940s consisted of ceding political office holding to middle-class representatives of the masses and encouraging industrialization, while preserving conservative sanctuaries in the countryside by barring the peasantry from mobilization and benefits.[10]

Among the Chilean reformers the Socialists were inspired by numerous foreign influences, including the Spanish and French Popular Fronts and the New Deal in the United States. However, the strongest alien influence was that of APRA. The Chilean Socialists met frequently with Aprista leaders such as Luis Alberto Sánchez. Learning from APRA's catastrophic confrontations with the Peruvian army, the Chilean Socialists tried to cultivate good relations with the military. The Chilean Socialists and APRA also felt kinship with Acción Democrática of Venezuela, the Socialists of Argentina, progressive factions of the Colombian Liberals, the revolutionary party of Mexico, and, later, some of the reformist currents of Argentine Peronism.[11]

Meanwhile, the Chilean Communists responded to international signals to establish a popular front in alliance with the Socialists and the centrist Radical party. Agents of the Communist International from the Soviet Union, Germany, Argentina, and Peru visited Chile to persuade the Communist party to adopt the Popular Front strategy. Subsequently, the Chilean Communist party moderated its ideology, broadened its social composition beyond the proletariat, and devoted itself to elections rather than rebellions. Like the Apristas the Communists argued that a socialist revolution had to await the completion of a bourgeois industrial revolution in semifeudal Latin America.

The Chilean Popular Front closely resembled APRA and other populist movements in the hemisphere. It boasted similar multiclass components and a programmatic emphasis on democracy, nationalism, and state intervention to promote industry and welfare. Apristas exiled in Chile backed the Front. Thus foreign influences helped Chilean popular forces both to moderate their objectives and to ascend to power.[12]

PERU, 1930S

In Peru the depression resulted in violent clashes between the Apristas and the armed forces that led first to dictatorship under Oscar Benavides, and then at the end of the decade to the stabilizing government of Manuel Prado. Although he professed himself an anti-imperialist, Aprista chief Víctor Raúl Haya de la Torre feared an American armed intervention in Peru like those in Nicaragua and elsewhere, and therefore he always approached the United States cautiously. As the 1930s wore on, Haya became increasingly friendly toward the United States. He responded favorably to the Good Neighbor policy, declared his support for the United States in the battle against fascism, and vainly hoped for U.S. support against his domestic adversaries. Earlier Marxist influences on APRA waned in the 1930s, as it established links with analogous nationalist and populist parties in Latin America. In its struggle against the armed forces, for example, APRA secretly requested financial assistance from socialists in Bolivia and from the Revolutionary party of Mexico.[13]

The military regime of Gen. Oscar Benavides (1933–1939) defended the interests of the oligarchy against APRA's populist challenge. Benavides outlawed both the Apristas and the Communists on the grounds that they were foreign parties alien to Peruvian interests, and he heavily repressed unions affiliated with those parties. In 1935 the tiny Peruvian Communist party adopted the Popular Front line and proposed a joint People's Front to APRA. The Apristas spurned these overtures, hoping that an anti-Communist position would win them greater acceptability. Although Haya de la Torre applauded the Popular Front in Chile, he opposed such coalitions in Peru because, as he claimed, APRA already represented a broad front in itself. In the semicompetitive 1939 presidential election, the Communist party threw its votes to Prado on the grounds of creating an alliance against fascism. Banned from running themselves, many Apristas too voted for the conservative, plutocratic Prado in the hope that he would legalize their party.[14]

World War II

The aims of the increasingly hegemonic United States in Latin America during World War II were to gain allies against invasion or subversion, to reduce the economic links between the Latin American nations and the Axis, and to obtain safe and reliable access to vital Latin American raw materials. Throughout the hemisphere the United States encouraged increased production of strategic commodities at controlled prices, improvements in communication and transportation, and smoother mechanisms for exchange transactions. To help the Latin American nations to surmount wartime disruptions, and to increase its own economic sway in the region, the U.S. government guaranteed the purchase of strategic and surplus exports, supplied minimal import necessities, and sent technical and military assistance, including lend-lease military equipment. To some extent the United States also became willing to grant public loans for the industrial development desired by many Latin Americans.

Washington believed that economic development would make the Latin American nations more politically stable and thus more reliable allies. Under the Good Neighbor policy the United States maintained neutrality toward authoritarian or democratic regimes so long as they were friendly toward its security and economic interests. Latin American progressives were favorably impressed both by the Good Neighbor policy and by the state planning involved in the New Deal and the war effort.[15]

CHILE, 1938–1945

In Chile the governments of Radical party leaders Aguirre Cerda and Ríos incorporated the Marxist left into a state capitalist program for import-substituting industrialization. Following the death of Aguirre Cerda in 1941, Ríos promoted national unity, social stability, and rising productivity under the conservative slogan To Govern Is to Produce. Although he had the backing of the Marxists, Ríos did not establish a formal pact with the leftist parties. However, they pressured him to join the Allies, which he finally did in January 1943 on the grounds of Chile's overwhelming economic interest in siding with the United States.[16]

The main agent in the efforts of the two Radical presidents to raise productivity, particularly in industry, was the new Development Corporation (Corporación del Fomento [CORFO]), which relied heavily on small credits from the U.S. Export-Import Bank. These loans were made available in part to attract Chile to the Allied side, but they were also devices to assist American exports, since under normal circumstances they could be spent only on goods and services from the United States. During World War II the Chilean government furnished more financial assistance for industrial development than any other in Latin America.[17]

The creation of CORFO pulled the Chilean left into a more conservative position. To win the approval of conservatives for the legislation that set up CORFO, the Communists and Socialists curbed labor mobilization, especially in the countryside. Government officials representing the Socialist party negotiated with the United States for loans for CORFO and for a stable and programmed schedule of purchases of Chilean exports, particularly copper.[18]

Events abroad both inspired and disrupted the Popular Front government. The Spanish Civil War, for example, convinced many members of the Front to exercise caution in order to avoid a similar conflagration in Chile. The Hitler-Stalin pact of August 1939 lessened the Communist party's willingness to cooperate with domestic rivals in the cause of antifascism. At this point the Communist party briefly revived the radical rhetoric of the early thirties, as it denounced middle-class reformers, especially Socialists, as deceivers of the proletariat. In October 1939, to the chagrin of the Socialists and the government, both of which desired loans from the United States, the Communists began assailing the United States when Chile repealed its neutrality laws in order to furnish arms to the Allies. Nevertheless, Aguirre Cerda vetoed attempts to outlaw the Communists.[19]

Castigating the Communists as antinational, antidemocratic, and insufficiently antifascist, in early 1941 the Socialists quit the Popular Front but remained in the government. Subsequently, the Socialists assumed a pro-American position, arguing that "democratic imperialism" was preferable to "totalitarian imperialism." Inspired by Franklin D. Roosevelt, Henry Wallace, and Haya de la Torre, many Socialist leaders proclaimed that World War II would result in greater peace and social equality among nations and classes. In the view of the Socialists industrial production had to be increased and the war concluded before class conflict and major reforms for the workers could be carried out. Referring to Haya de la Torre's pro-American position toward the war in 1941, Marmaduque Grove, the leader of the Socialist party, declared, "We follow the same line and are oriented toward the same propositions related to Latin American policy and the concept of our relations with the United States and the interpretation we give to the Good Neighbor."[20] Similarly, on the death of Roosevelt in 1945 Chilean Socialist Salvador Allende Gossens proclaimed: "the highest human value of the twentieth century has disappeared, the most solid guarantee for the small countries, especially for South America."[21]

Despite their professed adherence to revolutionary Marxism the Socialists upheld links with other populist, nationalist movements in the hemisphere. In 1940 they hosted the First Latin American Congress of Leftist Parties. They excluded Communists from this gathering, but included the Socialists of Argentina and Ecuador, the APRA of Peru, the Democratic Action of Venezuela, and the Revolutionary party of Mexico. Dominated by Aprista doctrines, all the parties endorsed solidarity with the United States against fascism, even though expressing their common longing for greater economic independence for their nations.[22]

When the Soviet Union joined the Allied cause in mid-1941, the Communists became more conservative. In Chile as well as Peru the Soviets promoted the international policy of National Unity, a program that pledged the Latin American Communist parties to almost any alliance and any sacrifice to further the war effort. Consequently, the Communist party backed the Ríos government almost unquestioningly. Between 1941 and 1944 the Chilean Communists accepted the view of Earl Browder, leader of the Communist party of the United States, that class collaboration would be the vehicle for progress both during and after the war. During the war the Chilean Communist party won prestige by virtue of its link with the Soviet Union, whose desperate and heroic struggle against Nazi Germany aroused widespread admiration in Latin America. This close identification backfired after the war, however, when old animosities toward the Soviet Union reemerged, intensified by rising nationalism and the Cold War.[23]

PERU, 1939–1945

In Peru, Manuel Prado found that he needed to use only relatively mild repression to hold the lid on an increasingly moderate APRA. World War II engendered a period of unity and tranquillity in Peruvian politics, buttressed by an export boom. Broad national support for the democratic side in the war strengthened democratic practices domestically while discouraging armed civilian or military uprisings against the government. Prado's pro–United States administration enjoyed widespread, nonpartisan support from civilian and military sectors alike following the brief war with Ecuador in 1941. At this point even APRA rallied around the flag. After decreeing neutrality in September 1939, Peru severed relations with the Axis in January 1942, although it waited until 1945 to declare war.[24]

The Prado administration outlawed and persecuted APRA, sometimes brandishing the quite unjustified accusation that the party was pro-Nazi. In fact, APRA supported the Allies, but it continually questioned U.S. aid to the Prado government in the form of Export-Import Bank loans and guaranteed purchases of the cotton crop. How, Haya de la Torre asked repeatedly, in the war for democracy could the United States embrace an undemocratic ally? Haya vainly lobbied the U.S. government to pressure the Prado administration to grant his party full rights as part of the Allies' international crusade against "totalitarianism." Although still opposed to the Prado government, APRA nevertheless restrained its criticisms of the administration in the interests of a broad consensus against fascism. Increasingly frustrated by his failures at home, Haya began to regard Chile's sturdy democratic system with envy.[25]

World War II caused the Apristas to tone down their anti-imperialism and to behave more favorably toward the United States.[26] They praised Roosevelt and Wallace for their commitment to end imperialism and to implement the "Four Freedoms." Their increasingly fervent opposition to fascism led the

Apristas to place growing emphasis on their own dedication to democracy, particularly in opposition to the oppression they faced in their home country. The Apristas continually drew analogies between the struggle led by the Allies against fascism and their own fight against dictatorship.

Although continuing to criticize economic exploitation by the United States, the Apristas softened their previous diatribes against international capitalism. In 1940 Haya de la Torre publicly acknowledged that the "twenty isolated and divided Indoamerican countries only subsist[ed] because the United States guarantee[d] their existence and sovereignty." Welcoming the Good Neighbor policy, he then called for "a democratic interamericanism purged of imperialism." Haya argued that Peru needed more capitalist development, fueled by foreign investment, before it could contemplate a transformation to socialism. Thus APRA echoed the Popular Front doctrine of its Communist adversaries, while remaining opposed to any pact with the Communist party because of that party's totalitarian orientations and principles. The Aprista program for industrialization and democracy aimed to create an alliance of the middle and working classes that would keep the former away from fascism and the latter away from communism. Like the Chilean Socialists the Apristas argued that the war demonstrated more than ever the wisdom of their program for state activism, for industrialization, and for the unification of Latin America as a counterweight to imperialist threats from Europe or the United States.[27]

Attempting to consolidate its base for the future, APRA strengthened its hold on organized labor, which was now expanding in size and militancy along with the growth of war production and the increasing impact of inflation. In 1944 APRA joined the Communists in organizing the Confederation of Peruvian Workers (Confederación de Trabajadores Peruanos [CTP]). When APRA finally regained legal standing at the end of Prado's administration, it urged restraint on organized labor so as not to interfere with the party's prospects for electoral victory in 1945.

Thus APRA and the Communist party replicated the alliance between the United States and the Soviet Union by cooperating briefly to consolidate the union movement. In this endeavor they were aided by the international Confederation of Latin American Workers (Confederación de Trabajadores de América Latina [CTAL]) led by Vicente Lombardo Toledano in Mexico, which at this point enjoyed the backing of both the United States and the Soviet Union. Nevertheless, even though both parties sustained a similar reformist vision for the worker movement, they remained bitter rivals. As the Apristas attacked the Communists, the latter replied with the accusation that APRA was dominated by cryptofascists.[28]

From mid-1941 Prado received solid support from the Communists because he shared the stances they were taking on the war. In return for this support Prado relaxed persecution of the Communists and granted them seats in Congress. Subsequently, the Communists increased their following among unions but curtailed labor agitation while heeding Browder's exhortations to support national production for the war effort. The Communists argued that their cooperation in Peru flowed logically from the wartime alliance between the socialist and capitalist nations. In the 1945 election the newly legalized Communists threw their support to the candidacy of José Luis Bustamante, who also had the backing of APRA.[29]

Victory for Democracy

World War II left the United States and its brand of liberal democracy and capitalism indisputably hegemonic in the hemisphere. To an even greater extent than during the war Latin America and its popular movements were now faced with the task of adjusting to the United States. In the early postwar period the United States faced no competition in Latin America and consequently took its supremacy for granted. The only potential rival, the Soviet Union, at this point possessed no significant economic or military ties in the region. Although the U.S. government later provided some capital through the World Bank and the Export-Import Bank, it expected Latin America to rely mainly on private investment and opposed any large-scale commitment of public funds to heavily statist and protectionist development programs. In short, the United States preferred Latin America to emphasize private enterprise and the free market and to develop as an active participant in an expanding world economy.[30]

Subsequently, the United States and the Latin American economic development plans, which had remained compatible during the war, now increasingly came into conflict. The United States pressured the Latin Americans to begin servicing debts they had defaulted on during the depression, to lower trade barriers, to curb economic nationalism, and to welcome foreign capital. In contrast, most Latin Americans wanted their export commodity prices stabilized or raised, their industries protected, their economies insulated from foreign control, tariff walls in the United States lowered, and financial assistance from the United States amplified.[31]

The defeat of Germany and Japan reversed economic relations between Latin America and the United States. During the war the scarcity of goods from the United States propelled import-substituting industrialization, while heavy demand for Latin American exports multiplied foreign exchange reserves. Following the Allied victory, however, imports from the United States threatened local industries. Meanwhile, demand in the United States for Latin American exports declined, as the former sought alternative suppliers and even reimposed tariffs on some Latin American commodities.

In the second half of the 1940s the terms of trade turned increasingly against Latin America. After a spurt of prosperity immediately after the war, recession came in 1947. As Latin America tried to satisfy delayed demands for consumer and capital goods, its surplus of foreign exchange evaporated quickly. At the same time, inflation escalated rapidly.[32]

Meanwhile, the United States compounded Latin America's difficulties by refusing to provide more than token economic assistance. Even so, the assistance that did arrive in the form of meager Export-Import Bank loans, and the appetite this inflow kindled for more, helped to convert the governments of Chile and Peru into staunch anticommunist allies. Following the reconstruction of Europe during the late 1940s, the United States turned its attention and resources to the Korean War. This conflict improved Latin America's export sales and balance of payments, which again convinced Washington the region did not require an injection of public funds from the United States. Meanwhile, foreign investment—nearly 70 percent of it from the United States—increased in both Chile and Peru.[33]

CHILE, 1945–1947

The death of Ríos was followed in 1946 by the elevation to the presidency of another stalwart of the centrist Radical party, Gabriel González Videla. Although on the campaign trail he sounded like a nationalist firebrand, González Videla realized the importance of cooperating with the United States. Between his election and inauguration he informed the U.S. ambassador: "I know that the future of Chile, its industrial development, its economic well-being, is dependent to a considerable extent on the friendship and collaboration of the United States. Chile needs capital and wants North American capital, and can guarantee fair treatment."[34]

At the time of his election González Videla and the Communists believed that they were still fighting the battles of World War II against fascism and the local oligarchy. Supported most strongly by the left wing of the Radical party and the Communists, the new president revived the social reform commitments of the original Popular Front. For the Communist party, fighting fascism translated into restraining extreme demands and backing centrist reformers against right-wing contenders. During González Videla's initial months as president, the Communist party occupied three cabinet posts for the first time, thereby emulating its counterparts in postwar Italy and France. In 1946 Communist strength among Chilean unions and the electorate ballooned.[35]

Exhilarated by the victory of the Soviet Union in Europe, the Communists declared that socialism was on the march. In their eyes the end of hostilities opened up new vistas for progressive movements. However, during the confusing transition of 1945–1946 from the collaboration of World War II to the confrontation of the Cold War, they vacillated between moderation and militancy. On the one hand they called for "a democratic bourgeois revolution" but on the other began to voice the view that national unity in the name of antifascism, if correct tactically, led to too many concessions to the upper class and too little commitment to proletarian demands. Many Communists now believed that the detour into moderation during the war explained their failure to grow more rapidly at the polls.

Following the line taken by the French Communist party, the Chilean Communists were soon denouncing Browder's disavowal of class struggle. Although a few Chilean Communists continued to endorse Browder's position, the majority wanted it stamped out and now rejected Browder's claim that the victory over fascism meant that the working class and the poorer countries could achieve their material needs peacefully in cooperation with capitalists.[36]

As the Chilean Communist party grew increasingly radical, tensions between Moscow and Washington contributed to clashes that eventually sundered the national labor federation. Taking their cue from the Soviet Union, the Communists grew increasingly determined to increase their control over the labor unions even at the cost of rupturing unity. Within months after the end of the war the Communists had launched an attack on the Socialist party and its labor affiliates.[37]

Meanwhile the Socialist party leadership was becoming increasingly social democratic and friendly to the United States. In 1944–1946 the head of the party was Bernardo Ibáñez, secretary-general of the national labor federation and a strong supporter and friend of the AFL-CIO in the United States. In Latin America Ibáñez emphasized fraternal relations with populist movements, specifically APRA, Democratic Action, Peronism, and the Brazilian labor party of Getúlio Vargas; in Chile Ibáñez turned the Socialists against the Communists and their unions.[38]

PERU, 1945–1947

Both the Apristas and the Communists backed the 1945 election of José Luis Bustamante y Rivero, who projected a more moderate reform image than González Videla. The members of Bustamante's National Democratic Front saw themselves as the victors over the oligarchy and as the bearers of the triumphant banner of democracy. Admirers of the achievements of the interventionist state abroad during the war, the leaders of the Front were committed to expanding the state's role in income distribution and industrialization. Like the Peruvian Communist party APRA now called for a "planned democracy," modeled on Roosevelt's New Deal. Bustamante himself hoped to repeat Chilean President Aguirre Cerda's success at incorporating and mollifying the leftist and popular forces through a broad coalition government.

In part APRA was persuaded to enter this centrist coalition—rather than struggle for power on its own—by Aprista exiles in Chile. APRA maintained frequent contact with the Socialist party of Chile through meetings like the 1946 Interamerican Congress of Socialist and Democratic Parties held in Santiago whose great highlight was the visit of Haya de la Torre. The delegates at the congress endorsed a struggle against imperialism and totalitarianism, as well as a campaign for democracy, economic planning, industrialization, and social justice.[39]

In Peru APRA promised "bread with liberty." It toned down its radical demands of the 1930s to placate its adversaries by stressing that it did not want to "take away wealth from those who [had] it but create wealth for those who [did] not have it." Thus APRA now placed little emphasis on social leveling. After enduring a decade of dictatorial repression, which its orators compared with the suffering of the European Allies during the war, APRA underscored its devotion to Western democracy.[40] In 1945 Chilean Socialist Senator Salvador Allende, en route to Venezuela to congratulate his friend Rómulo Betancourt of Democratic Action on taking over the presidency, visited his Aprista colleagues in Lima. During his visit Allende made a speech in the Peruvian Parliament saluting APRA and the National Democratic Front. He extolled their victory as a manifestation of the tide of democracy, economic liberty, and social justice rolling over Latin America in the wake of World War II.[41]

APRA had come to see not only democracy but also the United States as a progressive force that could help the party in its struggle against the oligarchy. Haya continually praised the New Deal and the alliance of capitalist and socialist powers during the war. A new era, he declared, had dawned of cooperation between North and South America alongside the "worldwide shift to the left." Although still wary of the possible effect of APRA's nationalism on foreign investments, the United States now viewed that party much more favorably as a bulwark of democracy against fascism and communism. The United States, however, paid little attention to Bustamante's government but focused instead on Peru's outstanding debt obligations, which in fact remained unresolved until the 1950s.[42]

In 1946, like the Communist party in Chile, APRA received three cabinet posts. Although it was also dominant in Congress, it proved unable to achieve major reforms for its constituents beyond a few enactments raising wages and benefits for the middle and working classes. During the opening months of the Bustamante government APRA increased its standing among the labor unions and took control of the national labor federation from the Communists. With government support unions expanded their numbers and demands. At this point, despite its setback among the unions the Communist party was also growing thanks to the legal freedoms it enjoyed for the first time in more than a decade, but it was soon distancing itself from the Bustamante administration and the hated APRA. Once again the convergence between the Communists and APRA had proved ephemeral.[43]

The Cold War

In the early postwar period the United States preferred democratic governments, parties, and labor organizations in Latin America and thus helped to open up a political space for popular movements. Yet these democratic preferences possessed a much lower priority than broader strategic and economic objectives. As the Cold War began, U.S. support for the Latin American democracies was quickly superseded by relentless opposition to Communists and those deemed "soft on communism."[44]

During the war reformers and leftists were able to discredit their conservative adversaries as fascists or cryptofascists. The Cold War, however, rapidly turned the tables and permitted the right to demonize all popular forces as Communists or fellow travelers. Armed with this weapon and encouraged by the United States, the conservative ruling groups in Latin America thus manipulated the discourse of the Cold War to discredit, then to disenfranchise, and finally to repress their opponents.

CHILE, 1947–1950s

Like the Peruvians the Chileans now drove the left out. They did so to place more emphasis on economic growth, price stabilization, foreign investment, and to achieve an alignment with the United States during the Cold War. Industrial development and social welfare were the tandem goals of populism inherited from the 1930s that now came into conflict with the growing emphasis on accumulation emerging at the end of the 1940s. At this point most Latin American governments decided to clamp down on labor and to restrain its demands on their fragile, inflation-ridden economies. By suppressing leftists and workers, rulers believed they were defending democracy by removing the conditions that would justify right-wing military plots.

Under pressure from conservative elites and the United States, after only five months in office González Videla threw the Communists out of his government and then into illegality. Having begun his presidency in the belief he was still waging World War II, he soon began to act as if he were fighting World War III. Indeed some of the president's advisers warned him that a new global conflagration was imminent and that he should now explicitly align his government with the United States against the Communists.

As the Cold War took hold, González Videla believed that the Communists were no longer his reformist allies but aggressive revolutionaries acting under the direct orders of Joseph Stalin. The Communists, he complained, were attempting to control him like "a useful fool." He resented their attempts to persuade him to follow the Soviet line in foreign policy and to oppose the various proposals and projects of the United States: the Truman Doctrine, the Marshall Plan, and the Continental Defense Pact for the Americas. González Videla especially worried about the strength of the Communists in the mines, which produced Chile's main exports and would be vital to the West in the event of war with the Soviet Union. Finally, he justified repression with the spurious claim that the Communists, at the behest of their Soviet masters, were planning an uprising to overthrow him; the Communists, he insisted, were attempting to take over in Chile as they had succeeded in doing in Eastern Europe and were attempting to do in countries like Greece and France.[45]

The United States helped persuade González Videla to move against the left and labor, especially in the mines, by withholding credits from the Export-Import Bank and from the International Bank for Reconstruction and Development. After González Videla had taken action against the Communists, the flow of technical assistance, loans, and investments from the United States began to increase. Chile now received credits for CORFO, loans to cover foreign exchange shortages, and lower taxes on copper imports. The State Department and the American copper companies became willing to accept slightly higher Chilean taxes on copper. Washington also signed a military assistance pact with Santiago.[46]

Following their expulsion from the cabinet in 1947, the Communists launched protests and strikes; the government lashed back with military repression. In response to a Communist strike in the coal mines González Videla obtained emergency coal shipments from President Harry Truman. Applauded by the United States, González Videla escalated the conflict by severing relations with the Soviet Union, Czechoslovakia, and Yugoslavia. He arrested Communist leaders and in 1948 supported the "Law for the Defense of Democracy," which effectively banned the Communist party for a decade.

The Communists blamed this bombardment on the global war against communism led by North American imperialism. But rather than fighting back, the Chilean Communists retreated into clandestinity. They continued to seek middle- and working-class alliances and to cooperate with the "patriotic bourgeoisie," and they still hoped to promote reform, industry, and democracy as the first step on a long road to socialism in what they saw as their semifeudal country. By the beginning of the 1950s the proscribed Communist party was upholding the same reformist and collaborationist position it had been defending since 1935. The only important differences were greater emphases on hostility toward the United States and on the need for the proletariat to lead any multiclass reform coalition to avoid another betrayal by the bourgeoisie and centrist politicians.[47]

Influenced by the United States, APRA, and the Venezuelan Democratic Action, the Chilean Socialists committed themselves to reducing the role of the Communists in the labor movement. Having strongly supported the Allies during the war, the Socialists and their unions received crucial support from the United States. From 1946 the United States government, the American Federation of Labor, the United Mine Workers, and their international representatives donated organizers and money to help divide Chilean labor into communist and anticommunist camps. The Socialists were denouncing the Communist party and its participation in the González Videla government even before the president turned against the Communists. Although officially neutral in the Cold War, the Socialist party described its struggle with the Communists as a battle between "democratic" and "totalitarian" forces.[48]

Alleging it was dominated by Communists, the Socialist party also broke with Lombardo Toledano's Confederation of Latin American Workers (CTAL) in Mexico. To counter the CTAL the Socialists and the Apristas helped the AFL-CIO to launch the rival Inter-American Confederation of Workers (CIT). Socialist Bernardo Ibáñez became the chairman of the confederation and the North American labor leader George Meany and Aprista Arturo Sabroso its vice chairmen. With the blessing of González Videla the CIT established its headquarters in Santiago. By 1948 international influences had played a major role in dividing and debilitating the Chilean left, as well as weakening leftist forces continentwide. The effects of these measures became particularly marked in Chile, where the leftist groups enjoyed unusual strength.[49]

The majority of Socialists sided with neither the United States nor the Soviet Union in the Cold War, accusing both of imperialist ambitions. Gradually distancing itself from past populist counterparts such as APRA, the Socialist party groped for alternative socialist models, such as Titoism in Yugoslavia. Officially the Socialists opposed the onslaught against the Communists led by González Videla, although Bernardo Ibáñez and a handful of his followers joined the government's anticommunist crusade, thereby splitting the party. This issue became another illustration of the way the Cold War further factionalized and weakened popular forces in Chile.[50]

In the 1952 presidential election Carlos Ibáñez del Campo, the ex-dictator from the late 1920s, offered to end the petty quarreling and the chaotic multiparty coalitions of the past twenty years. Ibáñez attacked the Radicals for having sold out to the United States and even managed to attract a few Socialists who were attempting to create a labor movement like that under Perón in Argentina. Other Socialists, along with many proscribed Communists, sought to stake out an independent Marxist strategy for the future and in 1952 supported the token candidacy of Salvador Allende. From their opposition to President Ibáñez in subsequent years, the Socialist and Communist parties began to construct the political alliance that in 1970 eventually led to Allende's fateful election victory.[51]

PERU, 1947–1950s

In Peru the democratic opening to the left under Bustamante proved equally short-lived. In a period of economic decline the government was soon under increasing pressure from conservative groups—especially the export barons—to squeeze APRA and the demands of the lower classes. The International Monetary Fund was recommending drastic budgetary reductions to stanch inflation. The government and APRA alike both increasingly favored North American investment but were unsure of how to use it and how to control it. When APRA proposed exploiting American support in its battle against the oligarchy, the latter joined the Communists in denouncing the Apristas for attempting to sell out to the United States. Meanwhile, rather than providing aid and moving in the directions Haya wished, the United States withheld loans and cut purchases of Peruvian exports. Haya became particularly disenchanted with the way Henry Wallace, the once powerful former U.S. vice president, abruptly disappeared from the political scene. Subsequently, the Apristas found it increasingly difficult to reconcile their progressive program with their willingness to cooperate with the United States under the wartime slogan "democratic interamericanism without imperialism."[52]

Although APRA officially supported democracy, it still contained violent elements that attacked opposition newspapers and plotted insurrections. As anti-APRA sentiments mounted, Bustamante found himself in a position similar to that of González Videla, trapped between the right and the left. He now turned against the party. Angry at APRA's attempts to usurp his powers, in January 1947 he ejected its members from the cabinet.[53]

Under Bustamante labor organization and activism grew. In 1947–1948 strikes proliferated in protest against rising prices and the persecution of APRA. In his war with APRA Bustamante, to the consternation of the United States, sometimes sided with the Communist against the Aprista unions. In this internal clash the United States began to favor APRA as the best instrument to support its campaign for an anticommunist labor federation in Latin America. In 1947 and 1948 Haya visited the United States as a guest of the AFL, and switched the support of the Confederation of Peruvian Workers (CTP) from the Mexican Confederation of Latin American Workers (CTAL) to the American-backed CIT (Inter-American Confederation of Workers). This body was founded in Lima in 1948 on the initiative of the Peruvian Apristas and the Chilean Socialists. Subsequently in 1951 the CIT became the ORIT (Organización Regional Interamericana de Trabajadores [Inter-American Regional Organization of Workers]), which became even more firmly dominated by the AFL-CIO.[54]

When a faction of APRA tried to mount an uprising against the government in late 1948, Bustamante again turned on the Apristas, this time destroying their revolutionary, insurrectionary segments once and for all. This purge left the banned party entirely in the hands of Haya and the more moderate, democratic elements. Bustamante's administration then hounded the national labor confederation into submission; it became an easy victim once the Apristas had been ousted from the government.

Finally, in late 1948 Gen. Manuel A. Odría, the instrument of the export aristocracy, overthrew Bustamante. Odría escalated the repression against APRA, prohibited all CIT activities in Peru, and forced Haya to spend no less than five years (until 1954) in asylum in the Colombian embassy. Other Aprista leaders fled to Chile, Argentina, and elsewhere. Observing the defeat of popular forces throughout the hemisphere, a leading Aprista concluded: "the year 1948 was terrible for everyone. Some sinister hand had decided to crush our hearts, not only mine, not only those of the Apristas, but the hearts of all Latin Americans. Every day brought the announcement of another calamity."[55]

At the end of 1948, reflecting the idea ingrained in the Peruvian military that the Communists and the Apristas were virtually indistinguishable villains, Odría outlawed the Communist party. This step helped him to win support from the United States. Like APRA the Communist party responded by retreating into moderation. During this period, as it lost the support of workers, the Communist party sought allies among reform sectors of the bourgeoisie. By the early fifties both Peruvian labor parties and their union adherents were severely weakened.[56]

Although the United States appeared to regret the failure of APRA in the Bustamante government, it soon came to accept Odría as a staunch anticommunist ally, particularly as he shifted the country toward laissez-faire, export-led growth and openness to foreign capital after the brief experiment with state activism and industrial promotion under Bustamante. The Peruvian elites now regarded themselves in step with the current global trend away from the state interventionism that had prevailed during the war. Odría's shift toward the free market, which received the enthusiastic support of the Peruvian upper classes, followed recommendations from the IMF and a financial mission from the United States. North American investment in Peru now greatly increased, especially in mining and petroleum. The ousted Bustamante complained that the international resolutions favoring democracy had failed to prevent the illegal and undemocratic Odría regime from winning diplomatic recognition. As he watched democracy wither throughout the hemisphere, Bustamante urged future international nonrecognition of de facto governments.[57]

Conclusion: International Crises and Political Resolutions

By the early 1950s, having survived the challenges of the depression, World War II, the onset of the Cold War, and the upsurge of antagonistic popular movements, the United States had fully consolidated its economic, military, and ideological hegemony in Latin America. Whether openly authoritarian or formally democratic, governments throughout the region turned toward the right. Popular movements were eviscerated, defeated, and bankrupted. The Communists were under ban while other leftist or reformist forces scrambled to adjust to the domination of the United States and the local elites. By the 1950s the aspirations for social change kindled in the 1930s had been pulverized.

In Chile Popular Front politics was discredited, although the earlier coalitions between Marxists and centrists were to reappear in different guises and to continue to influence the strategies of the left. Henceforward the approach changed: a sense of disappointment and frustration at their experiences in 1938–1952 persuaded the Socialists and Communists to abandon the multiparty coalitions led by centrists and to place greater emphasis on movements controlled by themselves and their worker followers. The leftist groups responded to the failures of the 1940s by focusing more narrowly on redistribution and taking up a much more hostile position toward capitalism and the United States. Turning away from the approach developed by the Apristas, they became less populist and more socialist.[58]

While the Chilean left believed that its experience in government in the 1940s showed that a more radical stance was needed, APRA concluded that the fiasco of 1945–1948 demonstrated the need for greater moderation. The Apristas now recognized that the boundaries of acceptable change were much narrower in Peru than in Chile, and they plotted their future course accordingly. Having failed to capture the executive branch directly in the 1930s, and having enjoyed only a limited share of power in the 1940s, APRA swerved farther to the right. In taking this position the Apristas were aspiring to gain respectability among conservative groups, hoping that this approach would eventually enable them both to win the presidency and to implement their programs.[59]

Between the 1930s and the early 1950s the profound shifts in the world arena continually altered the paths that became available and were taken by popular movements in Chile and Peru. Although the options available were mainly determined by the balance of internal political forces, they were also shaped and limited by external factors that filtered into the domestic economic structures, social hierarchies, political systems, and ideological lenses. Under these conditions there were both striking parallels and major differences between the histories of reform movements in Chile and Peru.

The strategies adopted by both the Chilean Marxists and the Peruvian Apristas eventually led them both to power, in Chile during the early 1970s under Salvador Allende and in Peru under Alan García during the late 1980s. During these periods both movements finally enjoyed the opportunity to implement their decades-old promises of economic nationalism and redistribution. But both these governments ended in disaster: externally they proved unable to challenge the dominance of the United States; internally they failed to deliver lasting power or benefits to their working-class followers.

Notes

I wish to thank my research assistants, Lisa Baldez and Susanne Wagner, for their help with this project. Charles Bergquist, Stephen Brager, Thomas Davies, and Rosemary Thorp made valuable comments on the manuscript.

1. I am particularly indebted to Charles Bergquist for the notion of "crisis" and "resolution" suggested here.

2. Cf. Mikael Bostrom, "Political Waves in Latin America, 1940–1987." Typescript, Umea, Sweden, 1988; Paul W. Drake, "Debt and Democracy in Latin America, 1920s–1980s," in *Debt and Democracy in Latin America*, edited by Barbara Stallings and Robert Kaufman. Boulder: Westview Press, 1989, 39–58.

3. See Fernando Henrique Cardoso and Enzo Faletto, *Dependency and Development in Latin America*. Berkeley and Los Angeles: University of California Press, 1979; and Peter Gourevitch, *Politics in Hard Times*. Ithaca: Cornell University Press, 1986.

4. Rosemary Thorp and Geoffrey Bertram, *Peru, 1890–1977: Growth and Policy in an Open Economy*. London: Macmillan, 1978, 152–53.

5. For a similar treatment of political and social coalitions in Latin America see Thomas E. Skidmore and Peter H. Smith, *Modern Latin America*. New York: Oxford University Press, 1984, 360–70.

6. Juan Manuel Reveco del Villar, "Los influjos del APRA en el Partido Socialista de Chile." Thesis, FLACSO, Santiago, 1989.

7. Norbert Lechner, *La democracia en Chile*. Buenos Aires: Ediciones Signos, 1970, 74–86.

8. Thorp and Bertram, *Peru*, 147–53; Baltazar Caravedo Molinari, *Burguesía e industria en el Perú, 1933–1945*. Lima: Instituto de Estudios Peruanos, 1976.

9. Most of the sections on Chile draw heavily on Paul W. Drake, *Socialism and Populism in Chile, 1932–1952*. Urbana: University of Illinois Press, 1978. Also see Brian Loveman, *Chile: The Legacy of Hispanic Capitalism*. 2d ed. New York: Oxford University Press, 1988; Ricardo Donoso, *Alessandri, agitador y demoledor*. Vol. 2. México, D.F.: Fondo de Cultura Económica, 1952, 1954; T. Ellsworth, *Chile, an Economy in Transition*. Westport, Conn.: Greenwood Press, 1945.

10. Paul W. Drake, "The Political Responses of the Chilean Upper Class to the Depression and the Threat of Socialism, 1931–1933," in *The Rich, the Well Born, and the Powerful*, edited by Frederic Cople Jaher. Urbana: University of Illinois Press, 1973, 304–37.

11. Luis Alberto Sánchez, *Testimonio personal*. Vol. 2. Lima: Ediciones Villasan, 1969, 573–81; Alejandro Chelén Rojas, *Flujo y reflujo del socialismo chileno*. Montevideo: Ediciones Vanguardia Socialista, 1961; idem, *Trayectoria del socialismo*. Buenos Aires: Astral, 1967; Julio César Jobet, *El Partido Socialista de Chile*. 2 vols. Santiago: Prensa Latinoamericana, 1971; idem, *El socialismo chileno a través de sus congresos*. Santiago: Prensa Latinoamericana, 1965; Alan Angell, *Politics and the Labour Movement in Chile*. London: Oxford University Press, 1972. On the influence of the Spanish

Civil War on Peru as well as on Chile see Mark Falcoff and Fredrick B. Pike, *The Spanish Civil War, 1936–1939: American Hemispheric Perspectives*. Lincoln: University of Nebraska Press, 1982.

12. Luis Alberto Sánchez, *Visto y vivido en Chile: Bitacora chilena, 1930–1970*. Lima: Editoriales Unidas, S.A., 1975; Carmelo Furci, *The Chilean Communist Party and the Road to Socialism*. London: Zed Books, 1984, 33–35; John Reese Stevenson, *The Chilean Popular Front*. Philadelphia: University of Pennsylvania Press, 1942; Ernst Halperin, *Nationalism and Communism in Chile*. Cambridge: Massachusetts Institute of Technology Press, 1965, 43–52; Marta Infante Barros, *Testigos del treinta y ocho*. Santiago: Editorial Andrés Bello, 1972; Ricardo Boizard, *Historia de una derrota*. Santiago: Ediciones Orbe, 1941; Eudocio Ravines, *La gran estafa*. 2d ed. Santiago: Editorial del Pacífico, 1954; Elías Lafertte, *Vida de un comunista*. Santiago: n.p. 1961, 298–304; Gabriel González Videla, *Memorias*. Vol. 1. Santiago: Editorial Gabriela Mistral, 1975, 155; L. A. Sánchez, *Testimonio*, 581.

13. Víctor Villanueva, *El APRA en busca del poder, 1930–1940*. Lima: Editorial Horizonte, 1975; Orazio Ciccarelli, "Fascism and Politics in Peru during the Benavides Regime, 1933–1939: The Italian Perspective," *Hispanic American Historical Review* 70, no. 3 (August 1990), 405–32.

14. Robert J. Alexander, *Communism in Latin America*. New Brunswick: Rutgers University Press, 1957, 227–29; idem, *Aprismo: The Ideas and Doctrines of Víctor Raúl Haya de la Torre*. Kent: Kent State University Press, 1973; Denis Sulmont, *El movimiento obrero en el Perú, 1900–1956*. Lima: Pontífica Universidad Católica del Perú, 1975, 151–74; Víctor Villanueva, *El APRA y el ejército, 1940–1950*. Lima: Editorial Horizonte, 1977, 7–20; Alberto Moya Obeso, *Sindicalismo aprista y clasista en el Perú, 1920–1956*. Trujillo: Librería Star, n.d.; Reveco, "APRA," 76.

15. R. Harrison Wagner, *United States Policy toward Latin America*. Stanford: Stanford University Press, 1970, 14–16; R. A. Humphreys, *Latin America and the Second World War*. 2 vols. London: Athlone Press, 1981, 1982, 2: 226–27; Irwin F. Gellman, *Good Neighbor Diplomacy*. Baltimore: Johns Hopkins University Press, 1979; George Soule, David Efron, and Norman T. Ness, *Latin America in the Future World*. New York: Farrar and Rinehart, 1945; Arthur Whitaker, ed. *Inter-American Affairs*. 5 vols. New York: Columbia University Press, 1942–1946.

16. William F. Sater, *Chile and the United States: Empires in Conflict*. Athens: University of Georgia Press, 1990, 113–20; Peter G. Snow, *Radicalismo chileno*. Buenos Aires: Editorial Francisco de Aguirre, 1972; Arturo Olavarría Bravo, *Chile entre dos Alessandri*. Vol. 2. Santiago: Editorial Nascimento, 1962, 29. For extensive information on industrialization throughout these decades see Oscar Muñoz, *Crecimiento industrial de Chile, 1914–1965*. Santiago: Universidad de Chile, 1968.

17. Michael J. Francis, *The Limits of Hegemony: United States Relations with Argentina and Chile during World War II*. Notre Dame: University of Notre Dame Press, 1977, 20–21; Whitaker, *Inter-American Affairs, 1944*, 130–32.

18. Ellsworth, *Chile*, 85–93.

19. Andrew Barnard, "Chilean Communists, Radical Presidents, and Chilean

Relations with the United States, 1940–1947," *Journal of Latin American Studies* 13, no. 2 (November 1981), 347–74; Florencio Durán Bernales, *El Partido Radical*. Santiago: Editorial Nascimento, 1958; Galo González Díaz, *La lucha por la formación del Partido Comunista de Chile*. Santiago: n.p., 1958, 20–42.

20. Quoted in Reveco, "APRA," 74–75.

21. H. Boris Yopo, "El Partido Socialista Chileno y Estados Unidos: 1933–1946," *Documento de Trabajo del FLACSO*, no. 224, October 1984, 1; Stevenson, *Chilean Popular Front*, 110–17; Oscar Schnake Vergara, *América y la guerra*. Santiago: Taller de Publicaciones del PS, 1941; idem, *Chile y la guerra*. Santiago: Ediciones Ercilla, 1941; Salvador Allende, *La contradicción de Chile*. Santiago: Talleres Gráficos, 1943.

22. Partido Socialista, *Primer congreso de los partidos democráticos de latinoamérica*. Santiago: Talleres Gráficos Gutenberg, 1940; Julio César Jobet, *El Partido Socialista de Chile*. Vol. 1. Santiago: Prensa Latinoamericana, 1971, 148–50; Reveco, "APRA," 89–90.

23. Barnard, "Chilean Communists," 347–74; Alexander, *Communism*, 15–29.

24. Humphreys, *Latin America*, 1: 124; ibid., 2: 99–105; Allen Gerlach, "Civil-Military Relations in Peru, 1914–1945." Ph.D. diss., University of New Mexico, Albuquerque, 1973, 501–5; James Carey, *Peru and the United States, 1900–1962*. Notre Dame: University of Notre Dame Press, 1964, 105–10; Thomas M. Davies, Jr., *Indian Integration in Peru: A Half Century of Experience, 1900–1948*. Lincoln: University of Nebraska Press, 1970, 129–31.

25. Waldo Frank, *South American Journey*. New York: Duell, Sloan, and Pearce, 1943, 266–67; Víctor Raúl Haya de la Torre, *Y después de la guerra ¿Qué?* Lima: Editorial PTCM, 1946; Villanueva, *El APRA y el ejército*, 27–34.

26. Reveco, "APRA," 69–77.

27. Harry Kantor, *The Ideology and Program of the Peruvian Aprista Movement*. Berkeley and Los Angeles: University of California Press, 1953, 98–114; Fredrick B. Pike. *The Modern History of Peru*. New York: Frederick A. Praeger, 1967, 277–278; Víctor Raúl Haya de la Torre, *La defensa continental*. Buenos Aires: Ediciones Problemas de América, 1942; idem, *Obras completas*. Vol. 1. Lima: Editorial Juan Mejía Baca, 1977, 268–99; Manuel Seoane, *Nuestra América y la guerra*. Santiago: Ediciones Ercilla, 1940; idem, *El gran vecino: América en la encrucijada*. Santiago: Editorial Orbe, 1944; Luis Alberto Sánchez, *Un sudamericano en norteamérica*. Lima: Universidad Nacional Mayor de San Marcos, 1968, 298–322; L. A. Sánchez, *Testimonio*, 586; Carey, *Peru*, 116–18; Moya, *Sindicalismo*, 87–88.

28. Sulmont, *Movimiento obrero*, 177–84.

29. Alexander, *Communism*, 229–31; Sulmont, *Movimiento obrero*, 171–87; Moya, *Sindicalismo*, 92–94.

30. See David Rock, "War and Postwar Intersections: Latin America and the United States," this volume.

31. Wagner, *United States Policy*, 17–20, 92; Humphreys, *Latin America*, 2: 215–16; James C. Tillapaugh, "From War to Cold War: United States Policies toward Latin America, 1943–1948." Ph.D. diss., Northwestern University, Evanston, 1973; Fre-

drick B. Pike, *The United States and the Andean Republics: Peru, Bolivia, and Ecuador*. Cambridge: Harvard University Press, 1977, 269–70.

32. On economic trends see Rosemary Thorp, "The Latin American Economies in the 1940s," this volume; Universidad de Chile, *Desarrollo económico de Chile, 1940–1956*. Santiago: Instituto de Economía, 1956.

33. Wagner, *United States Policy*, 46–49; Humphreys, *Latin America*, 2: 227–28.

34. Claude G. Bowers, *Chile through Embassy Windows*. New York: Simon and Schuster, 1958, 329.

35. Partido Comunista, *Ricardo Fonseca: Combatiente ejemplar*. Santiago: Talleres Gráficos Lautaro, 1952, 124–49; González Videla, *Memorias*, 467–69; Chelén, *Trayectoria*, 103–13; Halperin, *Nationalism and Communism*, 53.

36. Partido Comunista, *Ricardo*, 127–34; Barnard, "Chilean Communists," 348.

37. Lafertte, *Un comunista*, 330; Bowers, *Chile*, 159–62.

38. Ibáñez was an admirer of Haya de la Torre, and he had been a guest of the AFL-CIO in the United States during the war. Cf. Reveco, "APRA," 80; Whitaker, *Inter-American Affairs, 1944*, 72–73; Chelén, *Trayectoria*, 106–7; Bowers, *Chile*, 39; Bernardo Ibáñez, *El socialismo y el porvenir de los pueblos*. Santiago: Ediciones Difusión Popular, 1946.

39. The 1946 congress was also known as the "First American Congress of Parties of Socialist Tendencies." As in 1940 the Communists were excluded, and they denigrated this "American Social Democrat Congress" "to serve North American imperialist plans." Reveco, "APRA," 90–94; Jobet, *El Partido*, 194–95.

40. Gonzalo Portocarrero Maisch, *De Bustamante a Odría*. Lima: Mosca Azul Editores, 1983, 67–75, 90–92; José Luis Bustamante y Rivero, *Tres años de lucha por la democracia en el Perú*. Buenos Aires: n.p., 1949, esp. 11–25; Sulmont, *Movimiento obrero*, 185–87; Haya de la Torre, *Obras*, 5: 343–412; Moya, *Sindicalismo*, 141.

41. Reveco, "APRA," 81–83.

42. Nigel Haworth, "Peru," in *Latin America between the Second World War and the Cold War, 1944–1948*, edited by Leslie Bethell and Ian Roxborough. Cambridge: Cambridge University Press, 1993, 170–89; Fredrick B. Pike, *The Politics of the Miraculous in Peru: Haya de la Torre and the Spiritualist Tradition*. Lincoln: University of Nebraska Press, 1986, 200–203.

43. Pike, *Modern History*, 283–89; Portocarrero, *Bustamante a Odría*, 111–14; Haworth, "Peru"; Moya, *Sindicalismo*, 125–29; Haya de la Torre, *Obras*, 1: 300–320; Percy MacLean y Estenós, *Historia de una revolución*. Buenos Aires: Editorial E.A.A.L., 1953; Grant Hilliker, *The Politics of Reform in Peru*. Baltimore: Johns Hopkins University Press, 1971.

44. Sulmont, *Movimiento obrero*, 181.

45. González Videla, *Memorias*, 506, 603–4.

46. Gilbert J. Butland, *Chile*. London: Royal Institute of International Affairs, 1953, 108–9; Barnard, "Chilean Communists," 363–74; González Videla, *Memorias*, 573–765; Durán, *Partido Radical*, 426–29, 478–97, 549–89; Lafertte, *Un comunista*, 341; Partido Comunista, *Ricardo*, 152–78; Bowers, *Chile*, 166–75, 309–29.

47. Furci, *Chilean Communist Party*, 43–56; Partido Comunista, *Ricardo*, 15–19, 159–78; S. Cole Blasier, "Chile: A Communist Battleground," *Political Science Quarterly* 65 (1950), 353–74.

48. González Videla, *Memorias*, 529–31.

49. Ibáñez, *El socialismo*, 3–63; *El movimiento sindical internacional y la fundación de la C.I.T.* Santiago: n.p.., 1949; Serafino Romualdi, *Presidents and Peons*. New York: Funk and Wagnalls, 1967, 37–42, 73–139, 323–32; George Morris, *CIA and American Labor*. New York: International Publishers, 1967, 48–91; Moya, *Sindicalismo*, 198–200.

50. Chelén, *Trayectoria*, 116–31; Barnard, "Chilean Communists"; Oscar Waiss, *El drama socialista*. N.p., [1948].

51. Chelén, *Trayectoria*, 125–92; Lafertte, *Un comunista*, 348; Angell, *Labour Movement*, 174–82; Halperin, *Nationalism and Communism*, 57–61, 128–44, 192–201.

52. Pike, *Politics of the Miraculous*, 226–30; Moya, *Sindicalismo*, 133–35; Ray Josephs, *Latin America: Continent in Crisis*. New York: Random House, 1948, 173–76.

53. Portocarrero, *De Bustamante a Odría*, 138–64.

54. Romualdi, *Presidents and Peons*, 294–95; Portocarrero, *De Bustamante a Odría*, 161–72; Sulmont, *Movimiento obrero*, 226–28; Haworth, "Peru."

55. L. A. Sánchez, *Testimonio*, 864–65; Haya de la Torre, *Obras*, 1: 242–58; Bustamante, *Democracia*, 244–45; Pike, *Politics of the Miraculous* 232–41; Víctor Villanueva, *La sublevación aprista del 48*. Lima: Editorial Horizonte, 1973; Villanueva, *El APRA y el ejército*.

56. Moya, *Sindicalismo*, 152–54; MacLean, *Revolución*; Alexander, *Communism*, 231–33; Josephs, *Latin America*, 178–81.

57. Bustamante, *Democracia*, 319–27; Pike, *Modern History*, 290–91; Thorp and Bertram, *Peru*, 149; Sulmont, *Movimiento obrero*, 197–240; Portocarrero, *Bustamante, democracia a Odría*, 201–5. Haworth, "Peru."

58. Oscar Waiss, *Nacionalismo y socialismo en América Latina*. Santiago: Prensa Latinoamericana, 1954.

59. Hilliker, *Reform*, 125.

6 The Populist Gamble of Getúlio Vargas in 1945

Political and Ideological Transitions in Brazil

John D. French

The victory of the United Nations over the Axis powers in 1945 coincided with the end of the eight-year dictatorship of the Estado Nôvo (New State) in Brazil and the reestablishment of electoral processes. In late 1944, as pressures intensified to end a regime inspired by European corporatist and fascist models and installed by a coup d'état in 1937, a small group of opposition politicians and top military personnel began to raise the issue of a successor to the rule of Getúlio Vargas. Although the Vargas government had started to shed its most extreme authoritarian features following Brazil's declaration of war against the Axis in 1942, these changes failed to contain the resentment, frustration, and anger of the economic and political elites displaced by the revolution of 1930 and by Vargas's cancellation of the elections of 1938.

As the political drama of 1945 began, the opposition recognized that if it was to emerge victorious in the contest with Vargas it had to construct ties with the military—always the ultimate source of power in Brazil.[1] For these members of the self-defined "political class," mass mobilization was never an option, for they agreed that only a select few should be admitted into the hermetic corridors of power. Armando de Salles Oliveira, the former interventor of the state of São Paulo and the exiled candidate in the 1938 elections, captured their outlook when he wrote, "I do not belong to those who, disillusioned by the army. . .appeal to the people."[2]

As the end of the war approached, the most effective pressure for change came from the top levels of the military. Months of secret meetings came to a head on March 1 when Pedro Aurélio de Goés Monteiro, a general in the army and an ultraconservative widely known as a former Nazi sympathizer, called publicly for Vargas to step down.[3] Goés Monteiro quickly found support from Francisco Campos, the corporatist jurist who was the author of the 1937 constitution.[4] Simultaneously, Gen. Eurico Dutra, the minister of war under the Estado Nôvo, began cultivating the anti-Vargas politicians and military men.[5] Members of the liberal civilian opposition sought to turn military discontent to their favor by launching the presidential candidacy of Brig. Eduardo Gomes, a hero of the famous *tenentista* revolt ("Revolt of Lieutenants") in Copacabana, Rio de Janeiro, in 1922. Encouraged by Dutra's maneuverings, Gomes offered to make the minister the head of the transitional military junta that would replace Vargas.[6]

Vargas attempted to counter the threat from its very beginnings. On 28 February 1945 the president signed the Ninth Amendment to the 1937 constitution, which pledged that an election date would be set within ninety days. Two weeks later Vargas again sought to neutralize the threat of a coup by offering Dutra his support as the "official" candidate in the upcoming elections. Recent research, however, has suggested that Dutra's candidacy was initiated without the prior approval of Vargas and was in fact imposed on him.[7]

Subsequently Dutra adroitly exploited his unique position as a member of the government who had extensive ties with the opposition. He offered Vargas protection from a coup and from the revenge of his opponents; but to the supporters of Gomes he held out the enticing prospect of overthrowing Vargas before the elections took place. In an effort to ensure that the elections would indeed take place, Dutra declared his support for universal, direct, and secret suffrage; freedom of expression; and an amnesty for political prisoners. His most unexpected gesture was to back the release of Luis Carlos Prestes, the leader of the Communist party, which occurred on 18 April.[8]

Thus the stage seemed set for a transition to democracy in which the leading candidates for office were two generals likely to pursue highly conservative policies. Yet Brazil had undergone profound changes during the years of the Vargas presidencies since 1930. Between 1920 and 1940 the number of industrial workers in the state of São Paulo had risen from 80,000 to 275,000; by 1945 the overwhelming majority of Brazil's one million industrial workers were concentrated in urban areas such as metropolitan

São Paulo.[9] Even though a majority of the population of Brazil, now forty-one million in total, still lived in rural areas, the urban industrial areas, led by Rio de Janeiro and São Paulo, stood at the forefront of the nation's economic, social, and cultural development.

In 1945 Brazil stood at a political crossroads. Would the old *coroneis*, ("colonels"), the local-level political bosses, who controlled the rural vote again prevail and deliver a majority to the Partido Social Democrático or the União Democrático Nacional? Would the inhabitants of the cities, including the middle class and the industrial workers, follow the lead of the rural voters, or now strike out in new directions? Was the power of the urban population sufficient to determine the final outcome of the elections? Was any political leader in a position to capture their support?

Facing Brazil's Future: Getúlio Vargas and His Opponents

Since achieving power at the age of forty-seven in 1930, Getúlio Vargas had presided over a period of profound economic and social change. In 1930 Brazil possessed little more than its textile industry; fifteen years later it had developed a full range of intermediate factory products. The year 1943, which saw the establishment of the Volta Redonda steel plant, the first of its kind in Latin America and the underdeveloped world, marked the beginnings of heavy industry in Brazil.

As he approached his fifteenth year of office, President Vargas increasingly raised the banner of economic nationalism. He was pledged to "a struggle against economic colonialism"; before 1930, he argued, an unjust international economic order condemned Brazil to be "a simple semicolonial community." Trapped in this "primitivism of monoculture and the export of raw materials," the country had been forced to import nearly all its manufactured goods, and this system, Vargas believed, meant low profits and wages, and the impoverishment of the nation. The economic emancipation of Brazil, he declared, would be possible only through a policy of industrialization led by the state and protection of its industries from competition and interference from abroad.[10] Although he did not support rigid autarky, Vargas saw Brazil's new future being constructed primarily by its own people as opposed to foreign investors. His speeches warned constantly against allowing foreigners to take control of key industries and the strategic minerals necessary for military defense.[11]

Vargas thus repudiated the economic liberalism that had dominated Brazilian political discourse for the past century. He denied the validity of the concept of comparative advantage. The "disordered individualism" of liberalism, and the myth that labor was "a simple commodity," bred social injustice and communism, he declared. "Political equality alone" was insufficient for "social equilibrium"; the liberal prohibition against state intervention on social issues was a means for government to sustain "the rich against the poor, and the powerful against the weak."[12] To Vargas the attraction of industrial development was that it offered an instrument to break free of the zero-sum game that ruled relationships between the social classes. An expanding economy based on industry, he believed, might not lead to perfect equality, but it would ultimately benefit the whole population. Such populist policies and views were also part of a tide of social reform sweeping the United States and Western Europe, where liberal certainties had been shaken by depression and war. The landslide defeat of Winston Churchill, Britain's conservative wartime leader, in July 1945 astonished the world as the socialist Labour party took over the reins of power. In the words of Franklin D. Roosevelt, the architect of the New Deal, this did indeed seem to herald the move toward the "four freedoms," and "the beginning of the century of the common man."[13]

Stereotypes ill prepare us for the curious figure of Getúlio Vargas in 1945, the populist dictator who displayed neither the charismatic magnetism, the spellbinding oratory, nor the eclectic thinking that one tends to associate with populist politicians. Rather, we find a profoundly proud, intelligent, and private man, an enormously skilled politician with an integrated and coherent worldview, which he confidently believed to represent the collective interest and future of his country.

Aspiring to be a leader who embodied the interests of the nation and not merely one class, Vargas was willing to take risks, confident of his own judgment and ability to control the events he set in motion. Faced with strident enemies and dubious friends, the dictator decided on an unexpected course that was to profoundly affect both the 1945 electoral campaign and Brazilian history: reliance on the nation's working people.

To prevent the elections from becoming a means to turn back the clock to the era of the First Republic, Vargas sought to broaden the political arena by mobilizing the people of the new urban-industrial Brazil, who remained outside the Social Democratic party (Partido Social Democrático [PSD]) and the Democratic National Union (União Democrático Nacional [UDN]). Having now lost most of his conservative civilian and military supporters, he was free to formulate his populist appeal more categorically. Speaking to an audience of workers and trade unionists in the Vasco da Gama stadium in Rio de Janeiro on May Day 1945, Vargas placed the urban workers at the center of the succession issue. Today's self-proclaimed "champions of democracy," he declared, had never tried to implement the token social legislation of the period before 1930. For decades these "opportunists and reactionaries" had supported the "policy of the police state. . .to stifle by force the demands of the people and the workers, the true producers of the wealth of the nation." Vargas then hailed the social and labor legislation of his own administration: the legalization of the labor unions, the introduction of labor courts, the system of workers' compensation, the implementation of pension and vacation schemes, the regulation of conditions governing women and child workers. These measures, he claimed, constituted a "code of rights" that guaranteed the "economic emancipation" of the workers.[14]

As he launched this appeal, Vargas conveniently failed to mention that over the past fifteen years he himself had frequently used the methods of the police state against the workers. Under the constitution of the Estado Nôvo, which still remained in force in 1945, strikes were outlawed; the social legislation Vargas was now boasting about was inadequate, loosely enforced, or contradicted by other government measures. Even so, Vargas could accurately claim that the workers "had never received anything, nor could expect any benefits" from his conservative opponents. The stakes involved in the coming election, he warned his audience, were high. A victory for Gomes and the UDN, who represented the "backward mentality" of the First Republic, would be a disaster for both the workers and the nation, since it would spell the return of the "oligarchical groups [who had] made the country a colony of international finance." Vargas took a more restrained position on General Dutra, who deserved, he declared, the confidence of the nation because he acknowledged the "conquests of [Vargas's] social policy." But this was the last time Vargas mentioned the minister of war until the final weeks of the election campaign.

Vargas's rhetoric in 1945 was not, of course, totally new or untested in Brazilian politics. He had himself pledged the passage of social and labor measures in his 1930 presidential platform. And the social question had become the object of legislation and government regulation during the 1930s and was no longer treated as the exclusive responsibility of the police.

Populist rhetoric was not, however, the same as actually delivering concrete benefits. And much of Vargas's vaunted social and labor legislation of the early 1930s had remained so many paper promises during the first decade of his rule. Introduced on an ad hoc basis, they had been only sporadically enforced and lacked the coherence of systematic government policy until the Estado Nôvo.

Whatever their practical impact, however, Vargas's innovative social policies and rhetoric brought hope to the masses and had aroused the suspicion of many members of the conservative classes, especially after 1942. "I have never proposed," he had hastened to assure an audience in 1944, "to foment class struggle, but rather peace, harmony, and collaboration among them."[15]

All Brazilian politicians, naturally enough, shared this common rhetoric of "class cooperation" and "social peace." For most, however, "class peace" was a convenient shorthand for denying the legitimacy of any conflict between workers and their employers. But Vargas gave these clichés a different emphasis because he did not equate the interests of the state with the employers and workers. He recognized the divergence of sectoral interests between industrialists and workers but deemed both inferior to the collective interests of the nation as represented by the state.

Social injustice, class rivalry, and subversion, he believed, stemmed from a failure to meet the workers' legitimate needs. With labor's rights guaranteed by the state, class struggle would be eliminated and the "bonds of solidarity" strengthened as each group contributed to the supreme goal of national development.[16] In this approach the key concept was the social integration of workers but with the flexibility necessary to justify action against a strike or forms of workers' protest.

In his policy of working-class inclusion Vargas had the inevitable political objective of winning workers' support. He was conscious of the natural repulsion that existed between the potential working-class constituency and the PSD, which he had helped found, with its conservative politics and elitist style. To guarantee the desired popular participation, it was essential to establish a separate political vehicle.

On 15 May 1945 a new party was formed that would have an enduring role in the history of the following two decades. Although it could have simply been called the People's or Popular party, Labor Minister Alexandre Marcondes Filho chose a more daring and class-tinged name, the Brazilian Labor party (Partido Trabalhista Brasileiro [PTB]). The PTB was to be a classic populist party that spoke to class differences without proclaiming itself a class party. Its name, while excluding employers and the rich, was designed to appeal to a wide audience of urban laborers and members of the lower middle class. Getúlio Vargas, that "loyal and dedicated friend of the laborers," was named the party's "president of honor." The founding platform of the PTB declared that the interests of working people clashed with those of the "moderate right" and the "extreme left," by which it meant both the PSD and the Brazilian Communist party (Partido Comunista Brasileiro [PCB]). Having praised existing social legislation, the PTB called for greater union autonomy and the political representation of working people by the workers themselves.[17]

Vargas's ambitious plans for the PTB could easily have been frustrated by the political marginality and electoral inexperience of its proposed constituency. If the opening toward the workers was to bear fruit, it was necessary to foster their participation in the forthcoming elections, and to achieve this Vargas had to alter the terms on which the elections would be conducted. Decree Law 7,586, the electoral legislation issued on 25 May 1945, differed radically from all its predecessors. It was designed to enfranchise the working class and to favor urban over rural voter registration and electoral participation.[18]

In this way Vargas sought to prevent the return to power of the conservative landed classes.[19] To create an urban-industrial counterweight to the *coroneis*, Vargas maintained a literacy requirement for the vote. Although this restriction was opposed by the Brazilian left, it represented a means to favor urban over rural voting.[20] For all literate Brazilians except women who did not work outside the home, voting now became compulsory, and those who failed to vote were subject to a fine.[21] The law, which drew upon a plan prepared in 1943 by Marcondes Filho, also created a new voter registration system specifically designed to favor urban areas.[22]

These steps posed a serious challenge to the *antigetulistas* led by Gomes. In an interview on 17 April, soon after the announcement of future elections by Vargas, Gomes insisted that the only way to prevent government interference in the election process was for the president to resign. Brazilian soldiers were fighting for "the freedom of oppressed countries," Gomes declared, but at home they were "dominated by a regime identical" to those they were seeking to destroy in Europe.[23] In response Vargas mocked the "strange mentality of the enemies of the government. They demand democracy, the vote, elections; but when they are given the opportunity for democracy, their reply [is] to call for a coup d'état."[24]

Until around June 1945 Gomes focused almost exclusively on the deposition of Vargas prior to the elections. However, the links between Gomes and the military were now being checked by Dutra's intrigues to win military backing for his own efforts to secure the succession.[25] These conditions eventually forced the supporters of the UDN into searching for support beyond the military and therefore to confront the broader issues of national development policies. Gomes himself made this transition slowly and uneasily. In an interview on 3 May he continued to insist that the "illegitimate regime" should first be brought to an end by passing power to the judiciary, which he claimed was the only surviving institution from the country's last valid constitution of 1934.[26]

In these exchanges there was an ironic reversal of roles. Vargas, the large rancher who had originally been among the beneficiaries of the First Republic as a loyal member of the corrupt political machine of Rio Grande do Sul, was now the impassioned enemy of the old Brazil. Gomes, in contrast, the former *tenente* revolutionary who had fought to bring the First Republic down, was idealizing the agrarian oligarchical Brazil of his youth. In 1945 Gomes repeatedly attacked Vargas for blaming the "errors" of Brazil on the "representative regime in force until 1930." Gomes's rhetoric presented democracy as a restoration and reestablishment, but it was a return to a past that he himself had helped to destroy.[27]

As Vargas compelled him to address broader policy issues, Gomes began to campaign openly on behalf of the plantation owners and the export agriculture that had sustained Brazilian society for centuries. Casting himself as the defender of the "rural producer," Gomes posed as the leader of an aggrieved majority, neglected and exploited since 1930. Arguing against "currently fashionable ideas," he emphasized that "the basic wealth that sustained Brazil as a civilized nation" stemmed from its mining and agricultural exports. The million Brazilians who now subsisted on urban industry, he argued, lived and prospered only at the expense of the rural majority. Victimized by bureaucracy, deficit spending, and the "confiscatory foreign exchange rates" instituted in 1931, the "considerable influence" of the agricultural producer had declined with the recent growth of industry. After 1937, Gomes continued, the plantation owners became relegated to an even more secondary role since under a dictatorship that had abolished elections the votes they commanded no longer carried any political weight. Vargas's policies were based on the "false theory" that Brazil had to "break its armature as an agricultural country, because only industrialized nations [were] strong and rich." Reviving the old arguments in favor of free trade in Brazil, Gomes held that tariff barriers and the wartime disruption of trade had fostered an unnatural industrialization based on "excessive profits." Rural producers were thus forced to pay artificially high prices for inferior Brazilian manufactured goods.[28]

Gomes denounced the ill effects of the growth of industry and the cities on agriculture. Workers who were desperately needed on the plantations were being drawn into the cities by the government's public works and by "higher and higher" wages and shorter working hours offered by industry. The policy of "fascinating the multitudes in the cities with costly, luxurious projects" was provoking an "exodus" from rural areas and the "overcrowding" of the cities.[29]

Gomes took a stand against the nationalism represented by Vargas, stressing that an alliance with the United States should be at the foundation of Brazil's foreign affairs. Whereas Vargas repeatedly denounced foreign powers and influences, Gomes warmly acknowledged their contributions and argued that the support of foreign capital was essential to the development of both industry and Brazilian oil. Gomes denounced a recent antitrust law enacted by Vargas, the Lei Malaia, as a "Nazi-like" attack on free enterprise, and the "thoughtless opinion of a current hostile to foreign capital" that believed foreign investment made the country poorer.[30]

Gomes dismissed the president's recent "flattery" of the people as a "demagogic appeal." Yet, in a nine page interview on 3 May, Gomes devoted only three sentences to "the misery and hunger" of the "poorer classes." He qualified even that statement, however, blaming the problem on the disorganization of "public finances" and proposing no concrete steps to remedy it.[31] Not surprisingly, Gomes had few followers among the workers. His opening campaign rally held at the Pacaembu stadium in São Paulo on 16 June illustrated his weakness among urban workers, since the stadium was only half full and contained an exclusively middle- and upper-class audience. According to the radio publicity of the PTB, Gomes disdained the *marmiteiros*, a derogatory term for the votes of unskilled workers that derived from the metal pails in which they carried their lunches.[32]

Eager to counter these accusations, Gomes began to incorporate the workers, if not into his program, at least into his speeches. Praising the "resistance" to the Estado Nôvo among a number of groups including the workers, he claimed that the workers had never been seduced by the dictatorship and understood the need to "divorce themselves" from the fascist state. Invoking Catholic ideas, Gomes declared that Brazil must move toward a society in which "the sad spectacle of excessive wealth does not confront extreme misery, . . .in which the rich would be less powerful and the poor less suffering."

Beyond these paternalistic platitudes on the one hand Gomes pledged to perfect existing social legislation by eliminating its "fascist" features, while saying that workers needed "trade union freedoms and the right to strike." But on the other, he countered and undermined this commitment within a few sentences through language designed to appeal to employers: "state intervention should have in mind the stimulation of personal initiatives and activities and not its destruction."[33] Even if Gomes was sincere in upholding the right to strike, he failed to suggest that he would ever support this right in any practical terms.

A few middle-class Socialists in the small and ineffectual Esquerda Democrática (Democratic Left) founded in August 1945 supported Gomes for president, but the workers remained at a distance.[34] In a speech on 22 November in the São Paulo textile city of Sorocaba that he was subsequently forced to disavow, Gomes revealed his true attitude on the social question. The conflicts between labor and capital would be resolved, he said, when each side realized it needed and depended on the other, as the Church had for so long argued. Ignoring the past realities of repression, Gomes insisted that the workers of Brazil were not so weak and feeble that they required "vigorous" as opposed to "cautious and prudent" state intervention." Capital, he went on, required protection from "confiscatory assault by the state," and he suggested that the government should uphold only what was "beneficial" in existing social legislation.

Thus Gomes appeared to threaten even the small advances made by labor during recent years, and he assumed, in line with standard capitalist theory, that labor and employers stood in a relation of equality with each other, thus denying any objective basis for class conflict. The source of the labor problem, he argued, lay in the subjective and unfounded "belief" by both sides that their interests were opposed. The "free trade unions" in possession of the full "autonomy" he advocated would be led by men "conscious of their duties, not just their rights." Disputes would be resolved without "disturbing the social order or by recourse to the always-pernicious general or partial strikes." This attack on strikes appeared in clear contradiction with his earlier pledge to honor the workers' right to strike.[35]

Thus unlike Vargas, who recognized the inevitability of class conflict, Gomes wanted a system of labor relations in perfect harmony. It was not hard to imagine him responding to strikes by using the police to restore the "natural" nonconflictual state of affairs, or blaming strikes on agitators and their wrong "beliefs." This opponent of the "fascist" Estado Nôvo offered a kind of free enterprise trade unionism whose "independence" and "autonomy" would leave workers wide open to the depredations of their employers.

Gomes's opponent, Gen. Eurico Dutra of the PSD, showed an equal lack of sympathy toward labor. But while Gomes opposed state-supported unionism, Dutra saw himself as the beneficiary of Vargas's influence among the workers. He therefore contented himself with vague references to "economic unification" and the "complete assimilation of classes," while pledging that labor issues would be resolved through the "impartial organs" established by "social law."[36] Although it was based on the agrarian oligarchies, Dutra's coalition included the rising class of Brazilian industrialists who feared the backward-looking policies proposed by Gomes almost as much as Vargas's *trabalhismo*. Thus the great difference between Dutra and Gomes lay in the future role they ascribed to industry. When questioned on this issue Dutra declared that Brazil "was on the road to industrialization. The 'essentially agricultural' epoch [was] passing. Such countries. . .[were] countries of pauperism." This development-minded military leader called for the "industrial utilization" of the nation's natural resources and the mechanization of agriculture. Brazil should develop its exports of manufactured goods, he declared in an echo of economic nationalism, despite possible opposition from the already industrialized nations.[37]

Luis Carlos Prestes, Queremismo, and the Fall of Vargas

In mid-1945 neither of the declared candidates were attempting to appeal to the urban workers, whose potential impact on the election had been increased by the recent electoral legislation. Yet Vargas did not go unchallenged at the forefront of the new popular politics. On 18 April Luis Carlos

Prestes, the hero of the *tenentista* Long March of 1924–1927, was released after spending a decade in the regime's prisons. Now forty-seven years old, Prestes was soon to prove that he had lost none of his great popularity.

The release of Prestes, the most illustrious political prisoner throughout South America, occurred at a decisive moment in the international arena, when the rigid divisions between right and left had temporarily weakened. If the Western allies could work together with the Soviet Union for a common purpose, surely a similar tolerance was demanded on the domestic front in Brazil. In 1945 Prestes and the Brazilian Communist party were able to operate in a more open atmosphere than at any other moment in Brazilian history.

The contending parties eagerly awaited the pronouncements of Prestes on the succession while courting his support. But Prestes waited until 23 May and the spectacular rally organized by the Communists at the Vasco da Gama stadium in Rio de Janeiro. To the great surprise of the *antigetulistas*, Prestes rejected the demand of the UDN for the immediate resignation of Vargas. He decried the "spirit of unrestrained and threatening party feeling" with which the campaign had begun. The solution to Brazil's great problems, he declared, would not be found in "civil wars or in redemptory coups."[38] Unlike the followers of the UDN, Prestes detected different phases and turning points during the Estado Nôvo, and he drew a distinction between Vargas and the reactionary groups supporting the regime. Prestes spoke of the thousands jailed, tortured, and killed by the dictatorship. Yet "hatreds" and "personal resentments" had no place in his own politics so long as the regime was willing to liquidate the "decrepit remains of reaction." Prestes appeared extraordinarily generous in taking this position, since Vargas had been personally responsible for sending his German-born wife to her death in a German concentration camp.[39]

Prestes, however, positioned himself carefully to the left of Vargas and independently of him. Like Gomes he claimed that Vargas was exaggerating his concessions to labor, and he refused to condemn the 1935 revolt led by the Communists through the Aliança Nacional Libertadora. Prestes issued an unrelenting attack on the "painful" and "miserable" conditions of the poor and offered specific proposals for radical change. His program called for land reform, credits to increase the production of foodstuffs, the elimination of taxes on necessities, a doubling of the minimum wage, a progressive income tax, and a tax on excess profits.

In these measures, he declared, lay the keys to the unity of the popular masses and the foundation of democracy. While Vargas promised state intervention to resolve the problems of the working class, Prestes argued in favor of self-help. Grass-roots organization, he urged, was the way to reshape the country to meet the needs of the people. "Broad committees" should be established "in the workplaces, streets and neighborhoods." Uniting "bit by bit, from the bottom up," these democratic organizations, open to all except "reactionaries" and "the fascist fifth-column," would help to elect "genuine representatives of the people."[40]

During the next six months thousands of such committees did spring up, and the Communist party, now operating freely for the first time since 1927, gained tens of thousands of new supporters. Working with enormous energy, the followers of Prestes attempted to forge links with members of other classes and parties, and their conspicuous moderation dispelled any lurking fears of another revolt like that of November 1935.

Prestes had therefore sided with Vargas, partly because the Communists were aware of the president's popularity among those it regarded as its own potential constituency. "You can't throw stones at the people's idol," Prestes informally told his supporters.[41] Some leftist intellectuals were disenchanted by what they viewed as Communist collaboration with a loathsome regime, while many working people and trade unionists now viewed Prestes less an alternative to Vargas than as one of Vargas's allies.[42] As a result Prestes began to take a harder line on the Estado Nôvo. The upcoming presidential elections, he declared, would not guarantee the real "democratization of the country" since the constitutional amendment of February 1945 implied the recognition of the charter of the Estado Nôvo of 1937. The way forward, Prestes concluded, lay in nullifying the 1937 constitution and establishing a freely elected Constituent Assembly.[43]

The links between Prestes and Vargas, his former jailer, in 1945 have long been a subject of heated debate. Were they the result of a prearranged deal by which Prestes received his freedom in exchange for his support? Was this a case of two totalitarians brought together by their xenophobic nationalism and hatred of liberal democracy? Or was this coalition merely the Brazilian representation of a general policy directive of world communism? Lastly, was the deal a sellout by the Communists of their revolutionary calling?

With so much passion invested in the debate, it might seem less than satisfying to say that the links stemmed from the practical needs and congruent goals, however short range, of these two politicians and the urban masses they sought to lead. Both men had a common interest in overturning the political scenario dictated by the conspiracies among the elites in early 1945. Citing the "manifest disinterest" of the people, Prestes rejected the candidacies of Gomes and Dutra that were both built "from the top down" around a candidate rather than a party or a program. Prestes shared with Vargas certain nationalist prescriptions for Brazil's future, and both leaders were seeking to awaken the sleeping giant in Brazil—its people. Vargas was confident dealing with the Communists because, as he informed Adolph Berle, the U.S. ambassador, the masses supported him rather than Prestes and the Communist party.[44] Moreover, the support of Prestes would assist Vargas in gaining access to certain urban constituencies, labor in particular. Friendly relations with his regime's most persecuted opponent would further help to neutralize the "fascist" label that was the president's chief liability in 1945. Making contact with the Communists was less hazardous at this point than at any previous moment. After all, the U.S. ambassador himself had received Prestes in April, and photographs of the two men on the balcony of the embassy appeared to symbolize the newfound respectability of the Communists.

The cooperation between the two men, who never met personally, was a radical departure in Brazilian politics, but it fell far short of a true alliance. No Communist was allowed to speak at a *getulista* rally, and none of the PTB leaders appeared at the mass events and functions sponsored by the Communists. Conducted at arms length through intermediaries, the relationship was a matter of parallel action rather than formal agreements.[45] In an interview in August 1946 Prestes denied meeting with or entering into any formal agreement with Vargas. "The policies of Vargas and the CP," he explained, simply "ran along parallel lines. . . .Vargas was against a military coup because it would overthrow him, and the CP [was] against [it] because it would probably be aimed at them first. The army was primarily in the hands of fascist elements that hated the PCB."[46]

Vargas also set the terms under which the Communists operated. The Communists enjoyed an ambiguous status in that they were allowed to campaign but as yet had no legal standing to do so, at least until 27 October 1945, only two days before Vargas was ousted. For several months the Communist party's application for legal standing had been on hold on the grounds that the electoral legislation of May 1945 banned parties "whose programs violate the democratic principles, or the fundamental rights of man defined in the constitution." In this way throughout mid-1945 the initiative remained with the president, who kept the fate of the Communists in his own hands.

Vargas formally reentered the political scene in mid-1945 by means of the "We want Getúlio!" movement known as *queremismo*. The idea that Vargas himself might become a third presidential candidate first surfaced in late May in the president's home state of Rio Grande do Sul. But the appearance of *queremismo* as an organized movement was delayed until late July following the creation of a committee in Rio de Janeiro. Within days the organization spread to São Paulo, with employees of the ministry of labor taking a prominent part.[47]

In August 1945 *queremismo* burst onto the scene amidst large demonstrations of workers in the cities. At first the chief of police in Rio de Janeiro refused to grant the *queremistas* permission to hold marches and rallies, but the ban ended quickly following intercession from above. Addressing one of the *queremista* rallies in Rio de Janeiro on 30 August, Vargas hailed "the protest of the people" as a response to the "invective" of his opponents. His enemies, he declared, were those who, "living in abundance, [did] not wish to pay the men who work just payment for their labor."[48] The "laboring man," Vargas continued in a departure from his usual emphasis on the links between the state and the workers, was "no longer dependent on his boss or the state."[49]

The discourse of Vargas was strikingly different from that of Gomes. Vargas addressed an audience he defined as those who "labor[ed] and produce[d] in the fields and the cities, in the workshops, offices, factories, on the railroads, on board ship, . . .behind the counters of banks and in the places where public functionaries work."[50] Gomes directed his appeal, by contrast, at "the class of magistrates, public functionaries, the military men, the middle class, small commerce, the employees in all branches of activities, salaried workers in general, and manual workers."[51]

The *queremistas* practiced mass urban politics on a national scale, combining spontaneous popular action with careful organization.[52] The movement had ample financial resources, and one of its striking innovations, which the UDN failed to match, was the use of radio on a large scale. In an effort to reach a broader audience among the literate and to circumvent the opposition from the press, the *queremistas* also placed paid advertisements in the printed media.[53]

The unruly demonstrations, in which tens of thousands of urban working people were now taking part, took the conservative groups by surprise and produced an atmosphere of resentment and unease.[54] It now appeared that a dictatorship set up to put an end to class struggle and social disorder was now disintegrating in the wake of the largest popular mobilization in a decade. Vargas was now distancing himself from the Estado Nôvo, leaving Dutra and the PSD to inherit its legacy. Yet, as Adolph Berle noted, *queremismo* was also driving Dutra and Gomes "into a common camp, and probably with them the Army."[55] Indeed the army chief of staff, Gen. Christovão Barcelos, warned that the military would "oppose any action or the extremisms of creed or ambition that would lead [Brazil] into anarchy."[56] The conservative classes were fearful of and revolted by this unruly popular explosion. Speaking in Bahia, Gomes, for example, quoted Rui Barbosa, one of the most prominent figures under the First Republic, who had spoken of the "unconscious masses" that "oscillate[d] between bondage and disorder."[57]

In August 1945 in an incident at the Rio Law School, a traditional cultural redoubt of the upper class, the *queremistas* stoned supporters of the UDN. The latter replied by denouncing the episode as "one of the saddest, most degrading and grotesque spectacles" in Brazil's history as a "civilized nation." The UDN denounced the part played by the Communists in these disorders but believed Vargas was instigating them. "The rabble," they alleged, was now being greeted in the presidential palace. Vargas, who was a member of the Brazilian elite, was betraying his own class to its enemies, and practicing "subversive" behavior, dubbed *comuno-queremismo.*[58]

Communism itself became a major issue in September, as Gomes began to classify the Soviet Union, a wartime ally to which Brazil had recently accorded diplomatic recognition, with the regimes of Hitler and Mussolini.[59] In Brazil, therefore, the theme of anticommunism appeared almost immediately after the surrender of Japan and long before the onset of the Cold War. Gomes was now using this issue among his military colleagues to achieve his original goal of deposing Vargas prior to the elections. To remain silent in the face of the resurgence of communism in Brazil, Gomes told a group of graduating military officers, was to fail to meet "unavoidable responsibilities." He denounced the "radical materialism" of communism that denied God and sought to establish a regime based on compulsion and coercion.[60]

Despite the UDN's allegations that *queremismo* was merely a mask for Vargas's desire to stay in office, it is clear that Vargas had no illusions in late

1945 that he would be able to cancel the elections as he had done in 1937.[61] With his loss of military backing, Vargas could not fail to see that he continued in office only at the sufferance of the armed forces led by General Dutra.

Dutra resigned as minister of war on 9 August 1945, but he had chosen his own successor over Vargas's opposition. Gen. Goés Monteiro, one of the military strongmen of the 1937 coup, accepted the post only on condition that the elections be held and that Vargas avoid "ties of any sort" with the Communists.[62] At this point Vargas could draw some comfort from recent events in Argentina, where the triumph of Juan Perón in the events of 17 October 1945 demonstrated the power of the masses. But in Argentina it was the army that had allowed the people to act in the way they did; likewise in Brazil Vargas now recognized that he survived in office thanks only to the army. Dutra's candidacy was secure as long as he maintained his firm grip on the military. In September and October 1945 he concentrated on warding off Vargas's probing in military and political circles. The Estado Nôvo's top military man did not favor a coup unless absolutely necessary, especially if it meant a weakening of PSD control over the government. Nor did he share Gomes's degree of concern about *queremismo*, which he called "a sentimental movement."[63]

Yet *queremismo* had clearly unsettled Vargas's opponents and restored his political initiative. Unleashing new forces in the political arena, the movement had altered the terms of debate by encouraging the emergence of a third popular camp in national politics, following Vargas and not his elite opponents. *Queremismo* also increased the president's leverage over his "official" candidate Dutra, who was reminded of his need for the votes of Vargas's urban supporters. While placing Vargas squarely back in the center of the succession process, *queremismo* had deepened the rift with traditional conservative elites, both civilian and military.

In late September Vargas's own ambitions received a further blow when Berle, the U.S. ambassador, issued remarks that were widely understood as hostile to his candidacy.[64] A diplomatic incident followed, but by this point Vargas appeared to recognize that he could not bridge the chasm between the old elite politics and the new popular politics he was creating. His main object, it now seemed, was to maintain a popular following pledged to his nationalist agenda. In a rally attended by around one hundred thousand people at the Palacio Guanabara on 3 October, an impassioned crowd urged

Vargas to stay on in office. Vargas now stated that he was not a candidate, but he warned against the "powerful reactionary forces" that were opposed to a "genuinely democratic process."[65]

On 10 October Vargas issued Decree 8,063, which added gubernatorial elections to those for the presidency in December. This measure antagonized Gomes's UDN, which was strongly opposed to local elections and some months earlier had succeeded in having them postponed. Yet this measure had no discernible impact on the military and the PSD, and it was not a major issue, as some have claimed, in the downfall of Vargas only seventeen days later.[66] The more important issues were that in October Gomes increased his standing in the military, while Dutra began to suspect that Goés Monteiro, the new minister of war, was himself scheming for the succession.[67]

But the proximate cause of the fall of Vargas was the issue of growing popular mobilization. On 26 October the police in both Rio de Janeiro and São Paulo canceled demonstrations planned by the supporters of Vargas and Prestes. The following day Vargas ordered his brother, Benjamin Vargas, to take over as chief of police in Rio, but the appointment was rejected in an emergency meeting of the generals. When Vargas refused to rescind the appointment, the military summarily deposed him. Dutra stood out among the leaders of the coup, but fearing Goés Monteiro he finally agreed to the proposal from Gomes that power be turned over to the chief justice of the Supreme Court, José Linhares. Immediately after the "coup that restored democracy," as it was called, the regime struck at the new popular forces, arresting leaders of the PTB and PCB throughout the country.

Twenty-nine October marked a moment of triumph for Gen. Eduardo Gomes, who had finally achieved his year-long goal of overthrowing Vargas and passing the government over to the judiciary. Linhares appointed members of the UDN to the cabinet, to senior military positions, as state interventors, and as local *prefeitos* (prefects). For Dutra the coup was less welcome but survivable. Although he soon came to regard the Linhares government as "totally hostile," one of his own followers, Macedo Soares, became the interventor in São Paulo, the nation's most populous state.[68]

"Getúlio Says": The Newfound Power of the People

Vargas appeared the great loser on 29 October. Despite his strong popular support—with talk of strikes, demonstrations, and armed resistance—and some backing still in the military, he had chosen not to resist the coup.[69] Yet Vargas knew that he had created a new political force that in the future would enable him to create a massive new constituency. Refusing to endorse Dutra, his betrayer, Vargas retired quietly to his ranch in Rio Grande do Sul, urging the PTB to "fight and survive." The leaders of the PTB debated whether to run a third candidate in the elections, but it was finally agreed that the party's "enormous numerical force" was matched by its equally "enormous weakness as an electoral organization." As a result an alliance with the PSD in the December election, many argued, would facilitate the future consolidation of the PTB.[70]

The Communist party gained legal recognition only two days before the coup and quickly reemerged afterward following a brief outbreak of repression under the new government. On 3 November the leaders of the Communist party declared that the coup had only "apparently" been directed against Vargas; its real targets were "the people and democracy, . . .the proletariat and its organizations."[71] The followers of Prestes nonetheless pledged their support for the democratic elements in the government while criticizing Vargas for "betraying the people" by refusing to resist the "fascists." But these were far more the sentiments of the party leadership than those of the working class itself, which condemned the coup.

The Communists then attempted to tap this popular mood and decided to support a non-Communist candidate for the presidency. On 18 November they announced the nomination of Yedo Fiuza, a former *prefeito* in Petrópolis who had been close to Vargas.[72] In a two-week whirlwind campaign the Communists brought thousands out into the streets to support their candidate.[73]

Although the coup had dealt the PSD's campaign a blow, the party's local machines were too deeply rooted to be successfully dislodged by a few appointed officials in the month remaining before the election. Yet Dutra's backers had lost certain advantages and faced the hostility of Vargas's supporters because of their candidate's participation in the coup. João Neves, one of the PSD's most perceptive leaders, recognized that Vargas had unleashed "unknown forces," whose full strength was "not yet revealed," and that those forces could make the difference between victory and defeat for his own party. He appealed to Vargas to support Dutra to "impede a return to the old, ingrained conservatism" represented by the UDN and to the "oligarchical system of the politics of the governors" against which they had both fought in 1930.[74]

On 21 November Dutra's PSD concluded a formal alliance. Pledging to support Vargas's and the PTB's existing social and labor legislation, Dutra undertook to appoint a labor minister agreeable to the PTB, and to appoint its members to the administration in accordance with their share of the vote. Exploiting the furor that followed Gomes's speech at Sorocaba on 22 November, Dutra went so far as to pledge action against employers who defrauded workers of their rights.[75] On 27 November Vargas finally issued the message the PSD so badly needed. In a short text distributed in millions of copies under the title "Getúlio Says," Vargas called for an end to recriminations and blamed the coup on "errors and confusions." "One cannot win without a struggle," he declared and he urged the poor, the workers, and the people to vote for Dutra.[76]

The election of 2 December 1945 vindicated Vargas's vision that something radically new had appeared in Brazilian politics. During the 1930s only 10 per cent of literate adults voted; in 1945 the proportion grew to 33 per cent in a total population that was 50 per cent literate.[77] In the country's urban and industrial heartland, voting increased by between four and five times, and for the first time São Paulo replaced Minas Gerais as the state with the largest vote. Newly registered voters in the major cities of Rio and São Paulo also had a major role; although it represented only 23 percent of the population of the state, the city of São Paulo provided 44 per cent of the total vote.[78]

The final election tally was Dutra with 56 percent; Gomes, 35 percent; and Fiuza, 10 percent. It was therefore Gomes, and the liberal variant of old-fashioned oligarchical politics he represented, who ultimately became the great loser of 1945. Backed by the local machines of the PSD, Dutra assembled the winning combination by forging an alliance with the new urban forces represented by the PTB and by gaining the last-minute endorsement from Vargas. Dutra's victory was therefore unequivocal proof of the strength of Vargas's personal appeal.[79] The surprisingly strong vote for the Communists in 1945 also served to dissuade the military conservatives in Dutra's administration from carrying out their plan to strip Vargas of his political rights. If they did so, they realized, they risked driving the workers into the hands of an even more dangerous enemy: the Communists of Luis Prestes.[80]

Getúlio Vargas was aptly described as "the great elector" of 1945. Elected a senator by both São Paulo and Rio Grande do Sul, another nine states elected him a federal deputy. The PTB made a strong showing in its first-ever election, becoming the nation's third largest party. When Vargas declined the senatorship in São Paulo, the position fell to his former minister of labor, Marcondes Filho, the chief architect of the PTB.[81]

For Prestes too these elections marked a moment of personal triumph. Fiuza, the candidate he backed, had gathered 10 percent of the national vote, and the PCB emerged as the fourth largest party, a major accomplishment for an organization without financial resources, with fewer than a thousand members, and with no previous history of electoral successes. In a tribute to his own personal popularity Prestes received the second-highest number of votes in the country; he was elected senator by the Federal District (Rio de Janeiro), a federal deputy by three states, and an alternate deputy (*suplente*) in another three.[82]

In the highly industrialized state of São Paulo Dutra gained 58 percent of the vote, followed by Gomes with 28 percent and Fiuza with 14 percent; but in the industrial city of São Paulo Fiuza gained 26 percent of the vote against Gomes's 24 percent; and in the port city of Santos Fiuza won first place with 42 percent against Dutra with 32 percent and Gomes with 26 percent. In Santos a Communist dockworker, Osvaldo Pacheco, was elected a federal deputy.[83] In most major urban centers the PTB and the PCB received an absolute majority of the votes cast for federal deputy.

Thus working-class voters, who were participating in elections for the first time, signaled the coming of a new day in Brazilian politics. In a book published in 1945 the distinguished *antigetulista* jurist and socialist politician, Hermes Lima, recognized the full extent of the transition. Throughout Brazilian history, he observed, politics had been the exclusive preserve of the "educated classes," which viewed their dominance as a reflection of their cultural superiority. Until now there had always been a "fear of the people in public life," because the upper classes believed that the people lacked the education to exercise their rights and would quickly fall "into the camp of demagogy. . .or anarchy." Better the people remain, as he put it, "a species of sleeping volcano."[84]

In mid-1945, with the mass enfranchisement and mobilization of working-class people, new forces were unleashed that, despite a conservative counterattack in the late 1940s, could no longer be controlled in the manner of the past. Whether they were supporters of Vargas, Dutra, Gomes, or Prestes, contemporary observers correctly saw 1945 as proof of the forceful and irreversible entrance of urban working people into national political life.[85]

Notes

An earlier version of this essay was published in John D. French, *The Brazilian Workers' ABC: Class Conflict and Alliances in Modern São Paulo*. Copyright © 1992 by the University of North Carolina Press. Used by permission of the author and publisher.

1. Cf. Thomas E. Skidmore, *Politics in Brazil, 1930–1964*. New York: Oxford University Press, 1967, 58–59.

2. Armando de Salles Oliveira, *Diagrama de uma situação política: Manifestos, políticos do exilio*. São Paulo: Editora Renascenca, 1945, 95–96.

3. Salles, *Diagrama*, 23.

4. Cf. Helio Silva, *1945: Por que depuseram Vargas*. Rio de Janeiro: Civilização Brasileira, 1976, 113.

5. Ibid., 113–16, 260–63.

6. Cf. Osvaldo Trigueiro do Vale, *O General Dutra e a redemocratização de 1945*. Rio de Janeiro: Civilização Brasileira, 1978, 40–42; Silva, *1945*, 138. John W. F. Dulles refers to a conspiracy between Goés Monteiro and Dutra in late 1944. Cf. John W. F. Dulles, *Vargas of Brazil*. Austin: University of Texas Press, 1967, 255.

7. Cf. Trigueiro, *Dutra*; Stanley Hilton, "The Overthrow of Getúlio Vargas in 1945: Intervention, Defense of Democracy, or Political Retribution?" *Hispanic American Historical Review* 67, no. 1 (February 1987), 1–37.

8. Cf. Trigueiro, *Dutra*, 86, 94, 65–66.

9. Azis Simão, *Sindicato e estado (Suas relaciones na formação do proletariado de São Paulo)*. São Paulo: Atica, 1981, 40.

10. Getúlio Vargas, A *nova política do Brasil*. Vol. 11, *O Brasil na guerra*. Rio de Janeiro: José Olympio, 1947, 38, 27, 58, 56.

11. Cf. Vargas, *Nôva política*, 40.

12. Vargas, *Nôva política*, 37, 123–25.

13. Russell Landstrom, *The Associated Press News Annual: 1945*. New York: Rinehart and Company, 1946, 280.

14. Vargas, *Nôva política*, 141–51.

15. Ibid., 11: 19.

16. Ibid., 11: 125, 18.

17. Cf. Edgard Carone, A *terceira república (1937–1945)*. São Paulo: DIFEL, 1976, 453.

18. Cf. Angela de Castro Gomes, A *invenção do trabalhismo*. São Paulo: Vertice/ IUPERJ, 1988, 305.

19. Vargas, *Nova Política*, 103; Castro Gomes, *Invenção*, 296–97.

20. Cf. Boris Fausto, ed., *Historia geral da civilição brasileira*. Vol. 4. São Paulo: DIFEL, 1984, 236; Levi Carneiro, *Voto dos analfabetos*. Petrópolis: Vozes, 1964.

21. On the political role of women see John D. French and Mary Lynn Pedersen,

"Women and Working-Class Mobilization in Postwar São Paulo, Brazil, 1945–1948," *Latin American Research Review* 24, no. 3 (Fall 1989), 99–125.

22. See Castro Gomes, *Invenção*, 297–300, for a discussion of the secret Plan B drawn up in December 1943 in preparation for the impending postwar transition.

23. Eduardo Gomes, *Campanha da libertação*. São Paulo: Livraria Martins Editora, n.d., 331–35.

24. Cf. Vargas, *Nôva política*, 148.

25. Trigueiro, *Dutra*, 86, 110.

26. Gomes, *Campanha*, 115, 336–44.

27. Cf. João Almino, *Os demócratas autoritarios*. São Paulo: Brasiliense, 1980, 39.

28. Gomes, *Campanha*, 278, 46, 278.

29. Ibid., 278, 48, 266.

30. Ibid., 46, 30–33, 45, 51–52.

31. Ibid., 336, 342.

32. Cf. Maria Victoria de Mesquita Benevides, *A UDN e o Udenismo: Ambiguidades do liberalismo brasileiro (1945–1965)*. Rio de Janeiro: Paz e Terra, 1981, 45. This issue is also discussed in *Folha da Manhã*, 12 December 1945.

33. Gomes, *Campanha*, 16–17.

34. On the Socialists see Edgard Carone, ed., *Movimento operario no Brasil*. Vol. 2. São Paulo: DIFEL, 1979, 3–16.

35. For the Sorocaba speech see Carone, *Movimento*, 280–85.

36. Almino, *Demócratas*, 36–37.

37. Ibid.

38. For the text of this speech see Edgard Carone, *O PCB (1943–1964)*. Vol. 2. São Paulo: DIFEL, 1982, 25–40.

39. On the life and fate of Olga Benario Prestes see Fernando Morais, *Olga*. 14th ed. São Paulo: Alfa-Omega, 1987.

40. Carone, *PCB*, 2, 36–37.

41. Maria Andrea Loyola, *Os sindicatos e o PTB*. Petrópolis: Vozes/CEBRAP, 1980, 60.

42. Carone, *PCB*, 2, 40–57.

43. Silva, *1945*, 195–96; Carone, *PCB*, 56.

44. Adolph A. Berle, *Navigating the Rapids, 1918–1971*. New York: Harcourt Brace Jovanovich, 1973, 551, which recounts an interview with Vargas on 1 October 1945.

45. Ibid., 529–30.

46. Interview with Robert Alexander, 27 August 1946. Private archive of Robert Alexander.

47. Cf. Valentina da Rocha Lima, ed., *Getúlio: Uma historia oral*. Rio de Janeiro: Record, 1986, 155–56. *Queremismo* is discussed, but very sketchily, in Arnaldo Spindel, *O Pártido Comunista na genese do populismo*. São Paulo: Simbolo, 1980, 59–67.

48. Silva, *1945*, 136–37.

49. Vargas, *Nôva política*, 103.

50. Silva, *1945*, 136.

51. Gomes, *Campanha*, 40.

52. Castro Gomes, *Invenção*, 308–14.

53. John D. French, "The Communications Revolution: Radio and Working-Class Life and Culture in Postwar São Paulo, Brazil." Paper presented at the Third Latin American Labor History Conference, Yale University, April 1978; Elysabeth Carmona and Geraldo Leite, "Radio Povo e poder: Subserviencia e paternalismo," in *Populismo y communicação*, edited by José Marques de Melo. São Paulo: Cortez, 1981, 125–34; Silva, *1945*, 302; Trigueiro, *Dutra*, 178.

54. Cf. Lima, *Getúlio*, 157.

55. Berle, *Navigating*, 548; Almino, *Democratas*, 57.

56. Trigueiro, *Dutra*, 115, 145.

57. Gomes, *Campanha*, 57.

58. The latter term was used by the UDN in São Paulo in campaign advertisements; see also Trigueiro, *Dutra*, 120–22.

59. Gomes, *Campanha*, 81, 108–10,

60. Ibid., 148–50.

61. Luiz Vergara, *Fui Secretario de Getúlio Vargas: Memorias dos anos de 1926–1954*. Rio: Globo, 1960, 158.

62. Trigueiro, *Dutra*, 107–14; Lourival Coutinho, *O General Goés depoe*. Rio de Janeiro: Coelho Branco, 1956, 415–18.

63. Trigueiro, *Dutra*, 123, 144–45.

64. Silva, *1945*, 214–23; Berle, *Navigating*, 553; Bryce Wood, *The Dismantling of the Good Neighbor Policy*. Austin: University of Texas Press, 1985, 122–25 .

65. Vargas, *Nôva política*, 185–92; Trigueiro, *Dutra*, 151.

66. Cf. Coutinho, *O General*, 437; Trigueiro, *Dutra*, 151–54.

67. Trigueiro, *Dutra*, 154–64.

68. Ibid., 166–69.

69. Cf. Denis de Moraes and Francisco Viana, eds., *Prestes: Lutas e autocriticas*. Petropólis: Vozes, 1982, 109.

70. Silva, *1945*, 292–93, 204, 305–6, 309; Castro Gomes, *Invenção*, 315–18.

71. Carone, *PCB*, 2, 60–61.

72. Moraes and Viana, *Prestes*, 111.

73. Ibid.

74. Silva, *1945*, 297, 308.

75. Ibid., 312, 317–18; Trigueiro, *Dutra*, 177–80.

76. Trigueiro, *Dutra*, 181–84; Silva, *1945*, 318–19.

77. Cf. Kenneth Erickson, "Populism and Political Control of the Working Class in Brazil." *Proceedings of the Pacific Coast Conference of Latin American Studies* 4 (1975), 126; Glaúcio Soares, *Sociedade e política no Brasil*. São Paulo: DIFEL, 1973, 41.

78. Tribunal Regional Eleitoral, São Paulo [hereafter cited as TRE SP]: Serviço Informática, "1945: Resultado final do número de eleitores devidamente inscritos." Unpublished document.

79. Castro Gomes, *Invenção*, 318.

80. Almino, *Demócratas*, 68–69.

81. Silva, 1945, 286–87.

82. Moraes and Viana, *Prestes*, 112.

83. For election results see TRE SP: Serviço Informática, "1945: Resultado final," and "Quadro demonstrativo da votação obtido no estado de São Paulo, pelos candidatos a Presidencia da República." Unpublished document, [29 December 1945].

84. Hermes Lima, *Notas da vida brasileira*. São Paulo: Brasiliense, 1945. Reprinted in Luis Washington Vita, ed., *Antologia do pensamento social e político no Brasil*. São Paulo: Grijalbo, 1945, 404–8.

85. John D. French, *The Brazilian Workers' ABC: Class Conflict and Alliances in Modern São Paulo*. Chapel Hill: University of North Carolina Press, 1992, 256–60, 268–69.

7 Peace in the World and Democracy at Home

The Chilean Women's Movement in the 1940s

Corinne Antezana-Pernet

The 1940s were a crucial decade in the history of the Chilean women's movement. The middle years of the decade marked the high point of women's mobilization in the struggle for female suffrage and social reforms. During these years a national federation of women's groups was active that held street demonstrations and congresses and drafted petitions to improve the status of women. But this activism lasted for only about three years, and it was followed by the movement's division and decline. Soon after national female suffrage was introduced in 1949, the women's movement lapsed into a passivity that was to last for almost twenty years.

The development of this movement was shaped by a national political culture that strongly emphasized political parties as well as by specific political events. In Chile, always a highly politicized nation, the influence of this culture became much more pronounced than elsewhere, in that most leading feminists, despite their claims to the contrary, were strongly involved in and affected by party politics.

Women's political activism and organizations reached an apogee in 1938–1946 during the administrations of the reformist Radical presidents that were supported by center-left coalitions. This period of class collaboration created a propitious climate for the articulation of women's demands and for the formation of a broad front of women's organizations to pursue them. From 1942 on, however, the Chilean government, although resting on the same coalition as immediately before, abandoned its programs for far-reaching social reform and replaced them by policies emphasizing economic growth. In this atmosphere, in which domestic conditions tended to discourage political activism, World War II acted as a necessary catalyst in the formation of a broad, ambitious women's movement committed to the defense of democracy and its extension to women. Similarly, the demise of the women's movement can be related to international trends. With the beginning of the Cold War and the sharp turn to the right of the Chilean government in 1947, the progressive wing of the women's movement came to be viewed as a political liability by the centrist and right-wing women's groups. They now began to exclude the leftist feminists. These internal conflicts eventually led to the dissolution of the women's movement.

Early Organization

The first women's organizations appeared in Chile after 1915 during a period of rapid social change. The rise of the middle and working classes, and their increasing political assertiveness, brought to an end the era of oligarchic rule by the landowning and mining aristocracy by the early 1920s.[1] The following decade was a period of considerable political instability characterized by several military interventions. Despite the frequent changes in government the new leaders attempted to solve the social and economic problems besetting Chile through social welfare programs and increased state intervention in the economy to speed up industrialization. These efforts persisted after "Chile [returned] to the security of traditional modes and formal democracy" in 1932, since the working- and middle-class parties most strongly advocating state intervention were now important participants in electoral politics.

Part and parcel of this transformation of Chilean society was the increased participation of women in the Chilean labor force, especially in the developing industries, the national bureaucracy, and education. In 1907, 22 percent of Chilean women were economically active, of whom more than 70 percent were engaged in service occupations, working as domestics, laundresses, or seamstresses.[2] The rest of the women workers were mainly classified as artisans or as agricultural workers. The number of professional women barely went above 1 percent of women employed.[3] In the next decade the number of seamstresses and laundresses declined markedly. By 1920, 43 percent of all working women worked in manufacturing, while the number of teachers and other professionals more than doubled.[4]

A decade later, women accounted for 20 percent of the Chilean labor force, and their share grew to more than 24 percent in 1940, remaining at that level until the 1960s.[5] Women's distribution in the work force, however, had changed quite dramatically. In 1940 only 33 percent of women were employed in personal services, while more than 40 percent worked in manufacturing. More than 6 percent of working women were now classified as professionals or technicians, 5 percent as office workers, and another 7 percent as salespersons. Women thus accounted for 45 percent of Chile's professionals (reflecting their predominance in education and nursing), 21 percent of office workers, and 26 percent of salespersons.[6] Particularly in the urban society, women had become a highly visible component of modernizing Chile's work force.

Despite these trends women remained legally subordinate to men, and traditional gender roles designating a woman's place as the home remained strongly ingrained. Married women, for instance, had no power over their own property. There were some practicing women lawyers in Chile from 1892 on, but it was only in 1925, when some of the legal restrictions against women were abolished, that women were allowed to testify in court.[7]

The early women's organizations represented a reaction against these conditions, and they placed particular emphasis on the education of women in preparation for a fuller and more active participation in politics. In the 1920s the early women's groups issued the first tentative petitions for women's enfranchisement, but they were all ignored. During the late 1920s the women's groups found themselves hindered by the curtailment of civil liberties under the military dictatorship of Gen. Carlos Ibáñez del Campo, who ruled until 1931.

The fall of Ibáñez in 1931, however, led to the reinstatement of civil liberties and the return of a democratic system. The women's groups, although still small, began to make swift progress in their quest for civil and political rights. In 1933 a group of leading women, representing a broad spectrum of allegiances, established the Committee for Women's Rights (Comité Pro Derecho de las Mujeres). Among its members were Felisa Vergara, a Socialist leader, Amanda Labarca, an educator and member of the Radical party, and Elisa Doll de Díaz, an aristocratic member of the Conservative party.[8] In 1934 the committee persuaded Congress to grant women the vote in municipal elections.

Following this victory, differentiation and competition among the women's groups became more pronounced, and they began to mirror the divisions and rivalries of the traditional political parties. After the reinstatement of democracy in 1932 the political forces as a whole realigned themselves "on an explicitly Left-Right ideological continuum."[9] The result was the extreme fragmentation of the party system and highly competitive party politics, and by 1936 Chile had thirty-six political parties.[10] Henceforward it became essential for the various parties to form electoral alliances, but such alliances remained extremely unstable. During the 1930s and 1940s five parties commanded prominence: on the right were the two parties of the old elite—the Conservative party and the slightly more progressive Liberal party; the center was held by the middle-class, reformist Radical party; on the left the Socialists and the Communists competed for the support of the lower-middle and especially the working classes.

When the administration of Arturo Alessandri (1932–1938) became increasingly conservative and repressive, the reformist Radicals were driven closer to the Socialists and Communists, whose populist platforms enabled them to expand their popular support. In 1936 the center-left parties, along with a several small splinter parties, formed the Popular Front (Frente Popular), a coalition modeled on those in Spain and France that emerged as a result of the decision of the Comintern in 1935 to recommend that Communists form alliances with "bourgeois" parties to fight against fascism. In Chile, however, the chief objective of the Front was to combat the conservative elite.[11]

The Popular Front rapidly gained strong popular support through its slogan of "bread, roof, and overcoat." It elicited an "almost mystical" devotion among the common people and quickly became the "symbol of union. . .against oppression, union for achievements of all those things . . .[the masses] had always desired but were somehow always denied."[12] In 1938 the Popular Front achieved a narrow victory when the Radical Pedro Aguirre Cerda defeated the candidate of the conservative alliance in the presidential elections.

But the unity of the Popular Front was mostly a fiction, and there was heated competition among its various component parties. Rivalries between Socialists and Radicals were so intense that the two groups were continually sabotaging each others' activities; meanwhile, the Communists became increasingly critical of the Socialists.[13] Following the death of the popular Aguirre Cerda in 1941, the Front was formally abandoned, although the

Communists and Socialists continued to collaborate with the Radicals to gain access to government and administrative posts.

These conflicts found reflection in the competition among the representatives of different parties for control over the women's movement. During this period, however, women of different party backgrounds employed a similar feminist discourse that tended to obscure the competition among the parties. Like their early counterparts in Britain or the United States, Chilean feminists drew on traditional assumptions concerning women to justify the increasing participation of women in public life. The participation of women was thus portrayed as an extension of the woman's role as a mother: "generous by nature, the woman will extend her giving and capable hands wherever there is pain, injustice, a wound to be cared for, toward any human being in need of help."[14] On the assumption that women had special sensibilities and were morally superior to men, Chilean feminists claimed that the increased involvement of women in the public sphere would help the fight against political corruption and raise moral standards throughout the country in general.

A second strain of the Chilean women's movement emphasized that growing female civic participation was crucial to the creation of a modern and democratic state. Echoing John Stuart Mill, whose writings were well-known in progressive circles, Amanda Labarca, the first female tenured professor in Chile and a prominent member of the Radical party, argued for women's rights on the grounds that "the general progress of the country . . .cannot advance without the collaboration of women."[15] Extending the vote to women would "widen the foundations of democracy and the elected parliaments would represent the popular will much more effectively."[16] At the same time, women needed to become more involved in working outside the home to further economic and particularly industrial development, but without, of course, neglecting their duties as housewives and mothers.[17] These two lines of feminist argumentation were not mutually exclusive, and both were used by organizations with differing goals and political orientations.

In the 1930s there were numerous women's organizations in Chile, but multiplicity did not always help the cause since the various groups frequently worked independently and in direct competition with one another. Equally, many groups were short-lived, which again made concerted action difficult. Operating separately from each other, the women's groups failed to create a climate of opinion favoring their objectives.

One of the most important groups, which commanded a particularly prominent role during the 1940s, was the MEMCH (Movimiento Pro Emancipación de la Mujer Chilena). Founded in 1935 by members of the Association of University Women (Asociación de Mujeres Universitarias), MEMCH was designed as "an institution for struggle, one that would mobilize, be militant."[18] Under the leadership of Elena Caffarena, a lawyer and Communist, the organization pursued the economic, legal, and even the biological emancipation of women by advocating the use of contraceptives and limited abortions.[19] MEMCH called for an attack on poverty, prostitution, and the high rate of infant mortality and lobbied for equal wages and work opportunities for women. MEMCH was well organized and quickly established branches in many parts of the country. In the cities the organization led street demonstrations and workshops for women and petitioned the government for reform, sometimes successfully. An example of these activities was the requests by MEMCH to the foreign minister to include women in the delegations to international conferences. On one occasion, in response to a MEMCH petition, Aguirre Cerda vetoed legislation to allow only unmarried and widowed women to be employed in the state-owned post and telegraph company and to establish a 20 percent maximum for female employees.[20]

At the other end of the ideological spectrum stood the National Action of Women (Acción Nacional de las Mujeres de Chile), a conservative organization under the leadership of Adela Salas de Edwards. The National Action supported female suffrage in the hope that women would use their political power as a stabilizing force and to introduce limited welfare measures for the poor to arrest what they perceived as the moral decay of the population. The National Action vehemently attacked the programs advanced by MEMCH as "aberrations of sick brains" and warned women to stay away from an organization that adhered to "Communist principles."[21]

Between these two extremes there were many middle-of-the-road organizations, some oriented toward female suffrage, others toward social reform. For example, the Women's Civic party, founded in 1922, surfaced again in the late 1930s under the leadership of the prominent feminist Radical, Amanda Labarca, and published the magazine *Acción Femenina*. The magazine reported on the condition of women around the world, supported the campaigns of women candidates in municipal elections, and provided a forum for feminist ideas.

Wartime Growth of the Movement

Until around 1944 ideological and programmatic differences, and perhaps too inexperience, undermined efforts to achieve joint action, although before that date there was some collaboration among individuals. An example was the large exhibition "Women's Activities in Chile" held at the National Library in Santiago between December 1939 and January 1940. University women of all persuasions, such as the Radical Labarca and the Communist María Marchant, along with numerous artists and professionals, worked together in preparing the displays illustrating the history and the contributions of women in Chile.[22] Aguirre Cerda and some of his ministers were present at the opening ceremony, and the exhibition generated great publicity for women's issues. Public lectures and performances by local celebrities kept the publicity alive until the exhibition closed.[23]

Another event that helped to unite the members of different women's organizations occurred in August 1941 with the founding of a new Committee for Women's Rights under the leadership of María Correa de Irarrázaval, the president of the women's section of the Liberal party.[24] The sole purpose of this organization was to achieve political rights for women, a goal that women from diverse political backgrounds could agree on. Even though leftist women such as MEMCH leaders Marta Vergara, Angelina Matte, Clara Williams de Yunge, and María Ramírez worked on the committee, the participation of aristocrats such as the respected writer Inés Echeverría de L.,[25] Liberal Cleofas Torres, and Maria Correa de I. gave the committee a distinctive style of politics.[26] The small group met regularly in the conference room of the newspaper *El Mercurio* and used the social connections of its upper-class participants to win the ear of leading politicians. The appearance of the committee was timely, since in January 1941 Aguirre Cerda introduced a bill in Congress to grant women full voting rights in national elections.

Months later, however, the bill was still pending.[27] The political parties were reluctant to grant women the vote partly because they were uncertain which of them women's suffrage would favor and partly because they were unprepared for the task of recruiting women's support. At a rally in the Municipal Theater in Santiago in October 1941, Correa de I., who was seconded by Amanda Labarca and worker representative María Ramírez, appealed to the legislators to overcome their "selfish partisanship" and approve the legislation.[28]

Their efforts proved fruitless. The sudden illness and death of Aguirre Cerda in November 1941 left the country in a state of shock and confusion and launched the political parties on a frantic campaign for the forthcoming presidential election in January 1942.[29] The issue of the vote for women was quickly shelved, particularly as the new president, Juan Antonio Ríos Morales, a right-wing Radical, abandoned his predecessor's commitment to popular mobilization and social reform.

Following the failure of 1941, for the next few years the women's groups remained relatively inactive, and many women threw their energies into the work of the political parties. In an interview in 1943 Elena Caffarena complained that this focus on the parties had produced little progress on women's issues; strong independent women's organizations, she declared, were the "indispensable instrument" to advance the cause.[30]

In 1944 the women's movement began to achieve a new momentum, and there seemed little doubt that World War II stood out as a leading activating factor. Indeed the war proved an even more powerful mobilizing agent than the issue of the vote. Among leftist women the war tended to subdue the strong anti-imperialist sentiments of the 1930s. Vergara, one of the leaders of MEMCH, later explained that toward the end of the war she had no objections to representatives from the United States taking part in the Inter-American Commission of Women because "they fought against the Nazis, and [she] was on their side with all [her] heart."[31] In 1944 references to the war and the defense of democracy began to appear in great profusion in the speeches and writings of the leaders of the women's organizations.

The war supplied a set of new arguments to the supporters of women's rights and other social reforms. One common argument was that it was essential to enlist the support of the whole population, including that of women, in the struggle against fascism. Large numbers of women, declared the feminist leaders, were already gainfully employed, and they should now enter politics and broaden the base of democracy. "True democracy"—a democracy that included women—was portrayed as the panacea to deliver Chile and the world from fascism and to prevent future wars. Women, argued Amanda Labarca in 1944, must be active "in these bitter moments, at this bloody crossroads of Western culture," in the fight for "a world of peace, with democratic respect between big and small nations."[32]

At this point the women's movement attracted growing attention from the press and gained even greater impetus. Articles on the wartime contributions and activities of women both in Chile and in the outside world at least implicitly, and sometimes quite explicitly, questioned the rigidities of gender roles. The magazine *Zig-Zag*, for instance, featured an article in which "experts" asserted that women were as competent as men as workers in the war industries; *Ercilla* ran a piece lauding the efforts of Russian women, who it declared did all kinds of work and still remained sexually attractive.[33] The Chilean feminists, even the most radical among them, often issued the same claim: women could take part in the work force and in politics and still keep their looks and their appeal. They published articles that focused on the visible contributions by women, stressing their role as active citizens who merited full political rights.[34]

This publicity and propaganda had a galvanic impact. Even in the provincial rural areas women were organizing and following feminist leaders. In such far-off places as Coronel in the south and Tocopilla in the north, local MEMCH chapters organized celebrations for the 1944 International Women's Day.[35] In the city of Valdivia women established a Fraternal Union of Southern Women (Unión Fraternal de Mujeres Sureñas). Despite its ambiguous title the union led campaigns for the women's vote, better pay for women workers, and improved women's education. The president of the union declared that the war proved that the democratic nations could join together to defeat the "fanatics," adding that "in this moment of painful events the women of Valdivia want a place in the fight for a better and more humane world."[36]

The most important novelty of 1944, however, was the formation of a federation of women's organizations that quickly became the leading pressure group and instrument of mobilization. In early 1944 the veteran feminist Felisa Vergara, the Socialist who had been the president of the first Committee for Women's Rights in 1931, proposed a great celebration to mark International Women's Day.[37] The celebration took place on 23 March at the University of Chile. During the festivities and talks feminist leaders decided to organize a national congress of women. Vergara, María Garafulic, a member of MEMCH, and Luisa Vicentini, another leftist, undertook to organize the congress, which was to take place in October 1944.[38]

The National Congress of Women attracted more than five hundred delegates from all over the country. The agenda featured panels on such subjects as "The Constitution of the Family"; "Problems of Clothing, Nutrition, and Housing"; "The Protection of the Woman Worker" and "The Work of Children and Juveniles"; "The Unity of American Women"; and "International Problems." The delegates were also to debate and discuss the issues of divorce and the civil rights of women.[39]

The inauguration ceremonies and opening speeches at the congress proved a great success. But there were some difficult moments when it came to the election of a board of directors. The organizing committee had laid down the principle of "one woman, one vote," and the six women with the most votes were to become members of the board. This arrangement, the committee believed, was a democratic voting procedure that would allow minority groups some weight. When the congress was held, however, this procedure was overturned in favor of voting by lists. Subsequently, a list headed by Amanda Labarca that had been secretly assembled beforehand easily defeated by 194 to 78 votes a list headed by Felisa Vergara quickly improvised at the congress.[40]

What had happened was a prearranged strike of the well-organized Radicals and Communists against the Socialists and the splinter groups. *El Mercurio* wrote of a "Trojan horse" arriving at the congress, with the Radical and Communist contingents in its belly; the Communist *El Siglo* vaguely celebrated a "triumph of democracy" but omitted mention of the details of the procedural maneuver.[41] After the election around forty delegates walked out of the congress, including a workers' delegate who expressed her disappointment at the "unilateral, undemocratic current" in the assembly that failed to recognize the personal qualities of its organizers or the rights of minorities.[42]

The workshops held during the congress were less turbulent. Members of the congress resolved to fight for female suffrage in national elections. The women agreed to "repudiate all fascist regimes and to fight for the defense and strengthening of democracy." They called on the Chilean government to establish relations with the Soviet Union, to support the formation of the United Nations, and to nominate women as delegates at the International Peace Conferences.[43]

The Chilean press, with the exception of *El Siglo*, reported on the congress in superficial terms and dwelt patronizingly on the spectacles of women playing politics rather than on the substantive issues discussed and the resolutions taken. In the closing session of the congress the women agreed to "form an organization to propagate and publicize the resolutions of the congress and to attempt to carry them out." Women from all groups and social classes were invited to participate in this effort.[44] Following this agreement the FECHIF (Federación Chilena de las Instituciones Femeninas) was born, which incorporated 213 women's organizations from all over Chile.[45] Labarca became president of the organization, and the women on the directive board included María Correa de I., María Marchant, Graciela Mandujano, María Arancibia, María Aguirre, and Julieta Campusano.[46]

Despite the tensions surrounding its birth the creation of FECHIF provided a new impulse for the women's movement. The federation was particularly successful in organizing large demonstrations in the streets of Santiago, some of which attracted thousands of women. In another illustration of the central importance of World War II in the rise of the women's movement, by far the largest event organized by FECHIF was the great parade of early September 1945 to celebrate the return of peace. *Zig-Zag* reported that the speakers at this event (among them Labarca, Caffarena, and Correa de I.) "condemned the authoritarian regimes" (*"regímenes de fuerza"*) that brought armed conflict between the people.[47] Labarca depicted the parade as a commitment by Chilean women to "work united and untiringly for the consolidation of a just and lasting peace" through the protection of democracy and the abolition of "inequalities and hateful privileges."[48]

The concept of democracy that many activist women were advocating had a strong social content. Olga Poblete, a MEMCH member, argued that for Chile to be a true democracy its citizens needed not only political rights but also "opportunities for [individual] development" and "guarantees of a minimum of welfare." The famous journalist Lenka Franulic pointed out: "in Chile, there is no real democracy since the inequality of the classes is enormous."[49] In this way women's suffrage presented itself as an integral component of a far-reaching program of social reform.

The argument that involvement in public life was the way for women to improve their situation became the central theme in the celebration of the International Women's Day by FECHIF in 1946. During this event Irma Salas, a member of the Association of University Women, reported on the International Congress of Women in Paris in November 1945. Women had participated actively in the war effort, she declared, and this experience gave them new consciousness and self-confidence. Women had learned to join forces "to convert the principles of democracy into reality for women" and to overcome their subordinate position in society.[50]

As statements like these suggest, during the war feminist discourse underwent a sharp shift in emphasis. The earlier stress on traditional gender roles, and particularly motherhood, was now much less marked: women were now claiming to be full, equal citizens in possession of full rights and responsibilities in a democratic society. Labarca downplayed the role of the mother in the socialization of children, declaring unambiguously that "the predominant influence of the mother [on the child] is a poetic myth. Children are descendants of a couple. . . .we women are not the educators [*formadoras*] of humankind."[51]

Even so, some of the older rhetoric that portrayed women as morally superior and as purifying agents in politics still persisted. In one particularly emotional speech Labarca warned her audience that "Western civilization [was] playing its last card" and besought the women of Chile to "unite to help save it."[52] This more traditional approach that stressed the moral superiority of women was particularly marked in the Partido Femenino Chileno, the only women's political party to emerge during this period, which joined FECHIF in 1946. The founder of the Partido Femenino was María de la Cruz, a woman entering politics for the first time. De la Cruz, who was strongly influenced by Juan and Eva Perón in Argentina, put forward an idealistic platform stressing "justice and social harmony."[53] De la Cruz did not attempt to base the appeal of her party on the contributions of women to society and the economy but instead staunchly defended traditional gender roles and female attributes. She stressed and legitimated the "emotionality" of women, presenting it as a necessary counterpart to the "rationality" of men. Her party appealed strongly to the sense of solidarity among women that in her view was based on shared feelings. One of her slogans proclaimed: "men disagree because of ideas; women unite because of their feelings."[54] An outstanding orator, de la Cruz spoke at numerous rallies organized by FECHIF.

In addition to the moralizing rhetoric the women's organizations of this period employed other, more mundane techniques in the struggle for full political rights. In 1945 FECHIF led an energetic campaign to persuade leading senators to support a new bill to extend the vote to women. At a meeting held at the University of Chile, María Correa de I. insisted that all the party leaders, from right to left, supported women's right to vote.[55] On 21 June 1945 the bill was finally presented to the Senate. The measure won the support of numerous senators and was officially endorsed by five leaders in the Senate: Arturo Alessandri, the president of the Senate; Horacio Walker, a Conservative; Alfredo Rosendes, a Radical; Marmaduque Grove, a Socialist; and Elias Lafertte, a Communist.[56]

Some of the leaders of the movement were now convinced that the women's vote was close at hand, and they were already speculating on its likely impact on the next congressional elections in 1949. Elena Caffarena, however, warned against premature celebrations, arguing that although "no party want[ed] to stigmatize itself as anti-democratic" by openly rejecting the measure, the parties would nevertheless still try to obstruct it behind the scenes.[57] MEMCH now attempted to bring pressure on the government by rallying women behind the slogan "We women demand that the bill for female suffrage be approved in this legislative period."[58]

Caffarena's perceptions again proved accurate since it took the Senate until December 1946 to approve the bill, and two more years passed before the Chamber even began to discuss it. By this point the delaying tactics of the political parties were not the only problem facing the women's movement. Renewed ideological conflict and polarization in Chile that erupted in 1947 had severe adverse effects on FECHIF and the women's movement as a whole.

Conflict and Decline

Following the demise of the Popular Front in 1941, the rivalries between the parties of the left became intense. The Socialists and Communists, who were electorally weak on their own, continually competed to fashion alliances with the Radicals. During the 1940s, however, the Communists achieved some major electoral gains, and by 1947 they had increased their share of the national vote to 17 percent. In 1946 Gabriel González Videla, a right-wing Radical, was elected president with Communist support. He reciprocated by rewarding the Communists with cabinet posts, but the alliance did not last long. In August 1947 growing apprehensions among the Radicals at the recent electoral successes of the Communists, alongside new Cold War pressures from the United States, led to the expulsion of the Communists from the cabinet. Several Communist leaders were arrested, and the party newspaper, *El Siglo*, closed down.[59] These events coincided with the Inter-American Conference for the Maintenance of Continental Peace and Security in Rio de Janeiro. Chile was a signatory to this hemispheric defense pact and thereby became eligible for future military assistance from the United States.

As Francesca Miller has recently put it, following the Rio conference "the attention of the Inter-American diplomatic community shifted from social and economic reform to a focus on opposition to communism, a position embraced by governments throughout the hemisphere."[60] A year later, in September 1948, González Videla promulgated the "Law for the Defense of Democracy" known more popularly as the *ley maldita* (the law of damnation). It not only banned the Communist party and deleted its members from the electoral rolls but also led to increased levels of repression in general.[61]

The sharp turn to the right, and the heightened tensions among the political parties, had a decisive impact on the women's movement. Suddenly MEMCH and even many women activists in the Radical party found themselves on the far left of the political spectrum. In the climate that prevailed after late 1947 their slogans of "true democracy" and "social justice," although often merely echoes of the Perón regime in Argentina, appeared dangerously close to being denounced as subversive by the government.

MEMCH nevertheless maintained its leftist profile. In a treatise it submitted to the First Inter-American Congress of Women held in Guatemala City in August 1947, MEMCH criticized the plans for continental rearmament proposed in Rio and argued that the money would be better spent on the "rehabilitation of the people" in the form of schools, public works, and research centers for peace. The participants of the congress in Guatemala should "firmly repudiate the plans for the military collaboration of American countries. They [were] contrary to peace and to the sovereignty of the American peoples, and totally ignore[d] the economic, social, and cultural reality that these countries now confront."[62] Now that the war was over, anti-imperialism reemerged on the agenda as MEMCH deliberately distanced itself from the position of the Chilean government.

The resolutions of the women's congress followed closely the line of argument put forward by MEMCH. The first press release declared: "[the congress] has resolved in plenary session to denounce the hemispheric armament plan. . .and to insist that the costs of the arms program be used to support industry, agriculture, health, and education for our people."[63] In the Chilean press, however, the congress in Guatemala was largely ignored. *El Mercurio,* for instance, commented only on the declared opposition of the congress to atomic weapons. It then published a "letter of resignation" from the Costa Rican delegate, who complained the congress was "pro-Soviet" and ignored the threat that communism posed to the world.[64]

In contrast with MEMCH, FECHIF tried to adapt to the new environment in Chile by moving to the right. Conservative groups grew prominent in the organization, and the leftists were pushed into the background. Social reform and progressive politics were no longer on FECHIF's agenda. Hilda Mueller, a liberal who some years before had published traditionalist articles on women in *El Mercurio*, became editor of *La Orientación*, the magazine published by FECHIF.[65]

The tensions provoked by this shift to the right by FECHIF became visible in the Second National Congress of Women held in September 1947. At this point "true" democracy—the code expression for the alignment of the women's movement with social and educational reform—remained a prominent topic of discussion. But conflict arose concerning an invitation by a faction of FECHIF to González Videla to speak at the congress. According to Caffarena the invitation was issued without consultation with any of the member organizations.[66] During his speech the president caused more discontent when he accused the Communist press of seeking advantages for the Communist party by criticizing the extraordinary powers that González Videla had recently given himself.[67]

There were contrasting reports as to what exactly happened at this point. In one account these comments provoked "a temporary interruption" to the president's speech led by Communist sympathizers in the audience.[68] According to Olga Poblete, a member of MEMCH, González Videla was responding to a speech that expressed disillusionment with his government and hinted at the potential danger of popular discontent, with the remark that he would not hesitate to use the army to reestablish order should this become necessary. At this point, recalled Poblete, Elena Caffarena issued a loud vocal protest and then walked out of the hall with some forty other women in the midst of a general tumult.[69]

According to Caffarena and Poblete the resolutions adopted during the congress at first went unpublished and were then falsified to omit a resolution expressing opposition to Chile joining the Pact of Rio.[70] Shortly after the congress FECHIF expelled all the Communists from its ranks. MEMCH replied by withdrawing from FECHIF, thus leaving the umbrella organization without its mass base.[71] The expulsion of the Communists left the Radicals in control but deprived the FECHIF of experienced and prominent organizers such as Caffarena, Marchant, and Campusano. Subsequently, FECHIF dropped all its earlier demands with the exception of female national suffrage.

In late August 1947 Rosa Markmann, the wife of President González Videla, announced the creation of the National Association of Housewives (Asociación de las Dueñas de Casa), whose chief purpose was to prevent speculation in basic subsistence goods among producers, distributors, and retailers.[72] In addition, the government organized so-called Mothers' Centers (Centros de Madres) in different parts of the country that offered assistance and various services to working-class women.[73] Markmann then began to patronize a number of women's organizations and to express her support for female suffrage. In September 1948 she appeared at one of the events of FECHIF's "Pro-Women's Suffrage Week," assuring its participants that the president too favored women's suffrage.[74]

The activities of FECHIF during this "Pro-Women's Suffrage Week" illustrated the changing concerns and leadership of the organization. The women who were now prominent were far more conservative than the activists of earlier years. Among them were the new president of FECHIF, Ana Figueroa, a Radical who was closely connected to González Videla; María de la Cruz and Mimi Brieba de A. from the Feminine party; and Clara Williams de Yunge, who was secretary of Markmann's Association of Housewives. According to Caffarena there was a contest for the presidency of FECHIF between Labarca and Figueroa, but Figueroa had the decisive support of González Videla.[75] Instead of holding mass street rallies, FECHIF now invited participants to tour the graves of prominent Chilean women, visit maternity wards with gifts for newborn babies, and attend tea parties in big Santiago hotels.[76]

In a festive public event in January 1949 González Videla signed the law that gave Chilean women the right to vote in national elections. But for some the celebration left a bitter taste: Caffarena, who had actually written the legislation, along with other leftist leaders, were conspicuously absent from the banquets and receptions.[77] A few days after signing the law González Videla attempted to ensure that this "extension of democracy" would remain politically safe by purging Communists and other "subversive" women from the electoral registers. The authorities then began making life difficult for MEMCH by issuing a last minute ban on the workshops organized for the International Women's Day in 1949.[78] FECHIF was now plagued by new internal conflicts, and within less than a year of the enfranchisement of women both organizations had disappeared from the public arena.

The eventual collapse of this formerly strong women's movement was due to several factors. From 1947 on the women of leftist inclination, who had pushed for social reform and continuing militant action, found themselves increasingly marginalized. Women from the center and the right, who led the women's movement from late 1947, by this point had only one objective: the vote. When this objective was achieved, the movement quickly faded.

By the early 1950s the only sizable women's organization that remained was de la Cruz's Women's party with twenty-thousand members, and in 1952 María de la Cruz became the first female senator in Chile.[79] But this attempt to create an independent women's movement also failed eventually. Under fire for her sympathies toward Peronism, and tainted by accusations of smuggling watches into Chile, de la Cruz was expelled from the Senate in 1953 even though an investigating commission found her innocent of the charges. De la Cruz retired disillusioned, and her party immediately disintegrated.[80] The long silence that would last until the late 1960s had begun.

Conclusion

The development of the women's movement ran in striking parallel with that of Chilean politics in general. In the 1930s the broader struggle between the old elite and the center-left groups found reflection in the emergence of the National Action and MEMCH. In the early 1940s the center left emerged dominant in both national politics and in the women's movement. Equally, the shift to the right after 1947 manifested itself in the women's groups, culminating in the expulsion of the Communists from FECHIF and the taming of the organization.

The Chilean women's movement failed to achieve its high-sounding goals of peace in the world and democracy at home. Nevertheless, during the 1940s Chilean women achieved some substantial gains. The propaganda of the feminists made it virtually impossible for the politicians to oppose women's suffrage openly. Women drafted the legislation to change the electoral laws and persuaded key senators to support it. The enfranchisement of women was not the accomplishment of González Videla, since the measure had been pending in congress for some time before he became president. The president accepted the inevitable and tried to exploit it for his own purposes.

Conditions in Chile had a major part in shaping the political history of women in this period. Rivalries between different parties weakened the women's movement and eventually contributed to its rapid decline. The fear of what women's voting rights would bring proved the main factor in delaying the measure until 1949. At the same time, however, the development of the women's movement was closely related to the current of events outside Chile. First, the formation of a broad front of women's organizations coincided with Chile joining the Allies. The political atmosphere engendered by the war enabled the women's organizations to push their demands when the reformist currents represented by the Popular Front had largely disappeared. Indeed World War II served to mobilize women to a far greater extent than anything before it, including the Great Depression. Second, the beginning of the Cold War and the ban on Communists it provoked in Chile had devastating effects on women's activism. In sum, international conditions strongly influenced the formation and the dynamics of the Chilean women's movement in the 1940s, shaped its ideological directions, and initiated the process that led to its rapid dissolution at the end of the decade.

Notes

1. Paul W. Drake, *Socialism and Populism in Chile, 1932–1952.* Urbana: University of Illinois Press, 1978, 47.
2. Felicitas Alvarado Klimpel, *La mujer chilena: El aporte femenino al progreso de Chile.* Santiago: Editorial Andres Bello, 1962, 150.
3. Ibid.
4. Ibid., 151.
5. Alieto Aldo Guadagni, *La fuerza de trabajo en Chile, 1930–1960.* Santiago: Universidad de Chile, 1961, 56.
6. República de Chile, Dirección de Estadísticas y Censos. *Cifras comparativas de los censos de 1940 y 1952 y muestra del censo de 1960.* N.p., n.d., 9 (my pagination).
7. See Office of Inter-American Affairs, Research Division, Social and Geographic Section, *The Status of Women in Chile.* Washington, D.C., 1944, 1–5.
8. Georgina Durand, *Mis entrevistas: Escritores, artistas, y hombres de ciencia de Chile.* Vol. 1. Santiago: Editorial Nascimiento, 1943, 199.
9. Brian Loveman, *Chile: The Legacy of Hispanic Capitalism.* 2d ed. New York: Oxford University Press, 1988, 227.
10. See Sergio Bizarro, *Historical Dictionary of Chile.* 2d ed. Metuchen, N.J., London: Scarecrow Press, 1987, 400.
11. See John Stevenson, *The Chilean Popular Front.* Philadelphia: University of Pennsylvania Press, 1942, 69; Loveman, *Chile,* 241–42.
12. Stevenson, *Popular Front,* 72.
13. Ibid., 101–5.
14. Isabel Morel (Delia Ducoing de Arrate), *Charlas femeninas.* N.p.: Unión Femenina de Chile, 1937, 58. The book is a collection of the weekly columns she wrote for *El Mercurio.*
15. Interview with Labarca by Georgina Durand in Durand, *Mis entrevistas,* 226.

16. Amanda Labarca, *Feminismo contemporáneo*. Santiago de Chile: Ediciones Zig-Zag, 1947, 148.

17. This view is also advanced by contemporary writers Amanda Hermosilla Aedo, *La mujer en la vida economica*. Santiago: Soc. Imp. y Lito. Universo, 1936, and Luciano Pinto, *Como arreglar este pais*. Santiago: Imprenta Nascimento, 1949.

18. Interview with Elena Caffarena in María Angelica Meza, *La otra mitad de Chile*. Santiago: CESOC, 1986, 49.

19. *MEMCH Antología: Para una historia de movimiento femenino en Chile*. 2d ed. N.p., n.d., 14. The prologue of the first edition was dated August 1982.

20. Other petitions concerned equal work opportunities for women and working conditions of minors. See *MEMCH Antología*, 21–22, 25, 30–31, 71.

21. *El Mercurio*, 7 September 1935. *El Mercurio*, of liberal orientation, was the largest newspaper in Santiago.

22. Meza, *La otra mitad*, 50–51.

23. *El Mercurio*, 15, 16 December 1939; 2, 12 January 1940.

24. María Correa de Irarrázaval was described as an "aristocrat" by the magazine *Ercilla* (5 June 1945). Her good relations with the Edwards family publishing house, which published the *Mercurio*, corroborate this description.

25. Echeverría published under the pseudonym "Iris" and was well known for her novels *La hora de queda* (1918), *Entre dos mundos* (1918), and *Cuando mi tierra fue moza* (1943).

26. Cf. *El Mercurio*, 17 August 1941.

27. *El Mercurio*, 20 August, 6 October 1941.

28. *El Mercurio*, 6 October 1941.

29. Stevenson, *Popular Front*, 117–19.

30. Durand, *Mis entrevistas*, 199.

31. Marta Vergara, *Memorias de una mujer irreverente*. Santiago: Editora Nacional Gabriela Mistral Ltda., 1974, 237.

32. Labarca, *Feminismo contemporáneo*, 136.

33. *Zig-Zag*, 23 February 1945; *Ercilla*, 2 July 1946.

34. Amanda Labarca and Elena Caffarena in particular stood out as such writers, in *El Mercurio*, *La Opinión*, *Ercilla*, and *Zig-Zag*.

35. *El Siglo*, 7, 8, 23 March 1944.

36. *Ercilla*, 20 November 1945.

37. Amanda Labarca in *El Siglo*, 2 November 1944.

38. Ibid. Vicentini later became a member of the Women's Union, a last attempt of the left to hold up an independent women's group in the early 1950s. Cf. Klimpel, *Mujer chilena*, 245. The book is a valuable source since it lists women active in many fields. It is flawed, however, by blatant misinformation regarding some women's organizations that appears to be politically motivated.

39. *El Siglo*, 28 October 1944; *Ercilla*, 10 October 1944. The congress received most coverage from *El Siglo*, the organ of the Communist party. It was also covered extensively by Luis Hernández Parker, who wrote for *Ercilla*. His frequent articles

about women's activities are tinged by a certain paternalism, but he seems to have been a supporter of women's rights.

40. *Ercilla,* 31 October 1944.

41. *El Mercurio,* 1 November 1944; *El Siglo,* 1 November 1944.

42. The participation of working women merited a picture in *Ercilla,* with the caption "Authentic workers leaving the Municipal Theater." *Ercilla,* 31 October 1944.

43. *El Siglo,* 2 November 1944.

44. Ibid.

45. *El Mercurio,* 5 November 1944.

46. *El Mercurio,* 8 November 1944. The Liberals were: Correa de I., Aguirre; Radicals: Labarca, Arancibia; Communists: Marchant, Campusano.

47. *Zig-Zag,* 13 September 1945.

48. The speech was reprinted in Labarca, *Feminismo contemporáneo,* 110–14.

49. *Zig-Zag,* 26 July 1945.

50. *El Mercurio,* 11 March 1946.

51. *Zig-Zag,* 26 July 1945.

52. Labarca, *Feminismo contemporáneo,* 120.

53. The directory board of the Feminine party included Georgina Durand, the journalist whose interviews have been repeatedly cited in this paper, and Felicitas Klimpel. Klimpel and de la Cruz became politically active again in the early 1970s as organizers of the famous marches of the "empty pots," women's protests against the leftist Allende government.

54. *Ercilla,* 21 January 1947.

55. "They want to be representatives and senators," proclaimed the headline. *Ercilla,* 5 June 1945.

56. *Ercilla,* 19 June 1945; *Zig-Zag,* 5 July 1945.

57. *Zig-Zag,* 5 July 1945.

58. Quoted from a flyer distributed at a rally in May 1946. In Paz Covarrubias, "El movimiento feminista chileno," in *Chile: Mujer y sociedad,* edited by Paz Covarrubias and Rolando Franco. Santiago: UNICEF, 1978, 638.

59. Carmelo Furci, *The Chilean Communist Party and the Road to Socialism.* London: Zed Books, 1984, 39.

60. Francesca Miller, "Latin American Feminism and the Transnational Area," in *Women, Culture, and Politics in Latin America,* Seminar on Feminism and Culture in Latin America, edited by Francesca Miller. Berkeley and Los Angeles: University of California Press, 1990, 22.

61. Drake, *Socialism and Populism,* 288–91.

62. *Memoria del Primer Congreso Interamericano de Mujeres.* Guatemala: n.p., 1947, 12.

63. Quoted in Miller, "Feminism and the Transnational Area," 23.

64. *El Mercurio,* 27 August 1947.

65. Klimpel, *La mujer chilena,* 191. Mueller wrote under the pseudonym "Mme.

Veronique." See as an example her article "A Husband Who May Guide Us," *El Mercurio,* 7 January 1940.

66. Interview with Caffarena and Poblete, in Meza, *La otra mitad,* 62.

67. *El Mercurio,* 22 September 1947.

68. See Edda Gaviola Artigas et al., *Queremos votar en las próximas elecciones: Historia del movimiento femenino chileno, 1913–1952.* Santiago: Centro de Análisis y Difusión de la Condición de la Mujer, 1986, 76.

69. Caffarena says simply that González Videla had attacked the Communists and had called them traitors of the country. That angered her enormously and induced her to leave under protest. Meza, *La otra mitad,* 62.

70. Ibid., 63.

71. Gaviola, *Queremos votar,* 79; Meza, *La otra mitad,* 64.

72. *El Mercurio,* 26 August 1947.

73. Covarrubias, "El movimiento feminista chileno," 639.

74. *El Mercurio,* 18 September 1948.

75. Meza, *La otra mitad,* 64.

76. *El Mercurio,* 12, 13 September 1948.

77. *El Mercurio,* 10 January 1949.

78. *MEMCH Antología,* 8, 45.

79. Klimpel, *La mujer chilena,* 139–45.

80. Ibid.

8 Why Not Corporatism?

Redemocratization and Regime Formation in Uruguay

Fernando Lopez-Alves

In examining Uruguay, the smallest country in South America, I shall focus on the period between the late 1930s and the mid-1950s: the Baldomir and Amezaga governments of 1938–1946 and the first stage of the era of "neo-*batllismo*" from 1946.[1] The analysis suggests that political conditions, rather than structural variables or economic forces, fostered the transformations of this period. Economic trends and World War II had a major impact on Uruguay, but the previously established alliances within the two major political parties, and between these parties and labor, shaped responses to these external pressures. Thus the consensus among the elites in favor of industrial development was the result of prior political reaccommodations among these elites. In the 1940s transformations in the polity led to transformations in the economy.

Party politics had long played a major role in the country's development. For most of Uruguay's history its economy had lagged behind that of countries with similar resources, such as Australia, New Zealand, and Argentina, but more as a result of domestic conflict and civil war than as a reflection of changing trade conditions, for example, fluctuations in the prices of beef and wool. Some decades before the 1940s Uruguay had succeeded in creating a strong party system under the control of political elites who often possessed a quite separate identity from those which controlled the economy. On numerous occasions the state enacted policies that ran directly counter to the interests of landowners, merchants, or manufacturers. Indeed, for much of the nineteenth and early twentieth centuries the economic elites had little direct political power and relatively little influence over economic policy.[2] Unlike those in most of Latin America the Uruguayan political parties did not necessarily channel the interests of agriculture, commerce, or industry.[3] Instead, frequent revolts and long civil wars led to control over the parties and the state by an autonomous body of urban politicians and rural caudillos. The economic elites created institutions other than political parties to represent their interests, among them the Asociación Rural, the Cámara de Industria y Comercio, and the Federación Rural, entities founded in 1871, 1914, and 1916, respectively, but they often exerted moderate political influence.

The 1940s provide an example of a contrasting situation in which newly formed economic interests tied to commerce and small-scale domestic manufacturing were able both to create successful lobbying groups and to establish strong influence over the political parties, particularly the Colorado party. At the end of the decade urban-based economic interests became dominant among the Colorados. Similarly, the traditionally rural Blanco party began to respond more directly to the needs of large landowners and rural entrepreneurs. This process began during the Great Depression—particularly in the Blanco party—but gained strength during the 1940s. For almost the first time business groups found themselves able to influence Congress and to participate in the making of economic and social policy.

To some authors these trends suggested the growth of "democratic corporatism" in Uruguay, and along with the changing political role of the economic elites they have pointed to other changes of a similar tenor to support this thesis: the growth of labor union activity, the strong consensus among the economic and political elites in favor of industrial development, the absence of competitive capitalism, and the spread of the state into the private sector.[4] The argument presented here, however, is that rather than marking an upsurge of corporatism this period witnessed a liberal-democratic reconstruction.

In the late 1940s Uruguay was far from developing the corporatist institutions that emerged in Scandinavia. In this period Norway and Sweden introduced centralized systems of collective bargaining and converted the labor unions into active coparticipants in economic policy-making. Year-round negotiations between capital, labor, and government established a firm consensus on industrial policy and made corporate mediation one of the main activities of government. The labor codes in these two countries guaranteed the right of the labor unions not only to exist but also to participate in the running of business firms and to negotiate workers' fringe benefits. Similarly, the labor unions of both Norway and Sweden became closely tied to the ruling Social Democratic parties.[5] None of these basic features of "democratic corporatism" appeared in Uruguay.

Instead during the 1940s Uruguay adopted a loose system of collective bargaining with certain limited corporatist features. However, collective bargaining remained entirely separate from the political arena and the activities of the political parties and was, moreover, restricted exclusively to negotiations over wages. Thus in Uruguay, as distinct from Scandinavia and other formally democratic nations in Latin America such as Colombia, there was a total separation between the labor movement on one hand and the state and political parties on the other. Thus the Uruguayan practice differed from democratic corporatism, in which the state instituted closely prescribed and defined mechanisms of cooperation between capital and labor. Equally, in Uruguay the co-optation of labor by the government or by the political parties was entirely absent.

During the 1940s a system developed that was pluralist in the political arena and quasi-corporatist in the labor market. Throughout Uruguay pluralism became the means to achieve political conciliation. Yet negotiations between capital and labor had a corporatist flavor in that the two sides interacted on the basis of prearranged mechanisms of cooperation designed to promote agreement and to avoid conflict. Using Philippe Schmitter's definition, a system "licensed by the state [allowing] a monopoly of representation in their sphere" became the instrument to reconcile the interests of capital and labor.[6] But such institutionalized cooperation was again limited to wage bargaining, and it differed entirely from state corporatism, in which the state directly controlled the labor unions. Thus Uruguay followed a very different path from neighboring Argentina and Brazil. In sum in Uruguay the system that developed failed to achieve the conventional Latin American populist marriage between the labor movement and the state (as in Argentina and Brazil), or the European social democratic pattern of representing the labor movement in government through the political parties (as in Norway and Sweden).

The avoidance of corporatism in Uruguay suggested that there was no natural or automatic link between corporatism and industrial development and that the pursuit of industrial development in Latin America was possible under a pluralistic political system. In Uruguay too, again unlike in Argentina and Brazil, the military had little influence on the decision to attempt industrial development. The military establishment made no attempt to gain a broader constituency in civil society or to challenge the political parties. In contrast, the parties penetrated the military; the generals and the colonels were loyal to their respective services but even more loyal to the parties in which they became members. Thus members of the military played a role in politics but more often than not through the parties to which they belonged. In the 1940s this unusual arrangement prompted what I call "redemocratization by coup d'état."

Redemocratization by Coup d'État: Politics, Parties, and Alliances

During the government of Gabriel Terra between 1933 and 1938 the Blanco party achieved dominance. The succeeding period during the 1940s marked the resurgence of the Colorado party and the rise of a strong reform movement linked to the return to democracy that played a major part in the development of the Uruguayan political system for many years to come. The 1940s thus witnessed a transition from a relatively mild authoritarian system to democracy. The democratic system created during this period was similar to that of previous democratic eras, particularly the two Colorado administrations of José Batlle y Ordoñez in 1902–1907 and 1911–1915. Thus, it can be better described as redemocratization than as plain democratization. Batlle organized a reform faction in the Colorado party, and as president he pursued a number of progressive, populist policies. Under his rule elections were held at regular intervals, and urban interests increasingly dominated Uruguayan politics. The labor unions were allowed to engage in collective bargaining, and Uruguay became one of the world's first welfare states. Batlle died in 1929, but his legacy survived. In the words of M. H. J. Finch, *batllismo* defines the "national style or ideology of development within which Uruguayan public life [has been] conducted from early this century to the end of the 1960s."[7] Most of the features of this system were reproduced in the 1940s.

Thus the basic patterns of Uruguayan politics continually adhered to the mold established by Batlle that placed strong emphasis on the political parties. There were three periods in the twentieth century in which democratic party rule broke down: the Terra presidency of the 1930s, a brief authoritarian period under Alfredo Baldomir during the early 1940s, and the military dictatorship of 1973–1984. But only in the last of these periods, in which all political activities were banned and all individual rights eliminated, was the functioning of the political system drastically altered.

The military coups of 1933 and 1942 were led by generals who were also party members. On 31 March 1933 Uruguay suffered its first military coup of the twentieth century when Terra, a renegade *batllista*, established a de facto regime backed by the mostly rural Blancos and conservative sectors of the Colorados. Although Terra himself had earlier been a Colorado, as president he favored the Blancos and gave them the opportunity to dominate policy.

The origins of the 1933 coup lay in mounting dissatisfaction with the incumbent Colorado regime and in particular in the fear among the economic elites, led by the cattle interests, that the Colorados were about to introduce a radical reform program. The events of March 1933 bore some resemblance to those of 1916, when the cattle interests had succeeded in forcing President Feliciano Viera into vetoing *batllista* reform legislation in Congress. Similarly in 1933 the Terra administration stepped in to prevent a series of new reform initiatives. Under Terra, however, the political parties continued to function and were allowed to participate in the plebiscite of 1933 and in the national elections of 1934 and 1938. Although some political groups were banned from elections during the 1930s, or chose the path of electoral abstention, the regime failed to prevent both the parties and the popular vote from surviving as the primary sources of political legitimacy. Indeed Terra himself finally left office without protest in 1938 following his election defeat.

The elections of 1938 brought the reform party back into office under the leadership of Alfredo Baldomir, another Colorado-*batllista* general. But for a time the reform factions remained under the shadow of the Terra era and were unable to reassert their supremacy. Terra's followers remained dominant in Congress, and the Senate was divided into two groups, "*los quince terristas y los quince herreristas*." These "fifteen *terristas*" were survivors from the Terra regime, while the "fifteen *herreristas*" were the followers of Luis Alberto de Herrera, leader of the conservative wing of the Blanco party and for many years the most prominent opponent of the *batllistas*. The power-sharing formula between the two factions allowed each side to propose an equal number of legislative measures and divided government ministries and state appointments equally between them. Under this system Baldomir possessed relatively little room for maneuver. In February 1942, however, Baldomir led a revolt against the *terristas* and *herreristas* to increase his own power. The other objectives of this *autogolpe* (seizing of additional or dictatorial powers; literally, "self-coup") were to eliminate Blanco opposition in Congress, to restore the predominance of the Colorados, and to "reopen the doors," as Baldomir put it, to the *batllistas*.

Baldomir proved successful. When elections were held in November 1942, Baldomir's close associate, Juan Amézaga, won the presidency (see table 18). During subsequent years the Colorado party consolidated its dominance. In the next national elections of 1946 the *batllistas* gained an overwhelming victory, and they remained in power until 1958.

Amézaga, and the reform currents he represented, won the election by a large majority. Electoral abstention, a common practice during the previous decade, almost entirely disappeared, since 92 percent of voters opted either for the Colorados or the Blancos. The Communist and Socialist parties received only 4.1 percent of the vote, and the Communist share was significantly greater than the Socialist.

The *autogolpe* of 1942 strengthened the new political alliances that had

Table 18 1942 Presidential Elections in Uruguay

Party	*Votes*	*% of Total Vote*
Partido Colorado	328,599[a]	57.2
Amézaga	234,127	40.7
Blanco Acevedo	74,767	13.0
Lagarmilla	18,969	3.3
Partido Nacional	131,235[b]	22.8
Herrera	129,132	22.5
Partido Nacional Independiente	67,030	11.7
Partido Union Civica	24,433	4.3
Communist party	14,330	2.5
Socialist party	9,036	1.6
Total votes	574,633[b]	

Source: Ana Frega, Mónica Maronna, and Yvette Trochon, *Baldomir y la restauración democrática.* Montevideo: Banda Oriental, 1987, 131.

Note: The Partido Colorado total includes votes cast for Amézaga, Blanco Acevedo, and Lagarmilla.

[a]Includes 670 votes for Arquitecto Williman.

[b]Includes 2,051 votes for José P. Turena.

[c]Includes 40 votes for Tortorelli-Pagani, the candidate of the Partido La Concordancia.

formed during previous years. The Colorados saw democracy as a way of reducing the power of the livestock interests in Congress and the government. Following this transition Baldomir and his group were able to carry out the programs their opponents had earlier blocked. Their basic objectives were to ensure the predominance of urban interests and to pursue an industrial policy at the expense of the export interests.

This program, however, had been taking shape for several years. In 1939, for example, under pressure from the Colorado government elected a year earlier, Congress enacted two laws that imposed new taxes on the livestock sector. The first increased taxes on cattle and meat, and the second imposed a levy on the excess profits, or *ganancias extraordinarias*, cattle ranchers were earning as meat prices climbed at the beginning of World War II. Both these measures were designed to divert export revenues away from the rural sector toward the cities and the state.[8]

In 1939 the Federación Rural, as the chief organ of rural interests, strongly opposed the new taxes, attacking what it called the "privileges" of the "artificial" manufacturing sector supported by the Colorado administration. Seeking to escape the dependence of the ranchers on foreign meat-packing plants, in 1940 the Federación insisted on being given control over the single state-owned meat-packing plant, the Frigorífico Nacional. But for the most part these demands were ignored, and relations between the federation and the government became increasingly strained. After 1940, for example, members of the government rarely attended the federation's official functions, such as the annual show at which the great ranchers paraded their champion bulls.

A second indicator of the resurgence of the Colorado party during the early 1940s, and of its turning away from the landed and rural interests, was its use of the two-party system to strengthen its own position to an even greater extent than in the past. In earlier periods the Colorados were often weak in Congress. Throughout 1925–1942, for example, they failed to muster a majority in the Chamber of Representatives, while in the Senate between 1925 and 1933 their maximum representation totaled only 38 percent. From 1942 onward the picture was very different. Except in the Chamber between 1946 and 1948 they commanded large majorities in both houses, so that the two-party system in reality marked the strong predominance of only one party.

The Colorados benefited by alterations in the electoral law under Baldomir, who in May 1939 supported legislation to "strengthen the structure" of the political parties and to limit the scope for interparty alliances. Three years later, in 1942, these measures were followed by the *ley de lemas*, the "law of the [party] labels," which established a system broadly similar to the party primaries in the United States. Henceforward, the parties were permitted to register their candidates under party subgroups called "*lemas*," which enabled each party to represent a large variety of different factions and programs without the parties themselves suffering formal splits. The voters supported candidates (known as *sublemas*) in one of the *lemas*, and each party's candidate for the presidency was the person who among the *sublemas* won the most votes in the most strongly supported *lema*.

Baldomir used the *lema* system to overcome factionalism, to strengthen the local organizational party structures that had weakened under Terra, and to unite the Colorados. Both parties sought to gain from these changes, but the Colorados benefited the most since the more deeply divided Blancos found it more difficult to unify the *lemas* after the elections. By the end of the 1940s the Colorados had successfully overcome their internal divisions while the Blancos remained split. The *lema* system allowed vertical alliances within the Colorado party and prevented horizontal alliances between dissident Colorados and the Blancos of the type that were common during the 1930s. Neither party could adopt candidates who belonged to the other party, and the *lema* law banned the practice of creating new parties that used "names or labels similar to those employed by the two major parties."[9] Thus a dissident Colorado group that styled itself, for example, Renovación Batllista, could no longer function as a party, only as one of the groups within the *lemas*.

Many writers have suggested that the *lema* law tended to intensify divisions within the parties rather than help them to unite. Indeed the number of factions within the parties multiplied with the passing of time. Nevertheless, the Colorado party remained the broad coalition of forces that the 1942 legislation had intended. Equally, under this system Uruguay managed to uphold the two-party system. Without the *ley de lemas* the country might well have found itself with no less than six parties constituting the breakaway factions from the two original groupings plus the small leftist parties: the Partido Nacional Independiente, the Partido Nacional, the Partido Colorado, the *batllista* faction Avanzar, the Unión Cívica, and the Communists and Socialists.

In 1942 Baldomir carried out his *autogolpe* to prevent any possible challenge to his reforms by the Blancos, who possessed a potential veto power in Congress under the power-sharing formulas established under Terra. The Colorados were now determined to dominate Congress, to abolish the remnants of power sharing, and to put an end to what remained of the horizontal alliances between the parties. Subsequently, vertical alliances were encouraged.[10] The result was the progressive weakening of the *herreristas* and the disappearance of the last remnants of the Terra regime.

To what extent were external conditions responsible for the growing strength of the Colorados and the increasing weakness and division of the Blancos? In World War II the debate over foreign markets became one of the issues that destroyed the prewar party coalitions. From 1940, as the European markets disintegrated, Baldomir's Movimiento de Marzo (March Movement) began to seek closer relations with the United States. The Blancos, led by the *herreristas*, opposed this strategy on the grounds that the United States would continue to exclude Uruguayan goods by protection. To allow the traditional European connection to weaken, the Blancos argued, was suicidal.

This position reflected the historic ties between the livestock interests and the British beef market, and their long resentments toward the United States for having excluded imports of Uruguayan beef and wool. During this period the *marzistas* became strong supporters of Pan-Americanism, but the Blancos favored nonalignment and neutrality: closer connections with the United States, they argued, threatened the national interest.[11]

This issue provoked increasing divisions and became tied up with relations with neighboring Argentina as the Blancos became open supporters first of the Argentine right-wing nationalists who took power in 1943 and later of Juan Perón. In the eyes of the Colorados, however, Perón's Argentina came to be seen as "what happily Uruguay [was] not," and members of the Uruguayan government joined the chorus that denounced Perón for "leaning toward Nazism and Stalinism."[12] As 1945 approached, this posture helped the Colorados to increase their popularity.

There were thus some grounds for relating the growing dominance of the Colorados to the impact of World War II and for linking changing internal alliances with external forces. But important as they were, external conditions were insufficient to explain the new coalitions in Uruguayan politics.

In the 1940s Argentina and Uruguay had similar export economies and exported to the same markets, but politics in the two countries evolved in diametrically opposite directions: while Uruguay restored democracy and took a pro–United States position, Argentina opted for state corporatism and anti-Americanism. How can we explain these differences? The divergences sprang from party politics and the prior features of the political systems of both countries that World War II and its economic impact influenced but failed to change in any fundamental way. Relations among internal political forces, and the growing salience of urban politics in Uruguay, underlay the rise of Baldomir, Amezaga, and the increasing strength of neo-*batllismo*. The decreasing weight of the rural sector in Uruguay became a more important factor in Uruguayan politics than the influence of the Allies and explained, for example, why Herrera's group found itself unable to impose its own position on the issue of markets and international relations. In Uruguay the strong party system, and the weakness of the agrarian elites, brought about the decision to restore pluralism rather than take the same road as Argentina toward corporatism. In Argentina the political structure was quite different: the landed interests were much stronger, the urban political parties were much weaker, and both the church and the military commanded much greater influence than in Uruguay. As a result the closure of the European markets and the expanding influence of the United States provoked quite different responses in the two countries.

The party system and the relative weakness of the rural elites also explain the strength of the proindustry coalition in Uruguay during this period, the way the state promoted the formation of an industrial bourgeoisie, and how industry eventually became another instrument of democratic reconstruction. During the early twentieth century the *batllistas* did not regard the creation of an industrial economy as the essential route toward democracy, offering some sharp contrasts between the democracy of Batlle's day and that of the 1940s. In the early twentieth century an enlightened political elite imposed democracy from above; its methods were to confer voting rights on both men and women and establish a welfare state and a high-quality system of secular education. In the 1940s, in contrast, industrial development came to be seen as the magical formula to achieve democratization. The reformers of the 1940s believed that industry would sweep aside poverty and destroy the constraints of traditional society: modern industry would lead to modern man.

Industry and Democracy

In Uruguay the commitment to industrial development did not emerge in conjunction with corporatism and the co-optation of the working class by the state but from a perception that industry represented the material or structural foundation of democracy. Support for industrial development, however, did not imply any parallel faith in the invisible power of market forces. Instead, in keeping with a pattern established during earlier decades in Uruguay, the state had a crucial part in hastening and shaping the transformation to an industrial society. The 1940s marked the growth of a huge state bureaucracy that remains to this day a crucial element in the country's politics. In the political sphere the expansion of the state once more helped to strengthen the party system; in the economic sphere the growth of the state favored manufacturing.

Another key feature of this period was the emergence of a political alliance supporting both the expansion of the state and the development of industry, an alliance that coupled political pluralism with economic protectionism. Protectionism became an article of faith among the dominant Colorados, and it secured their success in enlisting the support of the bulk of the urban upper and middle classes: manufacturers and financiers, merchants and shopkeepers. During the late 1940s (and in contrast with the 1970s and 1980s) the two leading parties remained supreme, while the left continued to be small and isolated.

The Blancos and the Colorados alike reaped handsome profits from the growth of the state, receiving quotas of state jobs in large numbers, as state employment rose rapidly to around 15 percent in the late 1940s, and to more than 20 percent of the total labor force by the early 1950s. The highest rates of growth occurred among the employees of the central government as opposed to local government and the state enterprises.[13] In this period the growth of public sector employment not only exceeded that of all previous periods but probably occurred at a faster rate than anywhere else in Latin America. Although 90 percent of the economy remained private, the government nationalized a number of basic services and created several large state monopolies. Among these conglomerates were the UTE (Usinas y Teléfonos del Estado: State Electricity and Telephone Company), the SOYP (Servicios Oceanográficos y Pesca: Maritime and Fishing Services), and the ANCAP (Asociación Nacional de Alcohol y Portland, an alcohol, petroleum, and cement refinery). A large proportion of the railroad system was nationalized, along with many sectors of transportation in general. The government gained large shares in several foreign-owned meat-packing plants and established a state-owned plant.

Since the political party clubs handed out the state jobs, party members constituted the great majority of white-collar state workers. The distribution of the spoils typically followed the elections with the two parties determining the quotas by negotiation. Not surprisingly, the state employees quickly emerged as a new social class. Meanwhile, protectionism became the instrument to construct another, although much smaller, class of urban industrialists.[14] During the 1940s the industrialists became prominent in policymaking, and their organizations, led by the Unión Industrial Uruguaya (Uruguayan Industrial Union) and the Cámara de Industrias (Chamber of Industries), grew stronger.[15]

The expansion of manufacturing fed the growth of the urban working class. Despite the small size of most factories the workers achieved a high level of unionization in powerful national federations. Subsequently labor became one of the main partners in the protectionist alliance of the late 1940s along with the state, the industrialists, and some sectors of the agrarian elites linked with the processing of raw materials. In this period the associations representing the agrarian interests, led by the Rural Association and the Rural Federation, constantly criticized government policies in such areas as social reform, education, labor relations, and industrial development, but their complaints had little impact. For a large majority of Uruguayans the construction of democracy became virtually synonymous with the defense of industry, while the protectionist alliance developed as the main pillar of the neo-*batllista* movement that took power in 1946 on the election of Luis Batlle Berres, a nephew of José Batlle y Ordoñez, to the presidency.

Although labor formed part of this coalition, supported its agenda, and pledged to maintain industrial peace, the unions were neither tied to the government by any institutional mechanisms nor did they renounce the right to strike. In the 1940s the long-established right to strike remained sacrosanct, although strikes, in particular general strikes, remained far fewer in number than in earlier and later periods.[16] The link between labor, industry, and state was based exclusively on the support of the unions for the economic strategy of *batllismo*, which the unions perceived as a way to increase employment and their own memberships.

Many have argued that this period represented the golden era of the

Uruguayan economy. Rapidly rising export earnings during the war, along with the new tax on exporters' excess profits, bred a new sense of optimism among the urban sectors. Protectionism came to be seen as a way of resolving uncertainties over the future of traditional export markets. The optimists were encouraged by the early success of industry, which despite limited resources and restricted economies of scale, achieved an overall growth rate of 8.5 percent between 1945 and 1954. In this period some of the so-called dynamic industries grew at annual rates of up to 16 percent; between 1945 and 1954 the production of consumer goods increased 82 percent. In proportional terms Uruguay for a time possessed one of the largest industrial economies in Latin America.[17]

But the overall picture was more mixed. During this period the livestock sector did not enjoy the level of prosperity contemporaries imagined; other sectors prospered but only for relatively brief periods.

Between 1945 and 1949 the volume of cattle slaughtered for export declined by 20 percent, while imports fell as a percentage of total production, particularly after the mid-1950s (see table 19). The heyday of beef exports was the early 1940s, but even then the production of livestock was increasing at only 1 percent annually before permanent decline began. During the 1930s other sectors of the economy had been growing, particularly grains. For example, Uruguay had become the third-largest linseed producer after Argentina and India and had established strong markets for linseed in Belgium and the Netherlands. But the growth of grains and linseed ended following the outbreak of World War II and the closure of the European markets.[18]

The industrial development of the 1940s failed to create an independent,

Table 19 Volume of Cattle Slaughtered in Uruguay, 1935–1939 to 1955–1959

	Total Slaughter[a]	*Exports (%)*	*Average Price*[b]
1935–39	100.0	41.9	100.0
1940–44	101.4	46.4	133.5
1945–49	81.1	35.1	130.9
1950–54	103.5	31.8	134.2
1955–59	82.7	9.6	170.2

Source: M. H. J. Finch, A *Political Economy of Uruguay since 1870*. New York: St. Martin's Press, 1981, 145.

[a]Five-year averages (1935–1939 = 100)

[b]Per live kilo of steers bought by the Frigorífico Nacional.

innovative, and self-sustaining industrial class. Private industrial investment grew only slowly and with strong support from the state; in this sense Uruguay embodied a typical case of "dependent development." In this period there was no attempt to promote exports of manufactured goods, and planning went little beyond the vague aspiration for industrial self-sufficiency. Uruguay's petite bourgeoisie was mostly made up of state employees, and the industrial bourgeoisie that emerged created only small-scale mixed ventures heavily dependent on state subsidies for their survival. The state came to be seen as a source of unlimited benefits that asked for nothing in return.

These trends provoked increasing opposition from the ranching interests, and from the start the industrial project was accompanied by rising conflict between the state and landowners. In any event, agriculture ended up financing a project over which it had no control.[19] Unlike in 1933–1944, when agriculture had received many different kinds of state subsidies, industry, along with upper- and middle-class consumers, now became the great beneficiaries of state spending.[20] By the mid-1950s the heavy costs of this strategy were becoming glaringly apparent, as the economy entered chronic stagnation.

But in the 1940s, among those who supported and benefited from industrial development, Uruguay seemed to enjoy a special, privileged position in Latin America and the world. In his inaugural address in March 1947, President Luis Batlle Berres affirmed what he saw as Uruguay's enviable situation: "Let me urge all our citizens, as they observe the situation that prevails in the Americas, let alone that in Europe, to acknowledge the privileged situation of our Republic." Arguing that Uruguay had the most perfect and advanced democracy in the world, the prominent *batllista* Efraín González Conzi boasted, "There's nowhere like Uruguay" ("*Como el Uruguay, no hay*"), a phrase that captured the dominant mood of the time.

In this period Uruguay became the "Switzerland of Latin America," and *batllismo* came to be seen as a reform movement with unique features. Here was a democracy with its own civic culture that was entirely different from countries like Brazil and Argentina, not to mention the rest of Latin America. The civic culture and industry were perceived as being closely linked, since industry was promoting equality and pulling the country away from the backwardness associated with the old rural economy.

The differing roles of industry and the state in the democratic reconstruction of the 1940s and that of 1980s offer some striking contrasts. In contrast with the earlier decade, by the 1980s there was strong emphasis on foreign investment, the "rationalization" of the state bureaucracy, and an "outward-looking" strategy for industrial development. In addition, state participation in industry had come to be seen as a barrier to both economic growth and democracy, which by this point were equated with economic liberalization. In the 1980s, unlike in the 1940s, labor provided no support for the strategy for economic development; workers were willing to welcome the return of democracy but feared unemployment and falling incomes. Equally, the state bureaucracy, which became the vanguard of reform in the 1940s, opposed it in the 1980s.

There were also nationalist and statist components in the democratic reconstruction of the 1940s which were entirely absent forty years later in the programs that emphasized private initiative and the avoidance of state intervention. Thus, according to Luis Batlle in the late 1940s, key industries should not remain under the ownership of private capital because "whether they [were] nationals or foreigners, big capitalists [had] no nationality and [were] always dangerous."[21] In Batlle's era industrial development under state tutelage represented a new instrument to develop public education and the welfare state, to promote the interest of the middle class, and to widen the channels of social mobility.

In this era the idea prevailed that a strong democracy would be forthcoming so long as the masses followed, in John Stuart Mill's words, the "wise and virtuous" middle classes, whose numbers would increase alongside the growth of industry and the state.[22] Indeed by 1967 Aldo Solari estimated that the Uruguayan middle class, including those in the rural sector, made up 45.5 percent of the population, a slightly higher proportion than in Argentina.[23] Reviving the tradition established by Batlle y Ordoñez, the neo-*batllistas* of the 1940s laid great stress on the power of education in the formation of the middle class. While Juan Perón in Argentina let the church reestablish its grip over public education, Uruguay sought to strengthen and consolidate its tradition of a strong secular educational system. Historically this system had placed strong emphasis on pluralism, individual freedom, and the subordination of corporate groups such as the church and the military to civil society.

The view in Uruguay, again strongly represented by Luis Batlle, for example, was that state corporatism was to be avoided at all costs: corporatism would undermine the natural propensity of industry to foster democracy, and it was a recipe for military intervention and civic strife. Revolutions, Batlle maintained, originated in the aspirations of the masses for freedom, but freedom should be understood as embodying a strong economic component. "A plea for economic safety has replaced the plea of the masses for political freedom," he declared. "The political process must be directed at gaining the support of the masses for democracy [by demonstrating] that democracy provides both freedom and economic security."[24] There were strong populist overtones in the political discourse of this period, but they sprang from a commitment to pluralism rather than to corporatism, as the relationship between the state and organized labor once more demonstrates.

The Tacit Alliance between Labor and Neo-batllismo

Redemocratization combined with industrial expansion required the reconstruction of the system of labor relations. The scheme that now emerged in Uruguay was unusual in Latin America, since although labor remained autonomous from the state and the parties, it cooperated with them and with capital in a corporatist fashion. The system was based on a pact between labor and the state, but one with an entirely different nature from labor agreements in Argentina and Brazil under Perón and Vargas. The system differed too from that in Chile in that none of the Uruguayan parties attempted to create their own unions or to enlist the unions under party banners.

The autonomy of the Uruguayan unions was not entirely due to the activities and political skills of the left or to the existence of a strong anarchist or Communist tradition in the unions as is often argued.[25] These conditions helped to keep the unions autonomous, but the stances of the two major parties and the state toward organized labor offer a more convincing explanation. It became easier for labor to remain autonomous in a situation in which no group, apart from the left, was attempting to take it over. Even when industrial development and the expansion of the state bred a powerful working class, neither the state nor the Colorados and the Blancos made any attempt to establish their own unions. It was not that the state and the parties were ignoring labor; indeed it was their awareness of its presence that led them to support the tacit alliance between labor, the state, and capital.

The determination to avoid both state corporatism and party or state linkages with labor had a precedent in the early *batllista* movement. Earlier,

Batlle y Ordoñez had succeeded in converting labor into an ally without having to establish Colorado- or state-sponsored unions. Anarchist-led unions often supported *batllista* reforms by taking to the streets to back Batlle against his opponents and by agreeing to certain restraints on the use of strikes. Except for some of the Anarchist unions, which continued to urge abstention in national elections, by Batlle's second term as president in the late 1920s a large proportion of the working class was voting for the Colorados. Thus the *batllistas* managed to win labor support without resorting to organizing unions, competing with the left, or having to side with the working class on every single issue.

A generation later, the approach toward labor adopted by Batlle y Ordoñez still seemed the best one. At this point the unions were growing at a remarkable rate, while the Communist party, which now controlled the dominant labor central, the General Confederation of Workers (Confederación General del Trabajo [CGT]), was becoming the most powerful force in the Uruguayan labor movement. The CGT itself had begun as an alliance of Communist and Anarchist unions, although by the 1940s the Anarchists had disappeared. The top priorities of the CGT were to group unions by industry, to encourage the formation of federations in all trades, and to organize a national system of collective bargaining. By the middle of the decade the Communists controlled around two-thirds of all labor unions through the CGT. The transition to Communist dominance altered the political behavior of workers, because, unlike the old Anarchist leaders, the Communists encouraged union members to vote rather than to abstain: revolutionary change was to be achieved within the legal framework of bourgeois society.

The increasing centralization of the labor movement, and the position taken by the Communists on the vote, persuaded the *batllistas* that an extensive system of collective bargaining combined with a strong grass-roots Colorado party machine, would limit the unions to wage issues alone but still induce workers to vote for them rather than for the Communists. The *batllistas* therefore introduced changes in the labor code but proclaimed that the state alone would decide matters of social policy and legislation.

Law 10,449 of 1943 established tripartite commissions to set minimum wages in the private sector and issued some general statements in favor of collective bargaining between labor and capital. Subsequently the so-called wage councils appeared, but they were loose negotiating commissions that operated without written agreements and mostly on an informal and ad hoc basis. The labor legislation did not specify when agreements were to be concluded, the length of time they were to remain valid, or that collective bargaining was compulsory.[26] In practice the councils possessed certain corporatist features. The tripartite commissions, composed of three government, two union, and two employers' delegates, usually discussed proposals made by the government that were based on prior consultations with the unions. In practice, therefore, the deals were struck before the councils actually met.[27] Before submitting their requests to the councils, the unions customarily met with the employers as well, so that any conflicts in the councils usually reflected the refusal of one side or another to honor prior informal agreements. The agreements then became official once they were "approved" by the government.

This system gave a strong impulse to the growth of union federations and to the overall centralization of the unions. Because of the small number of union delegates allowed to participate in the negotiations, the smaller unions were continually forced to merge with others. By the end of the 1940s almost all unions in the private sector in the cities were covered by some collective agreement and belonged to a federation. These trends matched the long-run goals of the Communists, which were to increase the power of unions on the national level and to encourage a process of centralized collective bargaining. The shift toward much stronger labor unions during the 1940s paved the way for the creation of the National Workers' Convention (Convención Nacional de Trabajadores [CNT]) in 1964, which achieved the representation of 70 percent of the Uruguayan work force.

The labor unions possessed a powerful role in wage bargaining but virtually none in the sphere of fringe benefits. The wage councils tended to strengthen the organization of the unions but to weaken the power of their leaders. The labor legislation of 1943 instituted closer contact between rank-and-file workers, employers, and the state but laid down that only delegates elected *directly* by all workers, regardless of whether they belonged to a union or not, could participate in the wage councils. This measure prevented representatives from being designated by the unions. Similarly, the wage councils allowed the state to bypass the unions on the issue of social reform and the fringe benefits of workers. Thus, while organized labor increased its members, it became increasingly remote from the arena of policy-making.

The net result of the practices introduced by the Colorados was to establish two separate spheres for politics and labor and to encourage a strong demarcation between the role of the citizen and that of the worker. The parties, not the unions, represented the workers in their second identity as citizens, and none of the union leaders were able to represent their constituencies either to the parties or before Congress. Equally, the union leaders exerted no influence on social policy issues even in areas that closely affected workers' interests such as housing, health, and conditions in the workplace; none of these issues were decided through the system of collective bargaining.

Labor thus became incorporated into the process of redemocratization by relinquishing its political voice in exchange for the right to collective bargaining and the opportunity to grow in number and size. Because the major parties avoided attempting to co-opt labor, there were no alliances between the Colorado reformers and the left through the labor movement. Since it perceived state corporatism as threatening its autonomy, as had happened in Argentina and Brazil, the labor movement strongly supported political pluralism. Finally, the system of wage councils allowed the unions to participate in the benefits of industrial development through the expansion of employment and the growth of their memberships.

Conclusion

The democratic reconstruction of the 1940s differed sharply from that of the 1980s to the point that they became the reverse image of one another. The period of military rule in 1973–1984, followed by the years of renewed democratization after 1984, dismantled the political and economic system formed during the 1940s. In the 1940s protectionism and the growth of manufacturing provided the foundations for alliances between industry, the state, and labor; in the 1980s, in contrast, economic liberalization and privatization separated and divided the state from both the labor movement and most sectors of domestic industry. Policy in the 1940s was directed at exploiting the traditional agrarian export sector to support urban manufacturing; in the 1980s government attempted to develop agricultural exports as part of its effort to consolidate the restored democratic system.

These striking contrasts illustrate that the effort to restore democracy may stem from very different forces and factors and that democratic reconstruction does not result from any specific economic and political formula. In the 1940s redemocratization became part of the populist-reform movement led by the Colorados; in the 1980s the same goal was pursued under much more conservative guidelines. In the 1940s the neo-*batllistas* adopted a strongly progressive agenda; in the 1980s they tilted much more toward the right, and in this period the alliances typical of the 1930s between Blancos and conservative Colorados reappeared once more. Starting in the mid-1930s the Blancos underwent a succession of divisions that strengthened the conservative wing of the party. Henceforth this conservative wing set the party agenda, although the Blancos now fell far behind the Colorados in the national elections. Despite continuing splits, in the late 1980s the Blancos, as the more conservative of the two parties, won the presidency. One other difference between the 1940s and the 1980s was that the left now emerged as a significant contender, as the old two-party system gave way to three parties.

Finally, in another contrast with Argentina and Brazil, during the 1940s Uruguay illustrated a situation in which the political parties controlled the military, rather than vice versa, and excluded them from power and policymaking. Political history, particularly the way during the nineteenth century the parties had created and maintained their own armies, underlay this difference. From around 1910 the military became fully committed to civilian rule under the Colorados and Blancos. In the 1940s this particular commitment strengthened, as most military leaders renewed their pledge to civilian rule and deepened their ties with the Colorado party. The leading military figures of the 1930s and 1940s, for example, Baldomir, were reform-minded *batllistas*; even Terra called himself a *batllista* and never entirely abandoned the cause of progressive reform. The capacity of the parties to penetrate and co-opt the military reflected the absence in Uruguay of the strong links between the military and the agrarian elites that prevailed elsewhere in Latin America. Once more, Uruguay's strikingly different political tradition, not its social and economic base, which was very similar to Argentina's, explains why Uruguay opted for pluralism and largely avoided corporatism.

Notes

1. The dominance of neo-*batllismo*, whose features are examined at length in this chapter, extended from 1946 to 1958.

2. For a full account of political system formation and the role of economic elites in Uruguay see Fernando Lopez-Alves, *Between the Economy and the Polity, Uruguay 1810–1880*. London: Institute of Latin American Studies, University of London, 1993.

3. A contrasting case is Colombia. For a comparison between Uruguay and Colombia see Fernando Lopez-Alves, "Why Do Unions Coalesce? Labor Solidarity in Colombia and Uruguay." Ph.D. diss., University of California, Los Angeles, 1989, chs. 2–3.

4. See Jorge L. Lanzaro, *Sindicatos y sistema político: Relaciones corporativas en el Uruguay*. Montevideo: Fundación de Cultura Universitaria, 1986.

5. On democratic corporatist practices in Norway and Sweden see Peter Katzenstein, *Small States in World Markets*. Ithaca: Cornell University Press, 1985; and Gerhard A. Lehmbruch and Philippe C. Schmitter, eds., *Patterns of Corporatist Policy-Making*. New York: Sage, 1982.

6. Philippe C. Schmitter, "Still the Century of Corporatism?" *Review of Politics* 36 (1974): 90.

7. M. H. J. Finch, A *Political Economy of Uruguay since 1870*. New York: St. Martin's Press, 1981, 2.

8. The tax reforms of the late 1930s are discussed in Ana Frega, Mónica Maronna, and Yvette Trochon, *Baldomir y la restauración democrática*. Montevideo: Banda Oriental, 1987, ch. 4; Benjamín Nahum et al., *Historia uruguaya*. Vol. 7. Montevideo: Banda Oriental, 1989.

9. Quoted in Frega, *Baldomir*, 114.

10. For a detailed account of the 1942 constitutional reform see Frega, *Baldomir*, 114.

11. For a statement of the issues see *El Debate*, 2 July 1940.

12. Colorado attitudes toward Perón appear in *El Día*, the party newspaper. See particularly April–June 1946. See also Germán Rama, *La democracia en el Uruguay*. Montevideo: Arca, 1989, ch. 5.

13. Aldo Solari, *El desarrollo social del Uruguay en la postguerra*. Montevideo: Alfa, 1967, 32, 68–70.

14. The size and political weight of this bourgeoisie, however, has been exaggerated. Cf. J. Bonilla Sauns, "La restructuración capitalista del Uruguay: 1958–1976," in *Uruguay, dictadura y realidad nacional*, edited by América Latina, Estudios y Perspectivas. México, D.F.: ERESU, 1981.

15. After 1914 the Cámara de Industrias (Chamber of Industry) became the joint administrator of the Unión Industrial.

16. See Lopez-Alves, "Why Do Unions Coalesce?" 215–30.

17. Rama, *La democracia*, 67; Finch, *Uruguay since 1870*, 169.

18. Cf. Finch, *Uruguay since 1870*, 63–91.

19. Germán D'Elía has argued persuasively along these lines. See his *El Uruguay neo-batllista: 1946–1958*. Montevideo: Banda Oriental, 1986, 15 and passim. D'Elía reviews a range of hypotheses as to who financed industrial development in Uruguay.

20. See Luis Bertola, *Industrialization in Uruguay*. Ph.D. diss., Centro Uruguayo Independiente, Montevideo–University of Uppsala, Sweden, 1991; Raúl Jacob, *Breve historia de la industria en el Uruguay*. Montevideo: FCU, 1981, and *Modelo batllista:*

¿Variación sobre un viejo tema? Montevideo: Proyección, 1988; Rama, *Democracia*, 62–147.

21. Presidential National Address, 25 August 1949.

22. On Luis Batlle's economic ideas see Nahum, *Historia uruguaya*, 98–101.

23. Solari, *Desarrollo social*, 17. Gino Germani estimated that in 1947 the middle class of Argentina made up 45.4 percent of the population. In Solari's view 40 percent of the rural population of Uruguay could be considered middle class. (Cf. Solari, *Desarrollo social*, 15, 35.)

24. Batlle's speech to Congress, 3 September 1948, quoted in Rama, *Democracia*, 45.

25. See Alfredo Errandonea and Daniel Costabile, *Sindicato y sociedad en el Uruguay*. Montevideo: Biblioteca de Cultura Universitaria, 1969; also Pedro Alfonso, *Sindicalismo y revolución en Uruguay*. Montevideo: Nuevo Mundo, 1970; and Francisco Pintos, *Historia del movimiento obrero del Uruguay*. Montevideo: Gaceta de Cultura, 1960.

26. See Adam S. Bronstein, "The Evolution of Labour Relations in Uruguay: Achievements and Challenges," *International Labor Review* 128, no. 2 (1989), 28–42.

27. This information is based on interviews conducted in Montevideo in 1987 with the labor lawyer Leonel Bismark and the labor historian Germán D'Elía.

9 Internal and External Convergence

The Collapse of Argentine Grain Farming

Daniel Lewis

In many respects the modern history of Argentina hinges on the 1940s. Politically, socially, and economically, the events and the trends that shaped Argentine history during and after World War II ended the institutions that had survived from the country's "golden age" before 1910, establishing starting points for the conflicts and crises that followed.

Among the most important changes of this period was the spectacular decline of grain farming. Labeled, alongside cattle ranching, one of Argentina's "mother industries," grain farming had been critical to the country's rapid economic expansion between 1860 and 1910. By the 1930s Argentine grain farms occupied a maximum area of more than 20 million hectares, and record wheat, corn, and linseed crops made Argentina one of the world's leading grain exporters. But in the 1940s farming fell into crisis. Between the late 1930s and the early 1950s the average land area devoted to grains and oilseeds contracted from around 20 million to only 11.3 million hectares. Over the same period farm exports fell from 10.2 million metric tons to only 4.4 million.[1]

The most common explanation of the abrupt decline of farming points to the postwar policies of President Juan Perón. Echoing the complaints of the producers and their organizations during the mid-1940s, Perón's critics blame ill-conceived (or deliberately malicious) government intervention: by taxing farmers, government price controls provoked a reduction in output;

state regulation of rural labor practices and rental contracts led landowners to abandon farming for other types of rural activity.[2]

A second group of scholars, in contrast, has argued that structural flaws in the rural economy offer a less partisan, and therefore more satisfying, approach to the issue. This point of view emphasizes the subordinate position of farming in the rural sector as a whole. Grain farming had first emerged on the pampas during the late nineteenth century in response to the needs of ranchers, who settled tenant farmers on virgin land. The tenants grew grain on their parcels for two or three years but then, having seeded it with alfalfa in readiness for cattle, vacated the land. Later, as increasing numbers of ranchers hired tenant farmers on similar short-term contracts to improve their pasturage, grain farm acreages and production rose. Thus grain farming and ranching grew broadly in tandem.

Around 1914 the rural sector as a whole entered a second phase of development as the supply of new land suitable for agriculture became relatively scarce. Henceforth the expansion of ranching on one hand, or farming on the other, could occur only at the other's expense, and market conditions and international prices now determined the distribution of land between the two sectors. After 1918, for example, the collapse of foreign demand for meat hit ranching but encouraged the expansion of farming. During the late 1930s, in contrast, meat prices rose in relative terms so that farming began to stagnate. Seen from this perspective, the fall of farming during the 1940s occurred primarily as a result of the resurgence of ranching.[3]

Both these approaches are open to question. After 1948, for example, Perón scaled back the policies that discriminated against farming, yet grain production continued to slide. Similarly, the complete abandonment of economic populism after 1955 failed to reverse the process of agricultural decay.[4] Close scrutiny of land-use patterns challenges explanations stressing the total interdependence of ranching and farming. Before and after 1914 farming emerged in many areas, for example, southwestern Buenos Aires province and La Pampa territory, in which ranching was relatively unimportant.[5] Equally, changes in the land area used for grain farming were not always the result of shifts in the relative prices between grains and meat. During the late 1930s, for example, farm acreage and production reached record levels when world grain prices were falling but meat prices were rising.

Thus the decline of grain farming in Argentina is more complex than the standard explanations suggest. In this chapter I suggest a different approach to the issue. Among its principal arguments are the following. First, the adoption of new policies under Perón appeared to have such an enormous impact because of the progressive weakening of agriculture during previous decades. The disruptions of World War I, then protectionism and overproduction abroad afterward, followed by the turmoil of the depression in the 1930s, had already imposed severe strains on farmers. Second, during the 1930s and 1940s demographic shifts, in particular the accelerating flight of population from the land, progressively undermined the traditional, extensive methods of grain production. Finally, during World War II grain farmers faced an even greater crisis as a result of the near-total closure of the European markets. Seen against this background, the chief role of Perón's policies was thus to exacerbate conditions that were already extremely critical.

Two Successful Recoveries

Grain farming developed as one of the leading export activities from around 1880 under a system in which most farmers remained as tenants, sharecroppers, or laborers with only limited capital resources. Farmers worked under short-term and often unwritten contracts, and few remained on the same land for more than five years.[6] Yet these insecure conditions did not impede the rapid expansion of farming. Farmed on fewer than 2 million hectares in 1888, the three major export crops, wheat, corn, and linseed, expanded more than fivefold to reach a combined total of 10 million hectares by the eve of World War I.[7] By this point the value of farm exports was greater than that of livestock exports, and grain and linseed shipments provided more than half of Argentina's export earnings.

The period 1912–1918, however, often proved extremely difficult for farmers. Drought, locust invasions, and labor unrest disrupted planting and harvesting; farmers complained about increasing rents, freights, and other production costs. World War I exacerbated these problems by halting immigration, which provided the bulk of the agricultural labor force, and by reducing the supply of shipping, which limited Argentina's access to the European markets.[8]

Nevertheless, during this period the national and provincial governments successfully intervened to prevent any fall in production. Among the measures adopted during World War I were emergency loans to help the victims of drought or locusts; in 1918 a government agency, the Dirección de Defensa Agrícola, led campaigns to increase wheat production, using the argument that European demand would once more increase when the war ended. During World War I, unlike in World War II, Argentina continued to supply grains to both France and Italy, since both countries were on the side of the Allies. These measures helped substantially to keep farmers in the fields, and they were implemented without having to alter the existing extensive system of production.[9]

In the 1920s grain farming expanded once more. Many scholars have argued that the new expansionary cycle occurred as a result of the contraction of cattle ranching: with the end of wartime beef and mutton exports landowners shifted out of ranching and into farming. In reality, the resurgence of grain farming came as the result of a combination of factors. Over much of the Argentine pampas the contraction of ranching did clear the land for other activities, but farm acreages increased most rapidly in other, new areas, particularly southwestern Buenos Aires, western Córdoba province, and La Pampa territory. At the same time, foreign immigrants and internal migrants provided the abundant labor force required for renewed growth. Railroad companies organized new agricultural colonization schemes, and more liberal credit policies made it easier for farmers to buy land. Rural organizations, led by the Argentine Agrarian Federation, the Argentine Rural Society, and local cooperatives, introduced numerous other schemes to promote farming.[10] By the late 1920s the number of farms, farm acreage, and production stood at record levels.[11]

From the viewpoint of the farmers themselves, however, little had changed during the past decade. "The rural producer lives in isolation [and] struggles alone," commented a contemporary observer. "He is a speculator, not a producer, because he places all his hopes. . .in the kindness of the climate and in the timely fall of rain, rather than in the perfection of his labor or the organization of his enterprise."[12] These were complaints that might have been made thirty or forty years earlier, and they illustrated the survival of the old extensive farming systems. But despite the absence of change, foreign demand enabled Argentine farmers to maintain their competitiveness in the international markets.[13]

The Great Depression, however, quickly imperiled the gains of the previous decade. In 1928 and 1929 mounting international grain stocks and falling grain prices, alongside rising rents and production costs in Argentina, rapidly undercut farming profits. At this point the farmers' organizations, led by the Agrarian Federation and the leading rural cooperatives, continually urged the government to order cuts in railroad freights and set minimum prices to protect their share of the international grain trade. But during the early years of the depression farmers had to face these hard times almost entirely alone, since for some time the government remained narrowly preoccupied with the fiscal crisis provoked by falling tax revenues.

The farmers responded to the depression in several different ways. Those with any savings used them to cover their losses; they spent less on themselves and their farms and employed family members as opposed to hiring outside labor; they worked longer hours and took less time and care in the preparation of their fields for planting.[14] But the most common response was to attempt to increase production. During the early 1930s the acreages devoted to the three major crops, particularly corn, surged to record levels, with corn itself climbing from 4.7 million hectares in (the agricultural year) 1928/1929 to more than 7 million hectares in 1934/1935.[15] In this period larger harvests partially offset the steady fall in prices.

Farmers began to receive more assistance from the government on the accession of President Agustín P. Justo in February 1932. The Justo administration supported international treaties to control world grain markets and prices. It expanded its role as inspector and regulator of grain harvesting, transportation, and marketing in the hope of improving the quality, and therefore the marketability, of Argentine farm products. In August 1933 public officials and representatives of the railroads, grain trading houses, and banks proposed the expansion of short-term credit programs to farmers through a scheme known as the *prenda agraria* (agrarian loan). The plan also specified that all available barns, silos, and grain elevators were to be made available for the storage of grains, until bank employees and grain company agents determined the value of each farmer's harvest. With the harvest securely stored and catalogued, government officials would supervise the flow of grain to the ports.[16]

The extreme instability of the foreign grain markets, however, highlighted by the collapse of the International Wheat Agreement only weeks after its signing, rendered all these projects largely impractical. When farmers throughout the grain zone threatened to leave the 1933/1934 wheat and linseed crops unharvested, the Justo administration introduced a Grain Regulation Board (Junta Reguladora de Granos) that pledged to pay 5.75, 4.40, and 11.50 pesos, respectively, for each 100 kilograms of wheat, corn, and flaxseed delivered to port. The purchases made by the board would be financed by revenues from exchange control operations and by the devaluation of the Argentine peso.[17]

The administration claimed that the minimum prices were high enough to maintain farm production, and the scheme included measures to protect the profits of the intermediaries who bought the grain from the farmers and delivered it to the ports. The highlight of this plan was therefore its strong emphasis on preserving the existing organization of the farm sector, while keeping the farmers in production.[18]

The minimum price scheme succeeded in keeping most farmers afloat in 1934 and 1935. But then conditions suddenly changed. At the end of 1935 severe droughts in North America and Australia seriously imperiled international grain stocks. Prices now rose above the minimums prescribed by the Grain Board, and new markets suddenly appeared. Between 1935 and 1937, for example, the creation of the dust bowl forced the United States to import 2,925,700 metric tons of Argentine corn. During these years, with farmers in other countries still struggling to survive, Argentina once more became a leading supplier of grains to the world markets.[19]

The Price of Success

Although grain farming in Argentina emerged from the depression relatively healthy, its sudden apparent dynamism during the late 1930s disguised some growing weaknesses. Three key conditions had helped to protect farming during the previous twenty years: a continuing supply of unused arable land, a flexible labor force, and access to imported capital goods and technology. By the late 1930s these three conditions were disappearing, and along with them the opportunity to utilize the practices that had kept farming profitable and stable under adverse conditions.

Among these shifts the closing of the agricultural frontier was perhaps the most important, since it meant that farmers could no longer increase production by exploiting a reserve supply of land. After 1925 there were small increases in grain acreages in marginal regions, such as the La Pampa territory, but the dominant trend of this period was the expansion of agriculture in the province of Buenos Aires. Between the mid-1920s and the late 1930s Buenos Aires accounted for around two-thirds of the increase in grain acreages.[20]

Another indication that grain farming had reached its geographical limits appeared immediately before World War II. Along the western and southern margins of the Argentine grain zone, where climate and soil conditions made crop rotation unprofitable and forced farmers to specialize in wheat, barley, rye, and other grains, years of monocropping led to soil depletion and topsoil erosion. The damage proved so severe in some areas that it continued to block the expansion of grain farm acreage in the western and southwestern areas of the pampas until the 1950s.[21]

In addition, until the mid-1930s the flow of labor into the rural sector during periods of expansion and out of the sector during periods of contraction had provided grain farming in Argentina with considerable flexibility. But around 1935 the migrant inflow began to dwindle, as new social forces unleashed by the depression weakened the pull of the land but intensified that of the cities. Although the rural population continued to grow slowly until the mid-1940s, the pace of outmigration was growing simultaneously, from around two hundred thousand in the early 1930s to almost half a million in the mid-1940s. By World War II rural outmigration had reduced the net increase of the rural population to insignificant levels.[22]

With new land unavailable and labor flowing out of the rural sector, extensive production methods became increasingly unfeasible; what was now needed was a shift toward more intensive farming methods. But at the end of the 1930s international conditions increasingly conspired against change. During the previous decade the world market had moved away from the prewar system of relatively open commodity trading, as several European nations, including Italy, France, and Spain, raised tariffs and introduced subsidies to increase domestic grain production.[23] Although Argentina's share of export markets grew immediately after 1935, by the end of the decade its position was once more under threat, as the European markets became increasingly saturated with grain surpluses.

Meanwhile, in the United States the programs of the New Deal and a set of technological advances increased the international competitiveness of American farmers. These changes were particularly marked for the growing of labor-intensive crops, led by corn, in which improved planting techniques and new harvest machinery, combined with improved seed varieties, achieved large increases in yields. Argentine farmers attempted to respond to competition by adopting hybrid seeds tailored to local conditions. This strategy kept the wheat farmers on a par with their counterparts in the United States, but after 1940 the corn producers in Argentina fell rapidly behind (see table 20). By the mid-1940s corn yields in the United States outstripped those in Argentina by 30–40 percent.

To keep pace with their foreign competitors, Argentine farmers needed to adopt a range of new technologies but were unable to do so. Lacking an indigenous industrial economy, Argentina traditionally imported its agricultural capital goods and technologies. Low grain prices and the currency devaluation in 1933, however, made imports increasingly costly. A 30- to 40-horsepower tractor, for example, which cost 2,800 pesos in 1928, increased to 6,465 pesos in 1937 and to 8,650 pesos in 1940. Measured in a different way, by 1940 Argentine farmers had to sell seventy-nine more metric tons of grain than in 1937 to buy an imported tractor. With the prices of other imported agricultural capital goods increasing at a similar rate as tractors, it became increasingly difficult for Argentine farmers to maintain the necessary level of investment, and investment subsequently showed a sharp deterioration.[24] Another longer-term damaging trend was rising domestic consumption of grains provoked by the expansion of the cities. Between the 1920s and 1950s domestic consumption of agricultural goods doubled.[25]

By the late 1930s there were serious indications of growing crisis: an increasing glut of grain surpluses abroad and falling profits at home. In early 1939 one hundred kilos of wheat were trading at less than 7 pesos, a quintal

Table 20 Estimated Harvest Yields of Wheat and Corn in Argentina and the United States, 1930–1939 to 1950–1954 (In Kilograms per Hectare Harvested)

	1930–39	*1940–44*	*1945–49*	*1950–54*
Wheat				
Argentina	929	1,098	1,102	1,151
United States	844	1,098	1,061	1,123
Corn				
Argentina	1,842	1,998	1,766	1,529
United States	1,572	2,077	2,322	2,523

Source: Carlos F. Díaz Alejandro, *Essays on the Economic History of the Argentine Republic*. New Haven: Yale University Press, 1970, 194.

of corn at under 6 pesos, and linseed at under 13 pesos. Once more farmers were demanding public assistance. At this point the government responded by reviving the policies that had kept farming alive during the depression. The Grain Regulatory Board set new minimum prices for wheat and linseed, and the banks were directed to expand their rural credit programs. Advances to farmers under the *prenda agraria* program rose from 99,402 contracts valued at 337 million pesos in 1937/1938 to 129,933 contracts valued at 654 million pesos during the 1938/1939 agricultural year.[26]

Farmers' groups complained that these actions were not enough, and many farmers now turned to the tactics they had so often used in the past: once more they pushed the system of extensive farming to its limits by increasing the amount of land sown with grains. The resulting large harvests in 1939, alongside the depressed grain market abroad, however, forced the grain board to purchase more than 8 million metric tons of wheat and flaxseed—more than double its total purchases between 1933 and 1936.[27] In the first year of its renewed operations the board ran a deficit of 97 million pesos, and the high costs of the program quickly forced the government to review its policy.

In April 1939 Vicente Brunini, a director of the Grain and Elevator Commission in the province of Buenos Aires, outlined the new approach. According to Brunini, the way forward lay in the "diversification of cultivation in those zones where ecological conditions allow[ed] it, as well as promoting the transformation of marginal areas where the cultivation of wheat [was currently] unprofitable." Thus where conditions allowed, Brunini was arguing, farmers should replace wheat by other crops until wheat prices rose. In the southern, western, and northern fringes of the grain zone, where diversification was not feasible, he called for a shift from farming to ranching. Brunini admitted that this shift would force many farm workers and tenants into migrating out of the affected areas, but he promised, without going into detail, that the national government would help them move on to "new horizons."[28]

World War II and Its Aftermath

At this point came the shattering blow of World War II, which confronted the farmers with even worse conditions than those during the depression. First, the German U-boat campaigns and the ensuing shipping shortages, and then after mid-1940 the Nazi occupation of continental Europe, cut Argentina off from its European markets to an even greater extent than ever before. The sudden collapse of the markets in late 1940 occurred as the farmers were bringing in a record corn harvest of 10 million tons. Combined with leftover stocks from previous years, the new crop left the country holding more grain than it could store in the available silos and elevators.

In late 1940 the government attempted to keep the farmers afloat by once again expanding the grain-purchasing program. The grain board set a minimum price of 4.75 pesos for 100 kilograms of corn, bagged and delivered to port. But to reduce the vast expense of the program, it cut the minimum prices for wheat and flaxseed to 6.75 and 9.25 pesos, respectively. After 1940 the still-rising costs of the price support program forced further cutbacks in government support. In 1942, for example, the government reduced the minimum price for corn to 4.40 pesos and announced that the volume purchased in the following year would be cut by 40 percent; farmers were exhorted to reduce their sowings for the next harvest by the same amount.[29] Between 1940 and 1945 crop acreages plummeted by more than 3 million hectares (see table 21).

With less land in production, farm output fell steeply during the war (see table 22): wheat output declined by more than 4 million metric tons, corn

Table 21 Argentina: Acreage of Export and Forage Crops, 1940/1941 to 1944/1945 (In Thousands of Hectares)

	For Export				
Agricultural Year	*Wheat*	*Corn*	*Flaxseed*	*Forage Crops**	*Total*
1940/41	7,085	6,098	2,874	3,810	19,867
1941/42	7,300	5,000	2,730	3,299	18,329
1942/43	6,873	4,139	2,474	4,292	17,778
1943/44	6,811	4,412	2,283	4,691	18,197
1944/45	6,233	4,017	1,996	4,386	16,632
Net change (1944/45 minus 1940/41)	−852	−2,081	−878	+576	−3,235

Source: República Argentina, Secretaría de Agricultura, Ganadería y Pesca, *Estadísticas agrícolas retrospectivas*. Buenos Aires, 1987, 9–31.

*Forage crops include oats, barley, and rye.

output by more than 7 million metric tons, and flaxseed by almost 1 million metric tons between 1940/1941 and 1944/1945.

With tenants unable to pay rent and borrowers falling far behind on their mortgages, rural evictions grew increasingly common. Landowners converted some of the idle land to ranching and other activities, but bank and government surveys of economic conditions in the countryside during the war suggested that much of the abandoned farmland remained fallow. In 1942 the rapidly swelling rate of rural evictions forced the government to freeze existing tenant contracts. With economic conditions worsening and government support fading, by 1943 grain farming was in deep crisis.

Following the military coup of 4 June 1943, a new government, under Gen. Pedro Ramírez, at first expanded established aid programs and reversed plans to abandon grain price supports. But in 1944, as part of an effort to build up a political constituency amongst the rural lower classes, the military government reinforced tenant contract regulations and instituted a series of new statutes affecting rural labor organizations, wages, and working conditions. But these measures failed to halt the downward course of grain acreage and production.[30]

By 1945 Argentine grain farming had undergone a severe geographical contraction. With much less land devoted to grain farming, production lagged far behind prewar levels. But the farmers who had survived the wartime crisis found little relief in the postwar years. During the war, again helped by their governments, Argentina's competitors in the United States and Canada had become still more efficient. In Argentina itself, after years

Table 22 Argentina: Export Crop Production in World War II
(In Thousands of Metric Tons)

Agricultural Year	*Wheat*	*Corn*	*Flaxseed*	*Total*
1940/41	8,150	10,238	1,720	20,908
1941/42	6,487	9,034	1,600	17,121
1942/43	6,400	1,943	1,348	9,691
1943/44	6,800	8,730	1,573	17,103
1944/45	4,085	2,966	787	7,838

Source: República Argentina, Secretaría de Agricultura, Ganadería y Pesca, *Estadísticas agrícolas retrospectivas*. Buenos Aires, 1987, 9–31.

of single-crop farming, much of the grain zone displayed symptoms of land exhaustion. As acreages continued to contract, labor continued to flow out of the rural sector. Between 1937 and 1947 the rural work force fell from 1.2 million to only 624,000.[31]

With land and labor scarce, and foreign competition growing continually stronger, it was clear that the farmers could no longer pursue the path to recovery that had worked in the past. In order to thrive once more, farming now required a radical transformation of production methods: extensive operations had to give way to more efficient, mechanized farms that could produce higher yields with less labor. This path meant spending more on imported machinery or developing a domestic agricultural machinery industry. With the farmers exhausted by fifteen years of extreme hardship, only a comprehensive and far-reaching government program seemed able to execute the changes needed.

Immediately after the war state intervention in agriculture did expand once more, but instead of helping to promote the recovery of farming, it further accelerated its decline. Under Perón's government continued extensions of the wartime freezes on tenants' contracts discouraged new investment. By 1949, rather than continuing to collect rents made worthless by inflation, many landlords were either selling out to their tenants or illegally evicting them. Other Peronist measures encouraged the unionization of the rural work force and extended wartime regulations aimed at improving rural working conditions. By helping rural workers to organize and enforcing rural labor codes more strictly, the government made seasonal farm operations more complicated and costly for farm directors.[32] Moreover, the government took control over the marketing of agricultural goods by means of the notorious "IAPI" (Instituto Argentino para la Promoción del Intercambio [Argentine Institute for the Promotion of Trade]). By buying grains at around one-half or two-thirds of international price levels, the IAPI dealt another severe blow to the farmers.[33]

In the latter half of the 1940s acreage devoted to the country's three main export crops fell (see table 23). Production declined dramatically, except for wheat, which was less labor dependent and therefore less affected by the new government regulations than the other crops.

A decade or so after World War II Argentine grain farming became increasingly concentrated into two core areas: a zone dominated by wheat and other fine-grain products centered in southeastern Buenos Aires prov-

Table 23 Argentina: Acreage and Production of Selected Crops 1945/1946 to 1949/1950 (In Thousands of Hectares)

	1945/46	*1946/47*	*1947/48*	*1948/49*	*1949/50*
Land area					
Wheat	5,762	6,674	5,450	5,806	5,692
Corn	3,951	3,612	3,319	2,691	2,156
Flaxseed	1,865	1,905	1,573	1,305	1,078
Total	11,575	12,191	10,342	9,802	8,926
Production					
Wheat	3,907	5,615	6,500	5,200	5,144
Corn	3,574	5,815	5,200	3,450	836
Flaxseed	964	1,034	901	433	676
Total	8,445	12,464	12,601	9,083	6,656

Source: República Argentina, Secretaría de Agricultura, Ganadería y Pesca, *Estadísticas agrícolas retrospectivas*. Buenos Aires, 1987, 9–31.

ince; and a second area, spanning northern Buenos Aires and southern Santa Fe provinces, that specialized in corn and oilseeds.[34] But by this point the "mother industry" was close to eclipse. It could no longer compete on the world market, and in some years it was now failing to feed the domestic population. In 1952 Argentina, formerly one of the great exporters of grains, now suffered the humiliation of having to import large quantities of wheat and corn.

Notes

1. John Newton Smith, *Argentine Agriculture: Trends in Production and World Competition*. Washington, D.C.: U.S. Department of Agriculture, Economic Research Service, 1968, 18, 129.

2. The most comprehensive statement of his argument is in Carlos F. Díaz Alejandro, *Essays on the Economic History of the Argentine Republic*. New Haven: Yale University Press, 1970, 206–56.

3. Horacio C. E. Giberti, *Historia económica de la ganadería argentina*. 2d ed. Buenos Aires: Raigal, 1961.

4. Jorge Sabato, *La pampa pródiga: Claves de una frustración*. Buenos Aires: Centro de Investigaciones sobre el Estado y la Administración, 1981, 70–96.

5. For a critique of Giberti's view that ranching drove farming see Alfredo Pucciarelli, *El capitalismo agrario pampeano, 1880–1930*. Buenos Aires: Hyspamérica, 1986, 158–63.

6. See James R. Scobie, *Revolution on the Pampas: A Social History of Argentine Wheat, 1860–1910*. Austin: University of Texas Press, 1964, 27–70; Díaz Alejandro, *Essays*, 148–65.

7. For data on crop acreages see República Argentina, Comisión Nacional del Censo Agropecuario, *Censo agropecuario nacional, año 1937*. Vol. 1. Buenos Aires: Guillermo Kraft, Ltda., 1939, xxiii, xxv, xxix.

8. Bill Albert, *South America and the First World War: The Impact of the War on Brazil, Argentina, Peru, and Chile*. Cambridge: Cambridge University Press, 1988, 61–77, 142–56, 210–22, 239–55.

9. On these wartime measures see Daniel Lewis, "A Political and Economic History of Grain Farming in Buenos Aires Province, Argentina, 1914–1943." Ph.D. diss., University of California, Santa Barbara, 1990, 331–32.

10. Ibid., 350–75.

11. Ibid., 402–15.

12. José O. Dowling, "Resultados agrícolas generales y particulares: Una contradicción," *Gaceta rural* 21, no. 245 (December 1927), 435.

13. Leon M. Estabrook, *Agricultural Survey of South America: Argentina and Paraguay*. U.S. Department of Agriculture Bulletin, no. 1409. Washington, D.C.: U.S. Government Printing Office, 1926, 66–72.

14. Data on farmers' strategies during the depression appear in Banco de la Provincia de Buenos Aires, *Memoria y balance general*. Buenos Aires, 1931, 5–6; and República Argentina, Ministerio de Agricultura de la Nación, *Anuario agropecuario, año 1932*. Buenos Aires, 1932, v–viii.

15. For figures on acreages see República Argentina, *Estadísticas agrícolas retrospectivas*. Buenos Aires, 1987, 19, 21, 31.

16. *Revista del Ferrocarril Sud* 8, no. 98 (August 1933), 7.

17. On the Grain Board see Virgil Salera, *Exchange Control and the Argentine Market*. New York: Columbia University Press, 1941, 102–51; and Harry R. Woltman, "The Decline of Argentina's Agricultural Trade: Problems and Policies." Ph.D. diss., Stanford University, 1959, 87–117.

18. For details on the workings of the program see República Argentina, Ministerio de Agricultura de la Nación, *Memoria de la Junta Reguladora de Granos, campaña 1933–1934*. Buenos Aires, 1935, 40; and idem, *Memoria de la Junta Reguladora de Granos, 2 ejercicio, año 1935*. Buenos Aires, 1936, 15.

19. Export statistics appear in República Argentina, Ministerio de Agricultura de la Nación, *Almanaque* (1946), 78.

20. For data see Héctor Pérez-Brignoli, "The Economic Cycle in Latin American Export Economies (1880–1930): A Hypothesis for Investigation," *Latin American Research Review* 15, no. 2 (1980), 19; Curto E. Hotschewer, *Evolución de la agricultura en la provincia de Santa Fe: Su dependencia de factores geográficas y económicos*. Santa Fe: Province of Santa Fe, Ministerio de Hacienda, Economía e Industrias, 1953.

21. Antonio Arena and Antonio Román Guiñazú, "La erosión eólica de los suelos en el centro-oeste de la Argentina." In República Argentina, Ministerio de Agricultura de la Nación, *Publicaciones misceláneas* 65 (1939), 8–15.

22. For figures on rural population see Alfredo E. Lattes, "La dinámica de la población rural en la Argentina entre 1870 y 1970," *Cuadernos del CENEP*, vol. 9. Buenos Aires: Centro de Estudios de Población, 1979.

23. For a review of international farm and trade policies after World War I see Arturo O'Connell, "Free Trade in One (Primary Producing) Country: The Case of Argentina in the 1920s," in *The Political Economy of Argentina, 1880–1946*, edited by Guido di Tella and D. C. M. Platt. London: Macmillan Press, 1986, 74–94.

24. For investment data see United Nations, Comisión Económica para América Latina, *El desarrollo económico de la Argentina*. México, D.F.: CEPAL, 1959, pt. 2, 85.

25. Eprime Eshag and Rosemary Thorp, "Economic and Social Consequences of Orthodox Economic Policies in Argentina in the Post-War Years," *Bulletin of the Oxford University Institute of Economics and Statistics* 27, no. 1 (February 1965), 6.

26. Woltman, "Decline," 112–13.

27. Ibid., 108.

28. Brunini's comments appear in Ministerio de Obras Públicas de la Provincia de Buenos Aires, Dirección de Agricultura, Ganadería e Industrias, *La regulación de la producción agrícola: Consejos a los agricultores*. La Plata, 1939, 6, 7.

29. On the activities of the grain board in World War II see Woltman, "Decline," 164–73; on the policy shift in 1942 see "Los precios básicos del maíz y la política agraria nacional," in República Argentina, Comisión Nacional de Elevadores de Granos, *Boletín Informativo* 6, no. 5 (15 May 1942), 221–29.

30. Lewis, "Grain Farming," 523–32, 552–54.

31. On the rural population see Alfredo E. Lattes, "La dinámica de la población rural en la Argentina entre 1870 y 1970," in *Cuadernos del CENEP*, vol. 9. Buenos Aires: Centro de Estudios de Población, 1979, 35; for data on the labor force see Guillermo Flichman, *La renta del suelo y el desarrollo agrario argentino*. Buenos Aires: Siglo XXI, 1977, 179.

32. Humberto Mascali, *Desocupación y conflictos laborales en el campo argentino (1940–1965)*. Buenos Aires: Centro Editor de América Latina, 1986, 29–68.

33. Woltman, "Decline," 185–260.

34. Government measures of cattle production are unavailable for the years 1939–1951. For an alternative production series that suggests that ranching leveled off after the war see Lovell S. Jarvis, *Supply Response in the Cattle Industry: The Argentine Case*, Giannini Foundation Special Report. Oakland: Giannini Foundation, Division of Agriculture and Natural Resources, 1986.

10 The Origins of the Green Revolution in Mexico

Continuity or Change?

Joseph Cotter

The "Green Revolution" in Mexico originated in 1943 in the Mexican Agricultural Project (MAP) established by the Rockefeller Foundation. Previous scholarly works have treated the early stages of the revolution from the perspective of the economic or foreign policy interests of the United States, of which the Rockefeller Foundation is portrayed as an agent. To these authors Mexican interest in Rockefeller Foundation assistance arose from a new spirit of cooperation between the two nations during World War II and represented an abrupt shift from the proagrarian policies of President Lázaro Cárdenas (1934–1940) to the emphasis on industrialization under President Manuel Ávila Camacho (1940–1946). Further, the founding of the MAP has been portrayed as the abandonment of an autarkic and progressive agricultural science policy prevailing before 1943 in favor of one relying on foreign technologies inappropriate for Mexico's small-scale peasant farmers.[1] A recent monograph captures this interpretation well through the subtitle employed in discussing the origins of the MAP: "The Green Revolution and the Counterrevolution."[2]

Hitherto no Mexican archival sources have been used to illustrate how events and trends in Mexico influenced the origins of the MAP. Why did Mexico choose to abandon Mexican-directed agricultural improvement programs in favor of technologies imported from the United States? Did pre-1943 agricultural research and extension programs represent a successful, or potentially successful, attempt to develop an alternative agricultural technology more appropriate to the conditions of peasant agriculture? Did Mexico actually reject foreign agricultural science and technology before 1943? In this chapter I discuss pre-1943 Mexican agricultural research and extension programs and the development of Mexican agricultural research institutions during the same period. In particular I review the role of foreign agricultural science and technology, including direct technical assistance, in such programs and the attitudes of the Mexican agricultural research community toward such assistance.

Starting in the 1920s, and gaining strength during the Cárdenas administration, some agricultural researchers in Mexico adopted the ideology of "scientific nationalism": agricultural development programs had to be based on the results of research done in Mexico alone in order to be successful. Cynthia Hewitt de Alcantara's monograph *Modernizing Mexican Agriculture*, published in 1976, stresses the importance of this idea during the 1930s in discussing the agricultural research and extension programs of the Cárdenas administration. Relying on a 1971 interview with Edmundo Taboada, a plant genetics specialist, she argues that Mexican agricultural researchers were "little interested in importing technology from abroad."[3]

In this chapter, however, I illustrate that "scientific nationalism" was always more rhetorical than real. The lack of an experimental tradition within Mexican agricultural science continually undercut an autarkic approach to agricultural science. The Green Revolution is therefore better understood as the outcome of a long-term Mexican dependence on foreign agricultural science and technology rather than as an abrupt break from the past or an expression of the larger changes in policy led by the administrations of the 1940s. Moreover, from the perspective of agricultural science, the 1940s—so often in other respects seen as a major turning point in Mexican history—marked only a continuation, or at most an acceleration, of past trends.

Indeed, internal developments in Mexico set the stage for the arrival of the MAP in 1943. After twenty years of government-sponsored agricultural research and extension programs that had mostly failed, many concluded that Mexican agricultural researchers, particularly the *agrónomos* (agronomists), were parasitic bureaucrats rather than "scientists." By the late 1930s national corn production could no longer meet demand, forcing imports from the United States. In 1937 a banana disease began to destroy this profitable export industry, despite a government campaign to eradicate it.

Problems with the supply of other agricultural commodities also surfaced during the late 1930s. By this time various researchers and branches of the Mexican government had decided that foreign help was essential if progress was to be made toward improving agricultural productivity.

Agricultural Science Policy before 1933

The Mexican government first sponsored agricultural research and extension programs during the last years of the Porfirio Díaz dictatorship.[4] Between 1905 and 1910 the Mexican government sent study groups abroad, contracted a few European scientists, and introduced foreign varieties of wheat. During this period, and even earlier, the Escuela Nacional de Agricultura, founded in 1864, was training professional agronomists, although very few found employment in agriculture: most were shunned by the Mexican *hacendados* (landowners). Not surprisingly, most of the agronomists later committed themselves to the revolution that overthrew the Díaz regime in 1910 and participated in the first attempts at land redistribution. Among them was Marte R. Gómez, who served with the *zapatistas* and later as secretary of agriculture in the administration of President Manuel Ávila Camacho, who signed the agreement with the Rockefeller Foundation that established the MAP. Others rode with Pancho Villa or joined the ranks of Gen. Alvaro Obregón in Sonora. Many of the *agrónomos* held political office or served the ruling Partido Nacional Revolucionario during the 1920s and 1930s.[5] The close ties between the *agrónomos* and the Mexican state after the revolution significantly influenced the evolution of the profession, causing the public to associate it with specific policies, particularly the agrarian reform.

Meanwhile, the Mexican government again expressed interest in sponsoring agricultural research and extension programs under President Venustiano Carranza (1915–1920). Carranza founded the Dirección de Estudios Biológicos (Office of Biological Studies), a research institute within the Secretaría de Agricultura y Fomento (SAF) (Secretariat of Agriculture and Development), under the direction of Alfonso Herrera, a biologist. This agency, supposedly charged with conducting agricultural research, actually focused most of its attention on taxonomic projects of purely scientific interest, such as preparing catalogues of Mexican fauna and flora, but this situation led to conflicts with the Universidad Nacional Autónomo de México (National Autonomous University of Mexico) and the decay and eventual demise of the agency during the late 1920s.[6] The SAF also organized the "*trenes de maquinaria agrícola*" (trains of agricultural machinery), which toured the country promoting agricultural machinery manufactured in the United States.[7]

The commercial activities of the SAF, and its uninspiring overall performance, led to public criticism of both the agency and the agronomists, leading to a period of professional introspection during the early 1920s. At this point the *agrónomos* created the Sociedad Agronómica Nacional (National Agronomic Society) and sought to influence President Alvaro Obregón (1920–1924), who had some personal interest in agricultural modernization. During the organization's 1922 national convention, the agronomist Eustacio L. Contreras made a scathing attack on the corrupt practices, disorganization, and petty politics of the SAF, arguing that the guild had to develop a new sense of professional responsibility and closer relations with Mexican farmers to improve its public image.[8]

Members of the guild took Contreras's criticisms to heart. Several spoke of the profession's duty to modernize Mexico's backward agricultural practices. In meetings in 1922 and 1923 various *agrónomos* called for government programs to improve pest-control practices and fruit tree cultivation; to promote silk production, forest conservation, the practice of crop rotation, and the use of fertilizers; to rid the country of the Egyptian plow; and to disseminate "all the new trends the farmer must understand in order to implant them in his procedures."[9]

Other agronomists argued that the profession should engage in social, economic, and political activities such as improving rural health and education, organizing farmers into cooperatives, and helping them petition for land. These ideas led to the "*proyectismo*" approach to agricultural research and extension that became typical of almost all such programs until 1940.[10] The essence of *proyectismo* was that all Mexico's agricultural problems, technical and nontechnical, should be tackled simultaneously whatever the shortages of funds and trained personnel. Most members of the profession loudly advocated agrarian reform and called for Obregón to step up its pace.[11] During the mid-1920s the government employed more than twice as many agronomists in the Comisión Nacional Agraria (National Agrarian Commission), the agency responsible for carrying out the land refcrm, as it did in research and extension programs in the Secretaría de Agricultura y Fomento. Furthermore, the SAF's regional extension agents often spent their time organizing peasants and helping them petition for land.[12] Despite the plea of Juan de Dios Bojórquez, an agronomist, that the profession should avoid becoming "a new political group" that "would act in national life with partisan ends," by the end of the 1920s the public perception of the guild as professional bureaucrats and agrarian agitators had become solidly entrenched.[13]

The desire of the *agrónomos* to be more active in modernizing Mexican agriculture generated a commitment to "scientific nationalism." In 1923 for example, a SAF poultry expert, Rufino Monroy wrote:

> How to start? The question that all who begin poultry keeping ask. Unfortunately in Mexico, those who could give the answer have not done it, because the majority of writers on the subject have concentrated on the translation of articles from North American authors, which are hardly appropriate to our situation, given that they have been developed to confront the problems of another, in some cases very different, climate. Particularly if the article is not perfect for the locality it was written for, after it is poorly translated and put into practice outside its own locale, the advice turns out to be very bad and harmful because following it leads to disaster.[14]

This idea of scientific nationalism emerged during the early 1920s, and agricultural researchers continued to expound it during the 1930s.[15] However, the lack of an experimental tradition worked against an autarkic approach to science, and "scientific nationalism" did not go much beyond a purely rhetorical level.

The establishment of the *agrónomos regionales* (regional extension agents) in 1923 represented the first attempt by the Secretaría de Agricultura y Fomento at direct agricultural extension. Originally organized on the basis of the agronomist Gonzalo Robles's study of extension services in the United States, during its early years the program underwent several extensive reorganizations.[16] At the same time, the scarcity of funds led to continual reductions in the number of agents, until in 1933 only twelve of the originally budgeted thirty-five remained.[17] In 1925 the SAF appointed Juan A. González, an agronomist educated in the United States and a friend of Henry A. Wallace, to direct the extension service. He expanded the reach of extension programs by using prominent local farmers as agricultural promoters (*promotores agrícolas*), and establishing young farmer's clubs in schools (*clubes de fomento agrícola*).[18]

Extension programs under the direction of González attempted to improve cultivation of many different crops but resulted in an excessive dispersal of effort. The notion that the corn-based diet of the Mexican people was deficient, and a desire to increase peasant incomes by substituting more remunerative crops in place of corn, generated campaigns to promote the cultivation of fruits and vegetables. The Secretaría de Agricultura y Fomento encouraged farmers to import seeds of foreign-developed high-yield varieties, especially cotton and wheat. The extension agents often focused their efforts on arranging empirical tests of these imported varieties, examining their performance under Mexican conditions.[19]

From the mid-to late-1920s the SAF conducted a campaign to promote the use of agricultural machinery and iron plows.[20] After the onset of the depression in 1930 the SAF began several extension campaigns to promote the cultivation of export crops, such as melons, using imported seeds, in the state of Morelos.[21] In a similar vein, the agency promoted crops that aimed to reduce imports, such as sesame or grapes.[22] By 1934 the program with imported wheat strains achieved some success by encouraging the cultivation of "Marquis" wheat in the Bajío states and "Defiance" wheat in northern Mexico, especially Sonora.[23]

To increase corn production, the Secretaría de Agricultura y Fomento organized the *campaña en pro del maíz* (campaign in favor of corn). This approach involved using lectures, demonstrations, radio broadcasts, and articles in the national press to convince farmers to practice seed selection based on the morphological characteristics of standing plants, to disinfect seeds with commercial products, to store them properly, and to conduct germination tests to ensure their viability. Although the *agrónomos* were familiar with the corn-breeding experiments conducted in the United States, they had little experience or interest in experimental research. The peasant, not the agronomist, was supposed to become the plant breeder.[24] Alongside the methods of the *campaña* the SAF tried to introduce U.S. hybrid corn varieties and test planted them in various parts of the country. In the mid-1920s the government considered establishing an autonomous department to carry out an intensive program to improve corn cultivation, including the development of hybrids. However, the plan was rejected, partly out of recognition that Mexico lacked sufficient trained personnel for a program of this type.[25]

The SAF focused on extension programs and conducted relatively little agricultural research during this period. From 1928 to the early 1930s the Comisión Nacional de Irrigación (National Irrigation Commission) operated experimentation stations in the Don Martín irrigation district, near Rodríguez, Nuevo León, and in the "President Calles" project in Pabellón, Aguascalientes, but these stations limited their work to empirical tests of native and imported crop varieties in an attempt to ascertain which performed best under local conditions. An experimentation station established on the grounds of the Escuela Nacional de Agricultura likewise confined its works to empirical tests, usually of imported crop varieties.[26]

Between 1928 and 1930 the Secretaría de Agricultura y Fomento conducted tests of soil fertility using the Newbauer system of plant nutrient uptake and in 1933 with German assistance tested chemical fertilizers on coffee plantations in Veracruz and wheat fields in Jalisco.[27] Between 1926 and 1929 an SAF agronomist, Pandurang Khankhoje, who had been educated at the University of Oregon, developed a hybrid corn strain as part of his research on the genetic origins of the plant. However, the government displayed little interest in the project, and the assignment of Khankhoje to an SAF commission to Europe in 1930 disrupted the continuity of the research.[28] From 1920 to 1933 various private parties conducted agricultural research in Mexico, including developing hybrid plant varieties, but again the government expressed no interest in them and gave them no financial support.[29]

Regardless of "scientific nationalism," during the 1920s the Mexican government and agricultural researchers did not reject foreign agricultural science or technical assistance. Various Mexicans working in agricultural science spoke admiringly of the agricultural technologies of the United States and other foreign nations and called on Mexico to copy them.[30] By sending its technicians to the United States for training, the Mexican government sought to improve the agricultural statistics department of the SAF, its campaign to promote fruit and nut production and tree nurseries in the state of Chihuahua, and its rural secondary educational institutes (Escuelas Centrales Agrícolas).[31] Meanwhile, at the Colegio Agrológico in Meoqui, Chihuahua, the Comisión Nacional de Irrigación enlisted the aid of the University of California to train Mexican technicians in the science of agrology.[32] Thus in all these cases the Mexican government responded to failed programs by seeking assistance from abroad. Meanwhile, some of Mexico's more affluent and progressive agriculturists likewise sought technical advice from the

United States, and a few farmer organizations hired North American technical specialists to advise them regarding their agricultural practices.[33]

In 1928 the Secretaría de Agricultura y Fomento approved a request from the United States to establish a laboratory in Mexico City and a test plot in Tamaulipas when the Mexican fruit fly became a threat to North American growers.[34] After raising the idea in 1928, in 1929 the SAF gladly agreed to a U.S. proposal for a joint campaign to control the pink bollworm, which was threatening Texas cotton fields in the border areas while causing losses to Mexican growers in the La Laguna and other areas. The influential agronomists Gonzalo Robles and Luis L. León, minister of agriculture under President Plutarco Elías Calles (1924–1928), advocated importing foreign scientists to help to address the deficiencies in knowledge of experimental methods among the Mexican agricultural research community.[35]

From 1925, the first year in which fairly reliable statistics are available, to 1933 the yields of most important Mexican crops (corn, beans, wheat, henequen, coffee, bananas, cacao) stagnated, while the yields of crops whose seeds came primarily from imported sources such as tomatoes and potatoes either increased or, as with cotton, stood at the same level of those in the advanced agricultural nations.[36] This situation, combined with the crisis caused by the onset of the Great Depression, led to another outburst of debate regarding the future of agricultural development in Mexico.

Many important political figures, including former president and behind-the-scenes power broker Calles, along with prominent intellectuals decried the backward methods of Mexican farmers. Some called the agrarian reform a failure, and advocated terminating it.[37] The *agrónomos*, closely associated with the agrarian reform in the public's mind, likewise became subject to criticism because they were seen as responsible for the low agricultural productivity in Mexico. Between November 1931 and mid-1932 a series of articles appeared in the newspaper *El Universal* that accused the agronomists of ineptitude and corruption, argued they had contributed nothing to the improvement of Mexican agriculture, and demanded they end their involvement in the political cause of the agrarian reform.[38] Elsewhere, some argued that *agrónomos* preferred receiving financial rewards to offering any real social services and that they cared little for improving agriculture; they were content to be unproductive bureaucrats in comfortable offices in Mexico City. One report claimed the agronomists knew nothing about improving the productivity of farming; they were mere administrators or surveyors; foreign technicians should be brought in to take over agricultural extension services.[39]

The agronomists responded by launching a campaign to defend the profession. In 1931 various graduates of the Escuela Nacional de Agricultura revived the defunct Sociedad Agronómica Nacional, calling their new professional organization the Sociedad Agronómica Mexicana (SAM). The SAM vowed to continue the struggle to bring social, political, and economic redemption to Mexico's rural lower classes through agrarian reform and the application of modern science to farming practices.[40] The approach of the agronomists to the problems of Mexican agriculture was not restricted to technical issues like the use of fertilizers or crop varieties. It also involved rural hygiene and public health, organizing the farmers to increase the power of the producer relative to that of commercial interests, raising the education level of the peasantry, combating the hold of religion on the *campesino*, and raising political consciousness.[41]

Yet most agronomists agreed that the profession had accomplished little toward improving agricultural productivity. However, they denied they were to blame and instead attributed the failure of earlier programs to inadequate government financial support, poor planning and leadership, insufficient program continuity, and the personnel policies of the Secretaría de Agricultura y Fomento.[42] Once more the Sociedad Agronómica Mexicana requested the government to certify agronomy as a profession in the service of the state and to grant the *agrónomos* a greater role in the planning and execution of future agricultural research and extension programs.[43] The agronomists reiterated the sentiments of "scientific nationalism" from the 1920s.[44] Yet, despite the nationalistic fervor of this period, Mexico did not reject offers of foreign scientific aid or end its reliance on foreign agricultural science and technology. The joint campaigns against the pink bollworm and Mexican fruit fly continued uninterrupted, breeding a spirit of cooperation between the technicians of the two nations and public praise for the programs, and leading in 1934 to the establishment of the U.S.–Mexican International Pest Control Commission.[45] In 1933 Secretary of Agriculture Francisco Elías Calles expressed interest in a proposal by John A. Ferrell of the Rockefeller Foundation's International Health Division that urged the foundation to expand its activities from public health to include technical assistance in agriculture and a fellowship program for training Mexican researchers in U.S. universities.[46]

Agricultural Science Policy under Lázaro Cárdenas and the Origins of the Mexican Agricultural Project

In 1932 the government began to implement reforms in the Secretaría de Agricultura y Fomento that established the institutional structure for the agricultural research and extension programs of 1934–1940. In August 1932 President Abelardo Rodríguez (1932–1934) signed the Ley de Servicios Agrícolas Nacionales (National Law of Agricultural Services), which attempted to forge a close link between the development of agriculture and economic, social, and political issues. The legislation also established the Consejo Nacional de Agricultura (National Council on Agriculture), a body charged to advise the SAF, to develop a national plan to improve agricultural production and to organize state- and local-level agricultural improvement programs.[47]

In 1934 Rodríguez requested the agricultural science community to provide suggestions for future SAF research and extension programs. In response one report, prepared under the auspices of the Partido Nacional Revolucionario, advocated expanded research programs, a wide range of extension campaigns to improve fruit tree cultivation, livestock raising, pest-control practices, and measures to promote the cultivation of new crops that would be more remunerative than corn and beans. It also called for steps such as increased funds for agricultural credit, the formation of farmer organizations, and others reflecting the interest of the *agrónomos* in the economic and social aspects of agriculture.[48] Political leaders supported these recommendations, thereby assuring the perpetuation of the diversified, *proyectismo* approach to agricultural research and extension throughout the 1930s.[49]

In 1934 under the leadership of Enrique Beltrán, a Columbia University trained biologist, the Instituto Biotécnico (Biotechnical Institute) conducted research in various fields, including studies on plant pest-and-disease control, the development of regulations for commercial pesticides, and research on the genetics of purebred livestock. Pandurang Khankhoje continued his corn-breeding program, working with the strain he had developed during the late 1920s. In addition to research on topics with application to agriculture, the institute did taxonomic studies of Mexican flora, fauna, and natural resources, and reflecting its director's interest in marine biology studied the fish of Lake Pátzcuaro.[50] Even so the Instituto Biotécnico experienced many problems during its first year of existence. They included equipment and funding shortages, and interpersonal and professional rivalries with other SAF departments and employees. In 1935 Minister of Agriculture Tomás Garrido Canabal enacted and enforced various anticlerical measures within the agency, causing turmoil at the institute and provoking Beltrán's resignation.[51]

In July 1935 the new minister of agriculture, Saturnino Cedillo, appointed a veterinarian, José Figueroa, director of the Instituto Biotécnico. Reflecting his personal interests, Figueroa expanded livestock-related research, although the institute continued to conduct studies related to agriculture on topics such as plant pest control. Its list of projects also reflected the "diversified" approach to agricultural research that included studies related to human health and nutrition. It continued the taxonomic studies of the Beltrán period and conducted research on ecological topics such as "the advantages and inconveniences of importing and exporting wild mammals, birds, and reptiles."[52] Once more, however, personal favoritism at times took precedence over scientific ability in personnel decisions, and the turmoil in the Secretaría de Agricultura y Fomento caused by Minister of Agriculture Cedillo's dismissal and rebellion in July 1937 led to the ousting of several researchers in the institute. Tiring of the internal turmoil, in 1937 Pandurang Khankhoje left the institute, abandoning his corn-breeding research.[53]

Activities at the SAF's regional experimentation stations likewise reflected the "diversified" approach to agricultural research. In spite of the original plan to increase the range of its activities slowly under the scientific direction of the Instituto Biotécnico, the program became dominated by populist considerations. The number of stations increased from six in 1934 to fourteen in 1935, including two new ones in Minister of Agriculture Garrido Canabal's home state of Tabasco.[54] In 1935 Minister of Agriculture Cedillo announced that the SAF planned to establish two hundred stations throughout the country. Shortages of funds led to the closure of seven stations in 1936, but the SAF again increased their number in 1937, including two new stations in Minister Cedillo's home state of San Luis Potosí.[55]

The *agrónomos* believed the stations should perform many diverse functions, including plant-breeding experiments, empirical tests of foreign plant varieties, and the introduction of new crops. They were also intended to help to combat the hold of the Catholic church on the minds of the peasantry and to attempt to improve agriculture in all its aspects, economic and social as well as technical.[56] In practice, the stations concentrated on the empirical testing of various foreign crop varieties, especially wheat, but at the same time more unusual crops such as soybeans and sunflowers. They focused on the propagation of foreign fruit tree varieties by establishing tree nurseries and gave demonstrations of better farming practices based on their studies of agricultural theory rather than knowledge arrived at by experimentation. Only three of the stations conducted small-scale plant-breeding experiments with corn.[57]

Several of the experimentation stations were located on lands with poor drainage and lost their experimental plantings through flooding. Scarce funds often prevented or delayed necessary construction works and undermined their ability to operate. Understaffing exacerbated these problems.[58] In at least one instance the SAF used the personnel budget of an experimentation station to pay an individual who did not work there.[59] Although various projects were submitted to the SAF that involved using plant-breeding techniques to improve crop varieties, including one for corn, the agency expressed little or no interest in these proposals.[60]

Extension programs replicated the patterns of the 1920s. Despite increased government support for experimentation, they usually had little connection with research programs. The number of extension agents fluctuated annually, from a high of thirty-six in 1934 to a low of twenty-one in 1936, climbing once more to twenty-eight in 1938. When after 1934 President Cárdenas accelerated the pace of land reform, the number of agronomists employed in this task grew to outnumber vastly those employed in positions related to the technical improvement of agriculture. In 1937 the Secretaría de Agricultura y Fomento proposed that "ideology" be used as a criterion for hiring employees. Favoritism led the SAF to employ individuals as "agronomists" who lacked academic degrees. In one case in Chihuahua state, Minister Cedillo's hiring of an old *agrarista* (agriculture agency) crony as the agency's general representative led to serious unrest among the local peasantry and to a conflict between the state governor and the federal government.[61]

Despite the enormous importance of corn in Mexico to the peasantry and urban lower classes, the groups the Cárdenas administration claimed to support, between 1933 and 1937 the extension and research efforts of the SAF placed less emphasis on the development of corn than during the early 1930s. There were two principal reasons for this neglect. Some, including the prominent anthropologist Manuel Gamio argued that the predominance of corn in the Mexican diet "victimized" the populace. The Mexican Department of Public Health supported this argument, and provided support for SAF to promote the cultivation of other crops in place of corn.[62] But at the same time, after 1932 Mexico became self-sufficient in corn, and in 1934 and 1935 even managed to export some.[63]

In his address to Congress in 1937 Cárdenas claimed that Mexico's self-sufficiency in corn resulted from the success of SAF's campaigns to improve cultivation practices.[64] Meanwhile, spokesmen for the SAF used the national press to proclaim the success of previous corn improvement programs, claiming that great progress was being made toward the modernization of Mexican agriculture.[65] Yet this spirit of optimism, and the rising tide of nationalistic sentiments that culminated in the expropriation of foreign oil properties in 1938, did not result in a turning away from foreign technical assistance programs in agriculture or from importing agricultural technologies. People in agricultural science continued to admire the farming practices of the United States and called on Mexico to emulate them.[66] The SAF upheld the practice of granting permits for the free importation of foreign seeds, trees, and plant parts. By the mid-1930s the use of foreign seed was standard practice among the rice growers of Sonora, the potato farmers of the Bajío, and the majority of northern Mexico's cotton producers. In 1937 and 1938 the Banco Crédito de Ejidal purchased quantities of U.S. wheat and cotton seed for distribution to *ejidatarios* (members of peasant collectives) in the La Laguna and Mexicali valley.[67]

Meanwhile, the Mexican government continued to send its agricultural scientists to the United States and other foreign countries.[68] Some Mexican agronomists and Escuela Nacional de Agricultura students, the extremely left-wing National Congress of Agricultural Students (whose members insisted that their curriculum include instruction on the overthrow of capitalism), and the nation's orange growers all called for the government to allocate more funds to send Mexican technical specialists abroad for advanced training.[69] The pink bollworm and Mexican fruit fly campaigns pursued in cooperation with the United States continued without interruption, and the former expanded in scope. These programs once more created a spirit of cooperation and goodwill between technical experts in the two nations, even among the nationalist *agrónomos*.[70] During these years the Secretaría de Agricultura y Fomento codified the recommendations of U.S. technical specialists and used fines and other coercive measures to force Mexican farmers to comply with them.[71] In 1937 the Banco Crédito de Ejidal, a hotbed of leftist agronomists, hired J. H. Harrison, a cotton grader from the

United States, to offer advice on the purchase of ginning machines. Replying to a letter published in the newspaper *Excelsior* that criticized the bank for hiring technical experts in the United States, bank officials informed Cárdenas that "they [had] limited themselves to giving. . .their opinions on the activities of the *ejidatarios*."[72]

In 1938 shortages of corn, the need to import corn, and the resultant popular discontent shattered the earlier euphoria. In various parts of the country the *presidentes municipales* were now preventing corn from being sent to the market. Corn imports increased from 9,844 kilograms in 1936 to 3,662,500 kilograms in 1937, increasing sixfold to 22,062,330 kilograms in 1938.[73] The SAF responded by resurrecting the *campaña en pro del maíz*. Numerous articles in the national press exhorted the peasants to adopt the practices of the *campaña*.[74] The campaign appeared to have some impact, for by 1939 national average corn yields had increased 30 percent above those of 1937, although that had been a particularly poor year.[75] Nevertheless, in 1939 imports were still required to satisfy national demand.[76] The SAF devoted less energy to the campaign in 1940 and offered nothing more than the same productivity-improving ideas of the 1920s to the National Corn and Bean Growers Convention of 1940.

In late 1937 another crisis erupted when the banana plantations of Tabasco were hit by the Sigatoka disease, a malady caused by the fungus *Cercospora musae*. This disease had already done much damage in the banana plantations of Central America.[77] The SAF studied the procedures used by the United Fruit Company to fight the disease but concluded that the fixed tubing networks and high-pressure pumping required for liquid fungicides were too expensive for use in Mexico. Instead, it decided to conduct an eradication campaign using portable sprayers and a powdered fungicide.[78] The SAF publicly downplayed the significance of the disease, claiming falsely it had the situation under control.[79] But various difficulties delayed the onset of the eradication campaign, and by 1938 the disease was spreading to plantations in Chiapas, Veracruz, and Oaxaca.[80] Numerous farmers and their organizations pleaded for more government help to eradicate the disease, but the SAF failed to conduct a thorough spraying campaign, thereby ensuring that loci of infection remained to recontaminate the treated plantations.[81] By 1940 the situation reached crisis proportions, all but eliminating the export of bananas from Tabasco state.[82] There were accusations against the SAF of ineptitude and corruption.[83]

But the Secretaría de Agricultura y Fomento did not change its approach to agricultural research and extension during the last years of the Cárdenas presidency. During the late 1930s the crises in corn production, the banana industry, and others involving sugar cane, beans, and oilseed crops thus generated a flood of criticisms against the SAF, the *agrónomos*, and the land reform program itself.[84] Numerous studies and reports again asserted that the agency's research and extension programs had failed largely because the *agrónomos* lacked practical knowledge of farming and had inadequate training in science.[85]

It was at this point that the Mexican government and those involved in agricultural research began to turn to foreign sources in a much more intensive and systematic manner for assistance in the agricultural sciences. The SAF, the Banco Ejidal, and the Secretaría de Educación Pública (Ministry of Public Education) all initiated new programs for foreign training of Mexican agricultural specialists.[86] The existing pink bollworm and Mexican fruit fly control programs expanded in scope, and the Banco Ejidal warned *ejidatarios* who were lax in complying with the regulations of the pink bollworm campaign that their access to credit would be suspended for a month. These steps were taken in collaboration with U.S. experts. In describing the campaign, the *Memoria* of the SAF in 1939–1940 stated: "The works carried out, the legislation enacted, and the results obtained have earned the thanks of the phytosanitary authorities of the United States, who have given great help to the personnel of the border area districts."[87]

The success of these joint programs in pest control led to even closer technical collaboration between the United States and Mexico. In March 1939 Secretary of Agriculture Henry A. Wallace invited members of the SAF to a meeting in Matamoros, Tamaulipas, to develop a coordinated plan of action for cotton pest control in the border regions. The SAF responded favorably to the proposal.[88] In 1940 the two nations reestablished the U.S.–Mexican International Pest Control Commission, and several agreements for close cooperation and the exchange of technical personnel were reached. By 1939 the Banco Ejidal had hired J. H. Harrison as its full-time cotton expert, and the SAF requested the U.S. Department of Agriculture to loan the services of several of its cotton graders.[89] Also in 1939 the Comisión Nacional de Irrigación employed U.S. engineers to supervise construction at its Angostura Dam Project in Sonora and El Palmito Dam Project in Durango.[90] The same year the Mexican government asked the U.S. Bureau of Fisheries to loan the services of several of its experts to its counterpart in Mexico.[91] Tired of the

SAF's ineffectual campaign, in 1940 the governor of Tabasco traveled to the United States to obtain technical and financial assistance from North American business interests to control the disease.[92] In July 1940 Mexico reached an agreement with the Export-Import Bank to "encourage and promote research in the technology of agriculture."[93] At the same time the Mexican government gladly accepted the offer of technical assistance from the United States to develop a rubber industry.[94]

During the same period various agronomists, some of them leftists, argued that agricultural research and extension programs should be "depoliticized" and separated from economic concerns. In the future they wanted the SAF to concentrate on "science."[95] During the late 1930s even the "socialist" agronomists, the supporters of the collectivization of production along Stalinist lines, who were continually warning against U.S. "imperialism," became critics of agricultural science policy under Cárdenas and now supported technical assistance programs from the United States such as the Rockefeller Foundation's Mexican Agricultural Project.[96] To them, as well as to most other agronomists, saving the guild's public image through improving its skills as scientists, and producing scientific "successes" like the hybrid plants of the MAP, had now become more important than "scientific nationalism." Focusing on "science," the agronomists now believed, would improve the profession's public image: they would no longer be seen as agitators or bureaucrats but as skilled researchers and technicians.[97]

The annual reports of the Secretaría de Agricultura y Fomento now denounced the earlier association between technical agricultural matters and social, economic, and political questions. In 1941 the new minister of agriculture, Marte R. Gómez, implemented reforms in the SAF, seeking to avoid the mistakes and failures of the past. In an effort to place the extension programs on a more scientific foundation, Gómez disbanded the *agrónomos regionales* and assigned them to the experimentation stations. He also reduced the number of experimentation stations, concentrating efforts in a fewer number of locations.[98] At the suggestion of Henry A. Wallace, the stations began a plant-breeding program focusing on corn and beans.

However, Gómez's reforms could not erase the legacies of the past. Research efforts achieved more than in previous years, but they still suffered from shortages of trained personnel and a lack of program continuity; politics at times continued to interfere with agricultural improvement programs; scarce funds still disrupted various programs and had a particularly adverse effect on pest-control campaigns.[99] Despite the efforts of Gómez to bring the number of operating experimentation stations more closely in line with available resources, by 1946 the SAF had established seven new ones. When corn shortages returned in 1943, Gómez was forced to tell the president that his agency could do nothing to address the problem.[100] That same year, in February, Gómez and President Ávila Camacho signed the agreement creating the Mexican Agricultural Project.[101]

Conclusion

Many members of the Mexican agricultural research community used nationalistic rhetoric and held strong views against the United States during the 1930s and early 1940s.[102] However, these attitudes did not cause them to resist or attack U.S. technical assistance programs in agriculture. In this period Mexico tried and failed in the attempt to rely primarily on its own agricultural research to modernize its agriculture. The few agricultural scientists with some training in experimental methods in Mexico did not make SAF policy, which therefore lacked effective programs. The populist politics of the state, which sought to benefit all of Mexico's farmers, further contributed to the failure to achieve tangible results. *Proyectismo* all but guaranteed failure, and an autarkic approach to agricultural science was clearly doomed to failure from the beginning. By 1940 an affirmative answer to the question of whether or not to seek out foreign technical assistance for agricultural research and extension programs had already been made. The outbreak of World War II closed any options Mexico might have had in choosing the source of assistance, which now had to come from the United States. Even the agronomists were happy to receive the assistance of the Rockefeller Foundation.

The establishment of the Mexican Agricultural Project in 1943 became a logical outcome of Mexico's long-term dependence on foreign agricultural science and technology. Long before 1943 those in the field of agricultural science, along with research and extension programs, served mostly as conduits for the introduction of foreign science and technology, and it was only a short step from this point to that of bringing in the foreign scientists themselves, such as was to occur through the MAP. The origin of the Green Revolution therefore possessed strong roots in Mexico's past. The program was not born primarily as a result of the circumstances of the 1940s, nor did it represent a new form of dependence on the United States that resulted from the war and the swing to the right in Mexico during the early 1940s. The 1940s marked a major reorientation in Mexican public policy, particularly in the much stronger emphasis on industrial development. In the agricultural sphere there was more continuity, as Mexico retained its prior dependence on foreign science and technology in agricultural development programs.

Notes

1. Cynthia Hewitt de Alcantara, *Modernizing Mexican Agriculture: Socioeconomic Implications of Technological Change*. Geneva: United Nations Research Institute for Social Development, 1976; Bruce H. Jennings, *Foundations of International Agricultural Research: Science and Politics in Mexican Agriculture*. Boulder, Colo.: Westview Press, 1988; Deborah Fitzgerald, "The Rockefeller Foundation in Mexico, 1943–1953," *Social Studies of Science* 16 (1986), 457–83.

2. Angus Wright, *The Death of Ramón González: The Modern Agricultural Dilemma*. Austin: University of Texas Press, 1991, 171.

3. Hewitt de Alcantara, *Modernizing Mexican Agriculture*, n. 1, 19.

4. These Porfirian origins are discussed in detail in Joseph Cotter, "Before the Green Revolution: Mexican Agricultural Policy, 1920–1949," Ph.D. diss., University of California, Santa Barbara, 1993.

5. Luis L. León, "La actuación del gremio agrónomico en la reforma agraria," *Boletín de la Sociedad Mexicana de Geografia y Estadística* 78 (1954), 57–71.

6. Enrique Beltrán, "La dirección de estudios biológicos de la Secretaría de Fomento y El Instituto de Biología de la Universidad Nacional Autónoma," *Anales de la Sociedad Mexicana de Historia de la Ciencia y de la Tecnología*, no. 1 (1969), 105–41.

7. Eduardo Chávez, "El maquinismo agrícola exige la formación de obreros mecánicos agrícolas." Paper presented at the V Consejo Nacional Directivo of the Sociedad Agrónomica Mexicana (hereafter cited as SAM), in Sociedad Agronómica Mexicana, V Consejo Nacional Directivo, BCM #186–10.

8. Linda B. Hall, *Alvaro Obregón: Power and Revolution in Mexico, 1911–1920*. College Station: Texas A & M University Press, 1981, 217–18.

9. Juan de Dios Bojórquez, "Momento decisivo para el gremio agronómico." Paper presented at Segundo Consejo Nacional Agronómico (SCNA), 1 December 1922, BCM #168–40.

10. Eustacio L. Contreras, "¿Qué es un agrónomo?" *Agros* 1, no. 2 (July 1923), 6; idem, "El próximo Congreso Agronómico," *El Nacional*, 17 October 1935. Eyler N. Simpson used the term *proyectismo* to describe Mexican government programs of the 1930s; see *The Ejido: Mexico's Way Out*. Chapel Hill: University of North Carolina Press, 1937, 580.

11. "Acta de la inauguración de la ENA en terrenos de la hacienda de Chapingo, México," n.d., in Escuela Nacional de Agricultura, BCM #168–2.

12. Secretaría de Hacienda y Crédito Público, *Presupuesto general de egresos de la Federación para el año de 1925*, México, D.F.: 1925; Secretaría de Agricultura y Fomento (hereafter cited as SAF), *Memoria de la SAF correspondiente al periodo de 1° de agosto de 1924 al 31 de julio de 1935*, Tacubaya, D.F.: 1927, 69–70.

13. De Dios Bojórquez, "Momento Decisivo," 3–4.

14. Rufino Monroy, "La avicultura en México como se ha vista y como debe verse," *Agros* 1, no. 1 (June 1923), 5.

15. For examples, see "Campos experimentales para la resolución del problema agrario," *El Nacional*, 15 February 1935.

16. H. Vinberger to Gonzalo Robles, 11 August 1921, and others, Archivo General de la Nación (hereafter cited as AGN), FGR/Sección Correspondencia [SC]/41/34.

17. *Extensión agrícola* 1, no. 2 (March 1933), 34.

18. "Campaña del maíz," *Extensión agrícola* 1, no. 3 (April 1933), 115–16.

19. Translation, Circular no. 88, Mexican North Western Railway, General Freight and Passenger Department, "Free Transportation of Seeds, Bulbs, and Fruit Trees," n.d., National Archives, Record Group 166, Box 62, Washington, D.C. (hereafter cited as NA).

20. Antonio Rivas Tagle, *El cultivo racional del maíz*. Tacubaya, D.F., 1929, 261–73.

21. "Una nueva industria existe en Morelos," *El Nacional*, 27 March 1933.

22. "Es ya hecho el cultivo de la uva en el estado de Morelos," *El Nacional*, 17 June 1933; "Campaña de los plantas oleaginosas," *Extensión Agrícola* 1, no. 6 (July 1933), 261.

23. David S. Ibarra, "El trigo 'Marquis' en el Bajío," *Agricultura* 1, no. 2 (April–May 1935), 10.

24. Rivas Tagle, *Cultivo racional*, n. 26. The last chapter describes work on corn hybridization done in the United States. "El cultivo del maíz en México debe modernizarse," *El Universal*, 17 December 1933.

25. "Lo que debe hacer," n.d., AGN, FGR/SA/5/70; "Proyecto para la creación de un departamento autónomo para fomento de la producción del maíz," n.d., AGN, FGR/SA/13/118.

26. Alejandro Brambila, Jr., "La granja experimental en Rodríguez, N.L.," *Irrigación en México* 1, no. 1 (May 1930), 44–48.

27. Alejandro Brambila Jr., *El análisis químico y la fertilidad de los suelos*. Dirección General de Agricultura, México, D.F.: 1928; "Campaña para la explotación racional del suelo," *Extensión agrícola* 1, no. 3 (April 1933), 112–14.

28. Pandurang Khankhoje, *Maíz Granada 'Zea Maíz Digitata': Su origen, evolución, y cultivo*. Estación Experimental Agrícola, Boletín de Divulgación no. 1, Tacubaya, D.F., 1936, 9–13.

29. "Un limonero que da frutas sin semilla," *El Nacional*, 29 July 1931.

30. For an example of the former see División Estación Experimental, "El cultivo de secano es de gran porvenir en México," 30 November 1931, Archivo de Ramón Fernández y Fernández (hereafter cited as ARFF), Caja 5, Document 380, Zamora,

Michoacán. For an example of the latter see Alfonso Dampf, "Como defendernos contra las plagas de la agricultura," ARFF, 139/222.

31. For the program in Chihuahua see Francis H. Styles, "Agriculture Department: Excerpt from Annual Report on Commerce and Industries of the Chihuahua, Chihuahua, Consular District for 1932," 19 January 1933, NA, 166/308. For the Centrales see "Memorandum sobre las Escuelas Centrales Agrícolas," n.d., AGN, FGR/Sección Educación [SE]/49/23.

32. Miguel Alvarez Gleason, "La política de irrigación que más conviene a la agricultura Mexicana," in Partido Nacional Revolucionario, *Las problemas agrícolas de México*. México, D.F.: 1934, 132.

33. For the former see Herbert S. Bursley, "Excerpt from a Review of Commerce and Industries Quarter Ended September 30, 1927," n.d., NA, 166/151. For the latter see José Antonio Rivera, "El jitomate mexicano de exportación a los Estados Unidos," n.d., ARFF, 117/2.

34. Alfonso Dampf, "La importancia de la mosca de la fruta para el cultivo de la naranja y demas frutas cítricas en México," in Consejo Nacional de Agricultura (hereafter cited as CNA), *Memoria de la Primera Convención Nacional de Productores de Naranja*. México, D.F.: CNA, 1936, 2.

35. Gonzalo Robles, "Educación agrícola, propaganda," September 1921, AGN, FGR/SE/49/24; "Discurso presentado por el C. Ingeniero Luis L. León. . . ," in *Concurso de la mejor mazorca del maíz*. Tacubaya, D.F.: Imprenta de la Dirección de Estudios Geográficos y Climatológicos, 1926, 20.

36. SAF, Dirección de Economía Rural, *Boletín mensual de la dirección de economía rural*, years 1928–1933.

37. The debate is discussed at length in Jesús Silva Herzog, *El agrarismo mexicano y la reforma agraria*. México, D.F.: Fondo de Cultura Económica, 1959.

38. "Microscopio," *Agronómica* 1, no. 4 (January 1932), 10; Ramón Fernández y Fernández, "El fracaso de los agrónomos," *El Universal*, 4 February 1932; Ramón Fernández y Fernández, *Los agrónomos*. México, D.F.: 1933.

39. Eduardo Villaseñor, "Las zonas nuevas y el indio," *Revista mexicana de economía* 1 (1928–1929), 41–47.

40. SAM, *Exposición del criterio ideológico del gremio agronómico mexicano*. México, D.F., 1932.

41. "Microscopio," *Agronómica* 1, no. 4 (January 1932), 11.

42. Fernández y Fernández, *Los agrónomos*, n. 46.

43. Ramón Fernández y Fernández, "Los agrónomos y la reglamentación de las professiones." *Crisol*, March 1934; "Nuestra agricultura, los agrónomos, y la prensa," *Irrigación en México* 4, no. 2 (February 1933), 102–3.

44. Alfredo De León, "Técnicos! Técnicos!" *Irrigación en México* 1, no. 2 (June 1930), 33; George I. Sánchez, *Mexico: A Revolution by Education*. New York: Viking Press, 1936, 145.

45. For an example of the spirit of cooperation see Alfonso Dampf to Gumaro García de la Cadena, 17 March 1934, NA, 7/1394.

46. "Notes on Dr. Ferrell's Trip to Mexico March 15–April 21, 1933." Rockefeller Archive Center (hereafter cited as RAC), 2/323[stacks] Fer-1/3678.

47. SAF, *Ley de Servicios Agrícolas Nacionales*. México, D.F.: 1932; Antonio Martínez Barragan, "El Consejo Nacional de Agricultura," *Agricultura* 1, no. 2 (September–October 1937), 59–60.

48. Emilio Alanis Patiño, *Diversos aspectos de la situación agrícola de México*. México, D.F.: Instituto Mexicano de Estudios Agrícolas (IMEA), 1934.

49. "Proyectos para el mejoramiento a la agricultura," *Excelsior*, 12 August 1934.

50. Enrique Beltrán, *Medio siglo de recuerdos de un biólogo mexicano*. México, D.F.: Sociedad Mexicana de Historia Natural, 1977, 129–49.

51. Enrique Beltrán, "Instituto Biotécnico (1934–1940) de la SAF," *Anales de la Sociedad mexicana de historia de la ciencia y de la tecnología*, no. 1 (1969), 150–80.

52. SAF, *Memoria de trabajos de las Direcciones de Agricultura y Ganadería dependiente de la SAF durante el periodo presidencial de Lázaro Cárdenas*. México, D.F.: DAPP, 1940, 430–37.

53. Guillermo Gándara to Lázaro Cárdenas, 17 August 1937; Leopoldo de la Barreda to Cárdenas, 17 August 1937, AGN, FP/SLC/703.2/642.

54. Jacobo Aragón Aguillón, "Las estaciones agrícolas para la experimentación," *El Nacional*, 19 January 1935.

55. "Estaciones agrícolas en todo el país," *El Nacional*, 29 November 1934; José de Jesús Urquizo to Subsecretario de Agricultura y Fomento, 20 April 1936, AGN, FP/SLC/534.4/101.

56. Damién Correu, "Estaciones agrícolas experimentales, lo que son y las actividades que en ellas se desarrollan," *Jalisco agrícola y ganadero* 1, no. 9 (June–July 1934), 18; Gabriel Atie, "Estaciones agrícolas experimentales," *Chapingo* 1, no. 2 (September 1935), 22.

57. SAF, *Memoria de la SAF de septiembre de 1937 a agosto de 1938*. México, D.F.: DAPP, 1938.

58. Conrado E. Rodríguez to Director de Fomento Agrícola, 4 May 1934, Archivo Histórico de Jalisco, Caja AG-27bis-E, Expediente 22, Legajo 2, Guadalajara, Jalisco (hereafter cited as AHJ).

59. "Asuntos tratados por el Consejo de Agricultura del Estado, Sesión del día de 12 de junio de 1934," n.d., AHJ, AG-27bis-E/100/6.

60. Arturo R. Cuellar, "El cruzamiento del tomate," *El Nacional*, 27 December 1935.

61. Memorandum para acuerdo con el C. Presidente de la República, n.d., AGN, FP/SLC/606.3/164; Rodrigo M. Quevedo to Cárdenas, 12 January 1936, AGN, FP/SLC/702.1/84.

62. "La esclavitud del maíz," *El Universal Gráfico*, 7 February 1936; "Trigo en vez de maíz en la alimentación," *El Nacional*, 15 May 1937.

63. SAF, *Estudio agro-económico del maíz*. Pt. 3. México, D.F.: Oficina de Publicaciones y Propaganda, 1940, 142.

64. "Informe del general de división Lázaro Cárdenas, presidente de la República

Mexicana, ante el H. Congreso de la Unión, correspondiente al ejercicio comprendido entre el 1° de septiembre de 1936 al 31 de agosto de 1937. México, D.F., 1° de septiembre de 1937," in Lázaro Cárdenas, *Palabras y documentos públicos de Lázaro Cárdenas: Informes del gobierno y mensaje presidenciales de año nuevo*. México, D.F.: Siglo Ventiuno Editores, 1978, 107.

65. "Importación de cereales extranjeros," *El Nacional*, 17 November 1937.

66. For examples, see L. Iñíguez de la Torre, "El rancho americano y el rancho mexicano," *Jalisco Rural* 17, no. 7 (July 1937), 177–78.

67. For free imports see Cárdenas Decree, 22 July 1937, ARFF, 202/21. For farmer reliance on foreign seed see "Estudio presentado por la Delegación de Defensa Agrícola de León, Gto.," in CNA, *Memoria de la primera reunión nacional de productores de la papa*. México, D.F.: CNA, 1939, 40–41. Bernardo A. Avílez, *Cultivo y comercio del algodón en México*. México, D.F.: Dirección de Economía Rural, 1939, i–iii and 106–12. For the Banco Ejidal see "Importación de semilla de algodón," *El Nacional*, 4 February 1937. Horacio Mooers, "Wheat and Cotton Notes, Mexicali, B.C.," 9 December 1938, NA, 166/388.

68. For examples see Alfredo Tellez Girón, "El Instituto Nacional de Investigaciones Pecuarias y sus antecedentes," *Anales de la Sociedad mexicana de historia de la ciencia y de la tecnología* 2 (1970), 196.

69. J. Francisco Andraca and S. Gutiérrez Silva to Cárdenas, 8 May 1936, AGN, FP/SLC/506.22/2.

70. For examples see Lorenzo R. Jiménez to Hoidale, 10 July 1936, NA, 7/1393.

71. For examples see McDonald to Strong, 9 March 1936; "Weekly Report, Pink Bollworm and Thurberia Weevil Control," 4 October 1937; D. M. MacEachern, "Progress Report on Pink Bollworm Activities in the Lower Rio Grande Valley," 27 January 1937, NA, 7/1400.

72. "Numerosas despepitadoras de algodón serán adquiridos en el Banco de Crédito Ejidal," *El Nacional*, 1 July 1937.

73. Agustín García Rea and Isidoro Garibay Vázquez to Tranquilano Manríquez, 27 January 1937.

74. "Necesidad de aumentar la producción," *El Nacional*, 6 January 1938; "Selección de semillas para el maíz," *El Nacional*, 28 February 1938.

75. "Los cultivos del maíz en la República," *El Nacional*, 16 March 1938.

76. "Subsidio para importar catorce mil toneladas del maíz," *El Universal*, 31 October 1939. William P. Blocker to Secretary of State, "Rise in Prices of Essential Food Commodities," 7 March 1939, NA, 166/146.

77. Stacey May and Galo Plaza, *The United Fruit Company in Latin America*. Washington, D.C.: National Planning Association, 1958, 154.

78. Jeannot Stern, "El chamusco de plátano," *Agricultura* 1, no. 4 (January–February 1938), 43–50.

79. "Las plantaciones bajo la amenaza de nueva plaga," *El Nacional*, 11 September 1937; "La plaga del chumusco es combatida," *El Nacional*, 26 October 1937.

80. Guillermo Liera B., "Informe de trabajos de la campaña contra el chamusco

de plátano," in Primera Convención Resolutiva del Problema Platanero, patrocinada por la SAF del 25 al 30 de octubre de 1938. ARFF, 145/208.

81. "Plaga sobre los plantaciones en el Edo. de Tabasco," *Excelsior*, 29 January 1939.

82. Thomas H. Lockett, "Monthly Economic Review—Mexico, Conditions in Mexico during the Month of May, 1940," NA, 166/147.

83. For examples see Bruno Jiménez to Cárdenas, 25 February 1939.

84. For examples see Miguel García Cruz, "El fracaso de la experimentación agrícola en México," *El Popular*, 23 May 1939.

85. For examples see "Estudio formulado en la Oficina de Geografia Económico Agrícola por el C. Guillermo Rodríguez G. y sometida a la consideración del C. Presidente de la República con fecha de 2 de mayo de 1938," AGN, FP/SLC/437.1/556.

86. Jesús Patiño N. to Aaron Sáenz, 21 September 1939, AGN, FGR/SC/39/5. For the Banco Ejidal see "Los 5 futuros clasificadores del algodón," *El siglo de Torreón*, 26 May 1939. For the Secretaría de Educación Pública see "Estudios sobre la genética del maíz en EE UU," *El Nacional*, 13 April 1938.

87. SAF, *Memoria de la SAF de 1o de septiembre de 1939 al 31 de agosto de 1940*. México, D.F.: DAPP, 1940, 79.

88. "Memorandum que por el estimable conducto del Señor Secretario Particular, se somete a la respetable consideración del Presidente de la República," 14 March 1939, AGN, FP/SLC/425.5/134.

89. "Las siembras se apresurán," *El siglo de Torreón*, 24 February 1939.

90. Louis V. Boyle to Secretary of State, 15 April 1939.

91. "Interdepartmental Committee on Cooperation with the American Republics, Minutes of Meeting on April 28, 1939," NA, 353/29.

92. Francisco Trujillo Gurria, "Acuerdo con el C. Presidente de la República," 27 May 1940, AGN, FP/SLC/506.17/22.

93. "Convention on the Inter-American Bank," *Bulletin of the Pan American Union* 74, no. 7 (July 1940), 532.

94. Ramón Beteta to Josephus Daniels, 28 August 1940; Daniels to Secretary of State, 4 September 1940, NA, 166/151.

95. For examples see Ramón Fernández y Fernández, "La experimentación agrícola," *Germinal*, 28 June 1939.

96. For the "socialist" agronomists views on agricultural modernization see "Una revisión a nuestra política económica," n.d., ARFF, 180/356. For warnings about U.S. "imperialism" see Comité Ejecutivo a socios de la Liga de Agrónomos Socialistas, 28 October 1940, ARFF, 180/408.

97. José del Riego, Juan Francisco Kaldman, and Manuel Marcue P. to Manuel Ávila Camacho, 9 July 1941, AGN, FP/Sección Manuel Ávila Camacho [SMAC]/133.2/67; "Mayor producción con cultivos científicos," *El Universal*, 10 April 1944.

98. SAF, *Informe de labores de la SAF del 1° de septiembre de 1940 al 31 de agosto de 1941*. México, D.F.: Editorial Cultura, 1941, 23; SAF, *Informe de labores de la SAF del*

1° de septiembre de 1945 al 31 de agosto de 1946. México, D.F.: Editorial Cultura, 1946, 12–13.

99. For program continuity see Edwin J. Wellhausen, Oral History, RAC, Record Groups 13, 39, and 113. For politics see L. D. Mallory to Cordell Hull, San Jacinto Agricultural Exposition, 29 November 1943, NA, 166/302. For shortages of funds see José María Aguirre and Cesar Domínguez V. to Ávila Camacho, 7 November 1941, AGN, FP/SMAC/506.17/14. Mexican Agriculture, Annual Meeting, 17 October 1946, RAC, 6.13/1.1/32/359.

100. SAF, *Planeación agrícola*. México, D.F.: 1943, 1–5.

101. The SAF had been anxious for the program to begin since its proposal in 1941.

102. "El XXV aniversario de la fundación de la escuela," in *Ecos del aniversario de la plata de la Escuela Particular de Agricultura de Ciudad Juárez*. Ciudad Juárez: 1931, 6–7.

11 Labor Control and the Postwar Growth Model in Latin America

Ian Roxborough

In the 1940s, more precisely in the years 1944–1948, the institutional foundations of the postwar growth model in Latin America based on import-substituting industrialization (ISI) were established. At the same time, this period laid the contours of more than three decades of political and economic development, an outcome that was in large part a conservative response to the political and economic mobilization stimulated by World War II. Although there were significant trends toward ISI in the 1930s in response to the world depression and in some countries during even earlier decades, its adoption as a deliberate policy dates from around the mid-1940s.[1]

The 1940s marked the institutionalization of the systems of labor relations and capital accumulation that dominated the postwar era. Henceforth the development of Latin America was closely related to economic expansion worldwide based on the institutions created at the end of World War II. This system of political economy survived basically unaltered until the debt crisis, beginning in 1982, finally produced efforts to reorganize the Latin American economies. Thus as ISI unraveled during the late 1970s and early 1980s, the model of capital accumulation pursued by the larger, more highly industrialized Latin American countries lost viability and finally collapsed. By the early 1990s the ISI model had largely been rejected, and was being replaced by totally different economic strategies.

The Shocks of the Depression and World War II

At the onset of the world depression in 1929, the nations of Latin America were still overwhelmingly rural and their political systems dominated by agrarian or less commonly by mining elites. Urban middle-class groups had already begun to challenge the prevailing systems of oligarchic parliamentarism and personalistic dictatorship but without so far having any noticeable impact on policy.[2] The crisis of the 1930s brought into power regimes seeking alternatives to those systems, and so-called revolutionary challenges to oligarchic control became frequent. But apart from the sweeping transformation brought about in the aftermath of the Mexican Revolution, the movements supporting change were mostly unsuccessful: the Cuban insurrection of 1933, the Socialist Republic in Chile in 1932, the *tenente* movement in Brazil in 1922 and 1924, the rise of the Alianza Popular Revolucionaria Americana (American Popular Revolutionary Alliance) in Peru. Generally speaking, the ideological mainspring of these short-lived movements and regimes was an inchoate form of statism that drew inspiration from Mussolini's Italy and Catholic social thought, as well as from more conventional liberal sources. Some of the successful regimes, however, notably those of Brazil under Getúlio Vargas and Mexico under Lázaro Cárdenas, created novel and complex systems of corporatist intermediation whose principal aim was to control rapidly growing labor movements.

Except in these two countries the 1930s produced little change in economic policy or institutional innovation, and throughout the decade traditional types of regime remained in most of Latin America. Although the depression shook the Latin American societies and stimulated antioligarchic opposition movements, it failed to produce a new growth model. The absence of change reflected in part the lack of any self-conscious strategy for industrialization among Latin American policymakers and in part the unpropitious international economic climate. The industrial development that occurred during this period did so either as an unplanned response to external shocks or in conjunction with the export of primary products.

Toward the end of World War II the situation changed. Three sets of factors were important: (1) the structural shift in Latin America toward urbanization and away from the undisputed domination of agrarian or mining elites; (2) the diverse impact of the war in stimulating industrial and political mobilization; (3) the changing international economic and political context. These factors converged in complex ways to produce the institutional settlement adopted in Latin America during the late 1940s. At this point the ancien régime oligarchies were increasingly undermined as urbanization created a middle class whose leaders had their own ideas about how politics ought to be conducted; as a working class began to emerge and to push for social change; and as military modernization (or alternatively its frustratingly slow pace) heightened political concerns among the officer corps.

The challenge to the ancien régime took the form of the aggrandizement and autonomy of the state. Modernizing elites sought to use an expanded state apparatus as a countervailing force to liberate themselves from the oligarchies and to provide patronage for their new middle-class and working-class clienteles. Beginning in the 1930s the growth of the state often resulted in Bonapartist regimes, variously labeled "populist" or "corporatist," that reflected the efforts of political leaders to mobilize and to control a broad popular base to challenge to the oligarchies. But in most cases conservative forces were able to defeat the reform movements and to retain their power under the old forms. More important, as yet in none of the Latin American countries were the new institutional forms linked to a new model of capital accumulation: the linkage could be forged only following the emergence of a new international economic order after 1945.

World War II accelerated the challenge to oligarchic parliamentarism that had been beaten back in the 1930s. At this point globally rising expectations of democracy and reconstruction generated a strong momentum toward change in Latin America.[3] The war stimulated economic growth, industrialization, and a large expansion of the labor force. In countries in which the labor unions sought to contribute to the Allied victory by entering into no-strike agreements, inflation induced a decline in real wages. But as the end of the war approached, there was a burst of rank-and-file militancy, rapid growth in union affiliation, waves of strikes, and a general turn to the left.

These conditions formed part of a worldwide trend that began around 1942, following the defeat of the German armies at Stalingrad and the successful Allied offensives in North Africa. As the tide turned against the Axis powers, a wave of leftist mobilization followed, which in 1945 led the *Bombay Chronicle*, as far away as British India, for example, to remark: "the world is going to the left, as it must. The movement is both clear and irresistible."[4] At this juncture popular forces throughout the world began to demand major social change. In the areas caught up in the fighting, guerrilla and partisan units stepped into the vacuum left by the defeated Axis powers and challenged the old elites for control.

The outcomes of these struggles varied enormously and depended to a considerable extent on the role played by the Allied armies of occupation in each region. Thus in the areas taken over by the Soviet armies, the old ruling classes were rapidly pushed aside and Communist regimes installed. In France and Italy, in contrast, centrist forces supported by the Western Allies displaced the Communist-dominated resistance movements. In Germany and Japan the initial steps toward democratization and industrial deconcentration were soon reversed under the pressures of internal conflicts and mounting Cold War tensions.[5] Elsewhere in Asia and in the Pacific, where the war had created strong nationalist and revolutionary movements, the political situation became even more complex.

Latin America remained physically unharmed by the war but was nevertheless caught up in its embrace. There too the war produced a turn to the left, and the Communist parties in the region expanded their memberships fivefold.[6] Since this had been a war for "democracy," new democratic movements, often led by students and the middle classes, emerged in the countries ruled by dictators. In Nicaragua, El Salvador, Brazil, and Argentina mass rallies were staged to demand the overthrow or abdication of dictators or military juntas, and in several cases, notably Bolivia, Guatemala, Peru, Venezuela, and Brazil, the prodemocracy movements achieved at least temporary victories.

Thus the end of the war, combined with rising expectations and aspirations concerning a new world order, stimulated labor militancy, leftist radicalism, and prodemocracy movements. Reactions to these movements in the outside world often depended on the position each country had taken during the war. After the Japanese attack on Pearl Harbor, the United States pressured the Latin American republics to declare war on the Axis, and countries with neutralist foreign policies were generally regarded with suspicion as being pro-Fascist. The international Communist movement took a similar stance, describing regimes as "democratic" or "Fascist" according to their international alignments. In Argentina and Bolivia, for example, two countries where support for the Allies had been weakest, the new popular movements led by Juan Perón and Víctor Paz Estenssoro were seen by the U.S.

government (and by the Communist parties) as Fascist despite their working-class base.

Toward the end of the war past international alignments bred some strange political alliances. In Nicaragua, for example, the Communists and labor leaders joined with the dictator Anastasio Somoza against the prodemocracy movement of the urban middle class and parts of the agrarian elite. Somoza had supported the Allies and was therefore aligned with the "democratic" camp; opposition to him was automatically defined as oligarchic and reactionary. In addition, during the war Somoza had adopted an authoritarian populist stance, promulgating a labor code and looking favorably on union organizing.[7] Similar circumstances led much of organized labor in Brazil to support the dictator Getúlio Vargas in an unsuccessful bid to retain political power at the end of the war.

Postwar Options

When the war ended there was widespread discussion in Latin America of the place the region would occupy in the new world order. At this point segments of the reformist left in particular began to sketch out an alternative vision of Latin America's future development. The most articulate exponent of the new vision was the Mexican labor leader, Vicente Lombardo Toledano, who in 1938 used the large Mexican labor confederation, the Confederación de Trabajadores de México to set up the Confederación de Trabajadores de América Latina (CTAL). The CTAL gained the support of the largest union confederations of most of the Latin American nations, and by the end of the war around three quarters of the total organized labor force throughout Latin America, some three million workers in all, were affiliated with it.[8] Making due allowance for exaggeration and the unreliable measures of unionization, this was an impressive and unprecedented achievement. However, the CTAL lacked the support of the labor movements of Argentina and Brazil. Argentina did not join because Perón was now pursuing his own brand of unionism, and he eventually established a Peronist international union organization, the ATLAS (Agrupación de Trabajadores Latinoamericanos Sindicalistas). In Brazil labor law prohibited unions from establishing international links, and Vargas, who like Perón was seeking to develop his own union following, made sure the prohibition was enforced.

Lombardo Toledano intended the CTAL to become a vehicle to develop a new approach to Latin American development. He toned down his earlier anti-imperialism and urged national unity between labor and industrialists against what he portrayed as the twin menace of fascism and oligarchic reaction. His position became closely reminiscent of the "Browderism" supported by most Latin American Communists, who had now abandoned the notion of irreconcilable conflict between capital and labor in favor of a strategy of class compromise. Regardless of the merits or demerits of Browderism in the United States (where it originated), there was strong reason to support it in Latin America, where the emergent urban capitalists and the working class shared a strong common interest in industrialization. Lombardo Toledano and others saw workers and industrialists collaborating in a progressive development program based on protectionism. The intent was to clear away any remaining "feudal" remnants led by the landed classes and to provide a means to resist imperialist penetration. The state would coordinate and oversee this class alliance. The no-strike pacts during the war, despite their adverse impact on real wages, would serve as a model for future class compromise.

Leaders like Lombardo planned to harness the emerging corporatist institutions to the program of class compromise. Adopting themes later developed by Raúl Prebisch and the United Nations Economic Commission for Latin America (ECLA), Lombardo urged land reform and income redistribution to generate increased demand to fuel industrialization. The state would provide the infrastructure, protect domestic entrepreneurs, and remedy market weaknesses. This vision of the future drew heavily on the experience of the Mexican revolution, but it anticipated future ECLA doctrines and provided a Third World version of Keynesian demand stimulation. It appeared a brand of social democracy applied to Latin American conditions. Crucial to its success was a substantial redistribution of wealth and income from landed elites to the urban and rural poor. Such a transfer of resources, it was hoped, would provide the mass market demand to fuel a form of import-substitution industrialization based on a relatively egalitarian distribution of income and wealth.[9]

It is difficult to say whether the program would ever have succeeded had it been carried out. The program was credible and had the support of the Confederación de Trabajadores de América Latina, the Communist parties, and some members of the Latin American intelligentsia, such as Víctor Raúl Haya de la Torre.[10] Had it been put into practice in a sustained way after the war, the history of Latin America might well have been quite different. But the impact of the war on Latin America, important though it was, did not extend to the kind of disruption of elite control and mass mobilization that occurred in regions of the world where fighting had actually taken place. Indeed, in many ways, the Latin American elites emerged strengthened and invigorated after the war. As a result, instead of this approach a much more conservative version of ISI came to dominate economic strategy in the postwar period. The state continued to intervene to promote industrialization and resisted pressures from the United States for a return to free trade, but in an implicit compromise with landed elites, agrarian reform was removed from the political agenda. With agrarian relations of production largely unchanged, and with a relative neglect of agricultural exports, insufficient popular demand and perennial balance of payments problems marked the postwar experience of ISI. Without massive redistribution of income and wealth the conservative version of ISI that came to prevail in the postwar period was imbalanced and subject to recurrent crises. Latin American politics in the postwar period oscillated between populist attempts at income redistribution and inflationary growth that left intact the existing power relations, and authoritarian attempts to contain popular mobilization and to increase profitability.

The Hegemony of the United States and Its Economic Consequences

Despite strong opposition from those who wished to return to a growth model based on primary exports, at the end of the war several of the larger Latin American countries were ready to embark on a deliberate program of industrialization.[11] The supporters of primary exports gained victories over the reformers in Peru and in most of the smaller, less developed countries. At different points during the 1940s, however, the advocates of change triumphed in the larger, more developed countries.

At the end of the war there were discussions between the United States and the Latin American states concerning future economic links between them. At the Chapultepec conference in February 1945 the United States pressed for a liberal economic regime, despite insistent pressures from the Latin Americans, headed by Mexico, for protectionism, a preferential inter-American trading bloc, and agreements on commodities.[12] One of the central objectives of Latin American policymakers was to attract foreign capital, either in the form of aid or as direct investment. The Latin Americans preferred aid along the lines of the Marshall Plan, but at the inter-American conference at Rio de Janeiro in mid-1947 the United States delegation made it clear that aid on this scale would not be forthcoming.[13]

The Latin Americans therefore had to choose between the unorthodox and largely self-reliant development strategy supported by Lombardo and the left or reliance on substantial inflows of private foreign investment to stimulate industrialization. Both approaches possessed major consequences for political alignments: the former implied social democracy, but the latter a conservative restoration. To attract foreign capital, a favorable "climate for investment" had to be created. This climate required stabilization policies and devaluations and reorganizing the institutions of labor control and capital accumulation. It was essential to prevent rank-and-file labor militancy that would threaten political stability and thereby jeopardize the climate for investment. These objectives underlay the great onslaught against labor during the early postwar period.

In several Latin American countries, led by Argentina, Brazil, Chile, and Mexico, by the end of World War II the industrial labor force had expanded substantially. A relatively tight labor market had developed, and several governments were attempting to build a political base by incorporating organized labor into the political system. As a result the unions were in a position to exert a degree of power that would strongly influence the "climate" that emerged for foreign investment. The war had induced an almost general shift to the left; almost everywhere, oligarchic forces were on the defensive. An increase in strikes, the growing independence of the unions, the rise in the vote for the left, and a general sense of political uncertainty prevailed. None of these conditions were conducive to future foreign investment: labor therefore had to be tamed.

The campaign was waged in a variety of ways. Governments toughened their stance against strikes and sometimes passed legislation making strikes more difficult to organize and carry out. In much of Latin America there was a major onslaught on the Communist party. At the same time, state elites sought to utilize existing corporatist arrangements or to develop new ones to bring organized labor into the system. This combination of repression and incorporation led to a series of bitter internal struggles within the major union confederations between the supporters of moderation and compromise on one hand and those who advocated independent and confrontational unionism on the other.

These largely internal conflicts were overlaid by tensions arising from the international struggle for control of the world trade union movement that broke into the open in the immediate aftermath of World War II. At this point the world labor movement was riven by power struggles between Communists and pro-Communists and a range of anti-Communist forces. In 1948 anti-Communists led a campaign to split the World Federation of Trade Unions, which bore fruit in January of the following year. In Latin America the campaign took the form of persuading labor organizations to disaffiliate from the CTAL. The CTAL conference in Lima in January 1948 saw a split led by the Chilean and Peruvian federations, which effectively marked the demise of the CTAL as a powerful labor organization.

These divisions at the international level reverberated through the national labor movements. Thus in Chile, Socialists and Communists fought bitterly for control of the labor movement and their respective roles in the Radical party government of Gabriel González Videla. They accused each other of sabotaging strikes and damaging independent working-class action. In this climate González Videla promulgated the Law for the Defense of Democracy, which outlawed the Communist party.[14] In Cuba there were violent clashes between rival factions as the progovernment *mujalistas* moved to take over the Confederación de Trabajadores de Cuba.[15] In Peru the Alianza Popular Revolucionaria Americana and Communists struggled for supremacy against one another during the turbulent government of José Luís Bustamante (1945–1948).[16] In Venezuela union leaders loyal to Acción Democrática enjoyed the support of its short-lived government of 1945–1948 to oust the Communists from central positions in the labor movement.[17] In Colombia the leftist Confederación de Trabajadores de Colombia was pushed aside by the newly formed, clerically inspired Unión de Trabajadores de Colombia. In Mexico the Confederación de Trabajadores de México (CTM) survived, but the Communists and *lombardistas* were purged in 1948. Based to a large extent on the powerful national industrial unions in the transport and export sectors, the militant wing of the Mexican labor movement began to reorganize and to oppose the government's stabilization plan. Using dubious legal devices, the government backed up one of the conservative leaders of the railway workers union, Jesús Díaz de León, nicknamed "*el charro*" because of his penchant for dressing up in classical Mexican cowboy suits, when he accused the radicals of financial irregularities in transferring money to anti-CTM organizations. Díaz de León used goon squads and the police, and with government support he forcibly took over union headquarters and carried out a massive purge of rank-and-file militants. This *charrazo* (purge and takeover) was rapidly followed by similar events in the important oil and mining unions. Thus in one country after another the threat of independent and militant union opposition was removed or at least brought under control.

The Impact of the Cold War

The Cold War had a major impact on the Latin American labor movement, since it provided conservatives with an all-encompassing legitimation for the repression of labor. As a result, the requirements of capital accumulation coincided with the political dynamics of Cold War anticommunism. Beginning as early as 1946, but gathering momentum and reaching a peak in 1948, Latin American governments passed anticommunist legislation, intervened in labor unions, and took a hard line against strikes, often in the name of the "defense of democracy." Meanwhile, the American Federation of Labor (AFL), with backing from the State Department, embarked on a campaign to prevent the international labor movement from being dominated by leftists and particularly by Communists. During these struggles the AFL supported efforts by non-Communist forces to take over union organizations; when this approach proved impossible, the AFL encouraged splits and the creation of parallel unions.[18]

In Latin America the endeavor focused on attempts to divide and weaken the Confederación de Trabajadores de América Latina, which controlled some vital union confederations in key countries in strategically crucial sectors of the economy like docks and shipping. The United States was particularly concerned that in the event of another world war a Communist fifth column entrenched in the ports would wreak havoc on inter-American trade. As early as 1943 the State Department began a campaign to increase its influence in the Latin American union movement, and in July that year key anti-*lombardista* union leaders were invited to the United States to discuss alternatives to the CTAL.[19]

In 1943 these efforts proved premature, and nothing resulted from them, but the plots continued. Immediately after the war, with strong backing from the State Department, Serafino Romualdi became the AFL's "roving ambassador" in Latin America, and in 1946 he toured the region to line up support for a new confederation. Eventually, at a meeting of the CTAL in Lima in

January 1948 Romualdi successfully engineered a split that led to the formation of the Confederación Interamericana de Trabajadores (CIT). Although the CIT did not last very long, by splitting the CTAL it greatly weakened the influence of the left in the Latin American labor movement. There were similar splits in individual countries, some of them leading to considerable violence, as governments intervened in the labor unions to weaken radical labor activists. The *charrazo* in Mexico, for example, represented an attempt by the government to throw its weight behind the conservative forces in the railroad unions to oust the incumbent radical leadership. Purges of Communist and leftist union militants followed the adoption of anti-Communist laws. As a result in most countries by the end of the decade, and often earlier, labor militancy had been contained. The purge of the *lombardistas* in the Mexican CTM, and its takeover by conservative leaders in 1948, meant that an important source of funds for the CTAL dried up. The CTAL itself lingered on, but as a mere shadow of its former self until it finally disappeared in 1964. At this point, under the control of "responsible" leaders, most labor movements in Latin America had been domesticated, and they ceased to pose a threat to foreign investment.

The Specific Features of the Latin American Synthesis

In some ways these episodes can be seen as a Latin American version of the struggles in Europe, dubbed the "politics of productivity," that followed World War II.[20] In Europe, as in Latin America, the war led to the mobilization of the working class and heightened the influence of the left. The counteroffensive launched by political forces of the right and center, backed by the United States, focused on the need to "discipline" unions and to ensure they worked together with employers to improve productivity and rebuild the European economies. However, since rapidly rising productivity was to prove such an illusory goal in Latin America, it is more accurate to describe the effort to contain labor there as the "politics of labor peace and foreign investment." In Latin America the primary task of unions was less to collaborate with employers in the pursuit of enhanced productivity than to refrain from militant industrial action that would prejudice the inflows of foreign capital.

The postwar settlement in Latin America should be understood as a conservative consolidation rather than as a reactionary restoration, because attempts by the agrarian export interests to turn the clock back to the past were successful only in the less developed countries of the region. In the larger countries committed to industrialization, the institutional solution arrived at contained progressive elements: the state was to play an enhanced role in the economy, and the relatively small segment of the labor force that was unionized was to receive social security programs. Equally, the agrarian elites were displaced from the center of power and forced to share power with the emerging industrialists and the rapidly expanding state. But none of this meant that the interests of workers would be given high priority. Under the conservative version of ISI, in which foreign capital was critical and strict controls were placed on labor, income distribution would become increasingly regressive.

This outcome formed a striking contrast with that in Western Europe. There during the early postwar period intense conflicts over state ownership of industry, economic planning, social security, education, health, and welfare led to the emergence of social democracy as the dominant model of accumulation. Another quite different set of models emerged in much of Asia, where the war had weakened the old landowning elites and often created or stimulated armed popular rebellion. In Asia the nature of the postwar settlements varied greatly. They ranged from successful Communist revolutions in China, North Korea, and eventually Vietnam to defeated insurgencies in the Philippines and Malaya and U.S.–sponsored reconstruction in Japan and later South Korea. Even so, a common theme in Asia, notably in Japan, South Korea, and Taiwan, was the weakening of landlord control that led to land reform, income redistribution, a strong stimulus to demand, and changes in social structure which together ultimately provided a favorable environment for economic growth.

The contrast between these Asian nations and Latin America became particularly striking. In Latin America, which was physically untouched by the war, the agrarian oligarchy remained intact as a class, despite the structural shift in power away from it. Consequently, during the postwar period the landed interests found themselves still able to veto progressive development projects. As a result, one major component of postwar political instability derived from the continuing tensions over agrarian reform and peasant mobilization. This veto power among the landed classes persisted regardless of whether agrarians and industrialists continued as separate social classes or whether, by means of intermarriage and interlocking investments, the two became merged in a single dominant elite.[21]

Finally, the conservative consolidation in Latin America was different from the conservative consolidation in the United States. In the United States the war greatly strengthened American capitalism and gave liberal economic doctrines a new lease on life. At the same time, however, as in other parts of the world the war boosted both the left and organized labor. Even though the Communist party remained very small in the United States, at the end of the war it exerted considerable influence in important industrial unions such as the United Auto Workers (UAW) and the Congress of Industrial Organizations (CIO).

Immediately after the war the Truman administration embarked on a campaign to contain industrial militancy and in late 1946 successfully challenged the miners and their union led by John Lewis. The Taft-Hartley Labor Act of 1947, passed by Congress over Truman's veto, made it illegal for union leaders to belong to the Communist party and was significant in rolling back leftist influence in the labor unions. In 1947–1948 the Communists were displaced from their leadership positions in the UAW and the CIO and isolated within a limited number of relatively small unions.

Thus by 1949 American labor had been contained, and the stage was set for the spectacular economic growth of the postwar period. Despite the virulent anti-Communism of the McCarthy years, Americans subsequently basked in mass consumption and celebrated the "end of ideology." There was no similar transition in Latin America, which remained deeply fractured and riddled with conflict. There, the conservative consolidation remained fragile, subject to the strains that sprang from an expanding and mobilizing polity and vulnerable to the vicissitudes of continuing dependency.

The ISI model adopted in Latin America in the postwar period proved a success to the limited extent that it brought an expansion of industry, improvements in employment and real wages, and a transfer of technology into the region. The model also had certain political successes. The postwar period in Latin America was characterized by intense struggles over distribution, often led by populists, and by a rapid and explosive expansion of the political arena as urbanization and industrialization created large and increasingly powerful classes of workers, industrialists, middle classes, and the urban poor.

The eventual containment of these forces represented a triumph for the institutions established by the conservative consolidation of the late 1940s. Foremost among these institutions were the corporatist systems of labor control, which functioned effectively because they were never simply instruments to repress workers' demands; instead they structured these demands, defined the limits of legitimate action, and provided incentives to workers to operate within the system. Although the growth of real wages was slower than the rate of growth of national income as a whole, so that income distribution progressively worsened, (in most countries) average real wages were generally rising. While they lasted, these trends served to legitimize the system in the eyes of the organized working class, and in many countries labor leaders were incorporated into the status quo. Thus corporatism should not be seen simply as an instrument used by governments to control labor, but as a system in which workers and union leaders received real benefits as a reward for operating within the rules of the game. In spite of recurrent tensions the positive features of corporatism were perhaps most visible in Brazil and Mexico.[22]

Even so the ISI model established after the war exhibited numerous shortcomings and became plagued by inefficiencies, inequities, instability, and permanent political strains. The continuation of protection during the postwar period led to growing inefficiencies in industry; overvalued exchange rates failed to stimulate exports; government subsidies and transfers produced numerous allocative inefficiencies; extensive government regulation of the economy proved a disincentive to efficient growth; many government enterprises were badly managed; the expansion of state employment usually obeyed the dictates of clientelist politics rather than administrative efficiency.

The bloated public administrations of Latin America produced fiscal deficits and inflation but were unable to produce effective policies. The economies of Latin America staggered between balance of payments crises, inflationary episodes, and draconian stabilization programs, conditions that engendered an atmosphere more conducive to speculation and capital flight than to long-term productive investment. The highly inequitable distribution of income in the region not only led to an inefficient use of human resources and cramped the growth of a mass market for low-income consumption items but also contributed to accumulating political tensions.

Throughout the continent the recurrent economic crises that characterized the ISI model heightened distributive conflict, and labor militancy constantly threatened to break free from corporatist control. On numerous occasions recourse to military intervention became the only way to rescue the system from spiraling mobilization. The fundamental reason for the sad history of military intervention in Latin America lies there, in the tensions generated by the model of capital accumulation. Thus from a political perspective the distinctive feature of the conservative consolidation in Latin America was its fragility. In the postwar period none of the Latin American nations achieved an unbroken record of genuine democracy. Although the weaknesses of Latin American democracy had numerous historical roots, the linkages between import substitution, labor control, and political instability have been repeatedly documented.[23]

Eventually, the institutional arrangements established in the immediate postwar period failed to sustain the process of accumulation. In the late 1970s, when Eurodollars became increasingly available on the world market, Latin American governments sought to use foreign borrowings to continue economic growth and to ameliorate the distributive conflicts simultaneously. But this strategy collapsed in August 1982 when Mexico defaulted on its foreign debt. The ISI model was now disintegrating, and by the 1990s a quite different neoliberal model had displaced it.

This chapter has emphasized the ways in which three factors interacted to shape the pattern of growth and political conflict in Latin America in the postwar period: (1) the international environment that fostered the need to attract foreign capital, (2) national development strategies that led to the conservative version of ISI, and (3) the growth of corporatist modes of labor control. These three factors combined to shape the distinctive pattern of development in Latin America during the postwar period. The model of accumulation enjoyed some successes but possessed numerous tensions and points of stress, and it was particularly vulnerable to shifts in the international economic environment, to crises of legitimacy, and to labor mobilization.

Notes

1. Some revisionist historians have placed the origins of ISI as early as the 1920s. For Brazil see Warren Dean, *The Industrialization of São Paulo*. Austin: University of Texas Press, 1969; for Chile see Henry Kirsch, *Industrial Development in a Traditional Society*. Gainesville: University of Florida Press, 1977.

2. This terminology has been used by Nicos Mouzelis, *Politics in the Semi-Periphery*. London: Macmillan, 1986.

3. A more detailed version of this argument may be found in Leslie Bethell and Ian Roxborough, "Latin America between the Second World War and the Cold

War," *Journal of Latin American Studies* 20, no. 1 (May 1988), 167–89; Leslie Bethell, "From the Second World War to the Cold War, 1944–1954," in *Exporting Democracy*, edited by Abraham F. Lowenthal. Baltimore: Johns Hopkins University Press, 1991, 41–70.

4. *Bombay Chronicle*, 27 and 28 July, 8 August 1945. Quoted by Christopher Thorne, *Border Crossings*. London: Blackwell, 1988, 293.

5. There is an abundant literature on the postwar settlements. For Japan see Michael Schaller, *The American Occupation of Japan*. Oxford: Oxford University Press, 1985; for Korea, most useful is Bruce Cummings, *The Origins of the Korean War*. Princeton: Princeton University Press, 2 vols., 1981 and 1990. For Europe as a whole and "the politics of productivity" see Charles Maier, *In Search of Stability*. Cambridge: Cambridge University Press, 1987.

6. U.S. Department of State, Office of Intelligence Research, Report 4489, "The World Strength of the Communist Party Organizations," 1 October 1947.

7. Jeffrey Gould, "For an Organized Nicaragua: Somoza and the Labour Movement, 1944–1948," *Journal of Latin American Studies* 19, pt. 2 (November 1987), 353–87.

8. Víctor Alba, *Politics and the Labor Movement in Latin America*. Stanford: Stanford University Press, 1968, 325.

9. Vicente Lombardo Toledano, "Por la industrialización de México," in *El marxismo en América Latina*, edited by Michael Lowy. México, D.F.: ERA, 1982, 158–60; Confederación de Trabajadores de América Latina (CTAL), *Por un mundo mejor*. México, D.F.: Confederación de Trabajadores de América Latina, 1948; Víctor Manuel Durand, *La ruptura de la nación*. México, D.F.: Universidad Autónoma de México, 1986, 103–43

10. Víctor Raúl Haya de la Torre, *Y después de la guerra ¿Qué?* Lima: Editorial PTCM, 1946.

11. The debates between Gudin and Simonsen in Brazil over that country's "agrarian vocation" are an obvious example. Eugenio Gudin and Roberto Simonsen, *A controversia do planejamento na economia brasileira*. Rio de Janeiro: IPEA, 1978; Ricardo Bielschowsky, *Pensamento económico brasileiro*. Rio de Janeiro: IPEA, 1988,

12. U.S. Department of State, *Foreign Relations of the United States, 1945*, vol. 9. Washington, D.C., 1970, esp. 49, 64–65, 68–70, 83, 96–97, 103–105, 111–114, 138.

13. Stephen Rabe, *Eisenhower and Latin America*. Chapel Hill: University of North Carolina Press, 1988, 16–18; Forrest Pogue, *George C. Marshall: Statesman, 1945–1959*. New York: Penguin, 1987, 380–86.

14. See Paul W. Drake, "International Crises and Popular Movements in Latin America: Chile and Peru from the Great Depression to the Cold War," this volume.

15. Jean Stubbs, *Tobacco on the Periphery: A Case Study in Cuban Labor History, 1860–1958*. Cambridge: Cambridge University Press, 1985, 147–49; Jon V. Kofas, *The Struggle for Legitimacy: Latin American Labor and the United States, 1930–1960*. Tempe, Ariz.: Arizona State University Press, 1992, 126–44.

16. Gonzalo Portocarrero Maisch, *De Bustamante a Odría*. Lima: Mosca Azul, 1983; Piedad Pareja, *Aprismo y sindicalismo en el Perú*. Lima: Ediciones Rikchay Perú, 1980.

17. Steve Ellner, *Los partidos políticos y su disputa por el control del movimiento sindical en Venezuela, 1936–1948*. Caracas: Universidad Católica Andres Bello, 1980.

18. For a discussion of the international campaign to divide the union movement see Gary K. Busch, *The Political Role of International Trades Unions*. London: Macmillan, 1983. For Latin America see Kofas, *Struggle for Legitimacy*.

19. Kofas, *Struggle for Legitimacy*, 290.

20. Charles Maier, *In Search of Stability*. Cambridge: Cambridge University Press, 1987.

21. The empirical evidence on the social organization of dominant classes in Latin America is still quite limited. For a preliminary discussion see Ian Roxborough, "Unity and Diversity in Latin American History," *Journal of Latin American Studies* 16, pt. 1 (May 1984), 1–26.

22. See, for example, Ian Roxborough, *Unions and Politics in Mexico*. Cambridge: Cambridge University Press, 1984.

23. See, inter alia, Thomas Skidmore, "The Politics of Economic Stabilization in Postwar Latin America," in *Authoritarianism and Corporatism in Latin America*, edited by James Malloy. Pittsburgh: University of Pittsburgh Press, 1977; Guillermo O'Donnell, *El estado burocrático-autoritario*. Buenos Aires: Belgrano, 1982.

Conclusion

David Rock

The 1940s alone do not, of course, provide an exclusive point of departure into modern Latin America. Many of the themes of this period, among them the relations between Latin America and the great powers, the functions and scope of the Latin American states, and the tensions between "oligarchy" and "democracy," were a replay of perennial themes with often distant origins. Nevertheless, the 1940s brought to the fore issues that have frequently dominated the region's politics during the postwar period, at least until the profound changes that occurred in the international system during the late 1980s and the early 1990s.

In the 1940s many Latin American societies were changing more deeply, and at a faster rate, than ever before. The great issues facing the governments of Latin America sprang from the growth of the cities and from the increasing dependence of their expanding populations on urban and industrial employment. At this point the Latin American states deliberately opted for industrial growth through import substitution, which became the instrument "to raise standards of living of the masses and to transform weak, dependent states into strong, respected, viable nations."[1]

Writing in 1954 George Pendle saw the transition from "personal rule" as the most important development of recent years:

> Dictator and constitutional ruler alike now recognized that the support of the army, though still essential, was not enough; they also needed

> the backing of the increasing politically conscious workers, and therefore they were obliged to consider such awkward matters as wages, welfare legislation, land reform, food supplies, and all the many aspects of the national economy which affect the cost of living. Thus the outstanding characteristic of the Latin American political scene of the early 1950s was the adapting of personal rule to mid-twentieth-century economic and social requirements.[2]

Governments responded to these new conditions in several different ways. A common approach was to attempt to co-opt the masses by the extension of the franchise or, alternatively, to seek to exclude them by restricting it. Incorporation became a common trend during the mid-1940s, exclusion during the late 1940s and 1950s. Occasionally these two processes occurred almost simultaneously. Thus in Chile the proscription of the Communists in 1947–1948 was followed by the enfranchisement of women in 1949, although women who were also Communists continued under a ban.

Another common response to social change during the 1940s was to expand the role of the state as an employer through nationalizations, the growth of the bureaucracy, and increased state spending. This trend represented the most striking contrast between the democratic movements in Latin America of the 1940s and those of the 1980s and early 1990s when the state was contracting rather than expanding. In the 1940s the rise of popular forces and popular politics was almost invariably accompanied by a new brand of nationalism and a willingness to extend the activities of the state. These trends, epitomized in Juan Perón's slogan Social Justice, Political Sovereignty, Economic Independence in turn were in striking contrast with the neoliberal model of the early 1990s that expressed profound hostility toward social reform, national self-assertion, and interventionist economic policies. In the latter period the goal of policy was to emancipate market forces, not control or dominate them. In the 1940s Uruguay became a leading example of the growth of the state, as patronage became one of the main techniques of the Colorado party to consolidate its dominance. There were similar shifts elsewhere such as in Chile under the Popular Front, and in Mexico under the Partido Revolucionario Institucional (PRI).

A typical by-product of the growth of the state was the rise of "state corporatism," which represented an effort, often inspired by prewar European models, to neutralize social conflict through the creation of state-controlled mass institutions. Thus in Mexico the newly formed PRI established vast organizations representing the peasantry, the urban workers and labor unions, and the middle classes. In Argentina, Perón promulgated the "Organized Community," in which an even broader range of groups, among them workers, entrepreneurs, students, clerics, and soldiers, were to be brought under the tutelage of hierarchical state institutions. In Uruguay state corporatism remained weak by comparison with the systems in its giant neighbors, Argentina and Brazil. But in Uruguay there were echoes of corporatism in the ways government dominated the process of collective bargaining.

Among the other by-products of the growth of the state and of corporatist institutions was the rising impact and importance of inflation. During the war rising prices resulted principally from shortages of imported manufactures and from the declining supply of basic consumption goods like food as labor was drafted into export production. Soon after the war, however, inflation emerged in its "modern" form as a result of deficit-spending or populist redistribution policies. Among the foremost examples of this were Argentina under Perón, Chile under González Videla and Ibáñez del Campo, and Brazil under Vargas following his return to power in the early 1950s.

In the 1940s the political leaders of Latin America began to exploit the opportunities that came from the growth of the cities. When populists such as Vargas appealed to their new urban working-class constituencies, they were fashioning the discourse that subsequently dominated the "third world." Similarly, the Latin American populists and nationalists of the 1940s became the precursors of numerous political leaders in Africa and parts of Asia during subsequent decades. Vargas too became one of the first to articulate ideas subsequently developed in academic and theoretical directions by the ECLA (United Nations Economic Commission for Latin America) under Raúl Prebisch: juridical sovereignty would not necessarily eliminate international inequalities; colonialism could be succeeded by neocolonialism.

In the 1940s Latin America underwent a political cycle that recurred on numerous later occasions. Around mid-decade the "People," represented by the mass parties and the great labor federations, emerged as a major contender for power. Elected popular governments committed to social reform, some of them containing Communists, frequently displaced authoritarian regimes. These forces failed to consolidate themselves, however; reformism proved short-lived and unsustained, and by the end of the 1940s conservative and sometimes openly dictatorial regimes had regained control. During subsequent decades, as the Latin American states veered between short-lived democracies and hard-line autocracies, the basic pattern underwent continual repetition.

As we show in this volume, external conditions closely influenced the cyclical trend in politics. In 1939–1945 the United States extended its influence from its bases in middle America and the Caribbean into South America. During the war Latin America's trade, financial, and investment links with the United States grew rapidly, and wartime economic expansion, along with the social disruptions it provoked, helped foster the democratic opening of mid-decade.

Moreover, as Laurence Duggan declared in 1945: "the other American republics have the keen expectation of the continuance, but on a greatly expanded scale, of the assistance. . .rendered by the United States."[3] But after the war the United States proved unwilling to provide the aid the Latin Americans expected. The sharpening focus of the United States on Europe and Pacific Asia began during the early 1940s following the German conquest of Europe and the Japanese expansion in Asia. By the time of the Chapultepec conference in early 1945, the United States had already redefined its relationship with the rest of the world, and it now gave highest priority to Western Europe. Thus trends during the late 1940s, starting with the Truman Doctrine of March 1947, were not innovations prompted by the Cold War alone but logical consequences of the collapse of isolationism in 1940–1941. Nevertheless on the inception of the Cold War the interest of the United States in Latin America dwindled once more. Aid to Latin America quickly disappeared, and the wartime economic spurt in Latin America ground to a halt.

A parallel shift became visible in attitudes in the United States toward the political systems of Latin America. During the early 1940s, as the United States became embroiled in the defense of "democracy" in Europe and the world at large, it sought to propagate similar values in Latin America and strongly influenced the political transitions in Latin America in mid-decade. Support for democracy in Latin America from the United States became most intense immediately before the creation of the United Nations, but soon afterward ebbed. By 1946 the Latin American democracies were becoming tarnished in the eyes of the United States because of their association with nationalism and an expanding state; democracy also provided an unwelcome opportunity for the growth and consolidation of the Communist parties and Communist-dominated labor unions.

During the next few years the United States grew accustomed to supporting any government in Latin America opposed to Communism. Later, starting in 1953 under the Eisenhower administration, the policy of the United States was to uphold nondemocratic conservatives or military autocrats who were willing to defend its interests in the region. Support for conservative governments blended with the U.S. position on foreign investment, for which the right "climate" had to be created. Thus, economic trends worked in close conjunction with evolving political forces.

Toward the end of World War II the alliance abroad between the United States, Britain, and the Soviet Union found a reflection in Latin America, as the new emphasis on free elections coincided with the legalization and expansion of the Communist parties. The Cold War again cut short this trend: at the end of the decade the Communists were purged from governments, congresses, and labor unions, and in many countries the Communist parties were banned. Subsequently the Communist movement underwent a steep decline almost throughout Latin America, and "in some countries for all practical purposes the party ceased to exist." At the height of their influence in 1944–1947 the Communist parties of Latin America contained an estimated 375,000 members and polled more than one million votes. By 1952 membership had shrunk to fewer than 200,000, and the Communist vote was virtually zero.[4]

The economic forces stemming from the war, particularly inflation and industrial growth, became another conditioning influence on the transition. The drive to increase exports during the war, along with industrial growth provoked by falling imports, encouraged the new forms of democratic politics and promoted the emergence of a labor movement of unparalleled size and strength. Postwar economic problems, in contrast, further accelerated the fall or decline of the nascent Latin American democratic movements and organized labor. By 1947–1948 the wartime dollar reserves, and the bulk of the trade surpluses, were gone, as were the wartime exports of manufactured goods. The subsequent need for austerity to quell inflation facilitated the shift to conservatism during the late 1940s. As the constraints on economic growth increased, more authoritarian government emerged, although in the long run conservatives had no greater success in reviving stable growth than their leftist or populist predecessors.

The straitjacket that began to envelop Latin America at the end of the 1940s, as the new postwar system dominated by the Cold War took shape, had a profound impact on public policy and political debate. As a commentator observed during the late 1950s:

> Internal developments were closely connected with the broader currents of international affairs, because the main issues in internal politics determining the alignments of parties and factions involved such issues as the role of foreign capital, fear of and resentments against "economic colonialism," a nationalism scarcely less fierce than that which has invaded the Middle East, [but also] an admitted need for foreign capital on a large scale. It was, in the long run, the irreconcilable nature of these objectives which determined the fluctuations of Latin American politics.[5]

In sum, it had once more become quite impossible for Latin Americans to escape from under the shadow of the outside world. In Latin America newly arisen nationalist aspirations clashed continually with inescapable foreign linkages.

During this period external influences became visible in a variety of ways. As the origins and background of the ideology of the ECLA show, Latin and particularly Atlantic South Americans were constantly looking to Europe for answers to their own problems and dilemmas. Ideas from abroad sometimes came from surprising sources. Thus "unequal exchange," whose vogue in Latin America lasted from the late 1940s to around the 1970s, was based on European ideas popular among right-wing groups during the 1920s and 1930s. Similarly, in Mexico "scientific nationalism" never achieved the degree of intensity necessary to persuade Mexicans to abandon their willingness to utilize U.S. agricultural technology. Both these examples highlight the persistence of Latin America's deep-seated cultural and technological subordination.

Nevertheless in this period Latin Americans favored most strongly the ideas from abroad that led to the growth of the state, the welfare of the urban masses, and the consolidation of nationalism. Soon observers were noting "the widespread unrest among the Latin American masses, a fervent nationalism among all classes, and a resentment against the United States, . . .which [had] had a steady growth since World War II."[6] In the mid-1940s U.S. liberals like Sumner Welles were predicting this kind of reaction, as they sought to slow the U.S. policy shift toward Europe and away from Latin America. The best way to promote democracy and provide protection against communism, this argument ran, was for the United States to support the economic development of the hemisphere through a program of public aid like the Marshall Plan for Europe.

Yet there were some crucial weaknesses in this position, and the liberal claim that U.S. resources would be just as effective in creating new industrial economies in Latin America as in reconstructing old ones in Europe remained dubious in the light of later experience. In Western Europe the Marshall Plan achieved economic reconstruction in less than five years and fostered an unprecedented era of economic expansion. In Latin America the same basic approach appeared under the Alliance for Progress in the early 1960s, but in this venue it proved a complete failure.[7] Later, even greater financial and economic disaster followed the vast wave of private foreign investment in Latin America of the late 1970s. On this occasion the consequence of foreign intrusion was a decade of debt and economic decline.

The foreign aid issue provided an example of the way external influences could activate or intensify internal forces but could never supersede or derail them. Similarly, if the two pressures ran counter to each other, the internal forces invariably proved more powerful. Bill Albert has made a similar point in a recent study of the impact of World War I in Latin America: "In almost every case there were discernible prewar roots for wartime changes. . . .What the war did was hasten in hothouse fashion the emergence of these factors. . . .The war served as a powerful catalyst."[8]

Thus the separation of "internal" and "external" forces should not be pursued too far, since there were often close linkages between them. It is well known, for example, that industrial and urban growth in Latin America in the 1940s was intimately related to shifting patterns of foreign trade. A similar relationship prevailed in Argentine agriculture, whose decline illustrated a constant interplay between local and exogenous forces. Similarly, when in 1945 Vargas shifted from an authoritarian to a populist position, he was both appealing to the new working-class constituencies and adjusting to the new ideological climate fostered by the Allies from abroad that stressed freedom and emancipation.

The catalytic impact of external forces varied from country to country: in Brazil (as in Argentina) this influence was great, but elsewhere it was relatively low. A similar point might be made concerning the impact of the

1940s as a whole on different parts of Latin America. Brazil and Argentina had strong historical ties with Europe; change was less striking in many of the Pacific Rim or Andean states. Equally, change during the 1940s appeared less important in countries like Mexico and Chile that had suffered recent political turmoil (the former during the Revolution and more recently under Cárdenas, and the latter during the Great Depression). In Peru, where the landed oligarchies were stronger, the pace of change was less marked. Finally, change often appeared negligible in the most underdeveloped parts of the region, where peasant agriculture predominated, the cities were small, and foreign trade was minimal. In Paraguay, for example, there was a flicker of political activity in 1946, but it was quickly stifled by renascent *caudillismo.*[9] With the striking exception of Guatemala under Juan José Arévalo and particularly Jacobo Arbenz, these were the trends too in the Central American and Caribbean nations.

In sum, World War II and the coming of the Cold War underscored the close relationship between Latin America and the capitalist powers led by the United States. At the same time this period illustrates the complex, multidimensional nature of the relationship, as well as the limitations to it. During the 1940s the policies of the United States toward Latin America placed growing emphasis on conservative stability and increasingly less on economic development. In the short term this approach helped to open the gate to the dictators and authoritarians of the 1950s, but in the longer term it kindled the growth of a nationalist left committed to the destruction of "imperialism." Even so it is uncertain whether a different approach by the United States toward Latin America, if ever one were possible, would have altered the course of subsequent events very much.

All the contributors to this book stand a long way from the extremes of treating Latin America either as a cipher of the outside world or, alternatively, as a body entirely divorced from it. Our general consensus is that internal forces or "trajectories" provide the basic key to understanding the broad directions of Latin American society. However, these forces cannot be understood without reference to others from outside Latin America that constantly reshape the context or framework for their interplay.

Notes

1. Robert Burr, "United States Latin American Policy," in *The Dynamics of World Power: A Documentary History of United States Foreign Policy*, edited by Arthur M. Schlesinger, Jr., vol. 3. New York: Chelsea House Publishers, 1973, xix.

2. George Pendle, "Latin America," in *Survey of International Affairs, 1953*, edited by Peter Calvocoressi. London: Oxford University Press, 1956, 336.

3. See Laurence Duggan in George Wythe, *Industry in Latin America*. New York: Columbia University Press, 1945, viii.

4. Cf. Rollie Poppino, *International Communism in Latin America: A History of the Movement, 1914–1963*. Glencoe, Ill.: Free Press, 1964, 36, 224–31.

5. Geoffrey Barraclough, ed., *Survey of International Affairs, 1956–1962*. London: Oxford University Press, 1962, 304.

6. Ronald M. Schneider, *Communism in Guatemala, 1944–1954*. New York: Praeger, 1958, v.

7. On the intended scope of the Alliance for Progress see Lincoln Gordon, *A New Deal for Latin America: The Alliance for Progress*. Cambridge: Harvard University Press, 1963; for some of the basic criticisms of the Alliance see Víctor Alba, *Alliance without Allies: The Mythology of Progress in Latin America*. New York: Praeger, 1965.

8. Bill Albert, *South America and the First World War: The Impact of the War on Brazil, Argentina, Peru, and Chile*. Cambridge: Cambridge University Press, 1988, 5.

9. On Paraguay see Poppino, *Communism*, 83.

Select Bibliography

Abarca, Lt. Col. Mariano. *La industrialización de la Argentina*. Buenos Aires: Ministerio de Agricultura de la Nación, 1944.

Alba, Víctor. *Alliance without Allies: The Mythology of Progress in Latin America*. New York: Praeger, 1965.

———. *Politics and the Labor Movement in Latin America*. Stanford: Stanford University Press, 1968.

Albert, Bill. *South America and the First World War: The Impact of the War on Brazil, Argentina, Peru, and Chile*. Cambridge: Cambridge University Press, 1988.

Alcalde, Xavier. *The Idea of Third World Development*. Lanham, Md.: University Press of America, 1987.

Alexander, Robert J. *Communism in Latin America*. New Brunswick: Rutgers University Press, 1957.

———. *Aprismo: The Ideas and Doctrines of Víctor Raúl Haya de la Torre*. Kent: Kent State University Press, 1973.

Alfonso, Pedro. *Sindicalismo y revolución en el Uruguay*. Montevideo: Nuevo Mundo, 1970.

Allende, Salvador. *La contradicción de Chile*. Santiago: Talleres Gráficos, 1943.

Almino, João. *Os demócratas autoritarios*. São Paulo: Brasiliense, 1980.

Alvarado Klimpel, Felicitas. *La mujer chilena: El aporte femenino al progreso de Chile*. Santiago: Editorial Andres Bello, 1962.

Amin, Samir. *Accumulation on a World Scale*. New York: Monthly Review Press, 1974.

Angell, Alan. *Politics and the Labour Movement in Chile*. London: Oxford University Press, 1972.

Angell, Robert. *America's Dilemma, Alone or Allied?* New York: Harper and Brothers, 1940.

Arciniegas, Germán. *The State of Latin America*. Translated by Harriet de Onís. New York: Knopf, 1952.

Arena, Antonio, and Antonio Román Guiñazú. "La erosión eólica de los suelos en el centro-oeste de la Argentina." In República Argentina, Ministerio de Agricultura de la Nación, *Publicaciones misceláneas* 65 (1939), 8–15.

Arndt, H. W. "The Origins of Structuralism." *World Development* 13, no. 2 (1985), 151–59.

Ashworth, J. *A Short History of the World Economy since 1850*. London: Longman, 1975.

Avílez, Bernardo A. *Cultivo y comercio del algodón en México*. México, D.F.: Dirección de Economía Rural, 1939.

Baer, Werner. "The Economics of Prebisch and the ECLA." *Economic Development and Cultural Change* 10, no. 2 (1962), 169–82.

Banco de la Provincia de Buenos Aires. *Memoria y balance general*. Buenos Aires, 1931.

Barnard, Andrew. "Chilean Communists, Radical Presidents, and Chilean Relations with the United States, 1940–1947." *Journal of Latin American Studies* 13, no. 2 (November 1981), 347–74.

Barraclough, Geoffrey, ed. *Survey of International Affairs, 1956–1962*. London: Oxford University Press, 1962.

Bazdresch, Carlos. *El pensamiento de Juan Noyola*. México, D.F.: Fondo de Cultura Económica, 1984.

Beals, Carleton. *America South*. Philadelphia: J. Lippincott, 1938.

Beltrán, Enrique. *Medio siglo de recuerdos de un biólogo mexicano*. México, D.F.: Sociedad Mexicana de Historia Natural, 1977.

Benevides, Maria Victoria de Mesquita. *A UDN e o Udenismo: Ambiguidades do liberalismo brasileiro (1945–1965)*. Rio de Janeiro: Paz e Terra, 1981.

Berle, Adolph A. *Navigating the Rapids, 1918–1971*. New York: Harcourt Brace Jovanovich, 1973.

Bertola, Luis. *Industrialization in Uruguay*. Ph.D. dissertation, Centro Uruguayo Independiente, Montevideo–University of Uppsala, Sweden, 1991.

Betancourt, Romulo. *Venezuela: Oil and Politics*. Boston: Houghton Mifflin, 1979.

Bethell, Leslie, and Ian Roxborough. "Latin America between the Second World War and the Cold War: Some Reflections on the 1945–1948 Conjuncture." *Journal of Latin American Studies* 20, no. 1 (May 1988), 167–89.

———. "From the Second World War to the Cold War, 1944–1954," in *Exporting Democracy*, edited by Abraham F. Lowenthal, 41–70. Baltimore: Johns Hopkins University Press, 1991.

———, eds. *Latin America between the Second World War and the Cold War, 1944–1948*. Cambridge: Cambridge University Press, 1993.

Bielschowsky, Ricardo. *Pensamento económico brasileiro*. Rio de Janeiro: IPEA, 1988.

Bizarro, Sergio. *Historical Dictionary of Chile*. 2d ed. Metuchen, N.J., London: Scarecrow Press, 1987.

Blackhouse, Roger. *A History of Modern Economic Analysis*. Oxford: Blackwell, 1985.

Blasier, S. Cole "Chile: A Communist Battleground." *Political Science Quarterly* 65 (1950), 353–74.

Boizard, Ricardo. *Historia de una derrota*. Santiago: Ediciones Orbe, 1941.

Bonilla Sauns, J. "La restructuración capitalista del Uruguay: 1958–1976," in *Uruguay, dictadura y realidad nacional*, edited by América Latina, Estudios y Perspectivas. México, D.F.: ERESU, 1981.

Bostrom, Mikael. "Political Waves in Latin America, 1940–1987." Typescript. Umea, Sweden, 1988.

Bowers, Claude G. *Chile through Embassy Windows*. New York: Simon and Schuster, 1958.

Braun, Oscar. *Comercio internacional e imperialismo*. Buenos Aires: Siglo XXI, 1973.

Bronstein, Adam S. "The Evolution of Labour Relations in Uruguay: Achievements and Challenges." *International Labor Review* 128, no. 2 (1989), 28–42.

Brown, William Adams, and Redvers Opie. *American Foreign Assistance* Washington, D.C.: Brookings Institution, 1954.

Bulmer-Thomas, Victor. *The Political Economy of Central America since 1920*. Cambridge: Cambridge University Press, 1987.

Bunge, Alejandro E. *Una nueva Argentina*. Buenos Aires: Kraft, 1940.

Burr, Robert. "United States Latin American Policy," in *The Dynamics of World Power: A Documentary History of United States Foreign Policy*, edited by Arthur M. Schlesinger Jr., vol. 3, xix–xxxviii. New York: Chelsea House Publishers, 1973.

Busch, Gary K. *The Political Role of International Trades Unions*. London: Macmillan, 1983.

Bustamante y Rivero, José Luis. *Tres años de lucha por la democracia en el Perú*. Buenos Aires: n.p., 1949.

Butland. Gilbert J. *Chile*. London: Royal Institute of International Affairs, 1953.

Calvocoressi, Peter, ed. *Survey of International Affairs, 1947–1948*. London: Oxford University Press, 1952.

———. *Survey of International Affairs, 1953*. London: Oxford University Press, 1956.

Caravedo Molinari, Baltazar. *Burguesía e industria en el Perú, 1933–1945*. Lima: Instituto de Estudios Peruanos, 1976.

Cárdenas, Lázaro. *Palabras y documentos públicos de Lázaro Cárdenas: informes del gobierno y mensaje presidenciales de año nuevo*. México, D.F.: Siglo Ventiuno Editores, 1978.

Cardoso, Fernando Henrique. "The Originality of the Copy: CEPAL and the Idea of Development." *CEPAL Review* 4 (1977), 7–40.

Cardoso, Fernando Henrique, and Enzo Faletto. *Dependency and Development in Latin America*. Berkeley and Los Angeles: University of California Press, 1979.

Carey, James. *Peru and the United States, 1900–1962*. Notre Dame: University of Notre Dame Press, 1964.

Carmona, Elysabeth, and Geraldo Leite. "Radio Povo e poder: Subserviencia e paternalismo," in *Populismo y communicação*, edited by José Marques de Melo, 125–34. São Paulo: Cortez, 1981.

Carneiro, Levi. *Voto dos analfabetos*. Petrópolis: Vozes, 1964.

Carone, Edgard. *A terceira república (1937–1945)*. São Paulo: DIFEL, 1976.

———. *O PCB (1943–1964)*. 2 vols. São Paulo: DIFEL, 1982.

———, ed. *Movimento operario no Brasil*. 2 vols. São Paulo: DIFEL, 1979.

Chelén Rojas, Alejandro. *Flujo y reflujo del socialismo chileno*. Montevideo: Ediciones Vanguardia Socialista, 1961.

———. *Trayectoria del socialismo*. Buenos Aires: Astral, 1967.

Ciccarelli, Orazio. "Fascism and Politics in Peru during the Benavides Regime, 1933–1939: The Italian Perspective." *Hispanic American Historical Review* 70, no. 3 (August 1990), 405–32.

Clark, Colin. *The Conditions of Economic Progress*. London: Macmillan, 1940.

Collier, Ruth Berins, and David Collier. *Shaping the Political Arena*. Princeton: Princeton University Press, 1991.

Confederación de Trabajadores de América Latina. *Por un mundo mejor*. México, D.F.: Confederación de Trabajadores de América Latina, 1948.

Connell-Smith, Gordon. *The United States and Latin America: An Historical Analysis of Inter-American Relations*. London: Heinemann, 1966.

Cosío-Villegas, Daniel. *American Extremes*. Austin: University of Texas Press, 1964.

Cotter, Joseph. "Before the Green Revolution: Mexican Agricultural Policy, 1920–1949." Ph.D. dissertation, University of California, Santa Barbara, 1993.

Coutinho, Lourival. *O General Goés depoe*. Rio de Janeiro: Coelho Branco, 1956.

Covarrubias, Paz, and Rolando Franco, eds. *Chile: Mujer y sociedad*. Santiago: UNICEF, 1978.

Cumings, Bruce. *The Origins of the Korean War*. Princeton: Princeton University Press, 1981.

Dadone, Aldo Antonio, and Luis Eugenio di Marco. "The Impact of Prebisch's Ideas on Modern Economic Analysis," in *International Economics and Development: Essays in Honor of Raúl Prebisch*, edited by Luis Eugenio di Marco, 15–34. New York: Academic Press, 1972.

Davies, Thomas M., Jr. *Indian Integration in Peru: A Half Century of Experience, 1900–1948*. Lincoln: University of Nebraska Press, 1970.

Dean, Warren. *The Industrialization of São Paulo*. Austin: University of Texas Press, 1969.

Deane, Phyllis. *The State and the Economic System: An Introduction to the History of Political Economy*. Oxford: Oxford University Press, 1989.

D'Elía, Germán. *El Uruguay neo-batllista: 1946–1958*. Montevideo: Banda Oriental, 1986.

Díaz Alejandro, Carlos F. *Essays on the Economic History of the Argentine Republic*. New Haven: Yale University Press, 1970.

———. "The 1940s in Latin America," in *Economic Structure and Performance*, edited by M. Syrquin, L. Taylor, and L. E. Westphal, 341–62. New York: Harcourt, Brace, 1984.

Donoso, Ricardo. *Alessandri, agitador y demoledor*. 2 vols. México, D.F.: Fondo de Cultura Económica, 1952, 1954.

Dorfman, Adolfo. *Desarrollo industrial en la Argentina*. Buenos Aires: Escuela de Estudios Argentinos, 1942. Republished as *Historia de la industria argentina*. Buenos Aires: Solar Hachette, 1970.

Dowling, José O. "Resultados agrícolas generales y particulares: Una contradicción." *Gaceta rural* 21, no. 245 (December 1927), 435.

Dozer, Donald Marquand. *Are We Good Neighbors? Three Decades of Inter-American Relations, 1930–1960*. Gainesville: University of Florida Press, 1959.

Drake, Paul W. "The Political Responses of the Chilean Upper Class to the Depression and the Threat of Socialism, 1931–1933," in *The Rich, the Well Born, and the Powerful*, edited by Frederic Cople Jaher, 304–37. Urbana: University of Illinois Press, 1973.

———. *Socialism and Populism in Chile, 1932–1952*. Urbana: University of Illinois Press, 1978.

———. "Debt and Democracy in Latin America, 1920s–1980s," in *Debt and Democracy in Latin America*, edited by Barbara Stallings and Robert Kaufman, 39–58. Boulder, Colo.: Westview Press, 1989.

Duggan, Laurence. *The Americas: The Search for Hemisphere Security*. New York: Henry Holt, 1949.

Dulles, John W. F. *Vargas of Brazil*. Austin: University of Texas Press, 1967.

Durán Bernales, Florencio. *El Partido Radical*. Santiago: Editorial Nascimento, 1958.

Durand, Georgina. *Mis entrevistas: Escritores, artistas, y hombres de ciencia de Chile*. Vol. 1. Santiago: Editorial Nascimiento, 1943.

Durand, Víctor Manuel. *La ruptura de la nación*. México, D.F.: Universidad Autónoma de México, 1986.

Ellner, Steve. *Los partidos políticos y su disputa por el control del movimiento sindical en Venezuela, 1936–1948*. Caracas: Universidad Católica Andres Bello, 1980.

Ellsworth, T. *Chile, an Economy in Transition*. Westport, Conn.: Greenwood Press, 1945.

El movimiento sindical internacional y la fundación de la C.I.T. Santiago: n.p.., 1949.

Emmanuel, Arghiri. *Unequal Exchange*. London: New Left Books, 1972.

Erickson, Kenneth. "Populism and Political Control of the Working Class in Brazil." *Proceedings of the Pacific Coast Conference of Latin American Studies* 4 (1975), 117–44.

Errandonea, Alfredo, and Daniel Costabile. *Sindicato y sociedad en el Uruguay*. Montevideo: Biblioteca de Cultura Universitaria, 1969.

Escudé, Carlos. *Gran Bretaña, Estados Unidos, y la declinación argentina, 1942–1949*. Buenos Aires: Belgrano, 1983.

Eshag, Eprime, and Rosemary Thorp. "Economic and Social Consequences of Orthodox Economic Policies in Argentina in the Post-War Years." *Bulletin of the Oxford University Institute of Economics and Statistics* 27, no. 1 (February 1965), 1–44.

Estabrook, Leon M. *Agricultural Survey of South America: Argentina and Paraguay*. U.S. Department of Agriculture Bulletin, no. 1409. Washington, D.C.: U.S. Government Printing Office, 1926.

Falcoff, Mark, and Fredrick B. Pike. *The Spanish Civil War, 1936–1939: American Hemispheric Perspectives*. Lincoln: University of Nebraska Press, 1982.

Fausto, Boris, ed. *Historia geral da civilição brasileira*. Vol 4. São Paulo: DIFEL, 1984.

Fernández y Fernández, Ramón. *Los agrónomos*. México, D.F.: 1933.

Ferrer, Aldo. "The Early Teaching of Raúl Prebisch." *CEPAL Review* 42 (1990), 27–34.

Ferrero, R. A. *La política fiscal y la economía nacional*. Lima: Editorial Lumen, 1946.

Finch, M. H. J. *A Political Economy of Uruguay since 1870*. New York: St. Martin's Press, 1981.

Fitzgerald, Deborah. "The Rockefeller Foundation in Mexico, 1943–1953." *Social Studies of Science* 16 (1986), 457–83.

FitzGerald, E. V. K. "A Note on Income Distribution, Accumulation, and Recovery in the Depression," in *Latin America in the 1930s: The Role of the Periphery in World Crisis*, edited by Rosemary Thorp, 242–78. London: Macmillan, 1984.

———. "Kalecki on the Financing of Development." *Cambridge Journal of Economics* 14, no. 2 (1990), 183–203.

Flanders, M. June. "Prebisch on Protectionism: An Evaluation." *Economic Journal* 74, no. 294 (1964), 305–26.

Flichman, Guillermo. *La renta del suelo y el desarrollo agrario argentino*. Buenos Aires: Siglo XXI, 1977.

Floto, Edgardo. "The Center-Periphery System and Unequal Exchange." *CEPAL Review* 39 (1989), 135–154.

Francis, Michael J. *The Limits of Hegemony: United States Relations with Argentina and Chile during World II*. Notre Dame: University of Notre Dame Press, 1977.

Frank, Waldo. *South American Journey*. New York: Duell, Sloan, and Pearce, 1943.

Frega, Ana, Mónica Maronna, and Yvette Trochon. *Baldomir y la restauración democrática*. Montevideo: Banda Oriental, 1987.

French, John D. "The Communications Revolution: Radio and Working-Class Life and Culture in Postwar São Paulo, Brazil." Paper presented at the Third Latin American Labor History Conference, Yale University, April 1978.

———. "Industrial Workers and the Birth of the Populist Republic in Brazil, 1945–1946." *Latin American Perspectives* 16, no. 4 (Fall 1989), 5–27.

———. *The Brazilian Workers' ABC: Class Conflict and Alliances in Modern São Paulo.* Chapel Hill: University of North Carolina Press, 1992.

French, John D., and Mary Lynn Pedersen. "Women and Working-Class Mobilization in Postwar São Paulo, Brazil, 1945–1948." *Latin American Research Review* 24, no. 3 (Fall 1989), 99–125.

Furci, Carmelo. *The Chilean Communist Party and the Road to Socialism.* London: Zed Books, 1984.

Furtado, Celso. *A fantasia organizada.* Rio de Janeiro: Editorial Paz y Tierra, 1985.

Gardner, Lloyd C. *Economic Aspects of New Deal Diplomacy.* Madison: University of Wisconsin Press, 1963.

Gaviola Artigas, Edda, et al. *Queremos votar en las próximas elecciones: Historia del movimiento femenino chileno, 1913–1952.* Santiago: Centro de Análisis y Difusión de la Condición de la Mujer, 1986.

Gellman, Irwin F. *Good Neighbor Diplomacy.* Baltimore: Johns Hopkins University Press, 1979.

Gerlach, Allen. "Civil-Military Relations in Peru, 1914–1945." Ph.D. dissertation, University of New Mexico, Albuquerque, 1973.

Gerschenkron, Alexander. "History of Economic Doctrines and Economic History." *American Economic Review* 59, no. 2 (1969), 1–17.

Giberti, Horacio C. E. *Historia económica de la ganadería argentina.* 2d ed. Buenos Aires: Raigal, 1961.

Gomes, Angela de Castro. *A invenção do trabalhismo.* São Paulo: Vertice/IUPERJ, 1988.

Gomes, Eduardo. *Campanha da libertação.* São Paulo: Livraria Martins Editora, n.d.

González Díaz, Galo. *La lucha por la formación del Partido Comunista de Chile.* Santiago: n.p., 1958.

González Videla, Gabriel. *Memorias.* 2 vols. Santiago: Editorial Gabriela Mistral, 1975.

Gordon, Lincoln. *A New Deal for Latin America: The Alliance for Progress.* Cambridge: Harvard University Press, 1963.

Gould, Jeffrey. "For an Organized Nicaragua: Somoza and the Labour Movement, 1944-1948." Pt. 2. *Journal of Latin American Studies* 19 (November 1987), 353–87.

Gourevitch, Peter. *Politics in Hard Times.* Ithaca: Cornell University Press, 1986.

Green, David. *The Containment of Latin America: A History of the Myths and Realities of the Good Neighbor Policy.* Chicago: Quadrangle Books, 1971.

Ground, Richard Lynn. "The Genesis of Import Substitution in Latin America." *CEPAL Review* 36 (1988), 179–203.

Guadagni, Alieto Aldo. *La fuerza de trabajo en Chile, 1930–1960.* Santiago: Universidad de Chile, 1961.

Gudin, Eugenio, and Roberto Simonsen. *A controversia do planejamento na economia brasileira.* Rio de Janeiro: IPEA, 1978.

Gupta, Bishnupriya. "Import Substitution in Capital Goods: The Case of Brazil, 1929–1979." D. Phil. dissertation, University of Oxford, 1989.

Guzmán, Gabriel. *El desarrollo latinoamericano y la CEPAL.* Barcelona: Editorial Planeta, 1976.

Haglund, David G. *Latin America and the Transformation of United States Strategic Thought.* Albuquerque: University of New Mexico Press, 1984.

Hall, Linda B. *Alvaro Obregón: Power and Revolution in Mexico, 1911–1920.* College Station: Texas A & M University Press, 1981.

Halperin, Ernst. *Nationalism and Communism in Chile.* Cambridge: Massachusetts Institute of Technology Press, 1965.

Hanson, Simon Gabriel. *Economic Development of Latin America.* Washington, D.C.: Interamerican Affairs Press, 1951.

Harberler, Gottfried. "Los términos de intercambio y el desarrollo económico," in *El desarrollo económico y América Latina,* edited by Howard Ellis, 325–62. México, D.F.: Fondo de Cultura Económica, 1960.

Harrod, Roy F. *The Life of John Maynard Keynes.* London: Macmillan, 1951.

Haya de la Torre, Víctor Raúl. *La defensa continental.* Buenos Aires: Ediciones Problemas de América, 1942.

———. *Y después de la guerra ¿Qué?* Lima: Editorial PTCM, 1946.

———. *Obras completas.* Vol. 1. Lima: Editorial Juan Mejía Baca, 1977.

Hermosilla Aedo, Amanda. *La mujer en la vida economica.* Santiago: Soc. Imp. y Lito. Universo, 1936.

Herring, Hubert. *Good Neighbors: Argentina, Brazil, Chile, and Seventeen Other Countries.* New Haven: Yale University Press, 1941.

Hewitt de Alcantara, Cynthia. *Modernizing Mexican Agriculture: Socioeconomic Implications of Technological Change.* Geneva: United Nations Research Institute for Social Development, 1976.

Hilliker, Grant. *The Politics of Reform in Peru.* Baltimore: Johns Hopkins University Press, 1971.

Hilton, Stanley. "The Overthrow of Getúlio Vargas in 1945: Intervention, Defense of Democracy, or Political Retribution?" *Hispanic American Historical Review* 67, no. 1 (February 1987), 1–37.

Hirschman, Albert O. *Power and International Trade.* Berkeley and Los Angeles: University of California Press, 1945.

———. *Latin American Issues: Essays and Comments.* New York: Twentieth Century Fund, 1961.

———. *Journeys towards Progress.* New York: Twentieth Century Fund, 1963.

Hodara, José. *Prebisch y la CEPAL: Sustancia, trayectoria, y contexto institucional.* México, D.F.: Colegio de México, 1987.

Hotschewer, Curto E. *Evolución de la agricultura en la provincia de Santa Fe: Su dependencia de factores geográficas y económicos.* Santa Fe: Province of Santa Fe, Ministerio de Hacienda, Economía e Industrias, 1953.

Humphreys, R. A. *Latin America and the Second World War.* 2 vols. London: Athlone Press, 1981, 1982.

Ibáñez, Bernardo. *El socialismo y el porvenir de los pueblos.* Santiago: Ediciones Difusión Popular, 1946.

Infante Barros, Marta. *Testigos del treinta y ocho.* Santiago: Editorial Andrés Bello, 1972.

Inman, Samuel Guy. *Latin America: Its Place in World Life.* 2d ed. New York: Harcourt, Brace, 1942.

Jacob, Raúl. *Breve historia de la industria en el Uruguay*. Montevideo: FCU, 1981.

———. *Modelo batllista: ¿Variación sobre un viejo tema?* Montevideo: Proyección, 1988.

Jay, Martin. *The Dialectical Imagination: A History of the Frankfurt School and the Institute of Social Research, 1923–1950*. London: Heinemann, 1973.

Jennings, Bruce H. *Foundations of International Agricultural Research: Science and Politics in Mexican Agriculture*. Boulder, Colo.: Westview Press, 1988.

Jobet, Julio César. *El socialismo chileno a través de sus congresos*. Santiago: Prensa Latinoamericana, 1965.

———. *El Partido Socialista de Chile*. 2 vols. Santiago: Prensa Latinoamericana, 1971.

Josephs, Ray. *Latin America: Continent in Crisis*. New York: Random House, 1948.

Kantor, Harry. *The Ideology and Program of the Peruvian Aprista Movement*. Berkeley and Los Angeles: University of California Press, 1953.

Katzenstein, Peter. *Small States in World Markets*. Ithaca: Cornell University Press, 1985.

Kay, Cristóbal. *Latin American Theories of Development and Underdevelopment*. London: Routledge, 1989.

Kindleberger, Charles P. *The Great Depression*. Berkeley and Los Angeles: University of California Press, 1973.

Kirsch, Henry. *Industrial Development in a Traditional Society*. Gainesville: University of Florida Press, 1977.

Kock, Karin. *International Trade Policy and the GATT, 1947–1967*. Stockholm: Almquist and Wiksell, 1969.

Kofas, Jon V. *The Struggle for Legitimacy: Latin American Labor and the United States, 1930–1960*. Tempe, Ariz.: Arizona State University Press, 1992.

Korol, Juan Carlos, and Hilda Sabato. "Incomplete Industrialization: An Argentine Obsession." *Latin American Research Review* 25, no. 1 (1990), 7–30.

Krehm, William. *Democracies and Tyrannies in the Caribbean*. Westport, Conn.: Lawrence Hill, 1984.

Labarca, Amanda. *Feminismo contemporáneo*. Santiago de Chile: Ediciones Zig-Zag, 1947.

Lafertte, Elías. *Vida de un comunista*. Santiago: n.p., 1961.

Landstrom, Russell. *The Associated Press News Annual: 1945*. New York: Rinehart and Company, 1946.

Lanús, Juan Archibaldo. *De Chapultepec al Beagle: Política exterior argentina, 1945–1980*. Buenos Aires: Emecé, 1984.

Lanzaro, Jorge L. *Sindicatos y sistema político: Relaciones corporativas en el Uruguay*. Montevideo: Fundación de Cultura Universitaria, 1986.

Lattes, Alfredo E. "La dinámica de la población rural en la Argentina entre 1870 y 1970." In *Cuadernos del CENEP*. Vol. 9. Buenos Aires: Centro de Estudios de Población, 1979.

League of Nations. *Economic Stability in the Postwar Period*. Geneva: League of Nations, 1945.

Lechner, Norbert. *La democracia en Chile*. Buenos Aires: Ediciones Signos, 1970.

Lehmbruch, Gerhard A., and Philippe C. Schmitter, eds. *Patterns of Corporatist Policy-Making*. New York: Sage, 1982.

Lehoucq, Fabrice Edouard. "Class Conflict, Political Crisis, and the Breakdown of Democratic Practices in Costa Rica: Reassessing the Origins of the 1948 Civil War." *Journal of Latin American Studies* 23 (February 1991), 37–60.

León, Luis L. "La actuación del gremio agrónomico en la reforma agraria." *Boletín de la Sociedad mexicana de geografía y estadística* 78 (1954), 57–71.

Lerner, Abba. "Economic Liberalization in the Postwar World," in *Postwar Economic Problems*, edited by Seymour Edwin Harris, 71–103. New York: McGraw Hill, 1943.

Lewis, Daniel. "A Political and Economic History of Grain Farming in Buenos Aires Province, Argentina, 1914–1943." Ph.D. dissertation, University of California, Santa Barbara, 1990.

Lewis, W. Arthur. *Economic Survey, 1919–1939*. London: George Allen and Unwin, 1949.

———. "Economic Development with Unlimited Supplies of Labour." *Manchester School of Economic and Social Studies* 22, no. 1 (1956), 139–91.

Lieuwen, Edwin. *Arms and Politics in Latin America*. New York: Praeger, 1960.

Lima, Hermes. *Notas da vida brasileira*. São Paulo: Brasiliense, 1945.

List, Friedrich. *The National System of Political Economy*. London: Longman, 1909.

Lombardo Toledano, Vicente. "Por la industrialización de México," in *El marxismo en América Latina*, edited by Michael Lowy, 158–60. México, D.F.: ERA, 1982.

Lopez-Alves, Fernando. "Why Do Unions Coalesce? Labor Solidarity in Colombia and Uruguay." Ph.D. dissertation, University of California, Los Angeles, 1989.

———. "Informal Politics and Democracy: The Long Nineteenth Century in the River Plate." Paper presented at the 1991 Annual Meeting of the American Political Science Association, Washington, D.C.

"Los precios básicos del maíz y la política agraria nacional." In República Argentina, Comisión Nacional de Elevadores de Granos, *Boletín Informativo* 6, no. 5 (15 May 1942), 221–29.

Love, Joseph L. "Manoïlescu, Prebisch, and the Thesis of Unequal Exchange." *Rumanian Studies* 5 (1980–1986), 125–33.

———. "The Origins of Dependency Analysis." *Journal of Latin American Studies* 22, no. 1 (1990), 143–68.

Loveman, Brian. *Chile: The Legacy of Hispanic Capitalism*. 2d ed. New York: Oxford University Press, 1988.

Loyola, Maria Andrea. *Os sindicatos e o PTB*. Petrópolis: Vozes/CEBRAP, 1980.

Luebbert, Gregory. *Liberalism, Fascism, or Social Democracy: Local Classes and the Political Origins of Regimes in Interwar Europe*. New York: Oxford University Press, 1991.

Luna, Felix. *El '45*. Buenos Aires: Sudamericana, 1971.

McCormick, T. C., ed. *Problems of the Post-War World*. New York: McGraw Hill, 1945.

Maddison, A. *Phases of Capitalist Development*. Oxford and New York: Oxford University Press, 1982.

Maier, Charles. *In Search of Stability*. Cambridge: Cambridge University Press, 1987.

Mandelbaum, Kurt. *The Industrialization of Backward Areas*. Oxford: Blackwell, 1945.

Mannheim, Karl. *Estado y planificación demócratica*. México, D.F.: Fondo de Cultura Económica, 1945.

Manoïlescu, Mihail. *The Theory of Protection and International Trade*. London: King, 1931.

Mascali, Humberto. *Desocupación y conflictos laborales en el campo argentino (1940–1965)*. Buenos Aires: Centro Editor de América Latina, 1986.

May, Stacey, and Galo Plaza. *The United Fruit Company in Latin America*. Washington, D.C.: National Planning Association, 1958.

Mecham, J. Lloyd. *The United States and Inter-American Security, 1889–1960*. Austin: University of Texas Press, 1961.

MEMCH Antología: Para una historia de movimiento femenino en Chile. 2d ed. N.p., n.d.

Memoria del Primer Congreso Interamericano de Mujeres. Guatemala: n.p., 1947.

Meza, María Angelica. *La otra mitad de Chile.* Santiago: CESOC, 1986.

Miller, Francesca. "Latin American Feminism and the Transnational Area," in *Women, Culture, and Politics in Latin America,* Seminar on Feminism and Culture in Latin America, 10–26. Berkeley and Los Angeles: University of California Press, 1990.

Miller, James. *The United States and Italy, 1940–1950.* Chapel Hill: University of North Carolina Press, 1986.

Ministerio de Obras Públicas de la Provincia de Buenos Aires. Dirección de Agricultura, Ganadería e Industrias. *La regulación de la producción agrícola: Consejos a los agricultores.* La Plata, 1939.

Morais, Fernando. *Olga.* 14th ed. São Paulo: Alfa-Omega, 1987.

Morel, Isabel (Delia Ducoing de Arrate). *Charlas femeninas.* N.p.: Unión Femenina de Chile, 1937.

Morris, George. *CIA and American Labor.* New York: International Publishers, 1967.

Mosk, Sanford A. *Industrial Revolution in Mexico.* Berkeley and Los Angeles: University of California Press, 1950.

Mouzelis, Nicos. *Politics in the Semi-Periphery.* London: Macmillan, 1986.

Moya Obeso, Alberto. *Sindicalismo aprista y clasista en el Perú, 1920–1956.* Trujillo: Librería Star, n.d.

Muñoz, Oscar. *Crecimiento industrial de Chile, 1914–1965.* Santiago: Universidad de Chile, 1968.

Nahum, Benjamín, et al. *Historia uruguaya.* Vol. 7. Montevideo: Banda Oriental, 1989.

Niblo, Stephen R. "The Impact of War: Mexico and World War II." Occasional Paper no. 10, La Trobe University Institute of Latin American Studies, Melbourne, 1988.

North, Liisa, and David Raby. "The Dynamic of Revolution and Counterrevolution: Mexico under Cárdenas, 1934–1940." *Latin American Research Unit Studies* 2, no. 1 (October 1977).

Ocampo, José Antonio. "New Economic Thinking in Latin America." *Journal of Latin American Studies* 22, no. 1 (1990), 169–81.

O'Connell, Arturo. "Free Trade in One (Primary Producing) Country: The Case of Argentina in the 1920s," in *The Political Economy of Argentina, 1880–1946,* edited by Guido di Tella and D. C. M. Platt, 74–94. London: Macmillan, 1986.

O'Donnell, Guillermo. *El estado burocrático-autoritario.* Buenos Aires: Belgrano, 1982.

Office of Inter-American Affairs. Research Division. Social and Geographic Section. *The Status of Women in Chile.* Washington, D.C., 1944.

Olavarría Bravo, Arturo. *Chile entre dos Alessandri.* 4 vols. Santiago: Editorial Nascimento, 1962.

Oliveira, Armando de Salles. *Diagrama de uma situação política: Manifestos, políticos do exilio.* São Paulo: Editora Renascenca, 1945.

Pareja, Piedad. *Aprismo y sindicalismo en el Perú.* Lima: Ediciones Rikchay Perú, 1980.

Partido Comunista [of Chile]. *Ricardo Fonseca: Combatiente ejemplar.* Santiago: Talleres Gráficos Lautaro, 1952.

Partido Socialista [of Chile]. *Primer congreso de los partidos democráticos de latinoamérica.* Santiago: Talleres Gráficos Gutenberg, 1940.

Patiño, Emilio Alanis. *Diversos aspectos de la situación agrícola de México.* México, D.F.: Instituto Mexicano de Estudios Agrícolas, 1934.

Pazos, Felipe. "Cincuenta años de pensamiento económico en la América Latina." *El trimestre económico* no. 50 (1983), 1015–48.

Pendle, George. "Latin America," in *Survey of International Affairs, 1953*, edited by Peter Calvocoressi, 325–45. London: Oxford University Press, 1956.

Pérez-Brignoli, Héctor. "The Economic Cycle in Latin American Export Economies (1880–1930): A Hypothesis for Investigation." *Latin American Research Review* 15, no. 2 (1980), 3–34.

Pike, Fredrick B. *The Modern History of Peru*. New York: Frederick A. Praeger, 1967.

———. *The United States and the Andean Republics: Peru, Bolivia, and Ecuador*. Cambridge: Harvard University Press, 1977.

———. *The Politics of the Miraculous in Peru: Haya de la Torre and the Spiritualist Tradition*. Lincoln: University of Nebraska Press, 1986.

Pinto, Aníbal. *Chile: Un caso de desarrollo frustrado*. Santiago: Editorial Universitaria, 1958.

Pinto, Luciano. *Como arreglar este pais*. Santiago: Imprenta Nascimento, 1949.

Pintos, Francisco. *Historia del movimiento obrero del Uruguay*. Montevideo: Gaceta de Cultura, 1960.

Pogue, Forrest. *George C. Marshall: Statesman, 1945–1959*. New York: Penguin, 1987.

Pollock, David H. "Some Changes in United States Attitudes toward CEPAL over the Past Thirty Years." *CEPAL Review* 6 (1978), 57–80.

Poppino, Rollie. *International Communism in Latin America: A History of the Movement, 1914–1963*. Glencoe, Ill.: Free Press, 1964.

Portocarrero Maisch, Gonzalo. *De Bustamante a Odría*. Lima: Mosca Azul Editores, 1983.

Prebisch, Raúl. *Introducción a Keynes*. México, D.F.: Fondo de Cultura Económica, 1947.

———. *The Economic Development of Latin America and Its Principal Problems*. New York: United Nations, 1949.

———. *Algunos problemas teóricos y prácticos del crecimiento económico*. Santiago: Comisión Económica para América Latina, 1951.

———. "Five Stages in My Thinking on Development," in *Pioneers in Development*, edited by Gerald M. Meier and Dudley Seers, 175–91. New York: Oxford University Press, 1984.

Pucciarelli, Alfredo. *El capitalismo agrario pampeano, 1880–1930*. Buenos Aires: Hyspamérica, 1986.

Rabe, Stephen. *Eisenhower and Latin America*. Chapel Hill: University of North Carolina Press, 1988.

Rama, Germán. *La democracia en el Uruguay*. Montevideo: Arca, 1989.

Ravines, Eudocio. *La gran estafa*. 2d ed. Santiago: Editorial del Pacífico, 1954.

República Argentina. Secretaría de Agricultura, Ganadería y Pesca. *Estadísticas agrícolas retrospectivas*. Buenos Aires, 1987.

———. Comisión Nacional del Censo Agropecuario. *Censo agropecuario nacional, año 1937*. Vol. 1. Buenos Aires: Guillermo Kraft, Ltda., 1939.

———. Ministerio de Agricultura de la Nación. *Anuario agropecuario, año 1932*. Buenos Aires, 1932.

———. *Memoria de la Junta Reguladora de Granos, campaña 1933–1934*. Buenos Aires, 1935.

———. *Memoria de la Junta Reguladora de Granos, 2 ejercicio, año 1935*. Buenos Aires, 1936.

———. *Almanaque*. 1946.

República de Chile. Dirección de Estadísticas y Censos. *Cifras comparativas de los censos de 1940 y 1952 y muestra del censo de 1960*. N.p., n.d.

Reveco del Villar, Juan Manuel. "Los influjos del APRA en el Partido Socialista de Chile." Thesis, FLACSO, Santiago, 1989.

Rippy, J. Fred. *Latin America and the Industrial Age*. New York: Putnam, 1947.

Rivas Tagle, Antonio. *El cultivo racional del maíz*. Tacubaya, D.F., 1929.

Rock, David. *Argentina, 1516–1987: From Spanish Colonization to Alfonsín*. Berkeley and Los Angeles: University of California Press, 1987.

———. *Authoritarian Argentina: The Nationalist Movement, Its History and Its Impact*. Berkeley and Los Angeles: University of California Press, 1993.

Rodriguez, Louis. "A Comparison: U.S. Economic Relations with Argentina and Brazil, 1947–1960." Ph.D. dissertation, Louisiana State University, 1963.

Rodríguez, Octavio. "On the Conception of the Center-Periphery System." *CEPAL Review* 3, (1977), 195–239.

———. *La teoria del subdesarrollo de la CEPAL*. México, D.F.: Siglo XXI, 1980.

Romualdi, Serafino. *Presidents and Peons*. New York: Funk and Wagnalls, 1967.

Rosenstein-Rodan, Paul N. "Industrialization of Eastern and Southeastern Europe." *Economic Journal* 53, no. 3 (1943), 202–11.

Roxborough, Ian. *Unions and Politics in Mexico*. Cambridge: Cambridge University Press, 1984.

———. "Unity and Diversity in Latin American History." *Journal of Latin American Studies* 16, pt. 1 (May 1984), 1–26.

Sabato, Jorge. *La pampa pródiga: Claves de una frustración*. Buenos Aires: Centro de Investigaciones sobre el Estado y la Administración, 1981.

Salera, Virgil. *Exchange Control and the Argentine Market*. New York: Columbia University Press, 1941.

Sánchez, George I. *Mexico: A Revolution by Education*. New York: Viking Press, 1936.

Sánchez, Luis Alberto. *Un sudamericano en norteamérica*. Lima: Universidad Nacional Mayor de San Marcos, 1968.

———. *Testimonio personal*. 3 vols. Lima: Ediciones Villasan, 1969.

———. *Visto y vivido en Chile: Bitacora chilena, 1930–1970*. Lima: Editoriales Unidas, S.A., 1975;

Sater, William F. *Chile and the United States: Empires in Conflict*. Athens: University of Georgia Press, 1990.

Schaller, Michael. *The American Occupation of Japan*. Oxford: Oxford University Press, 1985.

Schmitter, Philippe C. "Still the Century of Corporatism?" *Review of Politics* 36 (1974), 85–131.

Schnake Vergara, Oscar. *América y la guerra*. Santiago: Taller de Publicaciones del PS, 1941.

———. *Chile y la guerra*. Santiago: Ediciones Ercilla, 1941.

Schneider, Ronald M. *Communism in Guatemala, 1944–1954*. New York: Praeger, 1958.

Scobie, James R. *Revolution on the Pampas: A Social History of Argentine Wheat, 1860–1910*. Austin: University of Texas Press, 1964.

Seoane, Manuel. *Nuestra América y la guerra*. Santiago: Ediciones Ercilla, 1940.

———. *El gran vecino: América en la encrucijada*. Santiago: Editorial Orbe, 1944.

Shafer, R. J. *Mexican Business Organizations: History and Analysis.* Syracuse: Syracuse University Press, 1973.

Silva Herzog, Jesús. *El agrarismo mexicano y la reforma agraria.* México, D.F.: Fondo de Cultura Económica, 1959.

Simão, Azis. *Sindicato e estado (Suas relaciones na formação do proletariado de São Paulo).* São Paulo: Atica, 1981.

Simpson, Eyler N. *The Ejido: Mexico's Way Out.* Chapel Hill: University of North Carolina Press, 1937.

Singer, Hans. "The Distribution of Gains between Investing and Borrowing Countries." *American Economic Review* 40, no. 2 (1950), 473–85.

Skidmore, Thomas E. *Politics in Brazil, 1930–1964.* New York: Oxford University Press, 1967.

———. "The Politics of Economic Stabilization in Postwar Latin America," in *Authoritarianism and Corporatism in Latin America,* edited by James Malloy, 149–90. Pittsburgh: University of Pittsburgh Press, 1977.

Skidmore, Thomas E., and Peter H. Smith. *Modern Latin America.* New York: Oxford University Press, 1984.

Smith, John Newton. *Argentine Agriculture: Trends in Production and World Competition.* Washington, D.C.: U.S. Department of Agriculture, Economic Research Service, 1968.

Solari, Aldo. *El desarrollo social del Uruguay en la postguerra.* Montevideo: Alfa, 1967.

Sombart, Werner. *Der Moderne Capitalismus.* Munich and Leipzig: Dünscker und Humblut, 1928.

———. *El apogeo del capitalismo.* México, D.F.: Fondo de Cultura Económica, 1946.

Soule, George, David Efron, and Norman T. Ness. *Latin America in the Future World.* New York: Farrar and Rinehart, 1945.

Snow, Peter G. *Radicalismo chileno.* Buenos Aires: Editorial Francisco de Aguirre, 1972.

Spindel, Arnaldo. *O Pártido Comunista na genese do populismo.* São Paulo: Simbolo, 1980.

Spykman, Nicholas John. *America's Strategy in World Politics: The United States and the Balance of Power.* New York: Harcourt, Brace, 1942.

———. *The Geography of the Peace.* Edited by Helen R. Nicholl with an introduction by Frederick Sherwood Dunn. New York: Harcourt, Brace, 1944.

Staley, Eugene. *World Economy in Transition.* New York: Council on Foreign Relations, 1939.

———. *World Economic Development.* Montreal: International Labour Office, 1944.

Stevenson, John Reese. *The Chilean Popular Front.* Philadelphia: University of Pennsylvania Press, 1942.

Stubbs, Jean. *Tobacco on the Periphery: A Case Study in Cuban Labor History, 1860–1958.* Cambridge: Cambridge University Press, 1985.

Sulmont, Denis. *El movimiento obrero en el Perú, 1900–1956.* Lima: Pontífica Universidad Católica del Perú, 1975.

Sunkel, Osvaldo. "La inflación chilena: Un enfoque heterodoxo." *El trimestre económico* 25 (1958), 570–99.

———. "The Development of Development Theory," in *Transnational Capitalism and National Development,* edited by José Villamil, 19–31. Atlantic Highlands, N.J.: Hassocks, Harvester, 1979.

Thirlwall, Anthony P. "A General Model of Growth and Development on Kaldorian Lines." *Oxford Economic Papers* 38, no. 2 (1986), 199–219.

Thorne, Christopher. *Border Crossings*, London: Blackwell, 1988.

Thorp, Rosemary, ed. *Latin America in the 1930s*. London: Macmillan, 1984.

Thorp, Rosemary, and Geoffrey Bertram. *Peru, 1890–1977: Growth and Policy in an Open Economy*. London: Macmillan, 1978.

Tillapaugh, James C. "From War to Cold War: United States Policies toward Latin America, 1943–1948." Ph.D. dissertation, Northwestern University, Evanston, 1973.

Triffin, Robert. "La moneda y las instituciones bancarias en Colombia." *Revista Banco de la República*. Bogotá, August 1944.

Tulchin, Joseph S. *Argentina and the United States: A Conflicted Relationship*. Boston: Twayne Publishers, 1990.

United Nations. *Yearbook of International Trade Statistics*. New York: United Nations, 1951.

———. *Foreign Capital in Latin America*. New York: United Nations, 1955.

———. *The Economic Development of Latin America in the Post-War Period*. New York: United Nations, 1964.

———. Comisión Económica para América Latina. *El desarrollo económico de la Argentina*. México, D.F.: CEPAL, 1959.

———. *Series históricas del crecimiento de América Latina*. Santiago de Chile: CEPAL, 1978.

———. Economic Commission for Latin America. *Economic Survey of Latin America, 1948*. New York: United Nations, 1949.

———. *Economic Survey of Latin America, 1949*. New York: United Nations, 1951.

———. *Economic Survey, 1951–1952*. New York: United Nations, 1953.

———. *Report on the First Session of the ECLA, 7–25 June 1948*. New York: United Nations, 1953.

———. Economic Commission for Latin America and the Caribbean. "Series históricas del crecimiento de América Latina." *Cuadernos estadísticos de la CEPAL*, no. 3. Santiago: CEPAL, 1978.

Universidad de Chile. *Desarrollo económico de Chile, 1940–1956*. Santiago: Instituto de Economía, 1956.

Urquidi, Victor L. "La postguerra y las relaciones economicas internacionales de Mexico." *El trimestre económico* 11, no. 2 (1944), 320–45.

Urquidi, Victor L., and Ernesto Fernández-Hurtado. "Diversos tipos de disequilibrio económico internacional." *El trimestre económico* 13, no. 1 (1946), 1–33.

U.S. Department of State. *Foreign Relations of the United States, 1945*, vol. 9. Washington, D.C., 1970.

———.*Memorandum of the United States among the American Republics with Respect to the Argentine Situation*. Washington, D.C.: Department of State, 1946.

Vale, Osvaldo Trigueiro do. *O General Dutra e a redemocratização de 1945*. Rio de Janeiro: Civilização Brasileiro, 1978.

Vargas, Getúlio. *A nova política do Brasil*. 11 vols. Rio de Janeiro: José Olympio, 1947.

Vergara, Luiz. *Fui Secretario de Getúlio Vargas: Memorias dos anos de 1926–1954*. Rio: Globo, 1960.

Vergara, Marta. *Memorias de una mujer irreverente*. Santiago: Editora Nacional Gabriela Mistral Ltda., 1974.

Villanueva, Víctor. *La sublevación aprista del 48*. Lima: Editorial Horizonte, 1973.

———. *El APRA en busca del poder, 1930–1940*. Lima: Editorial Horizonte, 1975.

———. *El APRA y el ejército, 1940–1950*. Lima: Editorial Horizonte, 1977.

Viner, Jacob. *International Trade and Economic Development*. Glencoe, Ill.: Free Press, 1952.

Wagemann, Ernest Friedrich. *Evolución y ritmo de la economía mundial*. Barcelona: Editorial Labor, 1933.

Wagner, R. Harrison. *United States Policy toward Latin America*. Stanford: Stanford University Press, 1970.

Waisman, Carlos H. *The Reversal of Development in Argentina*. Princeton: Princeton University Press, 1987.

Waiss, Oscar. *Nacionalismo y socialismo en América Latina*. Santiago: Prensa Latinoamericana, 1954.

Walters, Francis Paul. *A History of the League of Nations*. Oxford: Oxford University Press, 1952.

Weiler, Peter. *British Labour and the Cold War*. Stanford: Stanford University Press, 1988.

Welles, Sumner. *The Time for Decision*. New York: Harper and Brothers, 1944.

———. *Where Are We Heading?* New York: Harper and Brothers, 1946.

Whitaker, Arthur P., ed. *Inter-American Affairs, 1941*. New York: Columbia University Press, 1942.

———. *Inter-American Affairs, 1943*. New York: Columbia University Press, 1944.

———. *Inter-American Affairs, 1944*. New York: Columbia University Press, 1945.

———. *Inter-American Affairs, 1945*. New York: Columbia University Press, 1946.

Wilkie, James W. *Statistics and National Policy*. Supplement 3. University of California, Los Angeles, 1974.

Woltman, Harry R. "The Decline of Argentina's Agricultural Trade: Problems and Policies." Ph.D. dissertation, Stanford University, 1959.

Wood, Bryce. *The Dismantling of the Good Neighbor Policy*. Austin: University of Texas Press, 1985.

Wright, Angus. *The Death of Ramón González: The Modern Agricultural Dilemma*. Austin: University of Texas Press, 1991.

Wythe, George. *Industry in Latin America*. New York: Columbia University Press, 1945.

Yopo, H. Boris. "El Partido Socialista Chileno y Estados Unidos: 1933–1946." *Documento de Trabajo del FLACSO*, no. 224, October 1984.

Index

Designer: Barbara Jellow
Compositor: ComCom
Text: 10.5/14 Albertina
Display: Albertina
Printer: Haddon Craftsmen
Binder: Haddon Craftsmen